Networked Press Freedom

Networked Press Freedom

Creating Infrastructures for a Public Right to Hear

Mike Ananny

The MIT Press
Cambridge, Massachusetts
London, England

This book was set in Stone Serif by Westchester Publishing Services. Printed and bound in the United States of America.

Library of Congress Cataloging-in-Publication Data

Names: Ananny, Mike, author.
Title: Networked press freedom : creating infrastructures for a public right
  to hear / Mike Ananny.
Description: Cambridge, MA : The MIT Press, 2018. | Based on author's thesis
  (doctoral - Stanford University, Department of Communication, 2011) issued
  under title: A new way to think about press freedom : networked journalism
  and a public right to Hear in the Age of "Newsware" | Includes bibliographical
  references and index.
Identifiers: LCCN 2017038906 | ISBN 9780262037747 (hardcover : alk. paper)
Subjects: LCSH: Freedom of the press. | Online journalism. | Digital
  media--Law and legislation. | Social media--Law and legislation.
Classification: LCC K3255 .A958 2018 | DDC 342.08/53--dc23 LC record available
  at https://lccn.loc.gov/2017038906

10 9 8 7 6 5 4 3 2 1

Freedom is what you do with what's been done to you.
—Jean-Paul Sartre

Contents

Acknowledgments

This book has been a long time in the making, and although all of its errors are mine alone, I am deeply indebted to many people and institutions for helping it see the light of day. First, I want to thank the MIT Press—Margy Avery for first acquiring this project, Gita Manaktala for seeing it to completion, and Deborah Cantor-Adams and the entire editorial and production team. I am especially grateful for Gita's patience and supportive guidance as the project took shape and am deeply appreciative of her work as an editor and expert publisher. I am also grateful to the four anonymous reviewers who generously and thoughtfully helped me to improve the book in its final stages.

Although it has been entirely rewritten and updated, this project began as my doctoral dissertation in Stanford University's Department of Communication. I was fortunate to have as my adviser the indefatigably generous, inquisitive, and supportive Ted Glasser. In one of our first meetings, he taught me that any good project should be able to answer the questions "What is it?" and "Why does it matter?" With that deceptively simply starting point, he showed me how to be a scholar and how to think about journalism and the press in ways that are both critical and optimistic. I am grateful for his ongoing guidance and friendship. Similarly, Fred Turner was a member of my dissertation committee, a generous mentor, and a wise guide through the theories of science and technology studies that underpin this book. He taught me to think about technology and culture as intertwined, inseparable forces and pushed me to see news production as a world of contingencies, ideologies, and power struggles. I am also indebted to my other committee members—Jeremy Bailenson, S. Lochlann Jain, and Barbara van Schewick—who were supportive and thoughtful as I developed these ideas. My time at Stanford also was greatly enriched through an early relationship with the Stanford Center on Philanthropy and Civil Society (PACS), especially its faculty codirectors, Woody Powell and Rob Reich. Woody was the best mentor I could have hoped to have on questions of institutional sociology and organizational dynamics but also on ways to craft a project that was interdisciplinary and engaged with multiple communities of scholarship. Similarly, Rob helped me appreciate the broader ethical implications of the questions I was asking, gently forcing me to translate my work in different ways so it might speak to people concerned with civil society writ large, not just journalism. I am grateful for the community that they and the PACS students created; they became my indispensable, interdisciplinary, informal sounding board. At Stanford and in San Francisco, I was grateful for the friendship and camaraderie of Isabel Awad, Scott Cataffa, Jeannette Colyvas, Vince Fecteau, Seeta Peña Gangadharan, Janet Go, Dan Kreiss, Lise Marken, and Kat Murray.

While at Stanford, I was generously supported by a multiyear scholarship from the Pierre Elliott Trudeau Foundation. First welcomed into the Foundation by Bettina Cenerelli, Josée St-Martin, and Stephen Toope and later P. G Forest, it quickly became a key part of my professional network, a place for smart and kind feedback, and my Canadian touchstone. Through it, I met many friends and colleagues, including Jill Boyd, Lisa Freeman, Lisa Helps, Kate Hennessy, Myles Leslie, Leah Levac, Taylor Owen, Kate Parizeau, Chris Tenove, and many more. Directly and indirectly, the Foundation and its members intellectually framed this project.

Since leaving Stanford, I have been fortunate to be part many different communities that have made this work much stronger, either by engaging with it directly or providing social and intellectual homes where I could make connections, learn new literatures, and better understand how to do interdisciplinary scholarship. I am especially grateful to Microsoft Research New England's Social Media Collective. Founded by long-time friend, activist/scholar, and ongoing field guide danah boyd, the group has convened some of the finest minds in many different fields, many of which I was able to work with closely and continue to call good friends. In addition to a stellar set of people I overlapped with—Nancy Baym, Nicole Ellison, Eszter Hargittai, Cliff Lampe, Jessica Lingel, and Jason Schultz—several Collective folks stand out as key for this work. As a fellow postdoc, Alice Marwick was a fellow traveler in all things Microsoft and a keenly critical scholar who patiently explained myriad popular culture phenomena, and helped me understand how to write a book. I am grateful to Mary Gray for reminding me to foreground the people in my research by highlighting them, their experiences, and their expectations and contexts amid often abstract talk of technology and institutions. Tarleton Gillespie showed me how to look at a sociotechnical phenomenon from more analytical angles than I knew existed and has generously helped me puzzle through a host of questions related to platforms, algorithms, and journalism. Kate Crawford has been a consistently engaged and generous collaborator, helped me think about the ethics, histories, and politics of my research, and served as a key interlocutor for many of this book's ideas.

As a place to hone my thinking about the networked press, I could not have landed at a better institution than the University of Southern California's Annenberg School for Communication and Journalism. Its faculty—especially Jonathan Aronson, Francois Bar, Christina Dunbar-Hester, Tom Goodnight, Larry Gross, Henry Jenkins, Gabe Kahn, Andy Lakoff, Colin Maclay, and Allison Trope—are world-class collaborators and mentors. In particular, I thank Sarah Banet-Weiser and Christina Dunbar-Hester for their ongoing support, friendship, and good humor; they helped me remember the value of this project and provided me with the perspectives and resources I needed to see it through. I have also been fortunate to work with some of the finest doctoral students in the field—especially Leila Bighash, Renyi Hong, Cynthia Wang, and Sarah Meyers West—who have provided feedback on these ideas at various stages of their development. And special thanks go to Kate Miltner, who read the manuscript, caught many mistakes, provided constructive feedback, and helped me hone my thinking in several places. Annenberg staff members Allyson Arguello, Jordan Gary, Sarah Holterman, Christine Lloreda, and Billie Shotlow were also extremely helpful with various parts of this project's logistics and administration.

Beyond the communities already mentioned, I am indebted to a collection of communication and science and technology scholars who have, in various conversations over the years or through their own writing, helped me develop this book's argument: Chris Anderson (who read the entire manuscript and provided critically helpful feedback in its final stages), Lance Bennett, Rod Benson, Pablo Boczkowski, Josh Braun, Matt Carlson, Andy Chadwick, Nick Couldry, Dan Kreiss, Seth Lewis, Phil Napoli, Rasmus Kleis Nielsen, Zizi Papacharissi, Caitlin Petre, Victor Pickard, Matt Powers, Adrienne Russell, Michael Schudson, Keren Tenenboim-Weinblatt, Nikki

Usher, Karin Wahl-Jorgensen, and Barbie Zelizer. Two scholars in particular were excellent guides, made key interventions at critical moments, and were kind and generous comrades as we wrote our respective books: Kjerstin Thorson is one of the smartest, funniest, and truth-speaking collaborators I could have hoped for, and Megan Finn is one of the sharpest and most constructively supportive sources of sanity and critique I could have imagined.

I also have some family members to thank. Dad and Irene were early supporters of this project, and embody my ideals of informed and engaged readers who care about public life. As the first journalists I met, Uncle Frank and Aunt Linda were in my mind during much of this writing, as exemplary journalists working in the public interest. George and Ann Lawson provided me with more laughter, friendship, hospitality, and support than they may realize; from talking me through bumps along the way to knowing exactly when not to ask how the book was going, it all meant a great deal, and I am deeply grateful to them for helping me see this project through and becoming family along the way. Almost finally, John and M.B. have been the bee's knees, a formulation I know they will appreciate. John, especially, is a mensch. He read almost every word of this book, helped me clarify my thinking, and provided gut-checks at key moments, reminding me that this was a project worth doing and that might be helpful to nonacademics.

Finally: Wells. You have been my biggest champion, my most tenacious and understanding partner, and my best friend. You endured missed dinners, delayed vacations, compressed weekends, my short fuses, and my overabundant italics and love of em-dashes. You read every word of this book, literally made the spaces where I worked, and when I forgot or doubted, reminded me why this work matters and why I could do it. I am grateful beyond measure and dedicate this to you.

1 Introduction

What, exactly, is press freedom, and why does it matter? In the popular discourse of the United States, we do not ask this question very often or very deeply. The answers are obvious and almost cliché: the public has a right to know, journalists are the people's watchdogs, they afflict the comfortable and comfort the afflicted, democracy dies in darkness, and voters need objective information to be good citizens. Popular histories of modern U.S. journalism celebrate heroes who spoke truth to power and brought down institutions—Ida B. Wells, Nellie Bly, Ida Tarbell, Edward R. Murrow, I. F. Stone, Bob Woodward, Carl Bernstein, Walter Cronkite. They often are remembered as most effective when they were left alone to pursue their visions of what they thought the public needed. These virtuous, creative, public-spirited, hard-working storytellers occupy powerful positions within the modern mythology of press freedom. If we just get out of the way of good journalists and let them tell truth to power, they will produce the information that vibrant democracies need.

This myth is somewhat true, and these heroes were indeed expert storytellers who challenged each era's norms. But when we think about press freedom only or even mostly as the freedom of journalists from constraints, it becomes a narrow and almost magical phenomenon that depends on individuals and heroism. It says that journalists already know what the public needs, and just need freedom from the state, marketplaces, and audiences to pursue self-evident things like truth and the public interest. These brave journalists and publishers show their commitment to the public and the power of their independence by going to court and sometimes jail to protect sources and fight censorship. If journalists and publishers can get truth to the public, then individual readers and viewers will be able to make informed decisions about how to think and vote. Ultimately, the press wants to be left alone so that *you* can be left alone. The kind of democracy that dominates this common image of press freedom relies on a lot of independences—a lot of *freedoms from*.

This book tries to challenge this mythology. I want to complicate the idea of press freedom and show that it emerges not from individual heroes but from social, technological, institutional, and normative forces that vie for power, imagine publics, and implicitly fight for visions of democracy. I see press freedom as a concept to think with—a generative and constructive tool for looking at any given era of the press and public life and asking, "Is *this* version of press freedom giving us the kind of publics we need? If not, how do we revise the institutional arrangements underpinning press freedom and make a different thing that we agree to call 'the press'?" Alternatively, how do we adjust our normative expectations about what publics should be, creating a different image of freedom that we then might demand from institutions that make up the press? If we see press freedom not as heroic isolations—journalists breaking free to tell truths to the publics they imagine—but as a subtler system of separations and dependencies that *make* publics, then we might see each era's types of press freedom as bellwethers for particular visions of the public. Ideas of press freedom become evidence of thinking about publics. Rethinking press freedom can be a way to see how press power flows, a prompt to ask which flows produce which publics, and a challenge: what types of news, publics, or presses are we *not* seeing because our vision of press freedom is so narrow?

If you think press freedom is a particular thing, you will likely look for that thing when you want to see whether a democracy is healthy or whether journalists are doing their jobs. Assumptions about press freedom can shut down conversations about the press and democracy: "We have a free press, so the election result is what it should be" or "We have a free press, and corruption is still rampant!" or "If we had a free press, then we'd have a different government" or "A free marketplace is a free press because truth comes from competing viewpoints." Statements like these—coming from journalists, audiences, politicians, advertisers, publishers—assume that we already know what we mean by a free press and that our problem is just implementing it.

But if we can liberate the idea of press freedom from these assumptions and assumptions that equate it with whatever journalists say publics need, then press freedom becomes a generative and expansive tool—a way to think about publics, self-governance, and democracy. Because, as C. Edwin Baker (2007b) puts it, different democracies need different media, we can complicate democracy by thinking more creatively about press freedom.

Given this moment, when media systems are in a fundamental flux, this book offers a way to think about press freedom as sociotechnical forces with separations and dependencies that help to make publics. I aim to engage with and use this moment of fundamental change to show what press freedom could mean. Contrary to the dominant historical myth in the United States, I argue that press freedom should not be seen simply as journalists' freedom to write and publish. Rather, press freedom is a normative and institutional product of any given era: it is what people *think* press freedom should mean and how people have arranged people and power to achieve that vision.

Most simply, press freedom is the right and responsibility to create separations and dependencies that enable democratic self-governance. It is the power and obligation to know and defend the publics that its separations and dependences create. Today these separations and dependencies live in distributed, technological infrastructures with new actors and often invisible forces, so for the networked press to claim its autonomy, it needs to show how and why it arranges people and machines in particular ways. It needs to understand how its humans and nonhumans align or clash to create some publics but not others. It needs to be able to defend why it creates such meetings, and when necessary for a particular image of the public, it needs to develop new types of sociotechnical power that let it make new types of publics.

Rather than abandoning or collapsing the idea of press freedom—seeing it as naive or anachronistic—my aim is to revive and redeploy it. I trace the idea of press freedom through theories of democratic self-governance, situate it within the press's institutional history, argue that each era of sociotechnical change creates a particular meaning of press freedom, and ask how the contemporary, networked press might claim its freedom and make new publics. Instead of being seen as a holdover from a time that no longer exists, press freedom could be viewed as a powerful framework for arguing why and how the networked press could change.

Interspersed with this tour of institutional forces, I try to deploy my framework and use this new notion of press freedom to argue for a particular normative value—a public right to hear. I claim that the dominant, historical, professionalized image of press freedom—as whatever journalists say they need to be *free from* to pursue self-evident public interest—privileges an individual right to speak over a public right to hear. It confuses journalists' freedom to publish with publics' rights to hear what they need to hear in order to sustain themselves as publics—to realize the inextricably shared conditions under which they live, discover and debate their similarities and differences, devise solutions to predicaments, insulate themselves from harmful forces and nurture contrarian viewpoints, recognize the resources that hold them together, and reinvent themselves through means other than the rational, informational models of citizenship that dominate the traditional mythology of U.S. press freedom. For publics to be anything other than what unconstrained journalists imagine them to be, press freedom can be defensible only if it can be shown that the press's institutional arrangements produce expansive, dynamic, diverse publics.

In an era when many assumptions about communication and information are being reconsidered, it is difficult to say exactly what journalists can or should be free from. A better question to ask might be, "How is the networked press—journalists, software engineers, algorithms, relational databases, social media platforms, and quantified audiences—creating separations and dependencies that enable a public right to hear, make some publics more likely than others, and move beyond an image of the public as whatever journalists assume it to be?"

Three stories can help illustrate the phenomenon. First, in September 2008, high in Google News's list of results for a search on "United Airlines" was a story in the *South Florida Sun Sentinel* on United's recent bankruptcy filing (Zetter, 2008). The story detailed how United had lost significant revenue, could not meet market forecasts, and needed protection from creditors and time to restructure. A Miami investment adviser responsible for publishing news alerts through Bloomberg News Service saw the story and added it to Bloomberg's newsletter; United's stock dropped 75 percent in one day before trading was halted. Unfortunately for United, the *Sentinel*'s website displayed the current date (2008) at the top of its page; it did not include the story's original date of publication (2002). Google's Web crawler mistook the old story for a current story, creating a perfect storm of misinformation: the *Sentinel* displayed dates in a confusing manner; Google's crawler read the only date it saw and made an assumption; the investment adviser assumed that Google highly ranked recent information; Bloomberg subscribers and high-frequency traders assumed that the newsletter contained timely and actionable information; and the stock market assumed that its behavior was rational and based on true information. This is a story of networked press freedom because although the *Sentinel* may have tipped the first domino, the failure is the fault of no single actor. A sociotechnical failure of data, algorithms, individuals, and institutions together led to the creation of false news that drove action.

Second, in 2008, the *Pocono Record* published an online story about Brenda Enterline's sexual harassment lawsuit against Pocono Medical Center. In comments left by readers under the story, several people anonymously said that they had personal knowledge of incidents relevant to the lawsuit. When Enterline's attorneys subpoenaed the newspaper for access to the commenters, the paper refused, claiming that it had a right and obligation to protect the commenters' First Amendment rights to anonymity (Digital Media Law Project, 2009a). The Pennsylvania district court agreed, essentially extending a de facto shield law around the *Pocono Record*'s reporters and commenters. In contrast, also in September 2008, a grand jury in Illinois successfully subpoenaed the *Alton Telegraph* for the names, home addresses, and IP addresses of anonymous commenters who left responses to an online story the paper had run about a murder investigation. The paper argued that "the Illinois reporter's shield law protects the identities of the anonymous commenters as 'sources,'" but the court disagreed, saying that such a shield covers only reporters and not commenters (Digital Media Law Project, 2009b). Such cases have continued, with an Idaho judge ruling in 2012 that the *Spokesman-Review* had to reveal the identity of an anonymous commenter accused of libel, and a 2014 U.S. federal court ruling that the NOLA Media Group had to reveal names, addresses, and phone numbers of its anonymous commenters (Hare, 2014). Even though the First Amendment protects Americans' right to speak anonymously (Hermes, 2013) and several states have shield laws designed to protect newspapers from releasing information against their will (Digital Media Law Project, 2013), it is unclear exactly where newspapers stop and audiences begin. The press may sometimes be free from compelled testimony, but there is little clarity on what exactly the press is and therefore who can claim its freedoms.

Finally, in 2016, Norwegian writer Tom Egeland posted to his Facebook account a story that included Nick Ut's Pulitzer Prize–winning photo of

Vietnamese children running away from a U.S. military napalm attack. One nine-year-old victim was a naked girl. Facebook removed the post because it contained "fully nude genitalia" and "fully nude female breast," in violation of the company's community standards. When Egeland appealed the removal, his account was suspended. The Norwegian newspaper *Aftenposten* then posted the image and a story on the censorship to its company's Facebook site—and its post also was censored. The leader of Norway's conservative party then posted the image and a protest against the censorship—and her post was censored. Facebook initially defended its decisions saying that although it recognized the photo's iconic status, "it's difficult to create a distinction between allowing a photograph of a nude child in one instance and not others." It relented only after the Norwegian prime minister also posted the image with her own protest. Facebook eventually stated: "Because of its status as an iconic image of historical importance, the value of permitting sharing outweighs the value of protecting the community by removal, so we have decided to reinstate the image" (Levin, Wong, & Harding, 2016).

This is a story of networked press freedom. A Facebook user posts an image that has been recognized with one of journalism's highest awards. It triggers a review by Facebook's vast content-moderation operation tasked with policing millions of pieces of media in near real time (Chen, 2014). The user is suspended for appealing the decision. The incident attracts the attention of a news organization, political elites, and worldwide audiences. Eventually, Facebook relents after deciding for itself that the image is iconic, historically important, and worthy of sharing. In this incident, the journalist's right to publish and the public right to hear are not housed within any one organization or profession. They instead are distributed across an image with agreed-on historical significance, platform algorithms surfacing content, social media companies with proprietary community standards, vast populations of piecework censors implementing standards quickly, editorial protests of professional journalists and elite politicians, and an eventual reversal by a private corporation only after *it* thinks that an image should be shared. Here, press autonomy is not just the freedom of Nick Ut, Tom Egeland, or the *Aftenposten* to publish. It is the product of a *network* of humans and nonhumans that make it more or less likely that a public will encounter media and debate its meaning and significance.

There are many more such stories. This book is about putting them in context—to show how these seemingly idiosyncratic incidents are indicative of the larger challenge of figuring out what democratic self-governance requires, what kind of free press should help to secure it, and how such freedom is distributed across a network of humans and machines that together create publics. If nothing else, my hope is that readers will take away from this book both a skepticism about the idea of press freedom and a sense of its promise as a tool for interrogating the networked press. If someone says "We need a free press," my hope is that this book will nudge you to ask, "What kind of freedom, what kind of press, and for what kind of public?" Inspired by Michael Schudson's (2005) question "autonomy from what?," I try to ask "autonomy *of* what and *for* what?"

I develop this framework through four chapters that normatively ground the idea of press freedom, trace its historical roots, situate it within theories of technology, and examine how it plays out in the stories that members of the networked press tell each other about their profession. Chapter 2 argues that democratic self-governance requires more than an individual right to speak; it also requires a public right to hear. I revisit political theories of freedom to argue that democratic autonomy cannot be achieved by simply protecting individual speech and then assuming that a marketplace will somehow produce the quality, diversity, and relationships that people need to understand how and why to live together. Self-governance comes from encountering people and ideas that you have not chosen to consider, but that you *need* to encounter if you are to discover and manage the unavoidably shared consequences of communal life. The idea of democracy emerging from self-made individuals with unfettered rights to speak is an inadequate way of thinking about collective self-governance. Autonomy is about both negative and positive freedoms—a right to pursue ideas, relationships, and actions without unreasonable constraints *and* a capacity to realize versions of yourself that you could not develop independently and that come only through relationships with others (Berlin, 1969). Reviving a narrow and often overlooked body of research on the press's role as a guarantor of positive, affirmative self-governance (Baker, 2002; Emerson, 1970; Fiss, 1996; Meiklejohn, 1948),[1] I suggest that the press—as a public-facing institution of social communication with rights and obligations defined in constitutions around the globe—can be a counterweight to libertarian images of independent self-governance. With an admittedly narrowed focus on the United States, I trace how the U.S. Supreme Court has historically understood—and largely avoided—questions of press freedom and argue that we might look to newer and more controversial political theories of listening to motivate a renewed theory of press freedom.

Chapter 3 asks this double-barreled image of autonomy—as both freedom from and capacity to—to do double duty. I argue that both individual autonomy and institutional autonomy require positive and negative liberties. That is, just as individuals realize their full selves through a mix of individual and collective action, press freedom also depends on how journalists both separate themselves from and depend on nonjournalists. It is sociologically untrue to think that the press does its work by being free from states, markets, or audiences. At different times and in different ways, journalists depend on these entities to do their work. Further, the press *should* depend on them because doing so frees and prevents the press from pursuing only the kind of publics that it alone thinks are worth pursuing—one that is often dominated by an "information model" of citizenship (Schudson, 2003a) that is a small fraction of the democratic role the press could play (Schudson, 2008b). In this chapter, I use field theory and neoinstitutional sociology to show how press freedom has always entailed separations and dependencies and trace several other kinds of publics that a free press could help create if it acknowledged the relational basis of its freedom.

Chapter 4 connects this distributed model of press freedom to media technologies and to the role that digital, material cultures play in creating press separations and dependencies. I offer a brief history of how the press's image of what it thinks it is free from or dependent on is always bound up with questions of what media and communication technologies are thought to be. I connect to science and technology studies to suggest that if the press could see itself not just as a user of technologies but as an *infrastructure*, it would be better able to see how its social and material dynamics lead to different types of publics. The networked press does not convene audiences *through* technologies; its infrastructural dynamics create publics. To understand what kind of publics it could create, the networked press needs to understand how its separations and dependencies—powerful and invisible as infrastructural relations usually are—entail new kinds of meetings among humans and nonhumans, people and machines that together create the information under which people encounter ideas, consequences, tensions, and individuals they would not have sought out on their own. Thus, the networked press—as infrastructure—is not separate from publics but deeply intertwined with them.

Chapter 5 traces where the networked press exists today. Based on a seven-year corpus (2010–2016) of journalistic trade press focused on sociotechnical dynamics—the stories that journalists tell themselves about themselves, which Matt Carlson (2015b) calls "metajournalistic discourse"—I describe how the networked press's autonomy exists in twelve sociotechnical dynamics: observation, production, alignments, labor, analytics, timing, security, audiences, revenue, facts, resemblances, and affect. The typology is not exhaustive or exclusive (some networked press dynamics are not covered in the trade press, and many also exist in other sociotechnical domains), but it is both a snapshot of a historical moment and a generative framework for thinking about networked press freedom going forward. I argue not that the networked press should configure itself in any particular way or realize any particular public, but that by seeing itself as a set of sociotechnical separations and dependencies, the press may better be able to decide and defend what kinds of publics it can create.

In chapter 6, the conclusion, I offer some reflections on how this model of networked press autonomy might be used by journalists, technologists, regulators, designers, educators, and audiences. The networked press is infrastructure that touches on nearly all aspects of society, so any reforms that are made to the press will require engaging with a wide range of actors and various types of power.

My aim in this book is not to dismiss earlier theories of press freedom but to argue that they tell only part of the story. That the press is a product of multiple forces and many different kinds of power is nothing new. But if we want to understand the networked press's potential to create new publics, we might use the idea of networked press freedom as a kind of diagnostic. If we do not like the publics the networked press creates, we should examine its infrastructure and make changes. If we do not like the networked press's infrastructure, we need to show why it leads to unacceptable publics. If a new element of the networked press appears, we need to be able to say quickly and thoughtfully what its relationships are and how they create new publics. And if we have an idea for a new element that we think should be part of the networked press, we must be able to say why we need the new public it might help create.

2   What Kind of Press Freedom Does Democracy Need?

If press freedom is to mean anything, it needs a normative rationale. That is, for the press to claim that it needs cultural and constitutional protections—that its own decisions and contributions are somehow distinct from those of others—it must show why its vision of democratic life is realizable by no other institution. How does the press's unique set of professional standards, ethical values, publishing technologies, and public narratives produce a kind of self-government that others cannot create?

Most of this book is an attempt to trace the *how* of contemporary press freedom—to describe the tensions in tools, practices, norms, and infrastructures that collectively distinguish the networked press from other fields of communication and to show what types of structural controls and leverages are available for configuring the networked press and its freedoms. But first I want to focus on the *why* of press freedom—to trace reasons the press might give for its unique character and contributions, equipping press designers, advocates, and critics with some democratic theory with which to shape and debate the networked press. In the era of nearly instantaneous digital publishing and ubiquitous social network sites, the press is at an existential crossroads. It must demonstrate not just *how* it differs from other publishers but *why*—normatively, structurally, institutionally—it should be allowed and required be different and how its differences are essential to realizing a particular type of democratic life. As C. Edwin Baker (1998, p. 318) puts it, assessing "the media's service to democracy requires a theory of democracy," and conversely, different theories of democracy make different demands of the media.

In unpacking the *why* of press freedom, I want to suggest in this chapter that one way to think about the press's freedom is how well it ensures a public right to hear. That is, although the press might configure itself in a number of different ways (configurations I explore in subsequent chapters), it might most legitimately defend its unique identity and freedoms to the extent that it helps people hear in ways that markets, states, social networks, algorithms, and self-interest alone cannot create. In Baker's language, the press's value to democracy and therefore the legitimacy of its claims for freedom depend not only on how well it endures government oversight or meets the expectations of consumers choosing among viewpoints presented to them by their friends, search engines, or curiosity. The press also must create the conditions under which publics can hear—conditions that require the press to take the *public* as its primary concern, have a theory of why it matters, and an understanding of how it hears.

I develop this claim—that the press's freedom depends on how well it ensures a public right to hear—in four ways. First, I argue that the idea of democratic autonomy requires seeing individual freedom as a product of social relationships. Second, I review the demands that this view of autonomy makes on free speech, arguing that autonomy requires more than individual expression in marketplaces of speech. Third, I describe a structural, institutional model of the press, grounded in an affirmative interpretation of the First Amendment and a review of relevant U.S. Supreme Court cases to show that there is a basis in law for seeing the press as an institution that could be dedicated to ensuring a public right to hear. And finally, I use recent literature on the democratic value of listening to argue that the thoughtful absence of speech can be part of a rich system of public communication.

My aim in tying together these threads is to construct a *normative* case for press freedom grounded in the idea of a public right to hear, a little examined cornerstone of democratic life. That is, the press earns its own freedom by ensuring the democratic autonomy of its constituents—an autonomy requiring that institutions support public speaking and listening. Although the press's freedom is a matter of institutional design, professional practice, and audience relations (explored in subsequent chapters), the meaning of constituents' democratic autonomy is a problem for political theory that requires a close examination of what individual autonomy means in democracies.

The Idea of Democratic Autonomy

Although the concept of autonomy is "at the center of the modern demo-cratic project" (Held, 2006, p. 260) and frequently is invoked by theorists and activists of all stripes, there is little agreement on what it means. Sometimes it is seen as unfettered action—individual, physical motions unimpeded by others—and at other times it is seen as an ability to change preferences in the face of changing circumstances (M. J. Meyer, 1987). Some scholars argue that autonomy requires knowledge and anticipation—that autonomous action can be taken only if someone is aware of their circum-stances and available options and can reasonably foresee consequences of that action (Benn, 1988; Dworkin, 1988). Still others add that autonomy means making a decision independently because all forms of influence are potentially coercive (Arneson, 1985; Neely, 1974). Finally, other scholars distinguish between autonomy bracketed by global factors that are beyond a person's immediate control (for example, not being free to act because of legal or military force, cultural norms, or social traditions) and by local influences that are within a person's immediate, observable context and subject to individual interpretation (for example, personal relationships with friends or coworkers) (Dworkin, 1981). Randall Collins (1992, p. 77) goes so far to suggest that that individual agency is a "fantasy ... which we find pleasant to believe in"—an unfortunate result of naively misap-plying the findings of microsociologists like Erving Goffman and Harold Garfinkel to the powerful restrictions on individual freedom that are better explained by macrosociological accounts of sociopolitical forces. Collins claims that Anthony Giddens's (1984) theory of structuration—in which social structures and human agency continually reflect and recreate each other (Sewell, 1992)—presents a romantic and empirically unsupported vision of life because although people craft numerous folk theories about why society behaves as it does (D. Beer & Burrows, 2010; C. W. Mills, 1959/2000), "real-life individuals do not know very much of the social struc-ture which surrounds them" (Collins, 1992).

Nevertheless, especially among Western political ideals and traditions, autonomy is usually about the individual's power to self-govern (Christ-man, 1988, 1991). It is rooted in a Kantian desire for "freedom of the will from causal determinism" (Fallon, 1994, p. 878) and driven by a desire to use reason—as opposed to religious faith, naive spiritualism, or monarchical allegiance—to make decisions (Kant, 1785/2002). Autonomy is a future-oriented concept—a way to talk about what people can imagine and realize and a way to critique the extent to which their current circumstances let them create the world in which they wished they lived.

But this focus on an individual—on how preferences, knowledge, anticipations, and actions can be achieved unencumbered by others—is inadequate. It presumes that such individual freedom is possible in the absence of a social system, gives us few clues about how it might be achieved, and pits the individual against the forces of social and cultural enlightenment that people might use to decide what they want to know or be or do for themselves. Let me address each of these shortcomings.

First, the focus on the individual is a particularly Western one that presumes "everyone ... to be the best judge of his or her own good or interests" (Dahl, 1989, p. 100). In this idealized form, freedom comes from the *absence* of social relations. This presumption is consistent with a liberal political tradition in which equality is considered to be a private and individual matter focused on removing obstacles to personal realization:

The only freedom which deserves the name, is that of pursuing our own good in our own way, so long as we do not attempt to deprive others of theirs, or impede their efforts to obtain it. Each is the proper guardian of his own health, whether bodily, *or* mental and spiritual. Mankind are greater gainers by suffering each other to live as seems good to themselves, than by compelling each to live as seems good to the rest. (Mill, 1859/1974, p. 81)

Mill acknowledges that people live within associations, but his model of freedom requires that these relationships do not interfere with individuals' opportunities to make the lives that they see as desirable. Not only is a test for democratic autonomy passed at an individual level, but any role played by the collective is presumed to be, at best, an irrelevant distraction and, at worst, a serious impediment to personal liberty.

The liberal, pluralist tradition is principally concerned with ensuring that people have equal opportunities. It sees community and social associations as either tools for helping individuals advance or as sentimental tangents to the core project of individual, democratic liberty (Christians, Glasser, McQuail, Nordenstreng, & White, 2009, pp. 96–99). Whereas John Stuart Mill and Robert A. Dahl see autonomy as an ideal that individuals try to realize in the absence of interference, David Held (2006) agrees that people should be free from the "*arbitrary* use of political authority" but otherwise sees the idea of a priori personal independence as both theoretically un-realizable and empirically unfounded. Rather than being constrained by outside influences, he argues, personal autonomy always *emerges from* and *depends on* social, political, economic, and cultural circumstances. That is, people can achieve freedom *through* persuasive relationships (D. A. Strauss, 1991), not despite them. Democratic freedom and self-realization come from resisting others and being empowered by them (Rose, 1999, p. 65). The real challenge, Held argues, is for democratic institutions to create the right mix of influence, persuasion, resistance, and empowerment that best enables individual autonomy.

Democratic freedom is thus entangled with institutional design. For Held (2006, p. 263), the capacity "to deliberate, judge, choose and act upon different possible courses of action in private as well as public life" depends on a set of *resources*—material and symbolic goods that citizens must have access to and be able to use if they are to realize their potentials. Essentially, this model says that individual autonomy comes not only from having the power to realize preexisting preferences free of undue influence (such preferences rarely preexist, and such freedom is practically impossible) but also from being exposed to influences that you neither created nor chose for yourself. Autonomy comes from living within a set of circumstances that make it likely for you to encounter new perspectives that will, ideally, make future preferences richer and more complex.

Only by acknowledging and engaging with these external factors—essentially, being secure enough to learn things that might challenge but ultimately strengthen that security—can people realize *self-reflective* autonomy (Benn, 1988). Such self-reflexivity means acknowledging that we are

unique individuals, with our own identities created from the way we have taken up the histories, cultural constructs, language, and social relations of hierarchy and subordination, that condition our lives. (I. M. Young, 1997, p. 392)

Ignoring the power of these unavoidable influences means running the risk of becoming someone who is *heteronomously autonomous*: "dominated by his own prejudices, blinkered by unexamined ideology, or a slave to convention ... One looks for the causes of his decisions in the opinions and beliefs of other people which his own merely reflect" (Benn, 1988, pp. 124–125). Someone may seem independent and free of external influences but actually be simply receiving and uncritically recreating a system of values and influences he cannot see or appreciate.[1] (For example, this type of illusory autonomy may appear when people supposedly rationally choose a product or service without understanding that their choice has likely been influenced by a system of media advertising, a company's strategic positioning in relation to competitors, preexisting brand loyalties, or assumptions about what people like them usually buy.)

The underlying ideal here is that autonomy requires both *negative* and *positive freedoms*.[2] That is, someone has the right to be "left to do or be what he is able to do or be, without interference by other persons," but to be realized, that right needs "source[s] of control or interference" (Berlin, 1969, pp. 121–122). In other words, to do or be anything that I want, I need people to challenge and support me, to show me ways of being I never would have discovered on my own, to provide insights I cannot create in isolation, and to critique and check the ideas and actions that I think are right. Although this distinction is a powerful and helpful way to understand the dualistic nature of autonomy—as something that involves both the individual and the surrounding environment—it is too simplistic.

Notably, Gerald C. MacCallum Jr. (1967, p. 314) argues that democratic freedom emerges from a triad of relations: "freedom is always *of* something (an agent or agents), *from* something, *to* do, not do, become or not become something." That is, individual autonomy never exists as an abstract push-pull between constraints and action. Rather, there is a particular person in the middle—someone with myriad identities and relationships to others who reminds us to ask not just "Can people be free?" but "When do particular people have autonomy, and what does their balance of *freedom from* and *freedom to* look like?"[3] Richard H. Fallon Jr. (1994) similarly distinguishes between ascriptive and descriptive autonomy. *Ascriptive* autonomy is an ideal that we may strive for but know that we will never realize. This is the "the autonomy we ascribe to ourselves and others as the foundation of a right to make self-regarding decisions ... a moral entailment of personhood" (Fallon, 1994, p. 878). *Descriptive* autonomy, though, refers to people's "actual condition and signifies the extent to which they are meaningfully 'self-governed' in a universe shaped by causal forces" (p. 877). That is, autonomy is not a dualistic concept—a binary ideal of positive and negative freedoms—but rather a "matter of degree" that depends in part on how well someone understands what her relationships to others are, what influences her, and what action might look like in a particular circumstance. In this descriptive, pragmatic model, even "paternalism can sometimes be defended as a means of preserving or promoting autonomy" (Fallon, 1994, p. 877). Limits on fast-food advertising may be needed to curb the addictions of people who may *feel* like they are making independent eating decisions and who do not understand that their behavior is influenced by powerful advertising messages. Autonomy comes from making tradeoffs that limit some personal freedoms in order to secure broader autonomy and self-realization.

Understanding why such tradeoffs are necessary means accepting that social influences are crucial for realizing freedom, a strange notion in Western contexts that prize individuals' freedoms *from* others. This more complex vision of autonomy as a social construct means subjecting yourself and your thinking to others, appreciating that

to be autonomous one must have reasons for acting and be capable of second thoughts in the light of new reasons.... And for reasons one must have a system of beliefs from which action commitments derive and into which new evidence can be assimilated, yielding new commitments. How could anyone come by these bits of basic equipment except by learning them in the first instance from parents, teachers, friends, and colleagues? Someone who had escaped such a socialization process would not be free, unconstrained, able to make *anything* of himself that he chose; he would be able to make nothing of himself, being hardly a person at all. (Benn, 1988, p. 179)

Stanley I. Benn encourages us not to concentrate on whether people feel like they are free in their decision making (relying on self-reported satisfaction) but instead to examine the social conditions under which they make decisions and ask how meaningfully different their choices are. Testing whether someone can simply choose one option over another is a poor test of their autonomy if the options offered are few or practically identical. Autonomy based on choice is better seen as a probabilistic and pragmatic phenomenon in which someone's potential to think or act differently depends on their likelihood of encountering a meaningfully diverse set of choices. As Ulrich Beck puts it:

Opportunities, dangers, biographical uncertainties that were earlier predefined within the family association, the village community, or by recourse to the rules of social estates or classes, must now be perceived, interpreted, decided and processed by individuals themselves. The consequences—opportunities and burdens alike—are shifted onto individuals who, naturally, in face of the complexity of social interconnections, are often unable to take the necessary decisions in a properly founded way, by considering interests, morality and consequences. (Beck, 2002, p. 4)

That is, amid forces that privilege and force individualization, if people are to make choices with democratic value, they need supportive social structures that equip them with "full information and under suitable conditions of reflection" (Fiss, 1996, p. 23). My autonomy depends on how well *other people* articulate ideas and how diverse the resulting "space of possibles" (Bourdieu, 1993, p. 30)—within which I might think and act—is. The power of this space to "surpass the given toward an open future" (de Beauvoir, 1948, p. 91) depends not only on the rational exchange of truth claims in a marketplace of propositions. Rather, it comes from the messier but no less structured "power of redescribing"

the power of language to make new and different things possible and important—an appreciation which becomes possible only when one's aim becomes an expanding repertoire of alternative descriptions rather than The One Right Description. (Rorty, 1989, pp. 39–40)

Democratic autonomy is thus a communication problem that sits at an intersection of the individual and the collective, the private and the social. At first glance, we might judge personal autonomy simply in terms of what individuals do, but when it is more fully considered, we can see how such actions (and thus autonomy) emerge from "conditions of enactment" (Held, 2006, p. 260)—pragmatic institutional and organizational circumstances that make it likely for people to communicate about, experiment with, and realize versions of themselves that they could not achieve alone. Thus, communication creates the conditions under which individual autonomy can exist; personal freedom is a problem of free speech. But what kind of free speech does such autonomy require, how does this speech differ from unfettered personal expression, and what kinds of institutions might support such freedom?

Free Speech and Democratic Autonomy

If autonomy requires both *freedom from* unreasonable influence and a *duty to* engage with others, then we need to ask what kind of institutions help us become autonomous, "socialized individuals" (Benn, 1988, p. 179). The press is one such public-facing institution, but others also sit at this intersection between individual empowerment and socialization. Ideally, public schools "provide every child with an opportunity to choose freely and rationally among the widest range of lives" (Gutmann, 1987, p. 34), museums critically display cultural objects in order to teach visitors about the broader cultural histories that color their private lives (DiMaggio, 1991), and public libraries are civic-minded environments that offer group learning experiences to individuals and opportunities for borrowers to bring bits of curated collections into their private homes (Kerslake & Kinnell, 1998). Each institution helps individuals follow personal interests—people choose courses, select exhibits, borrow books—but they do so within larger traditions of professionalized curation that enable individual autonomy by selecting materials and experiences intended to help people imagine and choose ways of thinking and acting. That is, institutions are not impediments to individual autonomy but, in many circumstances, are vehicles through which people might realize different versions of themselves, which is a core feature of democratic freedom.

But what, exactly, does it mean for institutional circumstances to give rise to the kind of socialized autonomy outlined earlier—the mix of *freedom from* and *freedom to* considered essential for creating the space of possibles? Specific to the press, what demands might we make of how it understands free speech to ensure the kind of public communication required for individuals' democratic autonomy? Recalling the claim made earlier that the press earns its own freedom by helping to ensure the autonomy of its constituents, this question becomes doubly important. These institutional views of free speech are the conditions under which individuals might better achieve freedom, and they also are also a kind of litmus test for the press—a test it must pass if it wishes to enjoy the kind of cultural and constitutional protections that allow it the security it needs to reinvent itself continually. But what kind of role should the press play in free speech in order to engender democratic autonomy?

The relationship between speech and freedom is complex, but fundamentally it is based on the idea that speech is an other-regarding act (Schauer, 1982). Because speech affects others, it must be regulated on what Thomas Scanlon (1972, pp. 204–205) calls "consequentialist" grounds: speech acts are weighed for their ability to produce good and bad outcomes. These effects can be short-term and personal—"saying or printing something untrue (or true) about another person may damage his reputation, humiliate him, invade his privacy, offend him, or cause emotional distress"—or long-term and public—"the disclosure of military secrets, or the spread of lies (or truth) about government may impair the efficiency of the machinery of the state" (Schauer, 1982, p. 10).

In a democratic system, this speech "machinery" is critical for realizing a type of self-government in which individuals knowingly and freely submit to constraints on their freedom. The democratic legitimacy of this submission depends on how consequences have been discussed and debated and therefore on how speech is produced and circulates. As Franklyn S. Haiman (1981, p. 6) describes it, "Social order is a means to maximizing individual liberty and security," but for this order to function properly, it requires people to engage in "symbolic behavior" in which they express themselves, debate ideas, agree to resolutions, or maintain dissent.

Knowing that speech has both local and global effects (it matters both to individuals and to the autonomy they derive from their relationships to collectives), there are two main ways to think about the relationship between free speech and personal autonomy—an argument from truth and an argument from democracy.

The Argument from Truth

John Stuart Mill asserted that determining the truth requires the expressions of others. He argued that the "peculiar evil of silencing the expression of an opinion" (Mill, 1859/1974, p. 76) harms not only those who hold that view but also those who disagree with it: "If the opinion is right, [individuals] are deprived of the opportunity of exchanging error for truth: if wrong, they lose, what is almost as great a benefit, the clearer perception and livelier impression of truth, produced by its collision with error" (p. 76). Furthermore, the truly autonomous individual must be free even to experience harm that might result from encountering false statements; otherwise, he would "have to concede to the state the right to decide that certain views were false and, once it had so decided, to prevent him from hearing them" (Scanlon, 1972, p. 217).

Essentially, if truths are to be discovered and agreed on, they need environments for unrestricted conversation, debate, and claim making. This idea underpins the marketplace model of speech, a laissez-faire approach to speech regulation often embraced by the U.S. Supreme Court. Justice Oliver Wendell Holmes Jr. asserted that "the best test of truth is the power of the thought to get itself accepted in the competition of the market," and Justice Felix Frankfurter claimed that "the history of civilization is in considerable measure the displacement of error which once held sway as official truth by beliefs which in turn have yielded to other truths" (Schauer, 1982,

p. 15). And the U.S. Supreme Court's ruling in *Citizens United v. Federal Election Commission* (2009, p. 5) stated that "All speakers, including individuals and the media, use money amassed from the economic marketplace to fund their speech, and the First Amendment protects the resulting speech." By finding that "First Amendment protections do not depend on the speaker's 'financial ability to engage in public discussion'" (p. 5), the Court simultaneously accepted a marketplace model of speech and made no provisions for the fact that those with considerable resources to make themselves heard (such as corporations that have amassed large amounts of money from an economic marketplace) may drown out the speech of those with fewer resources.

This market-based theory of speech is powerful and ubiquitous, but as C. Edwin Baker (1989, pp. 6–15) shows, it suffers from three main weaknesses. First, adopting the theoretical perspectives of symbolic interactionism and social constructionism (e.g., see Blumer, 1969; Goffman, 1959; Mead, 1934/1967), Baker argues that the marketplace model assumes that all truths are objective and discoverable. It presumes that truths are unique (there is only one), binary (a claim is either true or false), and "out there" (preexisting and waiting to be discovered). The model also fails to explain why some claims may be considered more truthful than others by certain people at certain times. It has little to say about the value of sustained dissents by challengers who contest the truths presented as consensus by those with the power to do so. The marketplace provides no timeline for arriving at truth, no ethical accounting for the harms that people might have to endure as the market discovers truth, and no comment on how claims can be plausible and function as if they were true—not because they have been verified by a disinterested marketplace but because they "help us to get into satisfactory relation with other parts of our experience" (James, 1981, p. 30). Furthermore, a marketplace model erroneously equates freedom of speech with

liberty of the individual, where individual expression is treated like a *property*, to be defended and protected insofar as and as long as the rights of others are not violated in the process. (Lacey, 2013, p. 169)

Not only does this speech-as-property model focus only on the negative aspects of liberty (equating it with *freedom from* constraint), but it also ignores what Baker says is the "special nature of media products"—what makes them "not toasters" (Baker, 2002, p. 7). They are, for example, usually nonrivalrous, nonexcludable public goods that can provide significant positive externalities, distributing benefits to multiple people with little or no extra expense, regardless of whether everyone consumes the product (consider the benefits of living in a society where others consume media and gain knowledge, even if you do not).[4]

Second, he claims that the classic theory assumes that "people's rational faculties … enable them to sort through the form and frequency of message presentation to evaluate the core truth in the messages" (Baker, 1989, p. 7). The marketplace model assumes that people are already equipped with critical skills and are somehow already capable of stepping outside themselves and their own understanding to evaluate claims independent of their own identities and social positions. Such an assumption begs the question because it does not explain where such skills or capabilities come from. It suggests the preexistence of trusted agents who determine truth on our behalf (Coase, 1974) or some other space separate from a market that provides people with the facilities necessary to participate in markets.

Third, Baker claims that such a marketplace—even if it could exist—is of questionable value because people may not always want to discover a particular truth. A marketplace model does not allow for a kind of freedom not to be, for whatever reason, uninformed. Such ignorance may seem asocial or unethical (indeed, it may operate under different moral standards), but it also may be a strategic avoidance of information for some reasons that is simply differently efficient. (Consider Anthony Downs's 1957 theory of "rational ignorance" in which voters strategically decide that further enlightenment is not worth the effort.) People may also be guided by "irrational" desires to reach solutions that they do not consider "true" in any strict sense but that satisfice as good enough (Kahneman, 2003; Simon, 1978, 1983) for their particular circumstances.

Essentially, Baker's critiques undercut the assumption that a marketplace of speech—a lightly regulated space in which the state is mostly silent and takes little or no action to structure the conditions under which individuals encounter new ideas—is the desired ideal for ensuring democratic autonomy. There is a difference between seeing the marketplace as metaphor (an idealized space in which claims are thoughtfully contributed and considered by a wide variety of people equitably searching for plausible, workable, ethical understandings) and the marketplace as a gatekeeper (a structured environment in which speech is commodified and circulated according to dynamics that privilege rationality and speakers who possess the power to foreclose debate and thus make claims function as truths). If you see truth as a social construct reflecting the dynamics of institutions like the press, then a purely marketplace account of speech is inadequate. The failures of the marketplace model suggest a need for some other way of designing free speech—some other set of values that speak to role free speech plays in democracies, not markets.

The Argument from Democracy

The "argument from democracy" (Schauer, 1982, pp. 35–45) is less concerned with the role that free speech plays in discovering truths and more focused on its ability to sustain democracy. There are indeed different types of democracy that require different types of speech (more on this in chapter 3), but as this argument goes, free speech is a fundamental requirement if citizens are to engage in self-government. In the United States, for instance, the Constitution's main function is to delimit the state's power over self-organizing individuals, stating how and when the state may constrain individuals' personal freedoms. For constitutions to legitimately govern citizens, they must "derive their just powers from the consent of the governed" (Meiklejohn, 1948, p. 3), and citizens must have the autonomy and communication required to give such consent. As Alexander Meiklejohn argues, the

First Amendment is not, primarily, a device for the winning of new truth.... It is a device for the sharing of whatever truth has been won.... The primary purpose of the First Amendment is, then, that all the citizens shall, so far as possible, understand the issues which bear upon common life. That is why no idea, no opinion, no doubt, no belief, no counterbelief, no relevant information, may be kept from them. (Meiklejohn, 1948, pp. 88–89)

The argument from democracy is related to the argument from truth, but with a major difference. It says that the value of free speech is its capacity to achieve *public* ends—to help structure "common life." That is, free speech is not concerned only with people having the right to speak or individuals discover truths relevant to their private interests. The democratic function of free speech also must be concerned with how speech enables shared conditions and collective self-government—that is, public issues that may not attract private interests or survive marketplace dynamics. As Meiklejohn (1948, p. 25) famously wrote, the First Amendment's "point of ultimate

interest is not the words of the speakers, but the minds of the hearers.... [W]
hat is essential is not that everyone shall speak, but that everything worth
saying shall be said."

Although people certainly make individual communication decisions
that make informed citizenship possible—for example, by reading newspapers, voting in elections, writing letters to representatives, and arguing ideas
with neighbors—Meiklejohn's concern is more structural and is focused
on the conditions that might give rise to legitimate self-government. Put
slightly differently by another free-speech scholar concerned with structural
aspects of free speech, Owen Fiss claims that the

purpose of free speech is not individual self-actualization, but rather the preservation of
democracy, and the right of a people, as a people, to decide what kind of life it wishes
to live. Autonomy is protected not because of its intrinsic value, as a Kantian might
insist, but rather as a means or instrument of collective self-determination.... The critical assumption in this theory is that the protection of autonomy will produce a public
debate that will be "uninhibited, robust, and wide-open." (Fiss, 1986, pp. 1409–1410)

Such a relationship between self-government and free speech is certainly
open to critique. In an article titled "Meiklejohn's Mistake," Robert C. Post
(1993) argues that Meiklejohn's "collectivist" vision of free speech is fundamentally misguided because it assumes an end without specifying the
means. Meiklejohn's ideal, Post argues, is a "'traditional American town
meeting' [that is] 'not a Hyde Park' [or a] scene of 'unregulated talkative-
ness" (p. 1112). This town meeting model presumes the existence of a common agenda, set of goals, and subservience to the meeting leaders. It fails
to say exactly how such an agenda might arise, who would be responsible
for deciding whether everything worth being said had been said, and what
might become of citizens who either cannot or do not participate in what
Post calls the "managerial" structure of a town hall's authority. Post is
right to call out some circularity in Meiklejohn's reasoning: Meiklejohn's
ideal of self-government relies on the existence of a system of free expression in which there is some kind of shared communication, but it fails to
articulate exactly how this communication arises in the first place. Instead,
Post argues that we should reject overt attempts by the state to manage
public discourse on our behalf because, by doing so, we relieve ourselves of
the *individual* power to influence the conditions of public discourse and the
chance to realize the ideal of self-government that Meiklejohn envisions.[5]

This individual power, Jack M. Balkin claims in a further critique of Meiklejohn, is now with us because Meiklejohn's broadcast media world is being transformed by

technological changes [that make] it possible for large numbers of people to broadcast and publish to audiences around the world, to be speakers as well as audiences, to be active producers of information content, not just recipients or consumers. (Balkin, 2008, p. 114)

Meiklejohn's ideal, Post and Balkin claim, comes from outdated media worlds (the town hall and broadcast media) that no longer exist.

Judith Lichtenberg (1987) also critiques Meiklejohn's ideal but does so from a slightly different perspective. She emphasizes the need for equality among individual speakers rather than their independence from state control, giving three reasons why democratic free speech requires equality of opportunity to speak: "there is no way of telling in advance where a good idea will come from" (systematically and structurally excluding some speakers will prevent quality perspectives from entering into public discourse); "valuable contributions to arriving at the truth come in many forms, speaking the truth being only one of them" (democracies develop through more than the simple exchange of factually truthful or false statements); and "much of the value of a person's contribution to the 'marketplace of ideas' is its role in stimulating others to defend or reformulate or refute" (someone's mere presence, less than the rational value of their utterances, may surface differences that are critical for realizing autonomy) (Lichtenberg, 1987, p. 338).

Lichtenberg asks the designers and regulators of speech systems to see themselves not only as facilitators of free speech and self-government but as gatekeepers of particular *kinds* of self-government. She argues that the press, the state, and corporations—as public-facing collectives—enjoy free-speech rights and privileges only insofar as their actions serve to increase both individual opportunities to speak and also the overall diversity and equitability of speech within the public sphere.[6] That is, institutional actors like the state and press have both expressive responsibilities (to say some things but not others at certain times) and *structural* responsibilities to "establish essential preconditions for collective self-governance by making certain that all sides are presented to the public" (Fiss, 1996, p. 18).

Post's, Balkin's, Lichtenberg's, and Fiss's critiques help to distinguish between normative ideals and empirical conditions. That is, we can still

accept Meiklejohn's primary theoretical aim—a system in which the consent to be governed emerges when citizens knowingly and freely debate the
constraints they place on themselves—while accepting Post's plea to keep
dynamic and debatable the conditions of self-expression. Free speech is not
an end in itself (a static state of affairs in which expression is managed
by any central authority), nor does it adhere to any particular ideology (such
as one in which the individual's freedom to speak is privileged over a collective right to enlightened self-determination). Rather, as Thomas Emerson
puts it, free speech can best be thought of as a system of freedom of expression
that includes

the right to form and hold beliefs and opinions on any subject, and to communicate
ideas, opinions, and information through any medium ... the right to remain silent ...
the right to hear the views of others and to listen to their version of the facts [and]
the right to assemble and to form associations, that is, to combine with others in
joint expression. (Emerson, 1970, p. 3)

In his later work, Emerson (1981) elaborates on this system by arguing for
two types of government activity.[7] The first involves promoting the system
of freedom of expression—for example, by granting subsidies to electoral
candidates without preference; building cultural centers for use by anyone; regulating airwaves to ensure the sustained delivery of all messages;
and protecting individuals' rights to speech on streets, in parks, in open
spaces, and on privately owned land that looks and acts like public spaces.
The second entails government participating in the system of freedom of
expression—for example, when a government official issues information,
a state agency makes a report, or a representative delivers a public speech.
The only circumstance in which the state might legitimately exercise what
Post would call its "managerial" powers occurs when the state is promoting the overall system of freedom of expression, making possible "greater
opportunity for expression, increased diversity, or similar improvements in
the system" (Emerson, 1981, p. 799). The government, Emerson argues,
should always be expressly prohibited from holding an audience captive
for communication; communicating covertly or without disclosing itself as
the state; mobilizing citizens through grassroots efforts that pit one branch
of government against another; and promoting in even an implicitly partisan manner one religion or political candidate over another, especially
within institutions like schools and museums designed to educate citizens
(pp. 835–848).

Essentially, Emerson changes the focus of free speech from how individuals can speak or pursue private interests to how systems of free speech enable the achievement of public aims. For instance, in his ideal system of freedom of expression, the U.S. Constitution's First Amendment speech and press clauses ("Congress shall make no law ... abridging the freedom of speech, or of the press") work together to support both individual and collective aspects of democratic autonomy. Taken together, the clauses ensure people's (mostly) unfettered freedom to express themselves and pursue individual interests, *and* they expect the press to earn its unique constitutional privileges (it is the only industry explicitly mentioned in the Constitution) by both contributing speech to the system and investing in the circulation of speech with public value.

It is this understanding of the press clause—as a structural, institutional complement to the free-speech clause—to which I now turn, to trace when and why the press has enjoyed and asserted its autonomy, and how such autonomy has been interpreted and limited by the Supreme Court (in both bench opinions and extrajudicial writings).

A Structural View of the Press, Press Freedom, and an Affirmative First Amendment

Equipped with these rationales for free speech—the arguments from truth and democracy and the critiques thereof—we might ask what role the press can or should play in a system of free expression. How can the press be designed and enacted in ways that contribute to both the individual and collective aspects of democratic autonomy? That is, what are differences between the First Amendment's[8] speech clause and press clause, when has the Supreme Court recognized the press and afforded it privileges, and what might these press rights and responsibilities mean for understanding the press's own freedom?

For most of U.S. constitutional history, the press and speech clauses were used interchangeably and largely without distinction (D. A. Anderson, 1983, 2002). In the 1920s, the Supreme Court began to consider the press as a potentially distinct institutional actor with democratic functions. For instance, the Court heard but mostly rejected the press's arguments that it should be free to criticize the government and promote dissenting opinions (issuing decisions that largely upheld the Espionage Act of 1917 and the Sedition Act of 1918). It was not until *Near v. Minnesota* (1931) that the Court overturned a Minnesota state law prohibiting the press from publishing articles critical of police officers, finding that the state's prior restraint of the newspaper was unconstitutional (Garry, 1994, p. 15). This was an early instance of what would become a small series of Supreme Court cases mostly in the 1960s and 1970s that focused on deciding what, if any, rights or privileges the press should enjoy.[9]

As these court cases emerged, so did a body of legal scholarship arguing that the First Amendment could best be understood as a *structural* provision (Fiss, 1996). In addition to being concerned with particular news-gathering practices, this literature is focused on the broader institutional conditions under which citizens express and hear speech. The core idea is that the press and speech clauses ideally work together to create a system of expression that supports democratic aims (Fiss, 1986, p. 1411). Such a system includes both a *negative* interpretation of the First Amendment that guarantees *individuals freedom from* illegitimate constraints on their rights to speak and an *affirmative* interpretation of the First Amendment that ensures a *public's freedom to* hear how it is "affected by the indirect consequences ... and see to it that their interests are conserved and protected" (Dewey, 1954, p. 16). An affirmative, structural view of the First Amendment calls for the press to be judged according to how well it ensures both individual rights to speak and also public freedoms to hear. It rejects the idea that a disinterested marketplace of ideas alone somehow aggregates private, individual interests into public, collective concerns, making the public a necessary unit of analysis to consider alongside the individual. It asks journalists to care not only about how well they protect their own professional privileges and news-gathering practices but also about how well the press functions as a democratic institution that helps publics hear what they need to hear to achieve autonomy.[10]

The press (however it might be constitutionally defined at any moment in history)[11] is thus an institutional exemplar in a system of free speech designed for public needs.[12] Press autonomy might best be understood not by trying to reconstruct constitutional history (discerning what the constitutional framers meant by "the press")[13] but rather by examining the conditions under which the press envisions and serves publics, and therefore how it might legitimately earn its autonomy.

The Institutional Press

The institutional press has never been explicitly or consistently defined in U.S. Supreme Court jurisprudence. The court historically has been reluctant to hear press clause cases, to issue rulings that invoke the press clause, to distinguish journalists or news organization owners from other citizens, or to give them special privileges. To treat the press differently would mean creating a de facto two-tiered Constitution that assigns rights and responsibilities to some but not others—to define *journalism*.[14]

Instead, the Court historically has erred on the side of protecting most speech, no matter where it comes from. It limits speech rights on the bases of particular contexts and scenarios, not immutable identities like "journalist" or "not journalist" (D. A. Anderson, 1983; Bezanson, 2012; Schauer, 1998). It generally has done so using two broad logics. First, it has considered whether the speech in question is considered "low-value" (such as types of pornography, sexual and racial harassment, and threats) or "high-value" (such as political speech, deliberative discussions on current issues, and entertainment considered to be of public value). Second, the Court has evaluated whether speech restrictions are

• Content-neutral: Situations in which the "content of the expression is utterly irrelevant to whether the speech is restricted," (Sunstein, 1994, p. 11) as in a decision to ban all speech on billboards regardless of who purchased the space or what they said;
• Content-based: Limitations that consider the type or category of speech (for example, banning all political speech in a particular area); or
• Viewpoint-based: Restrictions that actively take sides in a debate, limiting the speech of those who disagree with a particular party's position.

The Court rarely accepts viewpoint-based restrictions, periodically approves content-based restrictions, and has most often accepted content-neutral "time, manner, and place" restrictions that are blind to who the speaker is or what is being said (Sunstein, 1994, pp. 1–23, 167–208).

Within these logics, the Court has readily differentiated among types of speech, distinguishing "incitement from advocacy, commercial speech from noncommercial speech, obscenity from indecency, public interest speech from personal interest speech, public forums from nonpublic forums and from 'designated' public forums" (Schauer, 2005, p. 1263). But with the exception of the broadcasting industry, it historically has not explicitly considered a speaker's institutional membership. Schauer offers three reasons for this reluctance. First, justices aim to make decisions according to legal distinctions rather than social theories:

What distinguishes categories like viewpoint discrimination, content regulation, public forum, and prior restraint from categories like universities, libraries, elections, and the press is that the former exist in the First Amendment but the latter exist in the world. (Schauer, 2005, p. 1265)

Second, courts are traditionally conservative entities focused on maintaining stability and avoiding radical change. And third, if the Court attempts to interpret the identities of institutions too closely, it may weaken the First Amendment, making it a less useful general instrument of law for regulating action across eras and contexts.

However, there is also a danger that institutionally blind decisions create *less* protection for the kinds of speech that are essential for self-government. If the Court ignores institutional particularities, it may create "institutional compression" (Schauer, 2005, p. 1272), artificially separating speech and speakers from contexts, norms, principles, and incentives of their circumstances. The First Amendment may be less powerful and increasingly irrelevant if the Court is reluctant to enter into the messiness of institutional action. A "Supreme Court [that is] unwilling to distinguish among the lone pamphleteer, the blogger, and the full-time reporter for the *New York Times* is far less likely to grant special privileges to pamphleteers and bloggers than it is, as it has, to grant privileges to no one" (Schauer, 2005, p. 1272). In the absence of clear distinctions, the Court may simply avoid getting involved for fear of making definitions where none exists.

An institutional middle ground is needed as a way for the Court to anchor its decisions in principles that affirm a broad interpretation of the First Amendment (making room for consistency with both past circumstances and unanticipated contexts) while staying relevant and timely (guiding citizens' and governments' expectations about what speech is more or less encouraged and protected). Frederick Schauer sketches such a two-tier system the Court might use to consider the institutional nature of speech:

We first locate some value that the First Amendment treats, or should treat, as particularly important. Then we investigate whether that value is situated significantly within and thus disproportionately served by some existing social institution whose identity and boundaries are at least moderately identifiable. If so, then we might develop a kind of second-order test. If there is a reporter's privilege, for example, we might ask not whether this exercise of the privilege serves primary First Amendment purposes, but instead simply whether the person claiming the privilege is a reporter. Obviously, defining the category of people who receive the privilege will be based both on the reasons for having the privilege and the reasons for locating it in a particular institution, but the case-by-case inquiry will largely consist of applying the rule, rather than applying the reasons lying behind the rule directly to individual cases. (Schauer, 2005, p. 1275)

Essentially, this model uses constitutional values as intermediaries—proxies that might be used to bridge legal language and particular actors. Given the court's reluctance to define reporters or distinguish them from bloggers (a largely fruitless exercise that appears periodically in the popular press), Schauer might better replace the word *actors* with *actions*. For example, the Court might consider how to connect First Amendment values such as reporting and publishing instead of reporters and publication. Such an action-oriented grounding might prevent the Court from becoming entangled in the subtleties of ever-changing technologies (for example, are bloggers and Twitter users journalists, and if so, how does blogging differ from tweeting?) and allow it instead to focus on practices and standards of reporting that are likely to produce the kind of speech that enables democratic autonomy, bringing these values to bear on particular technological moments.

As Justice Charles Evans Hughes wrote in a 1938 opinion, "The liberty of the press is not confined to newspapers and periodicals. It necessarily embraces pamphlets and leaflets.... The press in its historic connotation comprehends every sort of publication which affords a vehicle of information and opinion" (cited in Horwitz, 2006, p. 45). The question now is twofold: how might the Court continue to recognize the multiple ways in which speech is produced and disseminated, and how might the Court depart from considering particular forms of publication (blogs versus newspapers versus pamphlets) and instead establish standards for evaluating the democratic value of institutionally produced free speech? Answers to these questions might be found in a review of select Supreme Court cases that have—usually without mentioning the press clause—identified what it considers to be valuable roles for the press to play in democratic life, creating what Randall P. Bezanson (1999) calls a "developing law of editorial judgment."

The aim here is not to create a First Amendment that is too unpredictable for any one person or institution to expect its protections. An unstable

First Amendment is as useless as an antiquated one. Rather, the goal here is to describe how the Court might pay attention to the contingent, empirical, and institutional conditions under which contemporary speech is produced—to move toward an institutional view of the press that ensures *freedom from* and *freedom to*. If democratic autonomy is a question of institutional design, we need to interrogate the conditions under which the institutional press is allowed or required to circulate speech.

U.S. Supreme Court Press Decisions

Although the U.S. Supreme Court has never formally defined *the press* or based a decision exclusively on the press clause (D. A. Anderson, 1983; Bollinger, 2010), it has, at various times and for different reasons, assumed that something called the press exists, that its existence serves constitutional purposes, and that the state has an obligation to protect the press's First Amendment freedoms:[15]

A prime example is the Supreme Court's 1945 *Associated Press* [*v. United States*] case, in which the AP argued for antitrust exemptions based on its First Amendment rights. The Court dismissed this argument, stating that the First Amendment "rests on the assumption that the widest possible dissemination of information from diverse and antagonistic sources is essential to the welfare of the public." Since "freedom to publish means freedom for all and not for some," state-guaranteed public-interest press protections were legitimate: "It would be strange indeed ... if the grave concern for freedom of the press which prompted adoption of the First Amendment should be read as a command that the government was without power to protect that freedom." (Pickard, 2015, n.p.)[16]

Although not part of a Supreme Court decision, one of the most famous statements by a justice on the press comes from Justice Potter Stewart. In a 1974 address at Yale Law School, in the wake of the Watergate scandal and amid popular celebration about the press's role as an investigative watchdog,[17] Stewart (1975, p. 633) argued that "the Free Press guarantee is, in essence, a structural provision of the Constitution." Without such an institutional guarantee, he argued, the press could fall prey to one of two powerful forces—market forces that erroneously purport to create a "neutral forum for debate" (p. 634) and government forces that could require the media to "promote contemporary government policy or current notions of social justice" (p. 636). Although he expressed his opinions in a speech and not a ruling, Stewart's speech[18] suggests a need to look more closely at

Supreme Court decisions, examining them for clues as to how courts might think about the press as a distinct institution with a constitutional role. Such clues can help address two of this book's concerns: what democratic role might the press play, and how might *the press* be defined?

If the Court recognizes press clause privileges distinct from those guaranteed by the speech clause, it runs the risk of creating a two-tiered First Amendment in which not all clauses apply equally to all people.[19] This was the question that Chief Justice Warren E. Burger had in mind when he wrote that "the very task of including some entities within the 'institutional press' while excluding others … is reminiscent of the abhorred [press] licensing system," which "the First Amendment was intended to ban" (cited in Bollinger 2010, p. 10).

The modern Court's case law is concisely and thoughtfully summarized by Bollinger (1991, 2010), and it is his typology that I adopt here.[20] He identifies three broad ways of understanding the Supreme Court cases on the press clause—protecting publics against censorship, providing access to information, and regulating press structures in public interests. By offering this typology, I do not argue that the Court defines the press in these terms, that the Court should define the press these ways, or even that the Court is consistent in its reasoning (as several cases show). Rather, these are cases to think with— ways of seeing the constitutionality of an institutional press and starting points for debating the roles that the press might play in ensuring the pursuit of democratic autonomy.

Protecting Publics against Censorship

One set of cases focuses on ensuring that news organizations are not prevented from publishing (ensuring that they do not suffer what legal theory calls *prior restraint*). In *New York Times Co. v. Sullivan* (1964), the Court held—in an opinion by Justice Brennan a year before his speech supporting Meiklejohn's view of the First Amendment—that although Sullivan's personal reputation may have been damaged by a critical, error-filled advertisement run by *Times*, Sullivan was a public official who had voluntarily entered the public sphere, so the public had an overriding right to hear such criticisms. Unless a news organization publishes "defamatory falsehoods knowingly or in reckless disregard for the truth" (Bollinger, 1991, p. 8), public officials—and later, unelected public figures (*Gertz v. Robert Welch Inc.*, 1974)—enjoyed fewer protections against libel than other citizens.

False statements, the Court ruled, "must be protected if the freedoms of expression are to have the breathing space that they need to survive" (Bollinger, 2010, p. 16), and the press is "entitled to act on the assumption that public officials and public figures have voluntarily exposed themselves to increased risk of injury from defamatory falsehoods concerning them" (p. 18). Essentially, the press—acting in its role as a producer and distributor of potentially valuable public information—could privilege the public right to hear information about public officials over any concerns about libel.

In *Florida Star v. B.J.F.* (1989, p. 491), the Court similarly ruled that "If a newspaper lawfully obtains truthful information about a matter of public significance, then state officials may not constitutionally punish publication of the information." Two elements of this ruling are important to note in order to understand the press as a public service institution. First, although it failed to define the term, the Court granted a *newspaper* (not any other organization, medium, or individual) the right to publish. Second, the Court recognized that there are issues of *public* significance separate from the state's interests and that newspapers are thought to know the difference. The Court was essentially using similar logic as it had in the Pentagon Papers case (*New York Times Co. v. United States*, 1971) when it found that the federal government could not prevent the *New York Times* and *Washington Post* from publishing a classified Department of Defense report. The public's interest in knowing what the newspapers thought it should know overruled the government's interest in protecting what it considered to be state secrets.

Finally, in *Nebraska Press Association v. Stuart* (1976), the Court overruled a lower court's ban on allowing journalists to report a court case, ruling that part of what makes a trial fair is the public scrutiny provided by the press.[21] That is, if, on the public's behalf, a court is trying someone for committing a crime, the public—with the press as its proxy[22]—has a right to hear how justice is being administered. Although this ruling, like the others, does not define *the press* (nor does it ground its finding in the press clause), it effectively finds that something called *the press* can oversee the administration of justice and contradict the state's conceptions of public interest, ensuring what Vincent Blasi (1977) calls the "checking value" of the First Amendment. By reading the Constitution in a way that gives the press these publication rights, the Court aims to guard against the kind of structural, institutional censorship that prevents individuals from realizing their autonomy and from democratically self-governing.

Regulating Access to Information

As evidence that Supreme Court press law is more a collection of seemingly disjointed opinions than a coherent body of law, the Court assumes that the press will protect citizens against the forces of censorship, but it gives the press few special privileges with which to seek out information.[23] For example, although some state laws shield reporters from being compelled to testify in court,[24] in *Branzburg v. Hayes* (1972),[25] the Court ruled that reporters have no federal "constitutional right not to reveal the identities of their sources in grand jury or other criminal proceedings" (Bollinger, 2010, p. 25). Reporters counter by arguing that they need a shield from compelled testimony to prevent two kinds of speech chilling. First, they claim that because the stories with the most potential public value are usually sensitive and confidential and likely to attract litigation (R. E. Anderson, 1973), if editors and reporters knew that they could be subpoenaed, they would self-censor, pursuing fewer controversial topics and fewer enlightening sources. Second, if sources knew that their conversations with reporters were potentially matters of the public record, they would be far less willing to reveal information that might be of critical interest to the public (Murasky, 1974, pp. 851–862). Finally, reporters claim that they are most often called to testify in cases when the government wants to know the identities of suspected criminals, effectively deputizing reporters and making them agents of the state against their will (Guest & Stanzler, 1969).[26]

Two years later, in *Pell v. Procunier* (1974) and *Saxbe v. Washington Post Co.* (1974), the Court similarly found that reporters had no special right to interview prisoners who journalists thought may be being mistreated, failing to find that "the Constitution imposes upon government the affirmative duty to make available to journalists sources of information not available to members of the public generally" (*Pell*, p. 834). In both cases, the Court declines to define *the press*, but a weak definition can be reverse-engineered from comparing its rulings in these cases. In contrast to its earlier opinions that valued press oversight of criminal trials, in *Pell* and *Saxbe*, the Court decided that, whatever *the press* means, it has no legitimate public interest in telling the stories of posttrial inmates. Only *during* a trial does the press fulfill a public service by providing oversight of the judiciary. If the press is defined in terms of its interest in using particular inmates as sources in stories about incarceration, the state's interest in administering prisons—specifically its desire to avoid giving individual inmates the ability to increase their notoriety through press interviews—will prevail, and the press will have no special rights.[27]

Regulating Press Structures in Public Interests

Finally, in a series of decisions, the Court gave some constitutional rationales for prior restraint on news gathering and also for public interest in the press's institutional structures.[28] The trend began with the Communications Act (1934), which allowed the government to "take and to keep control over channels of 'radio transmission'; and to provide for the use of such channels, but not the ownership thereof, by persons for limited periods of time" (Bollinger, 2010, p. 29). Essentially, the state asserted its right to manage the technical systems of mass communication, recognizing that it needed to ensure, on the public's behalf, that the means of speaking and hearing opinions were structured in the public's interest.

The underlying logic of this act—a "fairness doctrine" that aimed to provide equal speaking time and reasonable access to airwaves for public office candidates—was first put to the test in the landmark case *Red Lion Broadcasting Co. v. FCC* (1969). In this case, the Court affirmed the fairness doctrine, finding that because radio and television spectra are limited and of great public value, the government has a constitutional interest in protecting their allocation and administration on the public's behalf. The Court thus waded into the empirical, structural conditions under which the press speaks and publics hear, finding that a "marginal interference" with broadcasters' free-speech rights "is justified when empirically calculated against the rights of the audience" (Streeter, 1996, p. 130). The ruling is significant because it suggests that a public right to hear exists—that "what is 'crucial' in this environment is the right of the public to receive suitable access to social, political, esthetic, moral, and other ideas and experiences" (*Red Lion*, p. 390). The Court has never more clearly suggested that a public right to hear exists, that the press has a role in securing it, and that the public's interests in "ideas and experiences" can override a private broadcaster's interests.

The Court's affirmative interpretation of the First Amendment—recognizing not only an individual's freedom from censorship but also a public freedom to hear—was short-lived, though. Five years later, in *Miami Herald Publishing Co. v. Tornillo* (1974), the Court found that no "right of reply" existed in newspapers and that editors and newspaper owners were free to decide what they would print in their publications. Essentially, *Miami* stopped in its tracks the *Red Lion* finding that press had a constitutional role in ensuring a public right to hear, a logic that tentatively emerged in *Near v. Minnesota* (1931) and matured in *New York Times v. Sullivan* (1964). The affirmative interpretation of the First Amendment apparently applied only to media that had limited spectra, and the fairness doctrine was not a philosophical critique of laissez-faire corporate liberalism or an embrace of the press's institutional role guaranteeing a public right to hear but instead was a technology-specific policy "useful for maintaining smooth relations between corporations and the consuming public" (Streeter, 1996, p. 195).

The Court confirmed this rejection of *Red Lion* in a series of cases. In *Columbia Broadcasting System v. Democratic National Committee* (1981), the Court found that a private broadcaster had no obligation to air a public-interest advertisement. Such an ad could be refused "for purely business reasons" (Fiss, 1996, p. 61). And in *Turner Broadcasting System v. Federal Communications Commission* (1994), the Court found that since cable technology offered virtually limitless bandwidth (technical infrastructures again trumped public interests), the government could not compel cable providers to carry channels. The only potential weakness of the cable industry, Justice Anthony Kennedy suggested, was its creation of *economic* monopolies that might interfere with free-speech markets. But the risk of market failure was considered an insufficient reason to regulate, essentially ending any hope that *Red Lion*'s affirmative interpretation of the First Amendment might translate into technologies other than television (Bollinger, 2010, p. 38).

The Court further confirmed this logic in *Reno v. American Civil Liberties Union* (1997), when it struck down parts of the Communications Decency Act (1996) that attempted to ban indecent material on the Internet. It ruled that because the Internet "provides relatively unlimited, low-cost capacity for communication of all kinds," no spectrum-scarcity rationale applies and that because the medium was not considered "invasive," people were free not to expose themselves to Internet content. Although it is certainly true that technological scarcity makes little sense in relation to the Internet, especially in light of research on the harms of multitasking and information overload (Ophir, Nass, & Wagner, 2009) and the fragmentation of online attention (Goldhaber, 1997; Terranova, 2012; Webster & Ksiaze, 2012; Wu, 2016), it is still difficult to classify people into publics in online environments. That is, although there may be no longer be a purely technological rationale for regulating spectrum, there remains a clear public interest in structuring the social and technological conditions (such as search engine rankings, newsfeed algorithms, and content moderation systems) that lead people to the "ideas and experiences" (as the Court wrote in *Red Lion*) that are critical for public life, self-government, and democratic autonomy.

Another structural element of the press's public role is how much the government funds broadcasters and whether such funding carries public obligations. In *Federal Communications Commission v. League of Women Voters* (1984), the Court found unconstitutional the part of the Public Broadcasting Act (1967) that prohibited publicly funded stations from editorializing. It ruled that broadcasters—regardless of their funding sources—could not be prohibited from "speaking out on public issues" because to do so would be a "substantial abridgement of important journalistic freedoms which the First Amendment protects" (*FCC*, p. 402). Again, we see the Court—without explicitly invoking the press clause or defining the press—implying that press freedom (in this case, news organizations' rights to interpret and not only report on public issues) is linked to a public's right to hear. Instead of supposing that publicly funded media might reflect the viewpoints of their state financers, the Court assumed that there was some kind of professionally monitored journalistic buffer between a news organization's financial and editorial interests, trusting editors to represent public concerns regardless of who paid them. The Court reaffirmed this finding in *Legal Services Corp. v. Velazquez* (2001), when it found that "prohibitions against editorializing by public radio networks were an impermissible restriction" (p. 543) and in *Arkansas Educational Television Commission v. Forbes* (1998, p. 673) when it ruled that "Public and private broadcasters alike are not only permitted, but indeed required, to exercise substantial editorial discretion in the selection and presentation of their programming." Again, *editorializing* and *editorial discretion* are never defined, although the Court finds them somehow integral to the press's First Amendment roles.

Across court decisions about journalism and the press (at both federal and state levels), there is less of a canon that defines the press or the press

clause and instead more of a "developing law of editorial judgment" Bezanson
(1999, p. 754) on:

• The subjective intent of editors (for example, whether news organizations
are guilty of libel),
• The effect of a news organization's decision to publish (such as whether
there seems to be a public interest in a particular story),
• The fact versus opinion nature of a story (for example, privileging stories
that contain verifiable, truth-oriented reporting over subjective, opinion-
based commentary),
• The accuracy of a story (such as favoring stories that later prove to be true
versus those found to have factual errors), and
• How journalists prepared a story (for example, looking positively on publishing decisions that show rigorous editorial thoughtfulness).

Considered alongside the typology of Supreme Court cases, it can be seen
that, even in the absence of clear definitions, legal thinking about press
freedom often assumes *public* interests—structural and institutional contributions the press might make to civic life. Although there are certainly
inconsistencies and dropped logics (the fairness doctrine and *Red Lion* logic
have largely fallen out of favor), the courts still leave open the idea that it
matters more what the press *does* than what it *is*—a vision of the press and
its freedoms as dynamic and contingent that is explored further in the following chapters.

The Democratic Value of Listening

I have argued that democratic autonomy requires not only that individuals
are free *to speak* but that collectives have freedom *to speech*. Although the
former is a key dimension of how freedom is usually thought of in the United
States (as an individual possession akin to a property right), the latter is better seen as a *public right to hear* that the press can help to realize—indeed, that
it should help to guarantee if it is legitimately to claim its constitutional
protections as a democratic institution of public communication and not
simply a private broker of individual information. But what, exactly, is the
democratic value of listening? What is this activity that the press should
guarantee, what role does it play in civic life, and why is it crucial to a normative defense of contemporary, networked news production?

The simplest but most fundamental point to make about listening is that it is both a necessary and sufficient form of democratic participation. Democracies need people who listen; "just listening" is a fully legitimate way of belonging to a public sphere. Although listening "tends to be taken for granted [as] a natural mode of reception that is more passive than active" (Lacey, 2013, p. 163), listening can be a political act. When you listen, you acknowledge the existence of others by literally giving them your attention— by "ceding the possibility of control" and the "quest for certainty" (Bickford, 1996, p. 5) and entering into a collective phenomenon that shows us how we are simultaneously individuals and members of societies. As Hannah Arendt (1958, p. 50) writes, the "presence of others who see what we see and hear what we hear assures us of the reality of the world and ourselves." Ideally, listening means temporarily suspending the pursuit of personal preferences and allowing the possibility of outcomes that come from others (Bickford, 1996, pp. 1–6) as you empathize with people and imagine what it might be like to adopt or help realize their preferences (Belman, 1977; Husband, 2009; Lipari, 2010). This kind of generous and thoughtful listening can help people engage with the sources of difference that Iris Marion Young (1997) says create us—the influences that we ignore at the risk of failing to achieve the kind of self-reflexive autonomy that makes us freer than simply being allowed to speak.

Listening is thus both a "private experience and a public activity" (Lacey, 2013, p. 17). Although individuals certainly interpret speech through the lenses of their personal identities and experiences, they often do so as part of a collective: "They become an aggregate entity—an audience—and whether or not they all agree with or like what they hear, they are unified around that common experience" (Douglas, 2004, p. 29).[29] A common listening experience creates the possibility for shared consequences. When individuals listen to the same perspectives on a common topic, through the same medium, and perhaps even at the same time, they are *brought into existence* as a public (Dobson, 2014; Evans, 2001). They are a public convened by their active attention to speech and "their awareness of absent others" (Lacey, 2006, p. 74). If Facebook reconstituted itself as a place for listening publics, it would not prioritize sorting people according to individually satisfying and commercially profitable information preferences; it would acknowledge and take normative responsibility for what its audiences are able to hear and what kind of publics such hearing creates. Such recognition and accountability would appear not only in the design of its algorithms and advertising markets but also in its relationships with news organizations and other social media platforms. This would mean acknowledging that it is more than a technology company that organizes the speech of others[30] and that it is a media organization with interests and values, speaking through curation—a dominant powerhouse creating conditions under which people hear and, thus, listening publics. What *kind* of publics people can become depends on *how* they listen—how they adopt or reject the speaker's views, share the speaker's interpretation of the world, and create consensus or splinter into dissenting subgroups with alternate interpretations. These public dynamics are visible only if we see listening to be just as critical as speaking.

Rather than seeing listening as a "preparatory stage" (Lacey, 2013, p. 16) for creating a public—where the goal is to convert listeners into speakers—we might instead see listening as participation in its own right, part of a "difficult and disciplined civic duty" to engage meaningfully with "opinions that contradict, challenge, test one's own opinion" (Lacey, 2013, p. 167). Indeed, the phrase "listening in" is used by educational researchers to describe "intent participation"—what can happen in learning environments that value "observation as an aspect of participation" (Rogoff, Paradise, Arauz, Correa-Chavez, & Angelillo, 2003).

Listening reminds us that democratic autonomy cannot come only from speech marketplaces that prohibit illegitimate restrictions on individual expression. Listening and autonomy are *collective* phenomena that require rejecting the idea that an individual freedom to speak automatically creates a collective freedom to speech.

There is thus a "second-order value of voice" that listening helps us realize. It is a way to see how "our stories [are] endlessly entangled in each others' stories," beyond a neoliberal model that "reduces politics to market functioning" (Couldry, 2009, p. 580). Understanding the democratic value of this kind of listening means studying how individuals encounter individuals through speech markets—a problematic reification of face-to-face dialogue as the ultimate form of democratic engagement (J. D. Peters, 2006; Schudson, 1997). And it also means studying how they understand the "conventions, institutions and privileges which shape who and what can be heard in the media" (Dreher, 2009, p. 445)—from tracing which stories institutions like the press tell and which entanglements they articulate.

There are at least two ways in which institutions can function as listening structures. The first, sketched above, highlights institutions' capacity to bring us information and interpretations we might not have encountered on our own—to listen *for* us and then orient our attention to experiences and ideas we probably would not have chosen for ourselves.[31] The second focuses on how institutions can give us *freedom from* certain kinds of speech, creating pauses for meaningful silences. Rather than being evidence of consensus, disinterest, antisocial lurking, failed participation, the nonuse of media technologies,[32] or dysfunctional speech markets, silence might be heard as a thoughtful absence of speech (Ananny, 2017) and even a way of exercising the freedom to *not* use language that may have oppressive connotations. As Wendy Brown (1998) argues, sometimes silence is preferable because it creates ambiguities that can resist oppressive speech. It can create pauses to reflect on and integrate what has been heard. Silence is "what allows speech to take place. It endows speech with the capacity to bear meaning" (Pinchevski, 2001, p. 74) and helps to create an "inner life"—somewhere between complete isolation and constant noise where one might "explore unpublic feelings in something other than solitude" (Nagel, 1998, p. 20). For silences to serve public functions, they must be *publicly motivated* absences of speech. They cannot result from people being barred from speaking or from people being compelled to listen or join forums against their will or under illegitimate terms (C. M. Corbin, 2009). Silences that come from censorship and coercion must be distinguished from those that come from participating by listening.

The press, for example, might not listen to audiences simply in order to discern their preferences (Crawford, 2009; O'Donnell, 2009; Willey, 1998), give them more information of a particular type, provide forums that work for certain debates, or disseminate information as quickly as possible.[33] It also might create spaces and rhythms that give publics time to listen to what they hear. By making listening and silence part of journalistic ethics (S. J. A. Ward & Wasserman, 2015), the press could provide the "proper distances" that Roger Silverstone (2003, p. 477) says give people time and space to consider "differences between neighbors and strangers."

The public right to hear is not in opposition to an individual right to speak, nor is it about an individual's right to gain access to speech. Rather, its focus is the public. I argue not that individuals need to say or hear particular things but rather that people can more fully understand themselves as collectives with intertwined dependencies if they live in societies not just where people say things but where people say things that *they* can hear. A public right to hear is a kind of group metaright (Garden, 2014)—a collective right that individual self-governance requires.

Positive freedom is not only having the courage to say things that liberate yourself and others (Hansen, 2014), but it is about living within social structures that make hearing such things possible and likely. Yes, it is essential that journalists are able to observe, to gain access to people and information, and to publish as they see fit. But for all this speaking to add up to democratic self-governance, it needs to rest on something other than faith in the eventual success of a marketplace of speech. When we shift our focus away from individual rights and the image of press freedom as journalists' right to report and publish, we start to see how we might also demand that "journalists should facilitate an awareness of which voices are not heard" (Hansen, 2013, p. 678) and see themselves as part of an institution that creates the conditions for speaking and hearing. Such a conceptual move may help us distinguish among legal rights to receive information, social contexts in which to hear information, epistemological conditions through which to understand information, and material forces that help people act on information. If, as John Dewey (1954) argues, publics are formed by realizing inextricably shared consequences—social conditions that individuals cannot extract themselves from—then they need more than just marketplaces of speech that may or may not surface consequences. They also need institutional conditions that help them hear *potential* consequences that they can talk about, share together, and act on.

Conclusion

I have tried to give normative and institutional shape to the idea of democratic autonomy and the press's role in securing it. I attempt to show how the idea of democratic autonomy depends on both separation from others (negative, *freedom-from* liberties) and reliance on them (positive, *freedom-to* liberties) and how such dynamics relate to the free production and circulation of free speech. Part of ensuring these dynamics involves creating public institutions that assume structural responsibility for free speech—for speaking *and* listening. The press is one such institution. Regardless of how we might define *the press* (the courts offer some hints but little clarity), one way to defend the legitimacy of its constitutional protections is to ask how it ensures a public right to hear—how it helps to create what Kate Lacey (2013) calls "listening publics" who can imagine and work to realize possible futures that exist outside themselves. The press might be held accountable, in part, for its capacity to create publics that both speak and listen.

An autonomous press is a kind of interstitial, institutional glue that works across multiple levels. It enables an individual's autonomy by ensuring that she hears everything she needs to realize her personal autonomy, it understands and depends on social relations to ensure that it presents individuals with truly diverse options, and it uses law, culture, and technology to distinguish and protect itself sufficiently well from other types of institutions so that it can do the work it needs to do to help democracies realize autonomy.

Most essentially, for the press to explain what kind of autonomy it wants and deserves, it needs to explain how its separations and dependencies help realize a public right to hear and how its autonomy both requires and involves balancing such distances. In the next chapter, I revisit some of the modern history of U.S. press freedom to show how—despite the assumption that journalists are most free when they pursue their own visions of the public independent of nonjournalists—the press has always negotiated its autonomy through a system of separations and dependencies.

3 How Has the Press Historically Made Its Freedom?

Before exploring how the networked press might earn its freedom by helping to ensure a public right to hear, I need to describe what it means to make *the press* a unit of analysis. First, I argue that the press has never been a singular thing. Rather, it always has been an institutional mélange of people and forces that, at different times and in different ways, have distinguished and intertwined themselves. One way of seeing any given era of the press is to look at how these things have separated and collided, ask why, and examine how their relationships matter. For example, at various points in its history, the press has aligned itself with or eschewed different goals and practices—facts versus values, objectivity versus subjectivity, state sponsorship versus circulation revenue versus advertising income, marketplace success versus critical achievement, expert sources versus audience involvement, and a variety of reporting techniques, organizational rituals, educational initiatives, professional associations, hiring practices, linguistic strategies, and institutional experiments—that added up to particular institutional arrangements.

This is how I think we should see the contemporary, networked, institutional press—as a dynamic set of separations and dependencies that create the conditions under which journalists work, news is produced, and audiences become publics. The press is less a single, discernible thing than an outgrowth of forces governing a field of expression, circulation, and interpretation. Intentional or not, these relationships let people and objects rely on and distinguish themselves from others, creating normative models of the press.

Mirroring the model of democratic autonomy described in the previous chapter—the mix of independence and dependence that self-governance requires—these *field-level* separations and dependences are how the institutional press manifests negative and positive freedoms. They are how the press shows what it thinks freedom is and why it thinks it needs that freedom. Just as individual autonomy is achieved not only through *freedom from* constraint (because self-realization is always relational), the press earns its freedom not only by separating itself from markets, states, or audiences but also by strategically relying on others—insofar as its separations and dependencies help to ensure a public right to hear. The idea of autonomy—as freedom from and reliance on—does normative double duty

• As the basis for the kind of individual self-realization and democratic self-governance that the press ideally exists to support (described in the previous chapter) and

• As a description of the institutional balances that the press must strike to be free from interferences that harm a public right to hear but not so isolated that it assumes this right can be ensured only by some preexisting, static notion of what defines *the press* (as this chapter argues).

My assertion is that the press most defensibly earns its freedom when its institutional separations and dependencies make possible the kind of hearing that self-governing publics require. This kind of press freedom might require it to be free from outside influences—with the reporting access, editorial independence, and publishing power that the press historically has protected—but it also may require the press to enter into strategic relationships with other actors, even if these relationships interfere with a purely negative, *freedom-from* conception of press autonomy. The press's normative legitimacy comes not from how well it distances itself from others—a kind of negative-only autonomy that brings with it all the institutional problems that a purely freedom-from conception of self-governance has—but from how well it creates the institutional conditions that ensure a public right to hear. This is why the first part of this chapter develops a conceptual framework for seeing press freedom as a distributed, *field*-level concept that can be earned only through relationships.

Second, I want to show how press freedom has *always* entailed institutionalized balancing of forces, not simply freedom from influences assumed to be interferences. I trace historical patterns in the press's relationships, analyzing how reporters, editors, and news organizations have traditionally both distanced themselves from and yet relied on markets, states, experts, and audiences. That is, although press freedom is often thought of as publishers' freedom *from* others, the press has a long history of pursuing aims *through* relationships with others. But to what aims? What kind of institutional autonomy has emerged from these relationships? And how close does this resulting autonomy fit with the previous chapter's call for press freedom premised on a public right to hear?

These two approaches to making the press as a unit of analysis—defining the press as a field of forces and tracing the kinds of autonomy these forces historically have created—entail seeing it not as a single, unified object of analysis that lives within any one profession, set of practices, regulatory regime, organizational type, or audience relationship. Rather—thinking ahead to the next chapter's tracing of *networked* press freedom as an ideal achieved through sociotechnical relationships—it means using a normative ideal—press freedom and, more specifically, a public right to hear—as a way to read and critique the intersecting forces that make up the press as a field.

The Press as a Field

Understanding the contemporary networked press means appreciating both the practice of journalism and the conditions under which it is practiced. The actions and assumptions of journalists, news organizations, the commercial market, advertisers, legal regimes, and audience expectations all reinforce and reflect the different types of news imagined as possible at any given time. This makes the study of the press in general and the study of press autonomy in particular a study of *mezzo* levels—spaces *between* micro, individual actions and the broader, macro forces in which *freedoms from* and *reliances on* are negotiated and resisted.

Such an investigation is thus a study of structure-agency negotiations. For example, journalists may be drawn to crime reporting because of personal experiences, but they must channel or reconfigure these passions into the objectivity and professional detachment demanded by their news organization's culture, their colleagues' expectations, and their desire to win reporting awards. As they frame issues, interview people, write stories, and work with editors, they reconcile personal perspectives with professional and cultural values that expect crime reporters to behave in a certain way. Like many professionals, they inhabit a *mezzo* layer that requires constant negotiation and reorientation to their own passions and the norms of those around them.

Press autonomy exists in such *mezzo* levels—not in the freedom of particular journalists to do what they please but in the forces that simultaneously separate them from and make them rely on social forces beyond their control. The study of contemporary press autonomy and its history is thus the study of how any given era of social science sees pieces relating to wholes—how it understands people as both products and agents of social systems and their interactions as the places where autonomy is negotiated. This dialectic between individual agency and social structure underpins several long-standing theories of communication and organization. For example, George Herbert Mead saw an individual's utterances not as "inner meanings to be expressed" but evidence of "co-operation in the group taking place by means of signals and gestures" (Mead, 1934/1967, p. 6), laying the groundwork for symbolic interactionism's view of language as material for people to create shareable interpretations (Blumer, 1969, p. 5) and structuration theory's (Giddens, 1984) argument that social structures are always both "the medium and the outcome of the practices [that] constitute social systems" (Sewell, 1992, p. 4).

These ideas of agency and structure grew out of efforts by early social scientists like Ernst Cassirer to create a "science of culture" that might explain how humans both interpret and structure their environments as they try to "give form to experience" (1923/1953; 1942/1960, p. 22). He challenged what he saw as a "crisis in the concept of evolution upon which the entire naturalistic philosophy of culture is built" (Cassirer, 1942/1960, p. 34) and argued that physical models of causality were being overapplied to the study of culture. He criticized the idea that "all events in the human world are subject to the laws of nature and that they are the outgrowth of *fixed* natural conditions" (p. 16), distinguishing between physical laws that are beyond human influence and social forces subject to human intervention and interpretation. He did not reject causality, determinism, or logical proof as social science epistemologies but was concerned that a social science rooted in naturalist philosophy would provide few clues about how a social environment might be changed and thus prevent people from realizing an "aesthetically liberated life" (Cassirer, 1946, p. 98). He warned that the "titanic creative power of the individual is in conflict with the forces with have as their goal the preservation and, in a sense, the immortalization of the *status quo*" (Cassirer, 1942/1960, p. 197). Individuals could never achieve freedom from social forces; the best they could hope for was equality with them.

Although Cassirer rightly saw people in tension with their social worlds, he seemed to hold onto the idea that a truly creative, liberated self could be realized if it could negotiate a better deal with external forces of status quo preservation. Social forces existed, he said, but they were pitted against individual agency.

This assumption was challenged by Kurt Lewin (1951), whose field theory saw a person not as an atomic, stable entity who could negotiate with the environment but as a series of "dynamic and nondynamic constructs" (p. 39) that, together, defined his or her position (location relative to a group, occupation, activity, including how near or far someone might feel or physically be from them), locomotion (the pattern of positions over time), force (a tendency for locomotion), goal (a field that distributes forces in space), conflict (clashes among the forces governing someone locomotion), fear (expectations of the present, hopes for the future, and guilt about the past), power (the likelihood of inducing forces), and values (the ways forces gain positive and negative valences). Missing from psychology, Lewin argued, was the recognition that the

individual sees not only his present situation; he has certain expectations, wishes, fears, daydreams for his future. His views about his own past and that of the rest of the physical and social world are often incorrect but nevertheless constitute, in his life space, the "reality-level" of the past. (Lewin, 1951, p. 53)

If individuals were never rational, unitary wholes striving to realize a preexisting self, then it made little sense to think of their autonomy as separation from social forces. Freedom was not distance from or closeness of one *thing* to another *thing*; it had to entail some other kind of configuration of elements that, inseparably, governed individuals and societies. The right unit of analysis for understanding intertwined individual and social developments was a *field*—a set "of coexisting facts which are conceived of as mutually interdependent" and that objectively define the variety of "possible life spaces" (Lewin, 1951, p. 240) available to us at any given time. Theses mutually interdependent spaces—not individuals or social forces— were the right unit of analysis for understanding human expression, learning, and organization.

Bourdieu's Field Theory

Motivated by Cassirer's philosophy of culture and Lewin's social psychology of fields, Pierre Bourdieu (1990, p. 25) created a new theory designed to bridge the "most fundamental, and the most ruinous" divide in social science—between subjectivism and objectivism. He aimed to understand how individual creativity intersects with social organization—how artists have historically influenced, recreated, leveraged, resisted, and adapted to the dynamics of cultural production that make their individual freedom possible. He found that cultural products—writing, paintings, music, architecture—need both "agents of consecration" (Bourdieu, 1993, p. 121) to confer legitimacy on small-scale producers who take risks developing new forms of art (the avant-garde painter survives through patrons' money and critics' approvals) and also large-scale markets that give artists cultural and economic stability by organizing popular approval into stable consumerism (the fiction writer contracts to produce books with predictable, well-selling literary structures, themes, plots and characters). Cultural production is never about solitary individuals with ideas or "sovereign viewpoints" (Bourdieu, 1990, p. 27) that are distributed to willing, open-minded audiences. Patrons and their artists co-cultivate novelty for audiences who need to be nurtured. The freedom to create becomes collectively meaningful and powerful only when it aligns with cultural infrastructures.

Instead of thinking that people form views through either first-person subjectivity or omniscient objectivity, Bourdieu's field theory calls for a *relational epistemology* in which taking a position—defined as having a perspective and interpreting others'—is the principal unit of analysis. Bourdieu (1990, p. 53) captures this ongoing balance between dispositions and structures in his concept of *habitus* as "systems of durable, transposable dispositions ... which generate and organize practices and representations that can be objectively adapted to their outcomes without presupposing a conscious aiming at ends or an express mastery of the operations necessary in order to attain them." In other words, individual perspectives work to the extent that they can make sense of and circulate among social structures that, in turn, create new perspectives.

Habitus thus shows people with freedom to express a variety of "thoughts, perceptions and actions" (Bourdieu, 1990, p. 55)—but only those relevant to a particular set of forces acting at particular times. These forces, in turn, create a *field*—a "space of possibles" (Bourdieu, 1993, p. 30) "within which agents occupy positions that statistically determine the positions they take with respect to the field, these position-takings being aimed at either conserving or transforming the structure of relations of forces that is constitutive of the field"[1] (Bourdieu, 2005, p. 30). Bourdieu argues that each field has its own dynamics. The literary field is "an independent social universe with its own laws of functioning, its specific relations of force, its dominants and its dominated ... where, in accordance with its particular laws, there accumulates a particular form of capital ... [and] entirely specific struggles"[2] (Bourdieu, 1993, pp. 163–164).

What does it mean for members of a field—or the field itself—to be autonomous? Autonomy, Bourdieu argues, depends on how habitus and position takings are encroached on (1) by influences that a field's dominant forces consider to be beyond its scope and (2) by actors from adjacent fields who are attempting to shift position in ways that a field and its members cannot avoid.

In his study of French artistic fields in the late nineteenth century, Bourdieu saw how writers and artists gained autonomy from the financier, commissioning patron, or state-sponsored "protector of the arts" who supported—and directed—their work (Bourdieu, 1996b, p. 49). Such domination was broken only when writers and artists learned to move between two modes of support—markets and durable links. Markets cast art as symbolic goods (with sales figures and revenue streams) while *durable links* were relationships with "apparatuses of consecration" (salons, universities, and elite journals) based on shared affinities and lifestyles among a small set of elite cultural producers. A field's autonomy, Bourdieu argues, depends on its ability to sustain both of these mechanisms for producing and evaluating symbolic goods. Markets use large-scale, commercial logics to produce low-risk symbolic commodities over short production cycles, creating goods with preestablished forms that are already accessible to "mass publics" with well-understood tastes (Bourdieu, 1993, p. 129; 1996b, p. 142). Restricted spheres of production give artists longer, higher-risk production cycles to create experimental "pure art" so they might compete for the "cultural consecration" of other producers, critics, and "privileged clients" (Bourdieu, 1993, p. 115).

If critically oriented, small-scale artists can work independently of market-oriented, mass-scale demands, then a distinct cultural product can emerge that does not depend on audiences but that eventually may reach them. Bourdieu avoids arguing that restricted production creates better or higher-quality works than large-scale production, but in calling such works novel, high-risk, experimental, and "pure," he gives "agents of consecration" the responsibility and power to change a field that mass audiences sustain in the meantime. A field's ability to sustain and create new positions requires both open, mass markets and closed, elite networks.

The field itself, Bourdieu argues, can change in two main ways, both of which reveal vulnerabilities in a field's autonomy. Its internal struggles, habitus, or networks of consecration and capital exchange may be subject to factional rifts among those not directly tied to the field in question. For example, the French revolution of 1848 briefly encouraged many artists to produce "social art" (Bourdieu, 1993, p. 58) before returning, post-uprising, to earning legitimacy from markets and fellow producers. Sometimes younger newcomers may enter the field, bringing with them "dispositions and position-takings which clash with the prevailing norms of production and the expectations of the field" (p. 57). Such new entrants bring with them a youth and sense of urgency that, Bourdieu argues, are not the direct challenges that factional rifts are but that nonetheless are powerful forces for change.

Both mechanisms for change locate field innovation mostly within the subfield of elite, restricted production where mass publics play one of two roles. Either they are recipients of "consecrated authors dominating the field of [restricted] production [who] also tend to make gradual inroads into the market, becoming more and more readable and acceptable [in a] more or less lengthy process of familiarization" (Bourdieu, 1996b, p. 159), or they are actors who are responsible for fast and often temporary changes when revolutions and political movements entail large-scale uptake.

Bourdieu does not see change originating from public spheres. He makes no mention of how cultural change might be brought about through democratically defensible systems of communication but instead sees field change as a "struggle between the established figures and the younger challengers" (Bourdieu, 1993, p. 60). In this battle for "contemporaneity" (Bourdieu, 1996b, p. 158), power is exercised through *illusio*, or an "aesthetic" (Bourdieu, 1993, p. 257) that categorizes actors either as forward-looking and avant-garde or as conservative and stagnating.

Bourdieu's field theory helps show freedom as a field-level concept that intertwines the individual and social—the habitus as the adaptable, acceptable principles that help people both make and make sense of new perspectives (for example, an artist's innovations always emerge from and are compared to earlier forms); the field as a place where individuals vie for capital and power in relation to a set of forces that determine the positions they might occupy; autonomy as a marker of a mature field's ability to balance elite, restricted production versus large-scale, mass production and to modulate the power that newcomers have to change a field's dominant habitus; and illusio as a set of values and aesthetics dominating members' acceptance and rejection of change.

How well is the field of journalism explained by these concepts? Since Bourdieu developed field theory, his ideas have been taken up, challenged, and adapted by scholars trying to explain how the press's field dynamics reflect and create publics (a concept Bourdieu largely neglected). Unlike artistic fields of cultural production, the press—ideally and principally—pursues its autonomy in order to advance *public* interests. It may exist economically as a two-sided market needing to earn revenue from both subscribers and advertisers (S. P. Anderson & Gabszewicz, 2006)—a narrow reading of its autonomy is simply the freedom to create content that succeeds in marketplaces—but it also has historically defined its autonomy, in part, as a freedom to let journalists "exercise independent professional judgment," even if it required owners to "let the norms of journalism occasionally trump concerns for maximizing profit in order to quiet the public criticism of the power of the media and stave off gathering movements to regulate newspaper ownership or wire service conduct" (Nerone, 2013, p. 450).

Press autonomy has always existed at an intersection of economics, journalistic professionalism, and perceptions of public interest. In Bourdieu's terms, the press's autonomy—and the illusio of values and aesthetics that should ultimately privilege its public mission over all others—depends on maintaining multiple scales that allow balances to be struck. These separations and dependencies entail both small-scale, restricted creation by elites who prioritize public over market interests and also mass-scale populist production that demonstrates news's viability in profitable marketplaces. Press freedom is not just journalism's *freedom from* anything that it does not define as journalism (a self-referential definition at best). Rather, it is the power to configure a field of forces to serve public interests. This may mean a smaller press (excluding actors and forces that traditionally have been considered part of journalism), but it also can mean making room for—and articulating expectations of—new entrants to the journalistic field.

This framing raises a number of questions: What qualifies as "public interest?" How can the forces that structure the journalistic field be traced and evaluated against a public interest? Which forces has the journalistic field traditionally managed, and what images of the public emerge from a balancing of those forces? These questions—which are critical for both understanding and challenging the historical roots of contemporary, networked press's institutional autonomy—have been taken up by a set of scholars concerned with how the journalistic field works and what kind of publics the field makes possible.

Bourdieu's Journalistic Field

Bourdieu's influence on journalism is primarily through a short book, *On Television* (Bourdieu, 1996a), a companion essay, and a series of secondary analyses (Benson, 1999, 2004; Benson & Neveu, 2005b; Neveu, 2007) in which journalism and journalists are critiqued from the perspective of field theory and, conversely, field theory is used to demonstrate the need for public sphere theories that account for media institution dynamics (Benson, 2009).

Bourdieu's main thesis is that as journalism (particularly television journalism) has become more dependent on large-scale commercial production, it has become less autonomous. First, he claims that the medium of television is driven by "structural corruption" (Bourdieu, 1996a, p. 17) that rewards people who produce spectacles without necessarily knowing what they want to say to an audience or why an audience should listen to them. Television's time constraints, he says, forces presenters to be "'fast-thinkers,' specialists in throw-away thinking" (p. 35) who "say banal things" (p. 18) and do "symbolic violence" (p. 17) as they comment simplistically on complex issues. Journalists, he says, are more motivated to report issues that are "exceptional *for them*" as they engage in a deadline-driven "relentless, self-interested search for the extra-ordinary" (p. 20). Although such journalists may act "in all good faith and in complete innocence," their positions within the field of forces governing television news make them "unleash strong, often negative feelings, such as racism, chauvinism, the fear-hatred of the foreigner, or xenophobia" (p. 21).

Bourdieu is clearly no fan of television, and his application of field theory to journalism reads more like a rant (albeit one that may viscerally resonate in political seasons especially), not a subtle, generative analysis.

Without supporting his claim, Bourdieu argues that journalism is at a structural disadvantage compared to other domains of cultural production because it is "much more dependent on external forces ... depend[ing] very directly on demand [and] the decrees of the market and the opinion poll" (Bourdieu, 1996a, p. 53). To Bourdieu, contemporary journalists can keep or shift their field positions—markers of autonomy in other fields of cultural production—only if they abandon the risky work rewarded by patrons of small-scale, restricted production and fully adopt the habitus and illusio of mass-scale markets.

Although Bourdieu extends Cassirer's "philosophy of culture" and Lewin's field theory into the study of distributed media cultures, his analysis of journalism has significant shortcomings.[3] The most obvious is a kind of circular logic as he a priori assumes the homogenization of journalism and journalistic practices while simultaneously arguing against their uniformity. He presumes that the press *was* once autonomous when he asserts without empirical evidence that its historical autonomy has dwindled. This romanticized view of journalism as a homogeneous and historically stable, independent profession in pursuit of shared ideals does not stand up to historical scrutiny (Barnhurst & Nerone, 2001; Nerone, 2013; Schiller, 1979; Schudson, 1978, 2003b). He also fails to distinguish among different kinds of journalists—such as beat reporters, feature writers, investigative journalists, and editorial commentators—as he moves quickly among critiques of television, newspapers, and magazines. In assuming homogeneity of a field he criticizes as being too homogeneous, he misses professional, commercial, and symbolic differences that may show evidence of balancing small-scale restricted production with large-scale mass circulation.

Bourdieu also only briefly touches on the public or democratic features of journalism when he criticizes its "de facto monopoly on the large-scale informational instruments of production and diffusion of information"—a monopoly through which he says journalists "control the access of ordinary citizens ... to the 'public space'" and "one's ability to be recognized as a *public figure*" (Bourdieu, 1996a, p. 46). In not further developing the public dimensions of his analysis, he avoids what is probably the most difficult and promising aspect of studying press autonomy as a field-level phenomenon—journalism's need to establish its autonomy by balancing the small- and mass-scale production that lets it practice and innovate its aesthetics and also by simultaneously serving and critiquing populist passions in ways that help publics thrive. When Bourdieu argues that the journalistic field should have a higher "entry fee" and that some of its actors have a "duty to get out" (Bourdieu, 1996a, p. 65), he leaves his theory open to charges of elitism. He later weakly defends himself by claiming that his ideal "social conditions of production" (Bourdieu, 2005, p. 46) make ideas possible that mass media cannot product. He also side-steps a core tension in journalism's relationship to democracy—its responsibility not only to influence masses by exposing them to ideas they might not seek for themselves but also to engage with them as people who can also produce novel and democratically valuable interpretations of social life.

In *Rules of Art: Genesis and Structure of the Literary Field* (Bourdieu, 1996a) and *The Field of Cultural Production* (Bourdieu, 1993), Bourdieu shows his affinity for elite production when he argues that a field is most autonomous when small-scale, restricted producers are symbolically privileged over those who produce for the market (Bourdieu, 1996b, p. 217). If a field treats elite producers as superior and gives them time and support to develop their ideas, he claims, then over time, their ideas will lead a field's change, "making gradual inroads into the market" (p. 159) that is unlikely to develop sophisticated ideas on its own. Although he never says so explicitly, to him, elites produce a level of quality that masses receive and eventually adopt.

This elitist autonomy is not democratically defensible. Its subjugation of mass-scale dynamics to small-scale patrons makes it a model of freedom ill-suited to journalism's democratic duties. Journalism—and thus the bases for its autonomy—is fundamentally different from other fields of cultural production because of its *public* dimensions. Journalism earns its autonomy not by balancing a binary (small-scale versus restricted production of products for aesthetic elites versus mass markets) but by simultaneously pursuing multidimensional priorities that all point to the press's unique position as a public institution whose legitimacy derives from principled brokerage.

Adopting an explicitly normative stance, Clifford G. Christians, Theodore L. Glasser, Denis McQuail, Kaarle Nordenstreng, and Robert A. White (2009) identify four key functions of the press that might be used to defend why it needs freedom from and obligations to others in adjacent fields. The press might adopt a *monitorial* role by scanning and interpreting a "real world of people, conditions, and events" (p. 140) that it sees as relevant or significant to its understanding of journalism's public function—equipping the "monitorial citizen" (Schudson, 1998) with the information (reports on public forums, government actions, corporate interests) that a journalist thinks she needs to act. The press might also play a *facilitative* role by creating, managing, and improving public forums; helping civil society groups learn to speak among themselves and to others; and working to create environments that "promote a mosaic of diverse cultures and worldviews" (Christians, Glasser, McQuail, Nordenstreng, & White, 2009, p. 159). Third, the press also might adopt a *radical* stance by insisting "on the absolute equality and freedom of all members of a democratic society in a completely uncompromising way" (p. 179) so that power can be redistributed "from the privileged (typically few) to the underprivileged (typically many)" (p. 181). This is a "revolutionary ideology" in which journalism is "an instrument for challenging and changing political and economic systems" (pp. 181–182). Finally, the press might serve a *collaborative* role by partnering with corporations, states, and civil society to create "mutual trust" and implement a "shared commitment to mutually agreeable means and ends" (p. 198). Collaboration can be synonymous with "compliance" (a weak form of autonomy in which the press is coerced into behaviors, disregards its own interests, or unreflexively follows its own traditions), "acquiescence" (a begrudging recognition of the pragmatic benefits of cooperating with others for strategic reasons), and "acceptance" (the strongest form of collaboration in which journalists decide that they should cooperate with others because doing so advances journalism's interests) (Christians, Glasser, McQuail, Nordenstreng, & White, 2009, pp. 198–200). Michael Schudson (2008c, p. 12) offers a more condensed, complementary model of press ideals in his list of "six functions journalism has frequently assumed in democratic societies"—information, investigation, analysis, social empathy, public forum, and mobilization.

Journalism scholars and democratic theorists perennially catalog and critique the press's normative roles in any given era of communication,[4] with all models at least implicitly acknowledging that the press cannot achieve its democratic duties without simultaneously serving, leveraging, reflecting, and critiquing all of the sectors it encounters. It is too simplistic for Bourdieu to argue that press freedom means balancing elite opinion and mass mobilization so that critical, minority expression might be sustained unsullied by commercial marketplaces. Such neat separations are neither possible nor desirable because the press's political relevance is inextricable from the social dynamics it describes, interprets, responds to, or tries to influence. Such dynamics (such as elites versus masses) are not simply relationships to balance and manipulate so that the press might carve out a privileged and critical distance from its audiences. These are the very tensions that normative models of the press require journalism to engage. As Schudson argues, what

> keeps journalism alive, changing, and growing is the public nature of journalists' work, the nonautonomous environment of their work, the fact that they are daily or weekly exposed to disappointment and criticism of their sources (in the political field) and their public (whose disapproval may be demonstrated economically as readers cancel subscriptions or viewers change channels). Vulnerability to the audience (the market) keeps journalists nimble in one direction, vulnerability to sources (the government) in another.... [A]bsent these powerful outside pressures, journalism can wind up communicating only to itself and for itself. (Schudson, 2005, p. 219)

For Bourdieu, other fields can contaminate and challenge journalism's autonomy, damaging an ideal of democracy as a social order led by informed elites. He has a "more ambivalent or at least indirect relation" to democratic normative theory and is more concerned with the social conditions by which "specialized knowledge" and "enlightened citizens" are produced (Benson & Neveu, 2005a, p. 9).[5] This environment is best created by an autonomous subfield of elites engaged in restricted production for other journalists or narrow audiences free of outside influences. But for Schudson and others who foreground journalism's public obligations, such influences are potential sources of accountability—ways to make journalism responsive to and engaged with the various forces that make it relevant.

Journalism is thus not an exclusive domain governed by any one organization or profession but an ongoing struggle for resources that its practitioners see as crucial to achieving the kind of autonomy that enables their understanding of the press's relationship to democracy: "economic capital is expressed via circulation, or advertising revenue, or audience ratings, whereas the 'specific' cultural capital of the field takes the form of intelligent commentary, in-depth reporting, and the like—the kind of journalistic practices rewarded each year by the U.S. Pulitzer Prizes" (Benson & Neveu, 2005a, p. 4).

But what does this struggle look like? How does competition for different types of capital—for different separations and dependencies—reveal different ways of conceiving press freedom and thus different visions of journalism's democratic value?

One set of answers to these questions lies in a newer body of work that traces how the press—as an ideal and a set of institutional arrangements—emerges from distributed, coordinated forces with the power to create, circulate, and signify the importance of accounts of social life. Grouped under the term *new institutionalism*, it argues that press freedom is less about striking dualistic balances—elites versus masses, patronage versus commercialism, journalism's democracy versus a marketplace's—and more about seemingly disparate actors vying for the power to determine what a public is or should be.

The New Institutionalist Press

The new institutionalist school of journalism studies (Benson, 2006; Cook, 1998, 2000, 2006; Kaplan, 2006; Sparrow, 1999, 2006) focuses on how journalism helps to create publics through relationships with political fields. For instance, in his account of how journalists, government officials, and politicians cocreate the news, Timothy Cook (1998, 2000, 2006) expresses no particular faith in journalists' ability to report the community's agenda, care for the public on its own, or become contaminated by the large-scale production logics of media marketplaces. Rather, he focuses on the press's ability to be a competent and critical partner of government. The press exists only through unavoidable codependencies with the state, even though journalists are "poorly equipped to assist in governance" (Cook, 1998, p. 4). No one elects reporters or asks any elected body to hold them accountable beyond what is expected of other citizens. Rather, press oversight is always intertwined with visions of democracy, aiming "to ensure that the news we receive gets us toward the politics and toward the democracy we want" (p. 4). Because the public is an ongoing, contested construction exclusive to neither government nor journalism, it makes little sense to define press autonomy as journalism's *freedom from* anything the press sees as incompatible with its definition of the public. New institutionalism says that journalism's public service is not secured through independence from the state or marketplaces. The press's public obligations develop according to how well it pursues public values through multilateral, institutional relationships—not how well it separates itself from anything it perceives as nonjournalistic or incompatible with its own definition of *public*.

This approach is grounded in a broader new institutionalist understanding of organizations, practices, and norms. It looks beyond any particular group, location, or profession and asks how the interplay between human agency and social structure emerges from multiple sites of action and power—formal rules and state-enforced laws (for example, in the U.S. press, consider First Amendment and libel law); the values and priorities embedded within social relations and professions (such as the largely unquestioned ideals of objectivity, balance, and public service that are adopted by many journalists); and the expectations and psychosocial processes governing people's relationships and perceptions of public service (consider the public's and journalists' assumptions about what constitutes a news story, what a credible source is, when news should be delivered and by whom, and what values drive the press's unique constitutional protections) (W. R. Scott, 2013, pp. 51–58).

A new institutionalist approach focuses not on instruments of formal organizational governance and policy but on how informal, implicit, networked understandings have the power to create, sanction, reproduce, and lend legitimacy to the taken-for-granted beliefs that invisibly underpin institutional actions (W. W. Powell & DiMaggio, 1991). Families, religions, professions, and markets all work not because members rationally and uniformly pursue self-evident aims but because they share (without necessarily consenting to) a persistent set of attributions, habits, and relationships that create and sustain what have come to be collectively recognized as institutions. Drawing on long-standing theories of socially constructed reality (Berger & Luckman, 1967; Blumer, 1939), Lynne G. Zucker defines *institutionalization* as

the process by which individual actors transmit what is socially defined as real and, at the same time, at any point in the process the meaning of an act can be defined as more or less a taken-for-granted part of this social reality. (Zucker, 1977, p. 728)

Neoinstitutionalism eschews the idea that institutions are "organic wholes" and instead asks how their "loosely coupled arrays of standardized elements" (DiMaggio & Powell, 1991, p. 14) combine to create actions that are then judged acceptable—or not—in any particular context. Institutions change when field actors expose "rules that had been taken for granted, calling into question the perceived benefits of those rules, and undermining the calculations on which field relations had been based" (Fligstein & McAdam, 2012, p. 22). Changes in institutions drive changes in collective governance because social problems do not exist a priori but are "only discovered and addressed when they fit within existing institutions" (DiMaggio & Powell, 1991, p. 28)—that is, when an institution's "classifications, routines, scripts, [and] schema" (p. 13) make relationships visible, relevant, and actionable.

Although this view of institutions complements Bourdieu's field theory— "much of [which] dovetails with and may contribute to a broadening and deepening of the institutional tradition" (DiMaggio & Powell, 1991, p. 26)—it presents a different image of institutional autonomy. Whereas Bourdieu saw field freedom as the power to balance small-scale patronage with large-scale commercialism in the pursuit of a dominant illusio that could withstand interference from new entrants, new institutionalism rejects the idea that there is a single or acceptably dominant illusio that is rationally protected from field-level forces. Instead, it favors carefully tracing multidimensional, networked forms of power among competing forces, acknowledging that institutional arrangements endure not because of utilitarian efficiency but because

individuals often cannot even conceive of appropriate alternatives (or because they regard as unrealistic the alternatives they can imagine). Institutions do not just constrain options: they establish the very criteria by which people discover their preferences. (DiMaggio & Powell, 1991, pp. 10–11)

If the press is not only a field but a neoinstitution, then it and its autonomy are constructed relationally. The press exists not because it has been found in nature, is required for self-governance, or enshrined in the U.S. Constitution. It exists because some set of actors, together and insofar as their imaginations allow, make, adhere to, and continually re-create rituals and categories that become taken-for-granted assumptions about what journalism is supposed to be. If the press is simply a set of institutional relationships that continually creates its legitimacy, it makes little sense to hold the press static and defend its autonomy as uncontestable. It makes more sense to (1) describe, as broadly and critically as possible, the institutionalized relationships that make up the press, (2) interrogate the assumptions and imaginations dominating its ongoing institutionalization, and (3) investigate whether this institutionalization helps to create normatively defensible publics. Press autonomy is not about freedom from interference but about a relational power to configure separations and dependencies in pursuit of public goods. Further, press autonomy is never finished but is an ongoing struggle among "loosely coupled arrays of standardized elements"—surely including government, markets, civil society, and journalism—that together create publics that no single actor could or should govern.

This image of networked autonomy as relationships among people, practices, and ideals with contingent separations and dependencies opens up a new way to think about press freedom. Instead of seeing it as enterprise journalism's independence from forces that *it* sees as corrupting, networked press autonomy becomes a field-level struggle among new entrants and established actors competing in different corners of a field, with different reaches across networks. In this ideal of networked autonomy, no single actor has complete power, no one part of the network has total command, and no particular vision of the public becomes unimpeachable. For example, the debate over whether a blogger is a journalist illustrates this point because it is simultaneously never-ending and elucidating. When Mayhill Fowler—as an Obama-supporting blogger for the *Huffington Post*'s 2008 presidential election spinoff *Off the Bus* (both new entrants to the field of journalism with contestable relationships to the mainstream press)— reported that then-senator Barack Obama said at a fundraiser that some Americans "cling to guns or religion or antipathy to people who aren't like them," there was no shortage of commentary asking whether Fowler was a legitimate journalist, whether the *Huffington Post* was a real publication, whether both had broken ethical rules by printing Obama's seemingly off-the-record comments (Seelye, 2008), and how exactly mainstream broadcasters should treat this person who did not fit into existing journalistic categories (Rosen, 2008).

Although the details of this incident have faded from popular memory and are difficult to translate into contemporary contexts, the perennial question "Is X a journalist?" remains useful. This is not because the question has a definitive answer but because responses to it show who thinks that a particular set of "loosely coupled arrays of standardized elements" in which a journalist finds herself is a category of networked press serving the public well enough to have its institutional autonomy recognized and defended. The conversation is worth having because it lets us see the forces creating and defending different types of journalism—and thus differently networked versions of press autonomy.

Amid these forces, Timothy E. Cook (1998, p. 7) describes how "journalists work hard to maximize their autonomy" as "professional communicators" trained to recast the words of sources into symbolic strategies that inform or persuade audiences (Carey, 1997, pp. 132–133). Some scholars have suggested that experienced journalists internalize this struggle as "bipolar 'interactional expertise'" (Reich, 2012, p. 339) that lets them shift between evaluating expert opinions and applying their own perceptions of audience interests. They do so while simultaneously "work[ing] hard to present a news account that seems largely beyond their individual control" (Cook, 1998, p. 7). Their autonomy, control, and professionalism, he argues, consist largely of "Taken-for-granted social patterns of behavior valued in and of themselves [that] encompass procedures, routines, and assumptions, which extend over space and endure over time" (p. 84).

This isolated, inward-looking model of individual autonomy requires separating (and assumes the possibility of separating) "news judgments (what's important)" from "moral judgments (what's right)" (Ettema & Glasser, 1998, p. 8). When journalists, bloggers, editors, or others with the power to make stories visible to audiences craft stories that they prefer and presume to have public value, they are certainly able to act free of any interference with their news judgment. But they bracket their autonomy within a negative sense of freedom. They lose an opportunity to develop a more sophisticated "mature subjectivity" (Schudson, 1978, p. 192) that acknowledges the impossibility of ever separating themselves from influences that inform, govern, care about, and may benefit from their judgment. The power of individual journalists to make unilateral and seemingly objective decisions consistent with their own vision of the public interest reinforces an image of the truly autonomous journalist as someone free to exercise professional judgment free of influence, but it fails on two counts. First, it erroneously presumes that normatively defensible visions of public interest and self-governance emerge only from a negative conception of freedom (this is the myth of the individual autonomy premised on *freedom from* critiqued in the previous chapter). Second, it ignores the empirical realities and historical arc of institutional press freedom—namely, that the press has never been completely free from external influences and has in fact always relied on others for its freedoms.

Cook (1998) argues that the U.S. press has never been autonomous from extrafield forces in the way that Bourdieu's field freedom calls for. Using three kinds of evidence, he reveals news media not as an independent, neutral institution that reports *on* government but as a political institution that reports *with* the government.

First, he catalogs government subsidies that historically have supported journalism: powerful political figures sponsored early newspapers; the Postal Act of 1792 made it cheaper to mail newspapers than other correspondence; Congress funded Samuel Morse's early telegraph experiments that eventually created news wire services; government information offices designed and timed their releases to be easily understood and reprinted by the news media; and even the seemingly restrictive government regulation of radio and television spectra helped the press standardize its use of the new media and rely on regular revenue streams.

Second, Cook shows how news organizations—even those having different owners, working with different media, and targeting different audiences—largely converged into a single institution with "shared processes and predictable products" (Cook, 1998, p. 3). For example, in order to prepare stories in predictable and timely ways, reporters "routiniz[e] the unexpected" (Tuchman, 1973, p. 110) by following particular beats (such as the White House, Congress, and police departments) and modeling their own organizational structures after those of the state. Without "some routine method of coping with unexpected events, news organizations, as rational enterprises, would flounder and fail" (p. 111). Such standardization lets beat reporters talk about their work with colleagues, find new jobs in labor markets that can compare and commodify their work in relation to others, pitch stories to editors and manage their expectations, and consciously or not, coordinate with their competitors to write leads that offer astonishingly similar interpretations of a what makes an event newsworthy (Cook, 1998, pp. 78–79).[6]

Third, Cook (1998, p. 12) shows how public officials and government sources "dictate conditions and rules of access and designate certain events and issues as important by providing an arena." By regulating press credentials (signaling certain events to be worthy of selection and exclusion) and providing quotes that easily fit within reporters' norms of newsworthiness, government officials suggest what is both interesting and important about state business, making it easier for journalists to organize their coverage and exercise seemingly independent judgment.

In defining the news media as a sociopolitical institution inseparable from those it reports on, Cook describes, in institutional terms, how journalistic autonomy is less about freedom from states and markets as they pursue an uncontestable public interest. Rather, press freedom is a relational phenomenon—with the power to participate in "negotiation[s] of newsworthiness" (Cook, 1998, p. 169) with those they depend on and report on.

Press Autonomy as Negotiated Separations and Dependencies

Combining field theory's notion of autonomy as the intersection of structure and agency with new institutionalism's theory of autonomy as socially situated relational power, it becomes possible to identify press freedom as the interplay of five dimensions—field interactions, capital competition, negotiated production, actor transitions, and public work. Independent of any particular vision of the public or any normative role for journalism, these dimensions highlight how the press might pursue field-level autonomy that is premised not on separation from external influences but on the negotiation of institutional relationships.

Press freedom does not come from journalism's unilateral freedom from outside interference as it pursues an uncontestable vision of democratic self-governance. Just as the theory of individual freedom fails when it is held up to the realities of collective self-governance, the idea of press autonomy as unilateral independence from nonjournalistic interference fails to account for the complexities of field-level struggle and neoinstitutional negotiation.

This model of press autonomy that emerges from the application of field theory and new institutionalism to journalism is an analytical ideal, not an empirical account. It describes how press autonomy *could* be realized through interplays of social forces, resource governance, professional practices, and public expectations. In reality, the press historically has pursued its autonomy in a less overtly coordinated fashion. In reading secondary sources and scholarly studies of how the press has defined itself as like or unlike others, an empirically nuanced view of press freedom appears to complicate this idealized model. We see an image of press autonomy—separations and dependencies in the often implicit pursuit of an illusio defined by relationships—coming from three sources: an institutionalized ideal of objectivity, organizational routines and ritualized practices, and publics bracketed as constructed audiences.

Autonomy through Institutionalized Objectivity

Before the 1920s, U.S. journalists (and most other social practitioners) saw little difference between facts and values (Kaplan, 2002; Mindich, 1998; Schudson, 1978). The generally held assumption was that the world—in

Table 3.1
Elements of press autonomy: Tracing autonomy through configured dependencies

Dynamic	Description
Negotiating with other fields	Press autonomy is a property not of journalism itself but of how journalism relies on or distinguishes itself from other relevant fields, including but not limited to political actors, government actors (state legislation, regulatory agencies, and courts), literary and artistic producers and taste makers, technological innovators, advertisers, financial capital managers, and social movements. In the pursuit of different illusios, the press may find itself more or less aligned with different fields at different times (growing or shrinking as interfield forces command), but its autonomy is always a function of its relationships to other fields, not a stand-alone, immutable property of journalism.
Competing for capital	Press autonomy requires commanding *economic capital* (resources derived from the market, state subsidies, and private funders) and *symbolic capital* (signals of legitimation from critical acclaim, circulation numbers, awards, and recognition from elite decision makers). Financial, material, cultural, and political support make it possible for the press to negotiate with other fields, sustain different types of production, securely evaluate new entrants, and realize public missions collaboratively.
Sustaining diverse production scales	Press autonomy entails balancing its two subfields of production, each of which provides the economic and symbolic capital that defines its position with other fields. In *restricted activity*, a small number of patrons have the power to fund and support high-risk, experimental journalism and new forms of illusio unable to find broader support, and in *large-scale information production*, consumer-oriented markets finance the press, signal its populist value, underpin its value as a constitutionally protected entity, and provide evidence of its ability to sustain mass publics. The autonomous press needs to be both insulated from and embedded within information markets.

Dynamic	Description
Appreciating new entrants	To be able to negotiate with other fields, command economic and symbolic capital, and balance its relationships with markets, the press must mediate between new and older entrants. Novel actors—defined by young ages, short durations within a field, or attitudes to institutional change—can come from other relevant fields (for example, they might have expert knowledge of how they are like and unlike journalism), attract new forms of capital (such as economic capital of investors looking to fund small-scale restricted activity and symbolic capital that can come with perceptions of novelty and innovation), and signal new types of illusio with the potential power to disrupt dominant norms and existing balances between restricted and large-scale activity. Autonomy is not the power to reject novelty but the ability to understand, include, and negotiate with the field positions of new entrants.
Pursuing public service	With unique constitutional protections and distinct cultural expectations intersecting every dimension of social life, the press's autonomy differs from other fields in that its illusio fundamentally depends on how well it imagines, articulates, and enacts *public* missions. This dimension of autonomy does not ask the press to pursue a particular type of public. Rather, its autonomy depends on how well its separations and dependencies enact publics that are pragmatically judged to work—how well its creation and circulation of informational goods and social associations produce self-governance, how accountable its activities are and to whom, how well it explains the need for private action and field-specific privileges, and how well it clashes with or reinforces other fields' conception of the public good. Because the press's information provisioning is situated distinctly within a model of public self-governance, its autonomy is not simply a matter of negotiating with other fields, sustaining capital, balancing production scales, and evaluating new entrants. It must articulate its autonomy in terms of collective self-governance.

both physical and social forms—could be described in terms of facts that were "not human statements about the world but aspects of the world itself" (Schudson, 1978, p. 6). Readers and reporters were seen not as active interpreters of the worlds around them and the information they received but as naive empiricists who discovered and acted on realities that were assumed to be largely free of human construction.

Although the history of journalistic objectivity has no exact beginning, Stephen J. A. Ward (2005) finds its roots in long-standing philosophical distinctions among *ontological objectivity* (truth independent of experience), *epistemic objectivity* (truth as a product of "people's beliefs and methods of inquiry"), and *procedural objectivity* (a pragmatic application focused on avoiding bias and irrelevant influences and justifying action through a "firm grasp on the facts of the case") (pp. 16–18). Most discussions of journalistic objectivity focus on it as epistemology and procedure playing out in professional practices and cultures of media. David T. Z. Mindich (1998, p. 11) claims that it "was certainly an issue at least since 1690"; Michael Schudson (1978, p. 4) argues that "before the 1830s, objectivity was not an issue"; and Mark W. Brewin (2013, p. 213) starts his history of journalistic objectivity during the "heroic," post–World War II era of the American press in which journalists "managed to extricate themselves from political partisanship and develop a truly professional ethos." Acknowledging this unsettled history and the varied ways of reading objectivity into any era of the press, I focus on Daniel C. Hallin's placement of journalistic objectivity in the "scientized" journalism following World War I, when a "habit of disinterested realism" (Hallin, 1985, p. 130) was grounded in "a faith in 'facts,' a distrust of 'values,' and a commitment to their segregation" (Schudson, 1978, p. 6).

First, in the aftermath of World War I, Walter Lippmann (1922) argues, journalists slowly realized that the accounts that they received from government sources of both specific battles and the war's underlying rationale were often not truthful descriptions of actual events but stories constructed to persuade publics and elites to hold particular beliefs or attitudes. Although it was commonplace for reporters to interview sources, take verbatim notes, and produce "fact-centered" accounts in the lead-up to the war, afterward journalists began to question whether facts were or even could be true (Schudson, 2001). The state's widespread use of propaganda suggested to journalists that the democratic institutions they assumed to be acting in the public interest were actually agenda-driven organizations that advanced their own priorities and values and were interested in convincing the press to circulate their versions of "facts." The press needed to become its own center of power and accelerated its search for new methods of reporting and an organizing ideology—a particularly journalistic epistemology that could let it produce accounts of and for publics in ways that were verifiably independent of the propaganda produced by governments that had sustained such a disastrous war. Its new ideology of objectivity—a commitment to separating the journalistic production of facts from outside influences and values—was both an aspirational epistemology and evidence of its professional maturity: "a natural and progressive ideology for an aspiring occupational group at a moment when science was god, efficiency was cherished, and increasingly prominent elites judged partisanship a vestige of the tribal 19th century" (Schudson, 2001, p. 162).

Lippmann, an already accomplished elite American intellectual, saw this new ideology as a key element of how the press could responsibly separate audiences from elites and prevent mass public opinion from being controlled and manipulated. In 1922, he warned the press against using its power to create dangerous "pseudo-environments" (Lippmann, 1922, p. 10) because when inserted between "man and his environment," they created "pictures which are acted upon by groups of people" that, in turn, become "Public Opinion with capital letters" (p. 18). He argued that the postwar press was simply a tool for *stereotyping* (his newly coined term). At best, it sloppily assembled half-truths that others were forced to explain to the unwitting public, and at worst, it trafficked in harmful manipulations that required real thought and power to overcome—thinking and power that he felt few people were capable of putting into practice. Lippmann wanted journalists to be able to derive facts about the social world in the same way that he believed physicists were able to discover truths about the physical world (pp. 227–229). In making such a critique, however, Lippmann did more than decry the professional practices of journalists. He made an epistemological assumption, equating the social worlds that journalists attempt to explain with the material worlds that physicists aim to predict.

The entire system of electoral democracy in which citizens choose representatives was unworkable without "an independent, expert organization ... making the unseen facts intelligible to those who have to make the decisions" (Lippmann, 1922, p. 31). Unlike the stereotyping journalists who let the country slip into a fraudulent war, the new professional, objective press envisioned by Lippmann would be driven by a new "political science" that could shape public opinion "in advance of real decision, instead of [being an] apologist, critic, or reporter after the decision has been made." To Lippmann, objectivity was an ideology for negotiated autonomy: it would help separate journalists from propagandists and simultaneously embed journalists within a science of politics that could, in turn, separate masses from the decisions they were ill-equipped to make.

Although seemingly elitist and anathema (Carey, 1987) to the critical, populist democracy that John Dewey (1954, 1963, 1997) said could be achieved through mass education, communication, and participation, Lippmann realistically and optimistically envisioned the press as an instrument of democracy. He was not an "antidemocrat" who envisioned an elite press as the sole caretaker of the public interest. Instead, he saw journalism as one of the many specialized domains that publics needed to navigate the complex information environments of modern, large-scale democracies. Just as the Census Bureau and the Department of Agriculture have their own areas of expertise (Schudson, 2008a)—and akin to Zvi Reich's (2012) "bipolar interactional expertise" that experienced journalists use to shift among the perspectives of sources, audiences, and colleagues—Lippmann saw journalists as privileged insiders and expert boundary workers. They could *use* the separations and dependencies that objectivity both created and required to translate political systems for those who would always be outside. In *The Phantom Public,* he wrote that

only the insider can make decisions, not because he is inherently a better man but because he is so placed that he can understand and act. The outsider is necessarily ignorant, usually irrelevant and often meddlesome, because he is trying to navigate the ship from dry land.... [C]ompetence exists only in relation to function; ... men are not good, but good for something. (Lippmann, 1925, p. 140)

Sounding like a student of yet-to-be-invented field theory and neoinstitutional sociology, Lippmann envisioned press autonomy not as a matter of elites policing borders but as a property of a journalistic system composed of actors with different roles, skills, privileges, and responsibilities.

In this way, Lippmann's search for the press's autonomy in a complex system of large-scale democratic governance that required communication was entirely consistent with Dewey's review of Lippmann's *Phantom Public,* in which Dewey wrote that the "modern state is so large that decisions made and the executions initiated are necessarily remote from the mass of citizens; modern society is not only not visible, but it is not intelligible continuously and as a whole" (Dewey, 2008, pp. 214–215). Dewey and Lippmann both envisioned a professional press that was close to elite decision making, separate from propaganda-driven stereotypes, embedded in local communities, and yet free from the passions of mass publics—an autonomous, objective press that would help publics "intervene occasionally" (Dewey, 2008, p. 216) in the business of self-governance.

Just as journalism was beginning to ground its autonomy in the separations and dependencies that the ideology of objectivity required, a new profession was emerging that resembled journalism but that explicitly collapsed facts and values—public relations. Public relations professionals were not disinterested reporters or accountable government officials. Rather, they represented a new kind of intermediary between powerful elites and mass audiences whose motivations were not driven by an adherence to democratic principles, an ideology of objectivity, or a history of wartime deception. They served bosses who wanted messages spread, beliefs changed, and behaviors modified. Journalists worried that their inchoate autonomy—grounded in objectivity—would be eclipsed by these new "parajournalists" who, to the uninitiated public Lippmann warned of, were indistinguishable from journalists. By the early 1920s, "50 or 60 percent of stories, even in the venerable *New York Times*, were inspired by press agents and that the new Pulitzer School of Journalism at Columbia University in New York City was churning out more graduates for the public-relations industry than for the newspaper business" (Schudson, 2003b, p. 83).

In the midst of this professional challenge, postwar journalism deepened its commitment to autonomy through a disinterested pursuit of the public good by investing in or bootstrapping three institutional projects that could distinguish it from other information professionals—journalism schools, professional bodies, and statistical techniques. First, although U.S. journalists require no license or degree to practice—indeed, they often hid their degrees from hiring editors who viewed college graduates suspiciously (Folkerts, 2014)—journalism schools have historically acted as gatekeepers of the profession (Josephi, 2009). They define a body of teachable knowledge distinct from other higher education units, are accredited by professional bodies that periodically audit their performance, demarcate expertise

levels in the form of entry-level and advanced degrees, usually espouse ethical commitments to ideals that define the profession's social value, and
produce graduates who, through practice, signify the profession's broader
cultural meaning (Abbott, 1988; Folkerts, 2014; Hatch, 1988; M. L. Larson,
1977; Schudson, 1988; Schudson & Anderson, 2008). Developing alongside
or emerging from English and literature departments and schools of social
science, speech, rhetoric, and communication, U.S. journalism schools
have always stayed close to both practices and ideas. They have aimed to
be homes for teaching vocational skills by providing an "old-fashioned
apprenticeship" that "duplicate[s] the atmospherics of a newspaper" (Carey,
2000), for doing social science research, and for making liberal arts reflections on journalism (Folkerts, 2014). The press's autonomy, as expressed
in its professional schools, arises when journalists learn how to distinguish
themselves from other disciplines—the practice and study of journalism has
always implicated different interpretive communities (Zelizer, 2004)—and
when they learn how to become employable and reflective practitioners
who can navigate the intersections of commercial news practice, social science research, and critical humanistic inquiry. The ideal graduate speaks all
three journalistic languages, although practice has always dominated the
triad (Folkerts, 2014).

Second, as the number of U.S. journalism schools rapidly grew—increasing
from ten in 1920 to fifty-five in 1928 (Folkerts, 2014)—professional bodies
emerged alongside. They provided quality control (by accrediting and rank-
ing journalism schools and conducting professional inquiries), convened
practitioners through yearly meetings and surveys, and published original
research on journalism designed to produce both best practices and intellectual contributions to the fledgling study of the news (Folkerts, 2014; Zelizer, 2004). Three organizations in particular illustrate the press's search for
autonomy through dependencies and separations that professional bodies
could govern:

• At its founding convention in 1922, the American Society of Newspaper
Editors (ASNE) created a member code of ethics espousing the principles
of sincerity, truthfulness, accuracy, and impartiality, declaring that news
"should be free from opinion or bias of any kind" (cited in Schudson,
2003b, p. 82). In 1947, outgoing ASNE president Wilbur Forrest used the
annual meeting to warn against looming threats to editorial independence

coming from labor unions and government regulators. He called on the ASNE to make its own definition of press freedom before the new Hutchins Commission did it for them (Pickard, 2014a, pp. 152–153).

• Formed in 1887, the American Newspaper Publishers Association (ANPA) was founded for "the advancement of the business interests of daily newspapers" and the adjudication of "conflicts with advertisers, with labor, with communications competitors, with newsprint makers, and with the government." To survive economic shocks to the newspaper industry, the association agreed "by voluntary secret agreement to limit industry-wide production, to allocate satisfactory quotas, and to stabilize selling prices" (Emery, 1950, p. 3).

• The progressive amalgamation of various associations of journalism school teachers and administrators created the Association for Education in Journalism and Mass Communication (AEJMC) for the "advancement of academic and professional education for journalism, encouragement of communication research, and cooperation with media practitioners in their efforts to raise the standards of their profession" (Emery & McKerns, 1987, p. 1).

These three bodies suggest different versions of press autonomy because of the separations and dependencies they prioritize. The ASNE convened editors around principles and defended them against what it saw as outside threats; the ANPA let press owners collude to withstand market forces that it saw as disruptive and nonjournalistic; and the AEJMC gathered teachers and researchers to define a body of knowledge that might shape press practices, businesses, and scholarship. As these organizations show, because there is no single vision of the press, there is no one definition of press autonomy. Press freedom is, instead, very much a property of how a field of forces—in these cases, arranged into organizational bodies—understands differently the value of editorial practice, commercial success, or intellectual rigor.

Third, in the interwar period, U.S. journalism began to both rely on and distance itself from the polling techniques, survey data, and logics of quantification that social scientists were using to create supposedly objective representations of public opinion. Akin to the role Lippmann envisioned for the press, pollsters saw themselves as scientific intermediaries between governing elites and mass audiences, challenging the idea that journalists, politicians, or anyone wedded to narrative modes of communication could represent the beliefs of a large-scale citizenry better than a survey researcher using objective techniques to sample a preinformed public. In 1939, Gallup wrote that "through the process of sampling referendum, the people, having heard the debate on both sides of every issue, can express their will. After one hundred and fifty years, we return to the town meeting. This time the whole nation is within the doors" (Gallup, 1939, p. 15). The press could give audiences information, but pollsters thought that their objective, scientific techniques could recreate, on mass scales, the kind of intimate conversations that traditionally had defined deliberative, participatory democracy. Their surveys could—at scale and with scientific rigor—do what the press was trying to do through individual stories that were written by biased reporters and that had to be interpreted by uninitiated audiences. Pollsters could say what the public really thought because their techniques aligned with the era's dominant positivist, bureaucratic epistemologies used by "a new generation of managers and technical specialists" to use "rationality, methodical processes, and standards of 'objectivity' in place of public deliberation" (Boyte, 1995, p. 427). Pollsters said that they did not have to worry about separating facts and values the way journalists did because they worked only with facts.

Journalists largely embraced polling techniques and survey results because they let them transform "the subjectivity of opinion into the objectivity of fact" (Salmon & Glasser, 1995, p. 444). As they buttressed their stories with polling data—or simply wrote stories *about* poll results—journalists could distance themselves from any discussion of public opinion quality (which was a matter for scientific methodologists) and from the content of public opinion (polls were not what journalists thought the public thought but what social scientists found the public to be thinking). This distancing was accompanied by a kind of closeness that gave scientific weight to the press's pursuit of objectivity. Polls, surveys, actuarial tables, margins of error, and stories that fit within the bounds of a questionnaire results became core components of reporting, especially in election journalism (Carey, 1995), with news organizations eventually creating their own polling operations. Without numerical backing, journalists' ability to write authoritatively about broad cultural forces was constrained, but with the "facts" that quantification provided, they were freer to explore the more qualitative, narrative dimensions of storytelling that gave context and color to statistics. *McClure's Magazine* (1893–1929) could headline an article "What Women Should Weigh" as it uncritically made insurance company actuarial tables the basis of a 1909 story, seeing correlation as a news peg and a "basis for action" (Bouk, 2015, p. 123). And the *New York Times* could confidently question a life insurance company treating the labor of men and women differently by stating that the "feeling that goes with" the services provided by women "ought to be worth at least the extra 25 per cent" (p. 168)—without ever questioning the wisdom or public consequences of accepting the premise that labor should be commodified in terms of gender.

By tying themselves tightly to the epistemologies of polling, journalists outsourced part of their objectivity and garnered a new kind of freedom. This outsourcing made possible an almost exclusive authority to interpret and frame polls, letting them rise above statistics and exercise a unique freedom to say what numbers meant.

These polling techniques also let the press position the separations and dependencies of its objectivity as instruments of two fundamental features of modern Western democracy—the notion that individual expression (aggregated in statistically defensible forms like polls) is the purest form of power in a democratic society made up of rational citizens (Salmon & Glasser, 1995) and the idea that modern democracies are so large and complex that they can be sustained only by systems of public opinion that use "quantification and statistics ... to routinize processes of observation" (Herbst, 1995, p. 12). Even if these aggregations bear little resemblance to how citizens themselves develop public opinions or discuss their experiences and perspectives (Gamson, 1992; Herbst, 1993; Igo, 2007), polls let journalists recast the public as "a statistical artifact" (Carey, 1995, p. 392)— "a demographic segment or data set rather than a realm of action" (J. D. Peters, 1995, p. 20).

Taken together, these three dimensions of how journalism tried to distinguish itself from other information professionals—by having journalism schools act as gatekeepers of the profession, by establishing professional bodies, and by relying on and distancing itself from polling techniques, survey data, and the logics of quantification—illustrate how press autonomy emerged from separations and dependencies in the service of objectivity. Journalists' uncritical echoing of state propaganda during World War I convinced them that they needed a professionalism premised on separating facts and values; the rise of the public relations professional highlighted the need to institutionalize the separation of facts and values; the creation

of journalism schools and professional bodies revealed a nascent press trying to carve out a unique identity amid demands for vocational training,
academic research, and commercial success; and the adoption of public
opinion polling and logics of quantification as ways to perform objectivity
placed statistics at the heart of objective journalism in a way that left journalists freer to assert their unique authorities as disinterested interpreters of
information.

Objectivity, in this sense, is not *freedom from* external influences but
the achievement of a field that sees facts as "consensually validated statements" about the world (Schudson, 1978, p. 7). It requires journalists to be
"reflective practitioners" (Schön, 1983) who can situate their factual claims
within a personal system of separations and dependencies—whom they
are close to, what they assume, what principles guide their actions, which
people and ideas they are disconnected from, and what they are unaware
of. As Judith Lichtenberg (2000, pp. 251–252) puts it, the "objective inves-
tigator may *start out* neutral (more likely, she is simply good at keeping her
prior beliefs from distorting her inquiry), but she does not necessarily *end
up* neutral." Journalists who naively and stubbornly adhere to neutrality
understand the separations and dependencies of their profession's ideology
of objectivity far less well than journalists who situate their actions within a
community of interpretation (Zelizer, 1997) that sees some separations and
dependencies as essential and others as corrupting.

It is not up to individual journalists to work out the significance of these
separations and dependencies and their relationship to press autonomy.
They are instead embedded in the routines and rituals that journalists have
historically shared and used to distance themselves from and embed themselves within the worlds they report on.

Autonomy through Organizational Routine and Ritual

This belief in objectivity was gradually standardized into the largely unexamined rituals and routines that news organizations used to codify and
standardize press autonomy. Instead of asking journalists to work out on
their own, in every situation, the salient differences between news and
nonnews, facts and values, numbers and narratives, U.S. news organizations built cultures that did this work for them. Journalists could outsource
any questions about how to identify news, treat sources, and convey expert
disinterest to a taken-for-granted system of separations and dependencies,

simplifying complexity and reducing the need for their conscious, idiosyncratic action (James, 1914). Their own understanding of freedom became intertwined with an almost unassailable set of shared rituals that defined what their profession meant or could mean in any context (Swidler, 1986). These rituals gave them the freedom to pursue and publish stories that fit within common expectations of what the press *should* do—but they also narrowed the meaning of press autonomy to a set of largely invisible separations and dependencies that came to define what the press *could* do.

Many studies show that journalists have historically crafted accounts of the world according to largely unspoken, shared heuristics about where they expect news to be (Ehrlich, 1996; Gans, 1979; Molotch & Lester, 1974; Tuchman, 1972, 1973, 1978); when they expect news to happen (Barnhust & Mutz, 1997; Bell, 1995; Berkowitz, 1992; Kielbowicz, 2015; Molotch & Lester, 1974; Schudson, 1986); what news is supposed to look like (Barnhurst & Nerone, 2001; Park, 1940); which sources "set the cultural definition of events and problems" (Carlson, 2009, p. 526) and are thus too important to offend and powerful enough to be granted anonymity (Boeyink, 1990; Carlson, 2009, 2011); what owners and publishers allow news to be (Bezanson, 2003b; Breed, 1955; Chomsky, 1999, 2006); and how editors and journalists expect news to be produced (Bennett, 2007; Ryfe, 2006, 2009, 2012).

Reporters "are entitled to select their own facts, draw their own conclusions, and come up with their own evaluations, although they may be edited later" (Gans, 1979, p. 101), but their independence is confined within the relatively narrow realm of operational decisions—who to interview, which quotes to use, and which leads to pursue (Murdock, 1977). This individual, story-level freedom from interference gives journalists considerable discretion within one aspect of practice, but equating it with press autonomy distracts from reporters' inability to control larger, more powerful allocative forces—fundamental dynamics about how news organizations operate, including which sections a newspaper should have, who should be hired or fired, and what kind of beats should exist (Murdock, 1977). Even when journalists claim that they have the right to make their own story-level judgments free of any hierarchical instruction, "the suggestions of powerful superiors are, in fact, thinly veiled orders" of senior editors (Gans, 1979, p. 101) or publishers whose identities are concealed from reporters (Catledge, 1971; Chomsky, 2006).

Reporters may have had real or imagined *freedom from* particular influences (Isaiah Berlin's individually felt and observable "negative freedom"), but their *freedom to* pursue journalism outside of the frameworks given to them (Berlin's collectively sustained "positive freedom") was largely curtailed by forces larger than themselves (Berlin, 1969). Their focus on individual freedom makes it hard to see autonomy as the power to direct collective resources.

Journalism also has historically bracketed the places where reporters expect news to be. Events, locations, and sources usually fit within well-structured rhythms—beats—that organize the production of news (Gans, 1979; Tuchman, 1978). With the exception of long-term, high-risk investigative reporting and earlier eras of foreign correspondence—when seniority and geography gave reporters distance from newsroom daily rhythms and license to exercise judgment (Ettema & Glasser, 1987a; J. M. Hamilton, 2009)—it is difficult for journalists to convince colleagues or audiences that a story can exist separate from a beat or from any of the other criteria that traditionally have defined enterprise news production, such as conflict, timeliness, proximity, prominence, and the unusual (Kovach & Rosenstiel, 2014; Stephens, 1988). Stories are far more likely to appear in the news when they can be easily understood "in the context of what has gone before and anticipated in the future" (Molotch & Lester, 1974, p. 101). Journalists are more likely to cover accidents, scandals, surprises, and event emotions that align with newsroom deadlines, editors' expectations, prize committee standards, and readers' expectations of what news should be (Wahl-Jorgensen, 2013).

These "strategic rituals" (Tuchman, 1972) of news production are not simply shortcuts for reliably meeting deadlines but also subtle institutional expressions of objectivity's dominance. When combined with the relationships that journalists cultivated with bureaucracies and reliable sources (M. Fishman, 1980; Sigal, 1973, 1986), these rituals served to "orient man and society"—bounding press freedom to what the profession's rituals, sources, and norms of objectivity all allowed the "actual world" (Park, 1940, p. 669) to be. Gaye Tuchman (1978) shows how journalists embed themselves within an ideology of objectivity through a set of practices that protects them against charges of bias:

• *Conflicting truth claims:* Journalists juxtapose statements from bureaucratically credible sources—high-profile politicians, elite doctors, professors from

Ivy League universities, CEOs of Fortune 500 companies—whose authority derives not from journalists' judgments of their expertise but from society's sanctioning of these positions.[7]

• *Attribution:* They overtly mark text as originating not from the story's writer but from sources. Whether quoted or not, named or not, anonymous or pseudo-anonymous, these attribution decisions let journalists strategically make some story elements closer to or further from their own voice.

• *Additional facts:* When reporters are uncertain of a story's lede or lack confidence in possible interpretations of a story, they overwhelm readers with information. By moving their stories closer to research, they simultaneously protect themselves against critiques that their stories lack rigor while offloading any misinterpretations to the research sources.

• *The inverted pyramid:* A news story's largely unquestioned hierarchy puts the most important information at the beginning of an article. It lets reporters simultaneously reenact professional norms (good stories have strong, clear ledes), meet readers' habits (many people read only headlines or opening paragraphs and expect news to be there), and exercise their freedom to highlight or downplay some story elements over others. The inverted pyramid is a constraint that reporters, editors, and readers rely on—but it also gives journalists the freedom to cast their interpretations selectively and strategically as objective organization.

The journalistic autonomy across Tuchman's practices is multidimensional—the freedom to cultivate relationships with sources but the need to negotiate with their interests and agendas for being sources; the power to invite sources into stories or broadcasts but the ethical duty to quote them directly or let them speak; the ability to construct balance and shape debates by combining sources with different viewpoints but the ultimate professional obligation to bracket your own interpretations and stay within the bounds of stories that are usually allowed to have only two sides.[8]

In a corollary to Tuchman's account of journalists' separations and distances and Cook's (1998) argument that the press cogoverns with the state, W. Lance Bennett (1990, 1996; Bennett, Lawrence, & Livingston, 2006, 2007) and others (Althaus, 2003; Ryfe, 2006; Zaller & Chiu, 1996) find that the elite press's celebrated freedom to critique governments is actually limited to what the branches of the state discuss among themselves. Studying press coverage of the Nicaraguan contras funding, the 1985–1986 U.S.-Libya crisis, U.S. foreign policy crises from 1945 to 1991, both Gulf Wars, and the Abu Ghraib prison scandal, researchers consistently find that journalists "base stories on official sources; index views according to the magnitude and content of conflicts between these sources; follow the trail of power; narrate stories according to the prevailing customs of the political culture"; and move beyond official sources only when given license by "credible dissenting icons" (Ryfe, 2006, pp. 204–205). The press's closeness to official sources leads it simply to "index" (Bennett, 1990) debates—tying its "story frames to the range of sources and viewpoints within official decision circles" (Bennett, Lawrence, & Livingston, 2006, p. 468).

If the elite sources that journalists regularly rely on for information do not debate an issue, it is ritualistically incomprehensible and thus virtually invisible to news organizations. To surface stories in the absence of elite debate would mean acknowledging that the press has its own interests that are separate from the discussions among those it covers. If the press separated itself from those it normally depends on, it would break a core ideological tenant of objectivity. This principle requires a different kind of separation—the idea that one of the primary responsibilities of "hard news" is to maintain a distinction between the facts themselves and the values that others use to give facts meaning.

Even when countervailing social movements have emerged that challenge elites, the press has had difficulty acknowledging the legitimacy of these challenges. For example, in studies of the U.S. media's coverage of the Vietnam War, Hallin (1986) found that most journalism fits within a "sphere of legitimate controversy"—defined by "the parameters of the debate between and within the Democratic and Republican parties" in which "objectivity and balance reign as the supreme journalistic values" (p. 116)—and Todd Gitlin observed the press adhering to a relatively small set of standardized "media frames":

persistent patterns of cognition, interpretation, and presentation, of selection, emphasis, and exclusion by which symbol-handlers routinely organize discourse, whether verbal or visual. Frames enable journalists to process large amounts of information quickly and routinely: to recognize it as information, to assign it to cognitive categories, and to package it for efficient relay to their audiences. (Gitlin, 1980, p. 7)

Political groups learned that, in order to gain the kind of power that comes with national media attention, they needed to submit their own goals, self-narratives, and events "to the implicit rules of newsmaking" and "journalistic notions" of "what a 'story' is, what an 'event' is, what a 'protest' is" (Gitlin, 1980, p. 3). The press's vision of autonomy as freedom from anything that interferes with its ritualized, objective indexing of elite discourse creates a kind of hegemony in which journalists' "picture of the world is systematically preferred over others'" (p. 257). The press's illusion of autonomy as independence thus requires an asymmetry—a dependence on the part of others who must anticipate and align with what they think reporters are expecting to see and with what kind of media frames they think journalists will be most willing to work within.

But not all journalists approach these logics in the same way, as highlighted by James W. Carey's (1997) distinction between the ideal of a journalist as a "professional communicator" versus "individual interpreter."[9] To Carey, professional communicators distance themselves from the story and use rituals of objectivity to claim that its validity comes not from their interpretations or judgments but from the veracity of the information provided to them by sources that they assume that their audiences see as authoritative. At each stage, their individual autonomy is a dance between closeness and distance—getting close enough to a story to understand which sources are relevant; backing away from the story as sources provide interpretation; assembling multiple sources and juxtaposing their accounts; knowing editors and audiences well enough to understand what they think counts as evidence; and backing away from the story, sources, and audiences after a story is published—leaving it to the ill-defined public to decide what should be done because of a story. The professional communicator adheres to an "information ideal" (Schudson, 1978, pp. 88–120) of news; writes stories in simple language that requires no special skill, knowledge, or socioeconomic status to be understood—"elaborated codes" to Basil Bernstein (1962); and strictly follows principles of "fairness, objectivity and scrupulous dispassion" (Schudson, 1978, p. 90). The autonomy of professional communicators is judged according to how well they assemble their separations and dependencies to make this ideal a reality.[10]

The individual interpreter, though, is a different kind of journalist who works within a "story ideal" of news (Schudson, 1978, pp. 88–120). In this model, newspapers are sources of entertainment, empathy, and foresight (Belman, 1977). They give readers "satisfying aesthetic experiences" that help them "interpret their own lives and to relate them to the nation, town, or class to which they belong" (Schudson, 1978, p. 89). Journalism was not simply "reporting that put the words and actions of others into simpler language" but principled sense-making that "invested the ordinary with significance" and helped audiences "come to terms with old realities in new ways" (Carey, 1997, p. 137). The authority of interpreters derived not from how well they dispassionately adhered to ideals of ritualized distance and objectivity but how well they situated themselves within stories and audiences. Autonomy was premised not on *freedom from* interference that corrupted the professional communicator but on a *freedom to* interpret that, ideally, helped readers relate to stories, understand possible interpretations, and appreciate their shared social conditions.

The professional communicator and individual interpreter, though, are analytical ideals, not empirical realities (M. Weber, 2007). There are, in practice, many ways for professional communicators to behave like individual interpreters periodically—complicating the idea that a professional communicator's freedom is exclusively individual and negative or that an individual interpreter's is strictly social and affirmative. Because the press enlists both of these roles (and many variants in between), press autonomy is a mix of people trying variously to be far from or close to practices of interpretation. For example, reporters subtly subvert the language of objectivity, and newsrooms embrace interpretation in the pursuit of workplace diversity.

Theodore L. Glasser and James S. Ettema (1993) describe journalists' use of irony to "quietly and discretely" (p. 334) pass judgment when "the facts do not 'speak for themselves'" (p. 322). They analyzed journalist Lou Cannon's reporting on President Ronald Reagan's 1985 visit to South Africa during which the president—one of the most powerful bureaucratically credible and socially sanctioned sources—erroneously claimed that the apartheid government had "eliminated" segregation. Cannon was faced with a choice—to echo Reagan's words (staying close to an ideal of objectivity that requires reporters to report facts and reprint statements while leaving audiences decide their meaning), to juxtapose Reagan's words with a source who could critique the president's claim (it would be hard to find an equally weighty source willing to go on the record), or to critique Reagan subtly within his stories using a technique that he knew only some readers would appreciate. He executed the third option by skillfully using quotation marks within the text of his story as "the equivalent of 'air quotes' used in spoken conversation to express ironic detachment or even contempt" (p. 332). Cannon's ironic distancing is a kind of double disinterest in objectivity. Not only is he subtly tearing the president's words from the context that the president intended (letting Cannon create his own frame), but he also is aligning himself with a more sophisticated subset of the audience that can appreciate the power of textual irony through selective quotation—a "restricted" style of communication that Bernstein (1962) argues is available only to those who have advanced language skills and share disdain for a president who is "not merely ignorant of the state of apartheid in South Africa but confidently unaware of it" (p. 331). Irony becomes a language game that shows the subtleties of press freedom. It frees reporters from the usual norms and standards of objectivity, leaves room for a professional defense ("I'm not biased; I just quoted the president"), lets reporters access an audience that understands the irony, shows how veteran reporters and skillful writers enjoy an extra dimension of autonomy, and invites the reader to see the newspaper as a genre that playfully mixes the information and story ideals.

Similarly, Lisbeth Lipari (1996) shows how journalists can skillfully use stance adverbs to achieve a kind of autonomy that lies somewhere between disinterested neutrality and overt interpretation. Akin to Cannon's use of irony, she shows how subtly modified action words can help sophisticated writers and attentive readers share interpretations. Her analysis of wire stories shows how reporters use words "such as *obviously, clearly, apparently*, and *presumably*" to "convey something about [their] attitude toward the facts at hand" (p. 821). She finds that writers use the word *obviously* to give "focus, emphasis, and legitimacy" to a reporter's story ("An obviously elated Marlon Brando hugged his eldest son"); signal "logical, causal, or common sense inferences" that they see as indisputable ("For President Bush, the stunning putdown of Saddam Hussein is obviously good political news"); or to "redirect or reorient [an] interpretation and information flow" ("The President obviously cannot make the U.S. decisions in a vacuum") (pp. 824–826). These interpretive moves—subtle and accessible only to those skilled enough to write and read them—let reporters simultaneously insert themselves into a story and align themselves with a set of unassailable facts.

Autonomy is not a disinterested separation from events, the freedom to overtly advocate, or a strict adherence to a subset of terminology deemed to be acceptably objective. Rather, it is the flexibility to use language to guide audiences toward events and ways of thinking about them.

Beyond individual reporters' freedom to skirt objectivity by creatively addressing sophisticated audiences, news organizations historically have struggled with the logic of reflecting diversity in style guidelines and in hiring policies in a profession that supposedly brackets the news and its practitioners within norms of objectivity. Facts are facts that reporters report, regardless of who they are. But the 1968 *Kerner Report*—commissioned by President Lyndon B. Johnson to investigate causes of civil unrest—"warned that the 'press has too long basked in a white world, looking out of it, if at all, with white men's eyes and a white perspective.'" The Society of Professional Journalists' 2002 Diversity Committee called multicultural newsrooms "'essential to an informed public and democracy itself'" (Glasser, Awad, & Kim, 2009, p. 58). The Associated Press and the *New York Times* have repeatedly updated their style guides in light of their perceptions of new norms for describing social groups—such as by changing how they describe members of lesbian, gay, bisexual, and transgender (LGBT) communities (GLAAD, 2014). And in 1988, the National Association of Black Journalists, the Asian American Journalists Association, the National Association of Hispanic Journalists, and the Native American Journalists Association united to form the group Unity, which was charged with "increasing the numbers of journalists of color to better reflect the actual composition of the American population and improving the 'representation' of people of color in the news" (Benson, 2005, p. 5). In short, the press itself—in its hiring practices, language policies, and professional associations—defines its autonomy not as generic reporters' independence from outside forces interfering with the production of objective news but as an ongoing, field-level conversation about which kinds of diversity it requires, which kinds it can ignore, and which kinds of public obligations it recognizes and hires for.

This brief history of the sociology of journalistic practices shows that press autonomy comes not from individual reporters breaking free of superiors or sources but through subtle, ritualistic negotiation of mutual dependencies. Reporters need beats, routines of balance, norms of language, and bureaucratic authority in order to organize their work, meet deadlines, cultivate relationships with sources, and perform their identities as professional communicators who let the public decide for itself. But if they can subtly interpret events and reflect changing social norms within the bounds of journalistic professionalism, they are sometimes able or expected to subvert the routines of objectivity—writing complex, nuanced stories that sophisticated audiences will understand, letting personal judgments of bureaucratically credible sources shine through, and diversifying their newsrooms with reporters who can situate neutral pursuits of stories and facts within personal investments and identities.

Autonomy through Bracketing Publics

As much as the press defines its autonomy through ideologies of objectivity and rituals of news making, it also shows why it thinks it needs institutional autonomy as it relies on, cultivates, and separates itself from the audiences that consume its news. That is, journalists have historically left clues about how they have understood the public purpose of their autonomy as they included and excluded audiences in their work or explanations of why they say they do their work.

Sometimes journalists have understood the public simply as those people who are interested in whatever they find interesting. They write "for their superiors and for themselves" (Gans, 1979, p. 230) or, as Robert Darnton (1975, pp. 182–188) describes it, for "the inner circle of a reporter's public." This circle includes not only other reporters and editors at the reporter's paper but those seen as competitors at other papers, friends and family members who might read the stories, reporters who are no longer practicing but who are seen as past masters of the craft, and sources and subjects who regularly appear in the paper's stories. This is the reference group for reporters' understanding of professional freedom—those that they see themselves responsible to as professional communicators and those that they imagine might be upset when they strike out on their own as individual interpreters.

At other times, though, journalists have a "fear of the audience" (Gans, 1979, p. 235). When reminded of the large, unknowable mass of people who may encounter their stories or the responsibility of providing "the democratic public" with what it needs to know, journalists demur and return to more familiar audiences: "If audience wants were considered, journalistic news judgment would go by the wayside" (p. 235) as they became paralyzed with responsibility.

Although they may seek informal feedback from friendly nonjournalists—a "known audience" of friends, neighbors, and family members (Gans, 1979, p. 236)—journalists cope with the responsibility of serving a large public by dismissing the audience members they do encounter. Readers who write letters to the editor are seen as a necessary evil. They serve as evidence that the paper is producing news that attracts attention and elicits feedback, but editors see those who write within an "idiom of insanity" (Wahl-Jorgensen, 2002) and see consideration of their feedback as a largely performative exercise.

Similarly, some papers bracketed much of their audience relationship within an "ombudsman" or "reader representative" position. First appearing in U.S. newspapers in the mid-1960s as part of an attempt to establish credibility with readers, the ombudsman was "typically a senior editor equipped with the authority to investigate complaints and get answers for readers" (Nemeth, 2003, p. 2). The ombudsman had to maintain sufficient distance from journalists, editors, and owners to sustain an ongoing critique of a particular news organization and the journalistic profession (Meyers, 2000) but could not appear overly sympathetic to all readers' concerns for fear of losing access to newsrooms. The ideal ombudsman, Andrew R. Cline (2008) argues, is not an "omniscient journalist" who simply tells journalists what they should have done or lectures readers on how newspapers "really" work. Rather, the ideal ombudsman is a self-reflective, "privileged reader" whose first mission is to critique the paper's integrity by critically examining its reporting practices as an experienced outsider.

More commonly, though, the ombudsman has been more symbolic than substantive. A national survey comparing the reporting of journalists who worked at papers with ombudsmen versus the reporting of those at papers without found that a reporter's age—not the presence of an ombudsman—was a better predictor of whether he or she would engage in what the survey described as "controversial newsgathering techniques" (Pritchard, 1993, p. 77). When papers do have ombudsmen, journalists tended not to share complaints they receive from readers and were more likely to ignore or hide negative feedback (Bezanson, Cranberg, & Soloski, 1987). This finding supports Kate McKenna's (1993) argument that ombudsmen isolate reporters from readers because they outsource the sense of public responsibility that, he argues, should be within a reporter's personal work ethic. Finally and perhaps most damaging, James S. Ettema and Theodore L. Glasser (1987b) found that ombudsmen's own understandings of their roles were so inflected with persuasive, public relations logics—stating, for example, that the "single most important aspect of their job" is to "give readers a sense that the newspaper cares about them" (p. 7)—that they were more likely to represent the paper's interests to the readers rather than be critical liaisons or cultural bridges between the news organization and its publics. In one high-profile moment when an ombudsman might have held his own paper accountable on behalf of readers, he was ignored. When the *New York Times* public editor Byron Calame asked executive editor Bill Keller to explain why he had held a story for over a year at the request of the George W. Bush administration, Keller replied: "There is really no way to have a full discussion of the back story without talking about when and how we knew what we knew, and we can't do that" (Calame, 2006, n.p.).

Perceived as a way to bring the press and audiences closer and foster professional accountability—an ostensible curb on the press's freedom from audiences—the ombudsman role was largely symbolic and performative.

Journalists defend such distancing as a practical way to manage the power that comes with being "self-appointed and unaccountable audience representatives" (Gans, 1979, p. 238). To exercise the judgment that it assumes to be correct, the press needs to bracket audiences as "a receptacle to be informed by experts and an excuse for the practice of publicity" (Carey, 1995, pp. 391–392). As long as it can contain public participation in news production and describe the public on its terms—making its accounts of the world appear natural and self-evident—the press can create strategically circular rituals that equate its interests with the public's interests. The press becomes a caretaker press that "justifies itself in the public's name but in which the public plays no [significant] role" (Carey, 1995, p. 391). Largely absent from a press predicated on sustaining its freedom by distancing itself from audiences is sophisticated professional self-reflection on the press's power to make—not reflect—publics through its uncontested rituals.

The type of autonomy the press says it needs reveals the type of public it thinks it is supporting (Baker, 2002, pp. 129–153). Beginning in the Progressive Era, the press came to be seen as a vehicle for informed citizenship. If audiences had good data produced by professional journalists, then citizens could claim their rights, hold elites accountable, and rationally assemble themselves into publics that gave informed consent to be governed (Schudson, 1998). The press is service-oriented. Its job is to sense, respond to, and meet public desires for information within a largely market-oriented system in which "consumers' desires drive news coverage" (J. T. Hamilton, 2006, p. 7). In market-oriented journalism (McManus, 1994, pp. 4–5),

• Consumers define news' quality and value through their choices;
• Products judged to be quality drive other products from the market;
• Self-correcting forces produce information that consumers lack when entrepreneurs identify market opportunities;
• Producers are under constant pressure to create the appearance of new, improved goods that are seen as better than competitors';
• Scarce resources like cultural and economic capital go to producers that consumers consider to be valuable; and
• Consumers are always free to choose among products without coercion.

In this model—most closely associated with a "competitive" model of democracy "through which individuals, acting alone or in concert with others, build support for what they want" (Christians, Glasser, McQuail, Nordenstreng, & White, 2009, p. 94)—the public is an aggregation of individual citizens expressing personal preferences. It consists of information clients for whom the press produces commodities—but only those commodities that consumers want. Market-based publics give news organizations a kind of autonomy consistent with the ideology of objectivity. Because journalists are beholden to no identifiable set of interests that might interfere with their editorial judgments—they follow market dynamics—their rituals of disinterested, factual reporting are simply institutional manifestations of what their clients demand. The press's objectivity-centered autonomy is intact because it can align itself with market forces that also are seen to lack ideology. As former Federal Communications Commission chair Mark Flower said: "the public interest is that which interests the public" (cited in Hallin, 2000, p. 234), and state regulators "should rely on the broadcasters' ability to determine the wants of their audiences through the normal mechanisms of the marketplace" (Fowler & Brenner, 1982, p. 210). The free press is a free market, and any malfunction is a market failure.

This separation from the state and alignment with the markets does give the press freedom from overt influence by government censors or nonmarket funders, but it creates a new set of dependencies that can hinder journalistic autonomy. First, markets tend to reward choice among goods but not necessarily diversity among products. It is easier for producers to earn market share and thrive if the number of competitors is small, if product differentiation is clear, and if competition centers on a few, discrete, easily measurable features. If products differ too much or if the differences cannot be discerned, then it becomes hard for producers and consumers alike to build a language of competition and choice. The result is a kind of "contract failure" (Hansmann, 1980; D. R. Young, 2015) between producers and consumers that drives producers to decrease product quality and leads people to make decisions based not on a rational self-interest in acquiring the information they need to consent to governance but on a host of other factors (for- or not-for-profit status, brand identity, peer recommendations) that fit poorly with the idea that audiences are focused on rationally seeking out, evaluating, and applying the objective information that journalists provide. Journalists' freedom to create publics is limited by the market's ability to prevent collusion, break up information monopolies, differentiate products, communicate meaningful differences among choices, distribute information equitably, and enable rational choice (Baker, 1998, 2002; J. T. Hamilton, 2006). It matters little if journalists want publics to emerge from informed citizenship if their autonomy depends on failing information markets that they lack the power to fix.

Second, when markets are working, journalists must confine their work within frameworks of competition defined by their peers. They must learn which factors their bosses, audiences, competitors, and coworkers see as proprietary and advantageous and orient their work toward these elements to ensure that their stories and reputation thrive in the market. This creates a "scoop and shun" phenomenon. Journalists are more likely to produce stories that are timely (it is easy to recognize which news organization published a story first, so time becomes an easy marker of market success) or stories that purposefully ignore what a competitor has reported or first discovered (to do so would be to acknowledge a competitor's dominance) (Glasser & Gunther, 2005). It is also hard for journalists to tell when a market has produced the definitive account, when competition should move on to a new topic, how authority on one issue translates to another, what standards markets must meet for certainty, and how long markets are willing to wait for such closure (Gentzkow & Shapiro, 2008). Largely lost in these dynamics is the bargain journalists make in tying their autonomy to competitive markets that are supposed to produce informed citizenship and enlightened self-governance.

Third, even if markets function and competition thrives, news is a fundamentally different kind of product compared to other commodities. It is nonrivalrous (consuming news does not prevent others from consuming news), largely nonexcludable (although subscribers often have first or privileged access, it is difficult to stop people from consuming news), depends on revenue from two-sided markets (advertisers and subscribers underwrite it), has benefits that extend beyond sellers and buyers (even those who never consume news benefit from living in societies with those who do), and its purchase both reflects and shapes preferences (people might seek out news they want, but consuming news often changes people and their ideas about what they think they want next) (Baker, 2002, pp. 7–19). If the press is to produce, circulate, and help audiences make sense of news, it needs freedom from thinking about itself as just an information marketplace and ways of framing the exceptional nature of its products.

Ensuring that the press had the institutional freedom to explore its unique qualities drove a major media reform movement in the United States in the 1940s. As Victor Pickard chronicles, a host of initiatives tried to limit the power of commercial media within normative, democratic aims:

a cluster of progressive court decisions and policy interventions, including the Federal Communications Commission's (FCC) 1943 anti-monopoly measures against chain broadcasters, which forced NBC to divest itself of a major network; the Supreme Court's 1945 antitrust ruling against the Associated Press, which affirmed the government's duty to encourage in the press "diverse and antagonistic sources"; the 1946 "Blue Book," which mandated broadcasters' public service responsibilities; the 1947 Hutchins Commission on Freedom of the Press, which established journalism's democratic benchmarks; and, finally, the 1949 Fairness Doctrine, which outlined key public interest obligations for broadcasters. (Pickard, 2014a, p. 3)

Indeed, the Hutchins Commission on Freedom of the Press (1947, p. 79) defined its mission as to "free the press from the influences which now prevent it from supplying the communication of news and ideas needed by the kind of society we have and the kind of society we desire." Instead of seeing markets as competitive mechanisms for disinterestedly producing, circulating, and evaluating information—a mission ostensibly aligned with the scientized press's goal to be an arm's-length curator of quality information that bracketed its role to truth telling without interpretation—reformers argued that a free press needed *freedom from* commercial forces that produced monopolies, minimize diversity, and limited to the press as yet another business.

The press's freedom, they argued, required relationships to commerce that subordinated the market's "egoistic concerns to the public good" and that prioritized "welfare, individual and collective" (Held, 2006, p. 43) over commercial success. The U.S. colonial press thought public interests surfaced through political partisanship (Nerone, 2015), the penny press used objectivity to appeal to mass markets that stood in for publics (Schiller, 1979; Schudson, 2001), and the "scientized" press served public interests by resisting propaganda through the professionalized, neutral segregation of facts and values (Hallin, 2000). Eventually, the ideal press envisioned by post–World War II media reformers ambitiously "prioritized the collective rights of the public's 'freedom to read, see, and hear' over the individual rights of media producers and owners" (Pickard, 2014a, p. 4).[11]

But what was this public, and how were its collective rights to be determined? As post–World War II social scientists and humanists showed, prioritizing "the public" could mean more than simply exposing people to information through markets. By moving from a marketplace model of press independence to one premised on cultivating the collective rights of publics, the press encountered an opportunity and challenge. Journalists and publishers were free to imagine their profession as more than just the production of information that markets could value. They had to have some idea of what collective welfare meant independent of markets and what their role was in creating publics. It was free to imagine audiences as being more than customers or citizens, and it was free to use its field of forces and forms of capital to advocate for one kind of public over another. But it also meant investing its authority and legitimacy in different meanings of *public* that were contingent, contentious, and carrying new expectations of the press. If press freedom was about separating from markets, then it simultaneously had to be about aligning with some other set of ideas.

An experiment in such alignment took shape in the United States in the 1990s under the auspices of the "public journalism" movement. Some newspapers invented new organizational forms, reporting techniques, and principles of audience engagement to bring journalists closer to the readers, ostensibly grounding their professionalism in the communities they served. For example, the beat system was replaced with a "reporting circle" in which reporters collaborated on a variety of broad themes identified through community consultation (including individual quality of life, city values and governance, and personal leisure) (Johnson, 1998). Reporters also were encouraged to convene focus groups to uncover issues not getting attention, solicit questions from readers that reporters could then ask of officials, look for sources with moderate views and not extreme opinions, frame coverage in terms of people's daily experiences instead of officials' policy priorities, use emotions to explain how people arrive at positions instead of merely as added "color," foreground the values that sources bring to issues, equally weigh the experiences of nonexperts with the knowledge of experts, explain why citizens should care about an issue, and encourage them to take action and design solutions (Gillmor, 2004; Glasser & Lee, 2002; Rosen, 1999; Willey, 1998).

These experiments largely assumed that community nostalgia for the processes of public journalism had inherent civic value, without critically asking what kind of publics emerged. By closely aligning itself with readers' priorities, nonexpert opinions, and community politics, the press certainly gave visibility to voices that had not been heard before, but in doing so, it left a vacuum. It ceded the journalistic expertise and professional judgment that underpinned its claims to professional autonomy without saying why the publics made by public journalism were better than the publics it could create through distance *from* audiences:

By denying the press the authority to set its own agenda, public journalism substitutes the community's judgement, however defined, for the judgement of journalists; it confuses "community" values with *good* values, as though the former always implies the latter.... It deprives the press of an opportunity—and diminishes the importance of its obligation—to set forth, clearly and convincingly, its *politics*. (Glasser, 2000, pp. 684–685)

It is exceedingly difficult to hold the press accountable—that is, to demand that it create an account of and take responsibility for its power—as an institution if its journalists are indistinguishable from their communities. Some separation *from* communities is required if the press is to do more than simply reflect community conversations.[12]

Public journalism's failure to enact a coherent vision of the public that was demonstrably better than what the press already had been making highlights a long-standing question in media studies research—how the press makes publics by convening and managing audiences.[13] For example, a negative view of liberty expects the press to uses its freedoms to be "partisan and segmented," mobilize members of preexisting groups, cover "crises and campaigns," and be a "check on power by alerting citizens to problems." But an affirmative view of liberty expects the press to use its freedom to facilitate deliberation, amplify particular debates, and serve "as a forum for debate and discussion" (Christians, Glasser, McQuail, Nordenstreng, & White, 2009, p. 97).

If the press sees its freedom as more than independence from markets and sees individual liberty as a collective achievement, then it implicitly has a normative image of the public that forms the basis of the test of whether that version of press freedom should be defended. The press must say exactly how it understands the potential for audiences to become publics if its separations and dependencies are to be normatively defensible. For example, the press might see the public it serves as some combination of these distinct but overlapping models:

• A rational, information-focused body that creates legitimate collective outcomes by making "occasions for consumers to identify with the public positions" (Calhoun, 1992, pp. 13–26) of those who agree to bracket their personal identities and follow procedures of deliberation, debate, and voting (J. Cohen, 1997; Fishkin, 2009; Gutman & Thompson, 2004; Habermas, 1989; Popkin, 1994);
• A social good achieved through multifaceted, participatory media cultures (Couldry & Jenkins, 2014; Jenkins, 1992; Jenkins & Carpentier, 2013; Kelty et al., 2015; Livingstone & Das, 2013; Mansbridge, 1999; Pateman, 1970) in which "individual and collective identities are reshaped" and "alternative conceptions of what is good are brought to the fore" (Calhoun, 1998, p. 21);
• A quantified aggregation of people constructed and sampled through survey techniques, opinion polls, voting, or citizen modeling that rationalizes social groups into discrete demographic patterns (Bouk, 2015; Herbst, 1995; Igo, 2007; Page & Shapiro, 1992);
• An outgrowth of symbolic and material associations (Fung, 2003; Marres, 2012; Warren, 2000) that people cannot individually extract themselves from and that motivate those "who are affected by the indirect consequences of transactions ... to have those consequences systematically cared for" (Dewey, 1954, pp. 15–16);
• A "sphere of publics" (Haas, 2004) or "decentered" space that is not a "comfortable place of conversation among those who share language, assumptions, and ways of looking at issues" (I. M. Young, 2000, p. 111) but a diverse body of "differently situated voices" speaking "across their difference" who are "accountable to one another" (p. 107);
• An "agonistic" body that rejects the "consensual approach" of "'dialogue' and 'deliberation'" in favor of a "sphere of contestation where different hegemonic political projects can be confronted" (Mouffe, 2005, pp. 3–4);
• Explicitly "alternative" (Atton & Hamilton, 2008) groups formed through "conflict with the norms and contexts of their cultural environment"

(Warner, 2005, p. 62) and in "parallel discursive arenas where members of subordinated social groups invent and circulate counterdiscourses, which in turn permit them to formulate oppositional interpretations of their identities, interests, and needs" (Fraser, 1990, p. 67);

• A private "enclave" of marginalized communication that survives by "hiding [its] counterhegemonic ideas and strategies in order to survive and avoid sanctions, while internally producing lively debate and planning" (Squires, 2002, p. 448); and

• A "recursive" social group defined by "a shared, profound concern for the technical and legal conditions of possibility for their own association" (Kelty, 2005, p. 185) whose existence is predicated on the power to imagine and realize new forms of itself.

Press freedom is both a requirement and diagnostic of publicness. The press needs to have an image of the public in order to explain why it needs the autonomy it claims, and conversely, whenever the press defines or defends its institutional freedom, such justifications can be read as evidence of the kind of public it thinks its autonomy makes possible.

Depending on which kind of public the press aligns itself with, it will see its power and responsibility to create separations and dependencies as in service of a particular public. If the press is a field of forces and if its freedom entails more than just a freedom from state interference or the limited commercial freedom afforded by marketplaces, then press freedom exists only as a network—as a set of separations and dependencies that configure the press into a field that makes certain kinds of publics more likely than others. That is, any defense of press freedom is inextricable from two follow-up questions: what kind of public does that network of press freedom make, and is that a normatively defensible public? If either question is answered unacceptably—or met with silence—it is impossible to know why press freedom is being defended at all.

Throughout these phases of U.S. journalism—an early embrace of professionalized objectivity, an encoding of objectivity within organizational routines, and a struggle both to account for and separate from audiences—the dynamics of press autonomy have been largely hidden and embedded in institutional relationships whose entirety cannot be viewed from any single perspective.

Conclusion

This chapter has argued that the press has never been a single, stable entity but instead has been an ever-changing product of a field of dynamic forces. The press is not a solitary entity that has freedom from anything but is an ongoing product of separations and dependencies. At various points in history, it has aligned itself with, interpreted, or eschewed facts over values, an ideology of objectivity, state sponsorship, marketplace legitimacy, audience engagement, and expert sources through a variety of reporting techniques, organizational rituals, educational initiatives, professional associations, hiring practices, linguistic strategies, and institutional experiments. It makes little sense to talk about freedom of the press when the press itself is a contingency and its freedom is made up of many dynamic separations and dependencies.

Press freedom is better thought of as a network state whose legitimacy depends on its normative conceptions of publics. In the spirit of Michael Schudson's (2005) question "autonomy from what?," I suggest asking "autonomy *for* what?" Instead of asking whether a static model of the press deserves its *freedom from* an unknown set of influences to pursue a right to speak, my aim has been to flip this question on its head: what subset of relationships making up the press creates a public we *want* to defend normatively, and how can we redefine press freedom as the separations and dependencies that make those relationships and those publics possible? Because the field of forces structuring the press is never static, the answer to this question is never settled. The question "freedom for what?" is not a test to be passed but a heuristic meant as a normative guide to networked forces.

In the previous chapter, I argue that democratic self-governance requires both an individual right to speak and a public right to hear. My aim was to highlight the idea that liberty is a collective achievement, not only an individual right—a dual reading of autonomy. As promised in the introduction to this chapter, I ask this dualism to do double duty: just as individual liberty requires conditions of collectivity, so too does the press's institutional freedom. As this tour of some of the press's historical, institutional dynamics has tried to show, the press's potential to realize a particular type of public is never about being entirely separate from states, markets, audiences, or sources. Its institutional power always depends on others—markets that fund its work, readers who understand a reporter's ironic wink, audiences whose interests respond to and align with what journalists care about, sources who quickly say what journalists on deadline expect them to say, colleagues and competitors who do not stray from professional patterns, and bureaucracies that reliably produce people and information understood as authoritative. And because press autonomy is, ideally, in the service of democratic governance, these dualistic notions of individual and institutional autonomy are further intertwined. Imagining and realizing a life beyond what a person can achieve individually requires an institutional press with a freedom to realize publics beyond what its freedom from others might let it create.

Today, this interplay between individual self-governance and institutional press autonomy is taking shape in a new context defined by forces different from those in past eras of the press. In this "state of permanent novelty" or "habitus of the new" (Papacharissi & Easton, 2013, p. 172), sociotechnical systems are designed and deployed by people who do not think of themselves as members of the press, organizations are driven by technological innovation and advertising revenue over journalistic missions, and hybrid media systems consist of boundary-spanning actor networks that resists any easy categorization as either journalistic or nonjournalistic. Autonomy as an ideal is still a tension between agency and structure—*freedom from* that enables individual action and *freedom to* that comes from inextricable relationships—but the form of the press's agency and structure is changing.

In the next chapter, I consider the idea of press freedom in light of these forces of structure and agency, read the contemporary networked press's sociotechnical infrastructures for evidence of separations and dependencies, and ask how well this new system of relationships helps achieve not only the right to speak (which historically has dominated liberal, individualistic notions of freedom) but also a public right to hear (which requires the kind of collectivity that the less popular affirmative interpretation of the First Amendment promised). Because the field of forces defining *the press* is now occupied and increasingly dominated by new entrants with different illusios, different types of capital, different scales of production, and different visions of publicness, the moment is ripe to reconsider the idea of press freedom beyond simple calls for "transparency, diversity and openness" (Karppinen & Moe, 2016, p. 115). Instead, press freedom might be defined more ambitiously as a network's responsibility to create affirmative, collective liberty—to create the kind of "proper distance" (Silverstone, 2003) that, depending on the type of public you want, you need the press to have.

Again, the dualistic concept of autonomy as *freedom from* and *freedom to* does double duty. For the press to help create both individual liberty and collective self-governance, its own institutional autonomy must be seen not simply as its freedom from undue influences that interfere with journalists' rights to report and publish but as the relationships it *needs* to have—most urgently, with new technologies and audiences—if it is to be an institution for democratic self-governance and not just content publishing. The next chapter tries to connect the ideals of listening and a public right to hear to the image of press freedom developed here as separations and dependencies, using an ideal of press freedom as a public right to hear as a diagnostic to ask: how can the autonomy of the networked press be understood and defended as the ability of its sociotechnical relationships to ensure a public right to hear?

4 How Is Networked Press Freedom a Question of Infrastructure?

Most of the press sociology explored in the previous chapter developed against the backdrop of twentieth-century broadcast media. Journalists, advertisers, technicians, policymakers, and audiences converged around one-to-many channels like newspapers, radio, television, and cable television.

The theories that scholars used to understand the news media's power were inseparable from the broadcast technologies that delivered messages to masses. Early studies' failure to find direct evidence of the media's power to create attitudes and opinions gave way to limited-effects theories focused on understanding why and how news exposure *sometimes* shaped opinions (McCombs & Reynolds, 2002)—the information flows and opinion leaders who have the power to persuade (Katz, 1957); the priming and agenda-setting effects (McCombs & Shaw, 1972) that mass media have when the social and cognitive conditions were right; the power that media have to influence thinking and change action (Bandura, 1986); the different effects that are possible when media focus on sex, violence, entertainment, or education (Bryant & Miron, 2002; Harris & Scott, 2002); the roles that identity, individual differences, and cultural affinity play in modulating mass media power (Ball-Rokeach, 1985; Oliver, 2002); the perceptions that audiences have about how media affect other people (Perloff, 2002); the explicit aims and rewards that people bring to their encounters with media (Rubin, 2002); and the role that media play in cultivating lifelong, macro-level interpretations of how the world works, beyond any particular media messages (Gerbner & Gross, 1976; Gerbner, Gross, Morgan, Signorielli, & Shanahan, 2002; Potter, 2014).

Although these studies often were motivated by different ideologies, used a mixture of empirical methods, variously impacted media policymaking, and sometimes focused on small-scale alternative media (Atton & Hamilton, 2008; McMillian, 2011), they centered on the social, political, cognitive, and cultural dimensions of broadcast media technologies.

My aim in this chapter is to trace the broadcast origins of press freedom, connect them to journalism's early computational tools and practices, and show how these influenced thinking about press freedom and social media. My main goal, though, is to argue that contemporary press freedom involves sociotechnical work. This is not only because today's news work involves connecting with diverse systems of people and machines but, more fundamentally, because the power to make publics—ideally, the press's chief concern—exists in subtle, often invisible, but always powerful relationships between humans and nonhumans that define the conditions under which shared consequences can be seen. I aim to show that because publics arise from infrastructures of people and machines, so too must press freedom.

Broadcast Era Press Freedom

Broadcasting can mean many different things—a method of distributing a product, a way to convene populations in space or time, a framework for adjudicating claims to the scarce resources of the electromagnetic spectrum and audience attention, a way to form normative expectations about what free speech is or should be in large democracies, and an ideology for defending the openness of a media marketplace and its potential to reach anyone, anywhere (Streeter, 1996). In essence, "before radio and television can be businesses, public institutions, or technologies, people must have ideas and hopes about them and seek to implement those ideas and hopes" (p. 7).

The meaning of press freedom in the broadcast era was wrapped up in the intimacies and separations of broadcast technology logics. The virtual impossibility of broadcast journalists knowing their audiences fit well with the ideological requirements of objectivity. Broadcast media let journalists think about one abstraction they made (objective truths created through neutral reporting techniques) in terms of another abstraction they sustained (the public that emerged from large audiences they could never really meet). The nineteenth-century economics that rewarded news organizations for using rituals of objectivity to secure audiences, advertisers, and revenue streams (Schudson, 2003b) needed to be reconciled with twentieth-century broadcasting technologies that convened large audiences through reporting designed for mass appeal—but that was also "a more intimate and conversational medium that needed its own forms of narrative" (S. J. A. Ward, 2005, p. 236). As people were able to afford receivers, became literate with broadcast genres and storytelling styles (J. A. Brown, 1998), and proved valuable to corporations and advertisers (Douglas, 1989), broadcast audiences grew quickly. People developed "associational listening" styles that helped them imagine who else was listening with them and lifelong "repertoires of listening" that made them nostalgic "not just for *what* they listened to but for *how* they listened to it" (Douglas, 2004, pp. 34–35).

Alongside the intimacy that broadcasting brought, audiences became "rationalized" as stable entities that could be measured, controlled, and managed into predictable aesthetics, revenue, and public opinion (Butsch, 2008; Napoli, 2011). The broadcast press was part of this rationalization in the face of intimacy as news organizations standardized audience expectations—what qualified as news that was worthy of airtime, when news was expected to occur, which crises qualified as breaking news interruptions, what authority should sound and look like on radio and television, how people should make sense of the intimacy of broadcasted, far-off events in terms of their local, daily lives (Baughman, 2006; Douglas, 1989, 2004), and how they could think of themselves as "broadcast publics" (Butsch, 2008, pp. 81–99). Radio shows like *Round Table*, *America's Town Meeting of the Air*, and *People's Platform* had different ideas about how to turn audiences into publics. Some used broadcasting to try to create a "Deweyan public that would assemble, collectively discuss, and act to petition their government," while others envisioned a "Lippmannesque public who would listen to the broadcast debate among the elite experts who represented public debate for them and to them" or an "individualized public who, once informed, would act individually rather than collectively" (Butsch, 2008, p. 90).

Tied to these rituals of consumption, rationalizations of audiences, and experiments with broadcast publics was a kind of journalistic autonomy that required the separations and dependencies that the print media had already been developing. Ideologies and rituals of detached objectivity were recast in the language of broadcasting, audiences were modeled and trained to expect certain experiences of news, and revenue-driven corporations learned how to neuter the diversity of audiences—to "use radio as a representative public sphere rather than a deliberative one, and envisioned audiences of attentive and obedient listeners rather than informed citizens actively participating in debate and politics" (Butsch, 2008, p. 96). The autonomy of the broadcast press—as a set of technologies, cultures, and economics—echoed the print press's reliance on institutionalized objectivity, organizational rituals, and bracketed publics. But added to this was a freedom to engage in a kind of "impure objectivity"—mixing "facts with daubs of interpretation, color, humor, and metaphor" (S. J. A. Ward, 2005, p. 237)—that better suited broadcast media that were both intimate and mass. This was not technological determinism: broadcast technologies did not invent a new type of press freedom. Rather, the forces that created broadcast technologies and intertwined them with new ways of thinking about publics that created new relationships between the journalists and audiences, advertisers, sources, and regulators. These new relationships—inseparable from the social and technological dynamics of mass media, broadcast technologies—created new networks of separation and dependency that, in turn, set new conditions of press freedom.

Computational Influences on Press Freedom

Alongside these mass media and broadcast technology-focused shifts, another set of sociotechnical conditions was starting to emerge around digital technologies. It brought journalism closer to statistical analysis, computational infrastructures, digital publishing and distribution platforms, and networked forms of reporting. Pioneering an approach he called "precision journalism," Philip Meyer (1973) in the late 1960s and 1970s began combining homegrown databases with social science statistical techniques and mainframe computer power to do a new kind of data-driven reporting. He and his collaborators invented new computer-assisted reporting (CAR) methods to turn data into news. Judicial sentencing records, surveys about urban riots, racial patterns in home loan programs, and school bus driver records are early examples of statistics that CAR transformed into stories. Journalism schools began teaching CAR, the Pulitzer Prize committee recognized CAR for the first time in 1989, and the National Institute for Computer-Assisted Reporting (NICAR) emerged as a new professional society (Houston, 2015). Alongside these CAR experiments, news organizations experimented with early, pre-Web forms of digital publishing and distribution—printing news through facsimile, posting digital versions of stories on computer bulletin boards and videotext, and gradually learning that such experiments were not commercially successful (Boczkowski, 2004a).

These techniques, though, were not simple matters of translation or republication. They raised new questions about how journalists knew what they knew. When should they build databases for themselves or trust the provenance of existing data? Were data sources to be interrogated (like interviewees) or ground truths on which to base claims (like polls and surveys)? What kinds of evidence should they and their audiences consider believable and authoritative, and should these standards be different from those of social scientists? Did reporters need their own visualization techniques that foregrounded journalistic forms of storytelling? Should the press's data-driven storytelling highlight broad patterns of data or delve into unique and idiosyncratic instances? Did the press have a responsibility to develop in its audiences the kind of data, visual, and interactive literacies their storytelling forms required? And finally, was it journalists' responsibility simply to describe the data-based findings of others, or did doing so come with a duty to interpret independently or gather competing data that could show the significance of trends?[1] Broadcast technologies forced the question of how press freedom existed at the intersection of mass media and intimate storytelling, and CAR and digital publishing platforms added epistemological and infrastructural wrinkles to press freedom: what kind of *freedom from* and *reliance on* audiences, computation, and social science did journalists need to make compelling, authoritative, data-driven arguments about the world?

Autonomy became not simply *freedom from* those who might interfere with objectively reporting data. The press's freedom to imagine and realize a public through data-driven journalism also *depended on* computational infrastructures that were often housed in universities, research techniques developed by social scientists, signs of authority and legitimacy that made some data more trusted than others, organizations and regulations that gave journalists access to data; audiences that were able to see and debate the significance of data, professional cultures that valued data-driven journalism, and publishers and bosses willing to invest in data-driven projects. Part of press autonomy is creating separations and dependencies that help data play a role in the press's ability to realize different kinds of publics discussed. That is, journalists need to understand how their data infrastructures work if they are to use them to make different types of publics—for example, the deliberative, participatory, aggregated, consequential, decentered, agonistic, alternative, enclave, and recursive publics described in the previous chapter. If the press is to help realize one or more of these publics through data-driven journalism, it requires not only negative freedom (separation from forces that interfere with journalism's power to practice objectivity on data) but also positive freedom (being in relation with others who, through their resources, traditions, infrastructures, and interpretations, help journalists make publics). As it has always been, the press was a product of field-level forces, but this field was increasingly intertwined with new computational actors—software engineers, digital publishing platforms, data-driven storytelling.

Social Media and Press Freedom

Press freedom's "computational turn" accelerated in the late 1990s as the World Wide Web moved out of research labs and universities and into homes and businesses. At first, newspapers simply re-presented their print content on rudimentary websites. Eventually, they created "personalized or customized [online] editions, new sites pulling together vast amounts of news and database information on a particular topic such as city guides ... nationwide classified ads, and archives of past editions" and began "taking advantage of the unique capabilities of the web" through "constant updates on breaking stories ... special multimedia packages of major events, new sections developed exclusively for their web sites, and user-authored content" (Boczkowski, 2004a, p. 51). Contrary to the idea that online news was disconnected from readers' geographic locations, early Web stories focused on events that were close to where publishers imagined their readers to be (Barnhurst, 2010b), and although it was technologically possible and easy to link to other news outlets, most early news sites kept traffic on their own servers (Barnhurst, 2010a). Although the early Web made it possible for enterprise news organizations to reimagine their relationships with audiences and create entirely new forms of storytelling, such experiments were largely undertaken by citizen journalist proponents and independent media activists documenting and mobilizing around international crises (C. W. Anderson, 2011b; Russell, 2001, 2007).

In the late 1990s and early 2000s, as news organizations experimented with Web-driven reporting and publishing techniques, journalism scholars began reorienting their research projects around explicitly digital questions (Mitchelstein & Boczkowski, 2009; Mitchelstein & Boczkowski, 2013). Was technology changing how journalists acted as gatekeepers (Livingston & Bennett, 2003; Shoemaker, Vos, & Reese, 2009)? Did the Web make possible an entirely new kind of democratized journalism that would finally achieve what public journalism was unable to do (Gillmor, 2004; Haas, 2005)? Were journalists' blogs like amateur blogs, and why did this question matter (Hermida, 2009; Johnston & Wallace, 2016; Perlmutter & Schoen, 2007)? What features of news websites did audiences use (Boczkowski & Mitchelstein, 2012; Chung, 2008; Chung & Yoo, 2008), how did Web forms of news different differ from print (Barnhurst, 2010b), how should user-generated content be incorporated into news work, if at all (Hlavach & Freivogel, 2011), and what kind of discourse did comments on online news stories lead to (Ruiz et al., 2011; Sunstein, 2001)? What new types of work and professional identities were emerging from online journalism (Deuze, 2004, 2005, 2007, 2008a, 2008b, 2010; Deuze & Marjoribanks, 2009)? What kind of digital skills should journalism schools be teaching? Should the Web be trusted differently than other sources of journalistic research (Machill & Beiler, 2009)?

This digital turn took on a new urgency with the dominance of Web 2.0 platforms like Facebook, Twitter, YouTube, Flickr, and others designed to encourage users to share digital content (John, 2012). This content emerged and became inseparable from a new class of social networking sites (SNSs) that distributed content and also defined the *conditions* under which people developed and expressed digital identities, established online relationships, participated in platform communities (Ellison & boyd, 2013), and tried to make sense of how this digital mediation aligned with the identities, relationships, and experiences they were developing in material worlds, a place derogatorily and inaccurately referred to as "real life" (Baym, 2015). As platforms and SNSs grew in popularity and economic power, websites shifted from being neutral "conduits for social activity" to being more complex sites of mutual construction in which "people use tactics to negotiate the strategies that are arranged for them" (van Dijck, 2013, p. 6) by the platforms. People populate platforms with their media and relationships, and platforms entrain people to make certain kinds of content and connections. A "real life" independent of media has never actually existed (Marvin, 1990), and audiences have always been active interpreters (Fiske, 2002; Jenkins,

1992), but the rapid proliferation of social network sites, user-generated content, online commerce, and play and gaming sites (van Dijck, 2013, p. 8) created new environments in which people encountered and made sense of news. Journalists had to think about those "formerly known as the audience" (Rosen, 2006) not just as people who accessed news through new channels, sometimes became citizen journalists, or challenged their professional authority. Rather, many audiences were increasingly swimming in vast amounts of media, hosted and surfaced by media platforms with few historical connections to the mainstream press. Many journalism scholars shifted their work toward explicitly digital questions (Mitchelstein & Boczkowski, 2009, 2013; Siles & Boczkowski, 2012), seeing social media not as simply distribution channels or challenges to professional traditions but as new contexts in which journalists and audiences (Ahva & Heikkila, 2016) encounter and make sense of each other. This work asks the following kinds of questions:

• Are social network sites generators of news stories (MacKinnon, 2012), research tools for journalists (Ahmad, 2010), sources of sources (Lecheler & Kruikemeier, 2016; Tylor, 2014), ways to verify information (Aitamurto, 2016; Brandtzaeg, Lüders, Spangenberg, Rath-Wiggins, & Følstad, 2016; Hermida, 2012, 2015; Pantti & Sirén, 2015; Schifferes, Newman, Thurman, Corney, Goker, & Martin, 2014) and to keep tabs on competitors (D. H. Weaver & Willnat, 2016), dissemination channels for news (Armstrong & Gao, 2010; Bright, 2016; Trilling, Tolochko, & Burscher, 2017), aggregators of news (C. W. Anderson, 2011c), sources of Web traffic metrics that can guide news work (C. W. Anderson, 2011a; Boczkowski & Mitchelstein, 2013), ways for journalists to develop personal brands (Canter, 2015), or entirely new ways of doing journalism that break with traditional thinking about who reporters are, what stories can be, and where audiences are to be found (Hermida, 2013; Russell, 2011)?

• Is online news really the diverse and empowering force that the Web's celebratory rhetoric promised it to be (Benkler, 2006; Shirky, 2008), or is it simply reinscribing longstanding mainstream media patterns of relatively few news organizations imitating each other and producing starkly similar content (Boczkowski, 2010; Hindman, 2008; Pariser, 2011; Sunstein, 2009)?

• What policies, laws, and guidelines seem to be governing journalists' use of social media, and what clues do they leave about how news organizations see their standards and ethical responsibilities as different from those of social media platforms (Ananny, 2014; Opgenhaffen & Scheerlinck, 2014; D. R. Stewart, 2013)?

• How are words like *national* and *foreign* problematic when describing geographically dispersed journalists and audiences who make and interpret news outside of traditional notions of nation-states, home markets, or colonial-era framings of the non-Western other? Many of those who make and interpret online news have increasingly cosmopolitan, multilingual, and multinational identities that span the time differences and geographic spaces that previously divided national and international news.[2]

• How are journalists, newsrooms, and entire news organizations reconfiguring themselves in light of audiences that can easily shift brand loyalties, are housed on platforms beyond news organizations' control, and develop relationships with reporters through myriad forums, tweets, photos, and posts that make letters to the editor seem almost quaint or contrived?[3]

• Methodologically and conceptually, how do you study journalism that is not bound within newsrooms, that spans networks that cannot be seen or accessed, and that involves people who do not even identify as news workers?[4]

• What kind of audiences do journalists see social media algorithms assembling? How do journalists understand their responsibilities to them? When do editors challenge or follow algorithmic suggestions, and what kind of interventions are needed to understand and influence their power?[5]

• And how should news organizations align themselves with—or differentiate themselves from—new entrants as varied as BuzzFeed (Tandoc & Jenkins, 2017), WikiLeaks (Benkler, 2011), Anonymous (Coleman, 2014), and Edward Snowden (Greenwald, 2014)? Each, in different ways, chastised the mainstream press for its cautiousness and conservatism, mimicked or partnered with journalists to increase their distribution, aligned with press autonomy as journalistic freedom to release information, and envisioned preexisting publics who were expected to interpret and act on data wisely (Coddington, 2012; Lynch, 2010).

Implicit in all of this work are questions of how the press is like or unlike social media and its users, how such similarities and differences are intertwined with places of news work, and how largely unquestioned ideals of participation, deinstitutionalization, innovation, and entrepreneurialism drive normative conceptions of digital journalism (Kreiss & Brennen, 2016). Journalism scholarship has rapidly expanded, with a greater number and diversity of topics appearing in leading journals (Steensen & Ahva, 2014).

But such approaches have largely traced *journalistic* practices, often using grounded theory to show how digital contexts affect news production and dissemination. It is vitally important that we understand such practices, but rarely have studies of them placed digital news production in larger institutional and normative contexts (Blumler & Cushion, 2014)[6] or asked whether this is the kind of press and press freedom that publics need. In an earlier, predigital era, Peter Dahlgren (1992) linked this discrepancy to the "metonymic character" of journalism scholarship that tends to let research on enterprise journalism *practices* represent understandings of the press as a whole. Barbie Zelizer (2004, p. 7) expands on this tendency to confuse actions of journalists with the conditions of the press to argue that professional journalists, when they do reflect on the meaning of their profession, "often repair to a sense of self that either draws on a romanticized, partial, and biased view of the news world or reduces news to a set of narrow, functional activities." This bracketing is made worse, she argues, by "the academy's move to professionalize journalism" and some professionals' claim that "journalism requires no qualifications because everyone in a democracy is a journalist" (p. 7). Focusing simply on what journalists do, what journalists say they do, and how academies train students to be journalists severely brackets journalism's potential to be a rich space of intellectual inquiry and anything other than a stubbornly undertheorized set of tropes or a seemingly obvious craft.[7]

There is a risk of this metonymy bracketing online journalism scholarship, too. The understandable focus on how journalists and audiences create, circulate, interpret, and act on digital news often stands in for studies of the networked press as a whole. There is a danger of confusing descriptions of what online journalists or audiences do online with critical interrogations of the conditions under which online journalism works—how its power is inseparable from a host of sociotechnical infrastructures and cultural expectations that are invisible to scholarship focused on local descriptions of journalistic practice. Scholarship that extends beyond the metonymic patterns of journalism research can identify new field-level, normative, and sociotechnical forces that, together, make press freedom something other than simply journalists' and audiences' *freedom from* restrictions on what they want to do. It might reveal the power that other forces—coming from outside of journalism—have to constrain the press and reframe its core affirmative purpose.

The reason to make this shift—to study the normative and sociotechnical conditions comprising the networked press—is more than an academic curiosity. Without this level of analysis, it is impossible to say what networked press freedom means. Without a framework for understanding these conditions, it is impossible to say which forces define the separations and dependencies driving digital news work. It is impossible to evaluate these forces against an ideal of what the press could be and what publics its networked separations and dependencies could create.

To trace a line of scholarship: Timothy E. Cook (1998) was right to see the press as a product of deeply intertwined institutional arrangements, but his concern now exists as hybrid media systems composed not only of state actors but myriad "technologies, genres, norms, behaviors, and organizational forms" (Chadwick, 2013, p. 4). They are all vying to define *the public* while constantly negotiating about what to publish, how, when, and for whom, with actors they cannot always see or understand (C. W. Anderson, 2013a). This lets us restate Michael Schudson's (2005) questions about press freedom—"autonomy from what?" and "How autonomous should journalism be?"—as "autonomy of what and for what?"

Put differently, if the press is no single, stable thing, then neither is press freedom. The press's autonomy is more like a likelihood—a possible balance between positive and negative freedoms that depends on how a field of actors is configured at any given moment. The challenge of understanding *networked* press freedom is to turn the press from "a heterogeneous set of bits and pieces each with its own inclinations" into "something that passes as a punctualized actor" that can be identified, analytically isolated, and seen as powerful (Law, 1992, p. 386). Networked press freedom is episodic and contingent and is visible only when the relationships among the components making up the press are articulated as balances between independences and obligations—that is, traced, critiqued, resisted, and reconstructed with some normative ideal in mind.

By making the networked press a focus of study, we can see different models of press freedom as diagnostics for tracing the networked forces of online journalism. For example, if press freedom rests on its ability to make possible a public right to hear, then the press's sociotechnical forces need to be configured to allow not just speaking but listening. If press freedom is premised on its ability to realize a more Habermasian ideal, then a different field of forces is required that brackets identities and rewards rationality.

After the idea of press freedom is liberated from the ideal that it is whatever journalists say they need to be *free from* in order to realize their vision of the public, then the question of press freedom becomes simultaneously broader and more generative. It becomes a way to diagnose a field of networked, sociotechnical forces and to ask several questions: What kind of public is being created by this particular network's mix of negative and positive freedoms? Is this public normatively defensible? If not, does the network's distribution of freedom—the sociotechnical forces driving news work—need to change? Or does its normative vision of democracy need updating? Conceived of as a distributed, sociotechnical construct that both contains and extends images of the press's role in self-governance, press freedom becomes a diagnostic—a reason to describe and a motivation to critique. As C. Edwin Baker (2007b) puts it, different democracies need different media.

This line of inquiry needs ways to talk about normative conceptions of the press (as chapter 1 does) and about the distributed and dynamic nature of press freedom (as chapter 2 does) and also ways to talk about the sociotechnical forces giving rise to the networks, practices, and norms that create either acceptable or unacceptable states of press freedom. The causes of media market failure are powerfully intertwined. They include everything from a collective inability to value public goods to "oligopolistic concentration and profit maximization" and uncompetitive markets, and yet "the vocabulary for describing such structural problems remains impoverished" (Pickard, 2014b, p. 4). I want to suggest here that the forces underpinning contemporary media system failures are not just conceptual, regulatory, or professional but sociotechnical and infrastructural.

Press Freedom as Sociotechnical, Infrastructural Work

This points toward another era in the study of digital media and the press that is related to but conceptually distinct from broadcast, computational, and social media eras. News organizations are still negotiating relationships to audiences through broadcast technologies and are still struggling to integrate with and distance themselves from social media, but they also are suffering and shaping sociotechnical, infrastructural forces that are regulating the press's negative and positive freedoms. These sociotechnical sites—many of them implicit, embedded, and visible only to particular communities—are where press freedom is being worked out today.

But before delving into empirical sites of sociotechnical press freedom, it is worth pausing briefly to ask: What are sociotechnical forces?

It is beyond the scope of this book to give a complete account of how science and technology studies (STS)[8] analyzes sociotechnical systems, except to say that many of STS's concepts are ripe for framing the study of the networked press's normative and sociotechnical forces:

• *Infrastructure:* Summarized by Geoffrey C. Bowker and Susan Leigh Star (1999, p. 47) as "scaffolding in the conduct of modern life," infrastructure is the embedded, standardized, and largely invisible relationships among materials and practices that are taken for granted and noticed only when sociotechnical systems break down (Star & Ruhleder, 1996).

• *Infrastructural inversion:* Infrastructural inversion is "recognizing the depths of interdependence of technical networks and standards" in order to interrogate their ubiquity (electrical sockets are exceedingly common), assumed materiality (electrical sockets are physical and difficult to redesign), and indeterminate pasts (the entire electrical system could have been designed differently with a different set of sociopolitical forces) (Bowker & Star, 1999, pp. 34–41).

• *Interpretive flexibility:* Before powerful forces mute controversies and force "closure," sociotechnical systems are "open to more than one interpretation" (Pinch & Bijker, 1984, p. 409)—interpretive flexibility. Finding such moments of openness and forced closure let people see that sociotechnical systems and our assumptions about them could have been different and that "the stability and form of artifacts should be seen as a function of the interaction of heterogeneous elements ... shaped and assimilated into a network" (Law, 1987, p. 113; Law & Callon, 1992). Sociotechnical systems are not inevitable, but realizing alternative interpretations or configurations means tracing the hard-to-trace forces that freeze flexibility and force coherence.

• *Boundary objects:* First observed in the jockeying of scientists and nonscientists who were vying for intellectual legitimacy, material resources, and professional autonomy (Gieryn, 1983), boundary objects are developed by many sociotechnical cultures that create and sustain objects that are both "adaptable to different viewpoints and robust enough to maintain identity across them" (Star & Griesemer, 1989, p. 387). Such objects may create boundary infrastructures to the extent that they make "stable regimes" that "allow for local variation together with sufficient[ly] consistent structure" so that a diverse community can meet its information needs (Bowker & Star, 1999, pp. 313–314).

• *Articulation work:* Developed through radical reinterpretations of healthcare work (A. L. Strauss, Fagerhaugh, Suczek, & Wiener, 1985) and feminist critiques of sociotechnical labor's gendered underpinnings (Wajcman, 2007), articulation work helps to create a "sociology of the invisible" (Star & Strauss, 1999) work required to maintain systems (Jackson, 2013). It shows the "artful integrations" (Suchman, 1994, p. 34) behind the "continuous efforts required in order to bring together discontinuous elements—of organizations, of professional practices, of technologies—into working configurations" (Suchman, 1996, p. 407). In the face of celebrations of technological innovation as the creation of the new, the labor that makes systems workable, reliable, coherent, and relatable is often devalued or ignored.

• *Values in design:* Values in design are rooted in long-standing debates about how ideas about authority, rationality, knowledge, power, and agency are inseparable from the material dynamics of tools, practices, and social environments (Feenberg, 1999; Hughes, 2004; Latour, 1993). Scholars of information technologies debate how values are ethics that guide designers and their professional communities, how normative criteria are used to judge sociotechnical systems and argue for reform, and how highly contextualized moments of intertwined people and artifacts defy separation into social versus material power (Flanagan, Howe, & Nissenbaum, 2008; Friedman, Kahn, & Borning, 2006; Nissenbaum, 2001; Shilton, 2012; Suchman, Blomberg, Orr, & Trigg, 1999; Verbeek, 2006).

• *Actor networks:* Actor-network theory (ANT) is one of the most popular sociotechnical concepts. Closely related to Gilles Deleuze and Félix Guattari's (1987) theory of how distributed systems of heterogeneous elements can be both coherent and dynamic, Bruno Latour's (2005) actor-network theory[9] rejects the idea that "social" is anything other than a *"tracing of associations"* (p. 5, emphasis in original) among "entities which are in no way recognizable as being social in the ordinary manner, *except* during the brief moment when they are reshuffled together" (p. 65, emphasis in original). Although he defines these entities as anything that "modif[ies] a state of affairs by making a difference"[10] (p. 71), he cautions against assuming "some absurd 'symmetry between humans and non-humans.'" Instead, he states that any account that prematurely divides social and technological dimensions of controversies ignores the fact that "the missing masses of our society are to be found among the nonhuman mechanisms" (Latour, 1992, p. 248). He asks sociotechnical scholars to include nonhuman actors in their accounts to tell richer accounts of the "social," show the contingent nature of human agency, illustrate the way that humans and nonhumans delegate tasks to each other, and show how powerfully political actor networks can be. Actor networks deployed during moments of controversy, he argues, help move us from "matters of fact to matters of concern" (Latour, 2004, p. 225), showing how a "critic is not the one who debunks, but the one who assembles. The critic is not the one who lifts the rugs from under the feet of naive believers, but the one who offers the participants arenas in which to gather" (p. 246).

It is in this spirit of reassembly that I examine these sociotechnical concepts—infrastructure, inversion, boundary objects, interpretive flexibility, articulation work, assemblages and actor-networks—in a book on press freedom. I use these ideas as framing for a way of thinking of press freedom rooted in its sociomateriality—how the field of journalism is defined by what people do and also by what is accomplished by the inseparable linkages among its people and technologies. This point has repeatedly been made by scholars who show how what seems like purely social activity emerges from interplays of people with tools, geographies, bodies, and senses. Organizations are inseparable from organizational technologies, cities are inseparable from urban landscapes, and human attention is inseparable from physiological senses (Hayles & Crofts Wiley, 2012; Law & Mol, 1995; Leonardi, 2012, 2013; Orlikowski, 2008, 2010). If a concept like press freedom is relational and sociomaterial, then we need to look for the press's "relational materialism" (Law & Mol, 1995, p. 277)—the ways in which its people and machines configure each other, make each other meaningful, and are sometimes fit together in unintended and unanticipated ways that John Law (1987) calls "heterogeneous engineering."

I am not alone in trying to think about journalism through STS lenses. A recent surge of scholars—far more than can be reviewed here—has used or been inspired by STS. One of the key early scholars who led journalism's "STS turn," Pablo J. Boczkowski (2004a, 2004b, 2004c), showed how news organizations' early experiments with multimedia involved the "mutual shaping" of journalists and technologies. It was not just that journalists used technologies or that technologies affected journalism. The character of news work at any given moment was a product of people and prototypes that were at different stages of development and were responding to and accommodating each other. Following Fred Turner's (2005) relatively early suggestion that actor-network theory (ANT) should be used to understand news work, Christopher W. Anderson and Daniel Kreiss (2013) use ANT to show how seemingly incomprehensible "black boxes" of political campaigning and online publishing—electoral maps and content management systems, respectively—stabilize and motivate different actions. Campaigns and newsrooms do not simply use these systems but discover what their work is, could be, and means as these systems are made, deployed, and repaired, a point similarly made by Matthew Powers (2012, p. 24) in his study of "technologically specific" forms of digital news work.

Likewise, Seth C. Lewis and Nikki Usher (2016) used STS ideas of boundary work and trading zones to characterize the work of journalists and software programmers participating in the Knight-Mozilla News Technology partnership; Amy Schmitz Weiss and David Domingo (2010) and Ursula Plesner (2009) used ANT and the idea of sociotechnical communities to trace newsroom cultures; and I argue that we might understand press-public collaborations as infrastructure, in part by looking at how news organizations use application programming interfaces to both include and exclude audiences from journalistic work (Ananny, 2013). Focusing on news distribution, Joshua A. Braun (2015) brilliantly inverts the digital infrastructures of contemporary television to show how dissemination is not simply a process of getting messages from point to point but is a highly contingent and dynamic process in which constantly evolving "transparent intermediaries" (Braun, 2014)—people, algorithms, databases, regulatory regimes, and organizational structures—ensure that news distribution is regular and reliable. He shows how much often invisible work goes into maintaining distribution networks and creating for consumers the appearance of engineered stability.

Finally, a 2014 special issue of *Journalism* (C. W. Anderson & Maeyer, 2015) showed how theories of materiality can be used to make sense of news work— how its documents encode persistent rituals (Neff, 2015), how copyeditors subtly vied for power by controlling particular newsroom objects (Keith,

2015), how international news organizations coordinate over vast geographical distances (Usher, 2015), and how historical photographs of newsrooms show architectures rife with social organizational power (LeCam, 2015). But it also cautioned that ascribing too much agency to journalistic objects might give the impression that journalists bear little responsibility for the systems they inhabit and create (Domingo, 2015), that the newsroom itself is no longer a center of editorial power (Boczkowski, 2015), or that the very nature of materiality is understood well enough to be neatly deployed into the domain of journalism (Schudson, 2015).

As media scholars increasingly show the infrastructural dynamics of the internet and media systems in general (Parks & Starosielski, 2015; Sandvig, 2015)—and of the social media platforms underpinning journalistic work (Gerlitz & Helmond, 2013; Napoli, 2015; Plantin, Lagoze, Edwards, & Sandvig, 2016; Thorson & Wells, 2016) in particular—the fundamental idea of the press becomes less bounded to any particular profession, tradition, or set of organizations. It instead resembles a digitally sociomaterial set of human and nonhuman actors held together in contingent, mutually shaping relationships. But the press's networked existence lacks a normative basis if we do not know why it hangs together as an institution that normatively deserves autonomy. We come back to needing a way to think about the press's institutional freedoms that connects to people's democratic freedoms.

Although Berlin's model of positive and negative freedoms is a good starting point for thinking about, as Christopher M. Kelty (2014, p. 217) puts it, "the human capacity to coerce or escape coercion," there is a "fog of freedom" among people and machines in which "our very ability to become free depends on our ability to design it into our technologies" (p. 218). As Kelty explains, this does not mean being free from technologies— some ideal of autonomy that could be achieved if machines would leave us alone—nor does it mean some libertarian ideal of being free through technologies. Both presume the preexistence of some ideal individual that exists outside of sociotechnical forces. Rather, the work of making publics[11] is inseparable from the separations and dependencies that both people and machines think are necessary for achieving some (often unstated) normative ideal of democracy.

The networked press exists in this sociotechnical fog of freedom. As discussed in the previous two chapters, the concept of autonomy does double duty as both an ideal of who individuals are, what they are capable of, and what they need for self-realization and as a vision of the institutional balances the press strikes as it tries to serve and define the public. This fog has individual, technological, and normative dimensions as well as institutionally situated sociotechnical dynamics. To think about networked press freedom, we need to see the "loosely coupled arrays of standardized elements" (DiMaggio & Powell, 1991, p. 14) (people, affiliations, norms, regulations, routines, myths, expectations) that structure organizations as inseparable from "the stability and form of artifacts" (databases, platforms, operating systems, algorithms, apps) that "are shaped and assimilated into a network"[12] (Law, 1987, p. 113). Further, the challenge is to move beyond descriptions of how sociotechnical elements interact to ask more normative questions about whether networks of elements are producing the diversity of publics—including the public right to hear—that political theories say democratic self-governance requires.

This is not only about asking what kind of values technologies contain or express (Flanagan, Howe, & Nissenbaum, 2008; Friedman, Kahn, & Borning, 2006; Friedman & Nissenbaum, 1996; Shilton, 2012; Shilton, Koepfler, & Fleischmann, 2013, 2014; Winner, 1986) but also about tracing what kind of self-governance is possible as humans and nonhumans together create what Nortje Marres (2012, p. 31) calls "material publics"—groups of people who are "affected by issues" but also "remove[d] from the platforms that are in place to address them." To Marres, the problem that material publics face is that they do not necessarily know what affects them and what is relevant to the conditions they share together—and they do not have control over the communication structures they would need to gain such knowledge. They are "strangers who do not have at their disposal shared locations, vocabularies and habits for the resolution of common problems" (p. 46).

Marres envisions publics that exist *before* people come together to manage problems they all agree they have. These are not publics where technologies are tools for rational deliberation applied to preexisting issues but publics in which technologies are part of the sociomaterial contexts that form publics—because some problems are relevant because materials and people make them so, regardless of interests or beliefs. Climate change is one example of the inseparable sociomateriality of publics. Even if you think you are unaffected by climate change (or do not believe it exists), its sociomateriality is inescapable. You are embedded in—and implicated by—relationships that make it a relevant public issue. For example, as Candis Callison (2014) persuasively argues, climate change existed long before journalists, politicians, and scientists decided it was an issue. Indigenous leaders and traditional knowledge communities have documented the ecological devastations for years. But it became seen as a public issue only after its material realities were fit within the epistemologies, ethics, and discourses that dominated Western political cultures. Andrew Barry (2013) tells a similar story in his study of the Baku-Tbilisi-Ceyhan oil pipeline. Communities along its path emerged as publics when the project became materially significant. Officials designated some people as affected, communities challenged the designation and the perceived risk of the pipeline to certain geographies, and experts and regulators from all sides used different types of evidence to demonstrate the project's safety or harm. As he puts it, "material objects should not be thought of as the stable ground on which the instabilities generated by disputes between human actors are played out; rather, they should be understood as forming an integral element of evolving controversies" (p. 12).

In different ways, Marres, Callison, and Barry alert us to the fact that people face problems that they do not know about and cannot see—not because they have failed to invent technologies to see them or because they do not understand a technology's effect on society but because issues stay dormant, invisible, and seemingly irrelevant until people recognize that humans and nonhumans—the social and the material—together make groups into publics.

Conclusion

In broadcast eras and the early days of the internet, the press could idealize its autonomy as *freedom from* influences that technologies brought them into contact with (such as audiences, markets, and states). It could see its freedom as the power to pursue its own vision of the public without coercion or contamination from those it saw as outsiders. But as such technologies have become more infrastructural—embedded in and inseparable from technological cultures that do not see themselves as journalistic at all—press autonomy has not disappeared but changed shape. Networked press freedom is arguably the infrastructural capacity to use sociotechnical separations and dependencies self-reflexively to realize new kinds of publics.

This extends the press far beyond an institution that simply needs to think differently about how it uses technologies as it performs public services (Napoli, 2015). Its task is not just to show people news that they or algorithms would not choose, to reveal both sides of a story, or to get people to "eat news vegetables" and pay attention to things other than crime, sports, and celebrities. Rather, it asks the press to appreciate how its sociotechnical configurations can create new publics and resist thinking that it, readers, or technology companies alone are responsible for creating publics. More technically, it means "direct[ing] our critical attention to the *devices* that are deployed to organize public relevance relations" (Marres, 2012, p. 55). The material public faces both a representational problem (getting public institutions like the press to take up causes or avoid bias) as well as an ontological one—figuring out which issues the public is "problematically entangled" with that it does not even realize are relevant (p. 56).

This extended discussion of material publics is meant to highlight an opportunity for the press—a way for it to think differently about itself and its need for autonomy. If press freedom is ideally premised on a notion of public service that is currently in flux,[13] then the networked press could see its autonomy as the power to arrange its sociotechnical separations and dependencies in ways that help new material publics form. Instead of seeing press freedom as the power to resist an emerging technological landscape, it could be a self-reflexive capacity to see it as a new "space of possibles" (Bourdieu, 1993, p. 30) that sees publics emerging when humans and nonhumans meet.

As Annemarie Mol (1999, p. 74) puts it, the press faces an existential question: "there are options between the various versions of [itself]: which one to perform?" I see the idea of networked press freedom—a system of sociotechnical separations and dependencies designed to help material publics hear more than what markets, states, friends, platforms, or algorithms define as interesting—as a diagnostic and a strategy for reinvention. The networked press's current system of sociotechnical relationships—and thus the kind of publics it has the capacity to realize—does not have to be the one we settle for. The questions Mol asks of politics are worth asking of the press: "Where are the options? What is at stake? Are there really options? How should we choose?"

The networked press should not pursue any single vision of the public and does not deserve more or less freedom if it pursues one public over another. As the previous chapter discusses, there are many different kinds of publics, each with different goals and forms. My claim is that press freedom is predicated on the power to realize publics and that, for the networked press, this power resides in its configuration of sociotechnical relationships. If it sees digital technologies as delivery mechanisms, as competition, as forces to be resisted, or as ways to outsource its work to audiences, it misses its power. But if it sees itself as an infrastructural institution embedded in and inseparable from a host of new and rapidly changing technologies, it can imagine and realize new types of publics that were not previously possible. The power to make new publics comes from the press's freedom to arrange its sociotechnical separations and dependencies—an understanding of autonomy that casts negative and positive freedoms in sociotechnical senses.

5   How Free Is the Networked Press?

What kinds of separations and dependencies organize the contemporary networked press, and what sociotechnical dimensions of autonomy emerge from them? That is, if press freedom has always been a balance of positive and negative freedoms and the press's power to convene publics has taken an infrastructural turn, what kind of autonomy does today's networked press have—and what kinds of publics can it make? By examining the trade press on networked journalism—essentially, the stories that the press tells itself about itself—I find twelve sociotechnical dimensions of networked press freedom and offer a typology of sociotechnical relationships.

In previous work, I examined how the networked press emerges from sociotechnical spaces that are neither entirely journalistic nor exclusively technological but a hybrid of the two. Kate Crawford and I (Ananny & Crawford, 2015) traced how mobile news app designers see themselves as part of what we called a "liminal press" that is somewhere between algorithm design and editorial decision making. Leila Bighash and I (Ananny & Bighash, 2016) examined how online news organizations reveal their public service mandates when they periodically choose not to use paywall technologies to meter news. I showed how the sociotechnical ethics of witnessing and Roger Silverstone's (2007) ideal of "proper distance" emerge from Google Glass infrastructure and design communities (Ananny, 2015), how the networked press's rhythms, deadlines, and timelines emerge from a mix of social and technological forces (Ananny, 2016b), and how news organizations' social media policies (Ananny, 2014) and application programming interfaces (Ananny, 2013) leave clues about how they see their work as both free from and reliant on audience participation. In each individual instance, the press was not found to be a set of journalistic actors pitted against software designers and their technologies. Rather, it was found to be a co-construction—a space of institutionalized communication that both depends on and distances itself from the people, norms, practices, and tools that live in an increasingly hybrid middle space between journalism and software.

There is a larger, field-level story to tell, though, about what *kind* of press autonomy exists in these hybrid spaces—what kind of networked press autonomy is emerging from these separations and dependencies. How does the press itself understand the field-level tradeoffs it finds itself making? Where does journalism see itself intersecting with technology, and what is at stake in these intersections? If the networked press's autonomy depends on—and exists to protect—its power to arrange human and nonhuman actors into configurations that allow new material publics to emerge, then we need to know where these configurations are, how they work, and what they assume. One way to understand the networked press's understanding of its own sociotechnical configuration is to look at how journalists describe their work among themselves and the conditions under which they say they do it.

Matt Carlson (2015b) calls this journalism's "metajournalistic discourse." Starting from the "premise that journalism should be understood as a cultural practice that is embedded in specific contexts, variable across time and space, and inclusive of internal and external actors" (p. 2), he shows how journalism's significance exists, in part, in stories *about* journalism. Such narratives show how "various actors inside and outside of journalism compete to construct, reiterate, and even challenge the boundaries of acceptable journalistic practices and the limits of what can or cannot be done" (p. 1). Indeed, although scholars have not reflected a great deal on the use of such coverage in academic accounts of media industries (Wilkinson & Merle, 2013), communication researchers have a history of studying trade press and journalistic self-coverage to understand where a technology industry thinks it is going and how journalists understand their own role in institutional upheavals (Liao, 2014; Napoli, 1997, 2011; Turow, 1994). Although such accounts can give limited and ritualistic images of media industries—falling prey to the same patterns that constrain and standardize journalism's coverage of other domains—and should not be mistaken for deep engagement with industry practices and actors (Wilkinson & Merle, 2013), they can act as "semi-embedded deep texts" that both "bring generalizing discussions of the nature and meaning of … production from one corporate media company or craft to another" and spur "discussion and eventual awareness in the public sphere of the consumer as well" (Caldwell, 2008, p. 203). These stories suggest how the press understands itself and how those outside of journalism might understand the field.

With these strengths and limitations in mind, I delve deeply into stories that the networked press tells about itself and to itself. I mine them to see how networked press freedom—as a system of sociotechnical separations and dependencies that gives rise to material publics—is being worked out in industry narratives of how and why journalism and technology intersect. (See the appendix for a discussion of the method that I used to build and analyze the corpus of trade press stories.) Within this chapter's analysis, whenever one of the primary sources is referenced, I provide an endnote to the URL of the corpus primary source. These dimensions of press freedom emerge from evaluating the primary sources as *metajournalistic* discourse, not as technical descriptions. Journalists, technologists, and scholars may disagree with how primary sources understand these systems and their significance. I treat them as stories that journalists tell each other—what *they* think systems do and mean—that, taken together, paint a picture of contemporary networked press freedom.

Dimensions of Networked Press Freedom

So far in the book I have developed three interrelated claims—that the networked press is infrastructural relationships among human and nonhuman actors, that it derives its normative legitimacy partly from its ability to realize publics, and that the power to realize publics requires the freedom to create separations and dependencies among its human and nonhuman actors. I do not argue that the networked press needs to use its autonomy to create any particular type of public (as chapter 3 shows, publics are always normative tradeoffs). But its power to create material publics that emerge from relationships among human and nonhuman actors and not just from what people alone find interesting or relevant depends on how well it understands its own sociotechnical separations and dependencies—that is, how its own arrangements of human and nonhuman actors make it more or less likely that a public right to hear is realized.

But what are these arrangements, what types of separations and dependencies do they entail, and what type of public right to hear do they suggest?

My aim here is to use stories that the networked press tells about itself as evidence of what Lisa Parks (2012) calls "infrastructural intelligibility"—the "process by which ordinary people use observations, images, information and technological experiences to infer or imagine the existence, shape or form of an extensive and dispersed infrastructure that cannot be physically observed by one person in its entirety" (p. 67).

Following the empirical approach described above, I identify twelve ways that the networked press reflects its institutional autonomy through stories about its sociotechnical infrastructure:

Observation: Watching social spaces for relevant people, events, and informational patterns.

Production: Creating the stories, representations, and interactions that circulate as news.

Alignments: Negotiating with platforms that deliver news and create the conditions under which people engage with news.

Labor: Defining operational roles and managing workforces.

Analytics: Measuring, describing, and creating abstracted accounts of networked news environments.

Timing: Setting and influencing the rhythms of networked news environments.

Security: Controlling conditions under which sources, journalists, and audiences are visible and protected.

Audiences: Defining news consumers and controlling their participation in networked news environments.

Revenue: Commodifying information and people to support networked news environments financially.

Facts: Defining the conditions under which information is seen as stable and legitimate.

Resemblances: Controlling the languages, media simulations, and international categories that make news seem familiar or foreign.

Affect: Setting stylistic and affective conditions of networked news environments.

I define each, offer examples from the journalistic trade press illustrating its sociotechnical separations and dependencies, and reflect on its stake in realizing a public right to hear. This purposefully exploratory and somewhat speculative approach does not claim to be a comprehensive image of the networked press but instead offers a typology of its dynamics to show how its autonomy is inseparable from its sociotechnical infrastructures.

Observation

Much of news work involves watching environments or *beats* where news-worthy people are expected to be and newsworthy events are expected to happen. In many ways, the networked press is no different, but its beats are sociotechnical observation systems of humans and nonhumans that scan environments, anticipate events, sense patterns, and watch locations. A mix of journalists and technologies perform acts of observing, and the sites they observe are hybrid spaces of people and digital infrastructure.

Observation takes one form in sociotechnical systems that news organizations have built to monitor social media.[1] For example, in 2014, the *New York Times* created a section called "Watching" that both automatically and manually observes headlines, tweets, and multimedia streams from around the social Web, giving readers "a carefully filtered window into rest of the world of news, all with the *NYT* stamp of approval."[2] Similarly, in 2013, *ProPublica* built a tool that lets its journalists monitor Instagram content for particular times and geographic coordinates (letting them see, for example, photos of the Boston Marathon finish line just before and after it was bombed[3]), and the *New York Times*, BuzzFeed, *Gothamist*, and the *New York World* were able to put reporters on the scene of a 2014 explosion in East Harlem because they were all using the CityBeat[4] program to search social media metadata algorithmically and be alerted to events it deemed newsworthy.[5]

Journalists are also using data tools to anticipate stories they think *might* happen. The Anomaly Tracker tool developed by the Center for Responsive Politics watches databases of lawmaker votes and campaign contributions and triggers alerts if anything happens that is considered out of the ordinary. The Center suggests extraordinary events to journalists, highlighting events that it sees as suspicious and that its database can observe. Derek Willis, "when he was at the *New York Times*, used to have an alert any time there was a vote in Congress after midnight. 'As I used to tell my kids, nothing good happens after midnight.' He had that programmed."[6]

ProPublica is a leader in data-centered reporting—making databases as part of reporting, reporting on databases, and creating databases that other organizations can use to find stories. For example, its Dollars for Docs database tracks payments that doctors receive from drug and medical device companies.[7] Its School Restraints project not only produced a publicly accessible of incidents in which children were physically restrained or secluded but also extensive guidance to other journalists on how to use the database and understand its limitations.[8] Finally, its Data Store project serves as a clearinghouse of raw datasets from government sources (available for free), hand-made vetted databases that it creates or acquires during its reporting (available for a fee), and application programming interfaces that provide regularly updated access to fresh data that can be queried according to rules it sets.[9] *ProPublica* is thus not only a data-driven news organization but a leading creator of what Michael Schudson (2010) calls "political observatories"—data collections that suggest, constrain, and empower journalistic work.

Finally, news organizations looking to observe geographic locations with drones must grapple with sociotechnical conditions.[10] A number of news organizations—including the *New York Times*, the *Washington Post*, NBCUniversal, the Associated Press, and Getty Images—are experimenting with using drones in their reporting and are learning about the regulatory and technological limits of drone reporting.[11] The Federal Aviation Administration (FAA) has issued rules on commercial drone usage,[12] but there are currently no special allowances made for journalists or news organizations.[13] Indeed, the company NoFlyZone maintains, for drone manufacturers, what it defines as a "comprehensive airspace database of critical infrastructure and sensitive sites" that include "airports, hospitals, schools, nuclear power plants, prisons" and other places it calls "sensitive locations."[14] What journalists are allowed to see with drones can be sociotechnically controlled. For example, databases can effectively create digital fences around sensitive locations (after one crashed at the White House, drones made by DJI now automatically land if they approach government locations),[15] and law enforcement officials can pressure the FAA to create no-fly zones that prevent coverage of protest events (as the St. Louis County Police Department did when it wanted to prevent journalists from using drones to cover the Ferguson, Missouri, protests).[16]

The networked press uses a variety of sociotechnical infrastructures to scan social media environments, anticipate newsworthy events, sense data patterns, and watch geographic locations. Its freedom to observe is not simply about human journalists gaining unfettered access to data or to places. Rather, its freedom requires the shared sociotechnical capacity to query social media and understand what such queries can and cannot show, appreciate the limits of what algorithms are able to anticipate and what anomalies databases are primed to reveal, and see physical locations as long as technologies index them and governments allow such indexing. The public right to hear—to discover new publics—is inextricable from the networked press's freedom to configure the sociotechnical separations and dependencies that enable observation.

Production

The networked press is also increasingly inseparable from infrastructures of humans and nonhumans that produce news together.[17] Such infrastructures let journalists tell or publish stories faster, and they sometimes use "structured data"[18]—collections of highly structured and predictably organized information—to semiautonomously create content that then circulates in ways that are often indistinguishable from news created entirely by humans. The trade press accounts of such news production infrastructures center on issues of authorship, interaction, and tailoring.

Three of the most highly discussed authorship infrastructures[19] are the Wordsmith platform that the Associated Press (AP) developed in partnership with Automated Insights to tell financial stories,[20] the Narrative Science Quill system that *ProPublica* used to report on educational data,[21] and the QuakeBot system that the *Los Angeles Times* uses to report data from the United States Geological Survey.[22] It is beyond the scope of this book to discuss these systems in detail, but they share a common process: journalists use their news judgments and domain-specific knowledge to create algorithmic processes that turn predictable, highly structured data— investment, educational, seismic—into human readable narratives. Authorship is a mix of human judgment, editorial tradition, data standardization, and algorithmic processing—with early research suggesting that people perceive "computer-written articles as more credible and higher in journalistic expertise but less readable" (Graefe, Haim, Haarmann, & Brosius, 2016, p. 1) and that algorithmically produced financial stories result in a greater number of trades.[23]

Another form of infrastructural production exists in the form of news organizations' semiautomated interactions with audiences—the creation of bots programmed to deliver news through interactive conversation-like experiences. For example, the *New York Times* used the Facebook messenger platform to create a bot that engaged readers conversationally about the 2016 presidential election, sending both prescribed messages and responses to users' queries for electoral predictions and poll data.[24] The *Washington Post* is similarly using the Facebook platform to develop a conversational news bot,[25] and CNN[26] and NBC[27] have both built applications for the Kik bot platform designed to engage younger users with content through conversation-like prompts and story recommendations based on users' responses. *Quartz* recently devoted its entire mobile news app to a chat experience that gives users "teases to stories in the form of chat bubbles, and then lets [them] select whether they want to get more information about a topic or move onto the next story."[28] (In November 2016, the Knight Foundation awarded *Quartz* $240,000 to further develop its "bot studio" and to create apps that deliver news through conversations with Slack messenger, Amazon Echo, and Google Home).[29]

The final area in which news production is intersecting with technological infrastructures is tailoring. News organizations recommend existing stories to readers and also create entirely new stories aligned with what their tracking systems record and different media require. For example, the *Washington Post* created personalized email newsletters with content related to stories that it observed users engaging with previously.[30] It also created a personalized reading experience called Re-Engage that tracks how readers interact with a mobile story, guesses when readers may be getting bored, and suggests at the optimal times alternative stories designed to keep that reader from closing the app.[31] And the *New York Times* created healthcare policy stories personalized for where it sensed readers were located ("Consider Los Angeles, our best guess for where you might be reading this article").[32] The experience of having the middle of a news story personalized was so unnerving that it prompted the *Times*'s public editor to muse whether "personalization could deprive readers of a shared, and expertly curated, news experience, which is what many come to The Times for."[33] Tailoring also appears as systems that automate translating a story from one medium to another. The AP created a system to solve the "manual labor nightmare" of translating a story written for print that needs to be rewritten for broadcast: "Stories are shorter, sentences are more concise, attribution comes at the beginning of a sentence, numbers are rounded."[34] The system is designed to give reporters more autonomy. Because relying on it frees them from tasks seen to be mundane and routine, embedded in such separations and dependencies are visions of what reporters are supposed to do.

The networked press does not use technologies only to accelerate the production or dissemination of stories. Through authorship, interaction, and tailoring infrastructures, it also blends humans and nonhumans into assemblages that speak to, converse with, and target audiences. And such infrastructures are fallible. Wordsmith erroneously reported a drop in Netflix's stock price (it had undergone a split, but the algorithm was not programmed to recognize this), and as Microsoft's crowdsourced chat bot Tay showed when it gave racist, Holocaust-denying replies to users' queries (reflecting what the crowd had taught its machine learning algorithm), designing artificially intelligent conversational agents with integrity is difficult.[33]

Autonomy does not need to mean freedom from authorship, interaction, and personalization infrastructures, which can be valuable ways to let journalists focus on less mundane stories, create relationships with audiences at scale, and help people see different ways that issues are personally relevant to them. Rather, autonomy means engaging with infrastructures of production to ask questions about data and audiences: What types of data are algorithmic stories relying on, and does the data meet editorial standards? When and why should news organizations engage audiences in conversations (Schudson 1997 argues that conversations do not always serve democracy)[36] versus other modes of communication? And when do personalized stories let people retreat into private domains of concern versus help them see the inextricable conditions and consequences of shared public life?

Alignments

The networked press also increasingly needs to align with "sites and services that host public expression." Such platforms do not "make [news] content, but they make important choices about that content: what they will distribute and to whom, how they will connect users and broker their interactions, and what they will refuse" (Gillespie, 2017, p. 255). Although companies like Facebook often eschew their roles as media companies (Napoli & Caplan, 2017)[37] and people find news through a variety of different media, audiences are increasingly using such platforms to access and share news (Bright, 2016; Gotfried & Shearer, 2016; Trilling, Tolochko, & Burscher, 2017).

News organization alignments with platforms discussed in the trade press take the form of partnerships (platform-centered strategic publishing agreements), resemblances (news that looks like the content that platforms find valuable), and breakdowns (moments when infrastructural meetings show how platform priorities and editorial values can collide and cause discord).

Partnerships   Much of the aligning described in the trade press comes in the form of guidance and collaboration agreements between news organizations and social media platforms. Facebook,[38] Google,[39] and Twitter[40] offer instructions on how news organizations should create and format news in order to align with the strategies that platforms use to find, rank, and suggest content. With other collaborations, platforms commission original content from news organizations: Facebook essentially hires news organizations to provide exclusive content for its Facebook Live channels,[41] and Twitter partnered with the BBC World Service's Global News Podcast to embed exclusive, sponsored video content within promoted tweets as part of its Amplify program.[42]

Other partnerships focus on creating what the trade press calls "distributed content"[43]—designing special formats and subareas of platforms specifically for news content. For example, in exchange for housing content on Facebook's servers, news organizations can join Facebook's Instant Articles program (originally for only a select group of publishers[44] but now open to all[45]) to load mobile content faster, reach advertising markets, and access exclusive interactive features.[46] (The *New York Times* demonstrated the value of distributing content around the Web before the Instant Articles program went live when it posted full stories to its Facebook page after its own website briefly went down.)[47] Google's Accelerated Mobile Pages project similarly offers publishers access to faster loading times, analytics tools, and interactive and revenue-gathering features, without requiring news organizations to place their content on Google servers;[48] Twitter's Project Lightning created Moments to let invited news organizations create digestlike summaries of tweets that they see as related to a particular news topic;[49] and several news organizations (from "BuzzFeed and Mashable to ESPN and National Geographic"[50]) produce custom content exclusively for Snapchat's Discover platform.

Finally, other partnerships focus not on producing content but on aligning customer bases and production work. For example, Amazon Prime subscribers get six months of free access to the *Washington Post* (owned by Amazon chief executive officer Jeff Bezos),[51] and CNN collaborated with Twitter to produce a custom tool for letting it sort and publish tweets in near "real-time."[52]

Resemblances   Other forms of news-platform alignment are less programmatic. They are instead ongoing sociotechnical dances in which news organizations create content that they think platforms favor and try to adjust their production processes quickly when they see platforms changing. This is understandable: different platforms attract different types of readers, and once there, people read, share, and comment on news differently depending on the platform.[53]

As with partnerships, the trade press describes different types of resemblance work. In the most extreme versions, news organizations decide to adopt platform formats entirely—as the *Wall Street Journal* did when it created a Facebook-only app in 2011,[54] as Vox did when it sequestered its Circuit Breaker within Facebook instead of as a separate Vox website,[55] and as many news organizations are currently doing as they create Flash Briefings customized for Amazon's Alexa voice interface.[56] In other circumstances, news organizations tailor stories for technologies. The Verge did so when it showed different versions of a story to Apple versus Google versus Microsoft users,[57] the *New York Times* did so when it heavily peppered a story with "tweetable phrases" to make it easy for Twitter users to comment on and share the story,[58] and the *Guardian* does so when it hovers a Twitter icon above any story text that readers highlight, encouraging them to tweet the passage directly from its site.

News organizations can be rewarded greatly for such resemblances. For example, news stories that appear as Facebook Instant Articles are shared more frequently and widely than other types of news links.[59] And National Public Radio (NPR) drew attention to local stations' stories when it used Facebook's location-based system suggestions[60] to geo-index stories it thought had local relevance.[61] Local traffic increased when Facebook's way of encoding "local" aligned with NPR's definition of a geographic news community.

When platforms change how they parse and rank content, news organizations pay attention and try to respond as quickly as possible. Facebook changed its News Feed algorithm in 2013 to limit what it called low-quality sites focused on spreading memes,[62] in 2014 to increase what it saw as partisan political sources,[63] and in 2016 to surface more content about "friends and family"[64] and fight what it defined as clickbait.[65] Although some news sites saw traffic increases in 2013,[66] the trade press debated[67] whether the change harmed legitimate sites like Upworthy that tried to *use* memelike formats as a way of disseminating quality news. (Facebook does not release detailed statistics on such changes, so the trade press is left with anecdotal evidence of their effect on the industry as a whole. *Mother Jones* saw its traffic increase as a result of aligning with Facebook's 2014 change,[68] but so did Mental Floss, a site that shares facts in memelike formats.)[69] Some news sites try to reduce their reliance on Facebook, as *Bleacher Report* did when it instead focusing on a partnership with Snapchat.[70]

As often happens with infrastructure, some resemblances appear in socio-technical forms that are largely invisible to end users or constrained to pre-defined categories. For example, Google News's Spotlight architecture gives prominence to stories its algorithms see as "in-depth pieces of lasting value,"[71] offers a "standout" metadata tag to let news organizations suggest pieces that they feel are high quality,[72] and asks news organizations to use a finite set of Google-defined genre tags (press release, satire, blog, op-ed, opinion, user-generated) to categorize stories for the search engine.[73] Other platforms also mediate their interactions with news organizations through algorithmic architectures: Facebook's Stories to Share feature alerts news organizations to content that Facebook thinks would circulate well but that it senses news organizations have not yet shared,[74] and Twitter has automatically promoted news articles that it determines have tweets embedded within them.[75]

Breakdowns   Finally, news-platform alignments often are most visible during moments of breakdown—when cooperation agreements or sociotechnical relationships seem to fail.[76] Such moments are diagnostics of networked press freedom because they reveal limits on news-platform alignment. We hear calls for the networked press to create more separation from technology companies, and technology executives have tried to distance themselves from news organizations by focusing on the supposed neutrality of their algorithms, disavowing editorial responsibility, promising to do better, but ultimately claiming that the days of hand-curated news experiences are over.[77]

There is no shortage of examples of such breakdowns, and they involve censoring or reformatting news or banning organizations and individuals. Some failures are accidental and quickly reversed, others are the product of platform policies and take considerable effort to overturn, others are unintended and inexplicable, and others are purposeful and defended. For example, in 2013, Twitter accidentally labeled an entire Philadelphia newspaper as spam and would not allow users to access the paper's site through tweets.[78] Reporters protested and used Tumblr instead, and Twitter apologized and reinstated the account about a week later. Also in 2013, Facebook deleted several news organizations' stories about same-sex marriage; the organizations received no explanation, and Facebook did not say why the stories had been removed.[79]

In 2016, Facebook censored two different news sites after news stories containing images of naked bodies were found to violate the site's community standards. In the first case, activist Celeste Liddle shared a story from the news site *New Matilda* that contained an image of Aboriginal women in ceremonial outfits that showed their breasts. The post was deleted, and Liddle's account was suspended. Facebook claimed that it had to maintain "uniformity in global policies"—although *New Matilda* showed images of nude U.S. models published in *Esquire* magazine that were circulating uncensored on Facebook. In the second case, Facebook censored a Norwegian writer's post containing Nick Ut's Pulitzer Prize–winning "iconic photo of a girl, screaming and naked, fleeing napalm bombs during the Vietnam War."[80] Facebook claimed that the post violated its community standards but eventually relented after the Norwegian newspaper *Aftenposten* reported on the suspension and included the story in its report; the paper had its own story removed and received a warning not to display nude images; the paper wrote an open letter claiming that Facebook was censoring the news; the leader of the Norwegian conservative party had her post removed for including the photo; and the Norwegian prime minister also posted the photo in protest over Facebook's actions. The company eventually decided the photo had iconic, newsworthy status.[81] Both the *New Matilda* and *Aftenposten* incidents highlighted the incompatibility of the platform's community standards and news organizations' editorial judgments and the idiosyncratic nature of how breakages are perceived and allowances for particular cases are made.[82] (In a different moment fueling trade press perception that technology company standards are incompatible with news values, shortly after Amazon CEO Jeff Bezos bought the *Washington Post*, the paper briefly displayed Amazon Buy It Now links within the article texts—a move that was widely ridiculed by journalists claiming that Bezos was turning the *Post* into a marketing arm of Amazon.)[83]

Although platforms usually claim that such incidents are unfortunate side effects of running global sites that serve massive scales of user-generated content in near real time and cannot be manually curated, sometimes a platform stands by its news censorship. In 2014, although some news organizations were showing the gruesome footage of the beheading of journalist James Foley, Twitter banned any accounts that displayed images of the murder, a move that many commentators said showed Twitter's power to override editorial judgment selectively and purposefully.[84]

Across different types of alignments—official partnerships, sociotechnical resemblances, and value-based breakdowns—news organizations and social media platforms find themselves in intricate and often inseparable relationships. Instead of seeing press freedom as the journalistic power to avoid aligning with platforms, we might trace what types of publics such alignments and breakdowns assume and create. Partnership agreements, sociotechnical resemblances, and failed collaborations show how the power is distributed unevenly between news organizations and technology companies. The networked press might demonstrate its need for autonomy—and what it could do with institutional freedom—by designing collaborations that ensure a public right to hear.

Labor

In his thoughtful study of digital news work, Matthew Powers (2012) observes that "Changes in the technologies of news production do not simply modify journalistic practices; they also introduce what might be considered *technologically specific* forms of work" (p. 24, emphasis in original). Such work, as we found in our study of mobile news app designers, is neither exclusively digital nor editorial but helps shape a "liminal press" (Ananny & Crawford, 2015) that both reifies and questions technological and journalistic traditions. If networked press freedom exists, in part, through envisioning and supporting different kinds of labor, what we see in the trade press are myriad initiatives, communities, and roles that attempt to balance separations and dependencies between journalists and technologists. What emerges is a complex story of how journalists both emulate and critique technological labor.

Some of these balances exist in entire news organizations centered on computational concepts and labor. Circa was founded on an "object-oriented" vision of news work that deconstructs the idea of the traditional news article, and it hired journalists who could think in "software development terms like forking and refactoring" in order to create a set of facts, stats, quotes, events or images that can be assembled and reassembled in the service of a news narrative.[85] The company is one of several news organizations trying to create blended workforces that see news work as the creation and manipulation of structured content.[86] This approach to news work is both relatively new (connected to software engineering notions of reusable and easily extensible code) and quite old (rooted in longstanding journalistic forms like the inverted pyramid, the standalone lede, and editing stories from the bottom). The trade press is filled with stories of people in these hybrid workforces reflecting on their identities as both journalists and coders,[87] advocating for others to develop hybrid skills,[88] and debating whether journalists should think of themselves as coders with software engineering skills or as general builders with the ability to tinker whenever their journalistic instincts suggest doing so.[89] The *New York Times* even built an in-house computational tool to track its own staff's Web browsing in an attempt to trace and summarize reporters' intelligence work automatically and avoid duplication among workers.[90]

These debates occurred alongside the rise of professional organizations designed to blend editorial and technological mindsets and offer networking opportunities for this new labor market. Akin to what Fred Turner (2005) calls "network forums"—entities that simultaneously convene and represent diverse people who may otherwise share little—the trade press contains many mentions of new groups designed to facilitate hybrid labor. Hacks/Hackers was founded to "help journalists (hacks) and developers (hackers) learn from each other and collaborate on projects,"[91] the Knight-Mozilla OpenNews group was designed to "strengthen the bonds between the worlds of journalism and software development"[92] and to execute open source journalism projects,[93] and the OpenNews initiative Source was designed to bring "wandering journonerds together under one roof" to share code and best practices.[94]

Newsrooms and platform companies alike trade in hybrid labor. When Joanna Geary left the *Guardian* to lead Twitter's UK news partnerships[95] and Liz Heron stepped down from head of news partnerships for Facebook to become HuffPost's executive editor,[96] several trade press stories reflected on increasingly blurred differences between news and platform companies. The *Wall Street Journal*, Condé Nast, Vox Media, and the *New York Times* have hired platform specialists and platform relationship managers to be liaisons with technology companies and to advocate for social media forms of storytelling within newsrooms.[97] And although they eschew their roles as media companies, both Facebook[98] and Twitter[99] have created positions that are designed to lead partnerships with news organizations and that call for several years of experience within newsrooms. A controversial aspect of such shifts has been the question of whether journalists who have built social media brands at one news organization or platform should be able to take them to a new job[100]—whether a journalist should be able to have a portable brand that travels easily between competitors and among editorial and technology contexts.

Visions of journalistic versus technological labor also play out in discussions about how and why to train the next generation of hybrid workers. There are calls for universities to change how they teach journalism students,[101] a Facebook program to teach new journalists how to report using the platform,[102] a focus in journalism schools on teaching students how to produce for social media,[103] scholarships to help software programmers learn about journalism[104] and journalism students learn to build technology projects,[105] an "in-house journalism school" at the *New York Times* designed to train future digital reporters,[106] and a traveling course where *ProPublica* and *Times* journalists teach technology skills to journalists in smaller media markets.[107] Each initiative is different, but they share an assumption that future journalists must have some literacy with technological concepts and systems. There is no sense that press freedom means sequestering journalism students from computational thinking.

Finally, there is evidence of some tension in this ideal of news organizations and platform companies educating the next generation of journalists together. When *Gizmodo* exposed the inner labor dynamics of the team behind Facebook's Trending Topics product, the trade press questioned whether news-technology partnerships are truly equitable and what power individual journalists have in the face of massively funded technology companies. *Gizmodo* describes how Facebook hired approximately a dozen journalists—people who had previously worked at the *New York Daily News*, Bloomberg, MSNBC, and the *Guardian*—to be "news curators" who decided what should appear on the Trending Topics part of Facebook, wrote short summaries of topics, and chose relevant media. After the team was disbanded, *Gizmodo* reported that Facebook managers told the curators not to list on their resumes that they had worked on Trending Topics so that the appearance that the list was algorithmically curated could be maintained.[108] Writing for *Forbes*, a former curator said that the team was always given the impression that their job "was essentially to train an algorithm to write the news."[109] The incident trigged a renewed discussion about how journalistic labor was valued by technology platforms and whether the much-heralded claims of partnership and cooperation were actually hiding technologists' more insidious goal of studying journalistic labor only for the purpose of algorithmically modeling it.

Networked press freedom thus is emerging not as neat separations in which journalistic work or education is distinct from the goals and practices of technology companies. Nor do we see evidence of journalists having the power to depend selectively on the parts of computational labor that they see aligning with editorial goals. Rather, a messier and more complex interplay between traditional ideals of journalistic work and newer forms of technological work is developing in professional organizations, career moves, educational initiatives, and perceptions of exploitation.

Analytics

Several academic studies have analyzed how newsrooms using Web analytics—quantified information about how content travels online—to shape news work, imagine audiences, and drive editorial policy (Hanusch, 2016; MacGregor, 2007; Petre, 2015; Tandoc, 2014, 2015; Tandoc & Thomas, 2014; Usher, 2013; Vu, 2014; Welbers, van Atteveldt, Kleinnijenhuis, Ruigrok, & Schaper, 2016; Zamith, 2016). There is little doubt that such metrics are increasingly ubiquitous and powerful, but beyond calls for such tools not to overwhelm traditional editorial judgment, there is little understanding of how the press perceives the role such systems play in shaping its autonomy.

The trade press has long been tracking the appearance of Web analytics in digital news work, with companies like Google (Analytics), Chartbeat, Omniture, Newsbeat, and Parsely all promising news organizations the ability to provide rich and often real-time images of how audiences interact with their content[110] or might interact with content.[111] Not long after they appeared, commentators and analysts began wondering whether knowledge about how stories were spreading would simply impact how stories were featured on news sites[112] or whether it would affect more fundamental thinking about which stories were told at all and how a story's impact might be measured.[113] The trade press conversation progressed from general worries about the influence of analytics on seemingly pure journalistic work that editors could direct to more specific questions: What is the right thing to measure? Where do analytics systems come from? And how should they be used within newsrooms? As the field struggled with each question, it left clues about what it thought its autonomy meant—how it could or should be free from knowledge about audiences and technology companies eager to provide rich metrics.

The first question—what is the right thing to measure?—is important to track because as the networked press evolved its vision of the ideal metric, it revealed what kind of knowledge it was willing to be influenced by. Counting page views for a story was an early and crude measure of how popular the story was and what reach editors imagined the story to have.[114] This method was relatively quickly replaced with more sophisticated ways of measuring unique page views and sources of page views as the number of new readers and their origins became a more influential metric.[115] Another metric became the time spent on an article[116] as news sites tried to argue that time was a proxy for a reader's interest and learning as well as a sign of an increased likelihood that a reader might click on a site's advertisement.[117] (Facebook agreed, publicly saying that its News Feed algorithm would use the time spent on a news story as a "signal" it would use to surface content.)[118] These emphases on page views, unique visitors, and time on a page were gradually replaced with attention—an indication that readers were actually focusing on news stories. Focus was something that both news organizations and advertisers agreed could drive the news: the *Guardian* centered its analytics platform on attention,[119] the analytics firm Chartbeat focused its dashboard on attention,[120] and the Media Ratings Council certified and endorsed Chartbeat's model of attention as one that could be trusted to measure potential advertising impact.[121] Other news organizations added the idea of engagement to the metrics mix, with the *Daily Signal* creating a platform to track how people commented on, shared, tagged, and otherwise interacted with its content across multiple social media platforms.[122] The *Christian Science Monitor* interpreted the word *engagement* slightly differently, offering readers ways to take action after they read a story (by visiting a relevant organization, giving the *Monitor* feedback, or contacting an elected representative)—and then defining those actions as engagement.[123]

The desire to understand engagement motivated a small-scale analytics platform called NewsLynx[124] (built by Columbia University researchers) to try to connect a story's quantitative reach (such as number of tweets and Facebook posts) with its qualitative impact. It let news organizations add tags to a story's analytical report indicating whether the story had—in the news organization's judgment—increased awareness of an issue, spurred a government investigation, or prompted a policy change. This tool married an approach to analytics with a model of what it thinks news impact *should* mean (that is, more than a number of page views or unique readers, time spent on an article, attention paid, or social media engagements).

NewsLynx's unique origin story and implicit normative goal suggest a second question to ask of the trade press's discourse on news analytics: where do metrics systems come from, and why might such origins matter to networked press freedom? Some news organizations have enough resources to build their own analytics platforms and imbue them with their own editorial values. The *Guardian*'s Ophan system[125] was designed around its own understanding of engagement (the page "has to be in the foreground tab, and you have to be moving the mouse or scrolling, or clicking, or doing something like that") and the ability for its editors to make changes to the system as theories occurred to them they wanted to test. The *Financial Times* wanted its metrics platform, Lantern, to be understandable to its journalists. It gives journalists access to information like "average time on page, retention rate, scroll rate, social performance, and what type of devices readers are coming from" as well as breakdowns "between subscribers and non-subscribers who are accessing a particular story."[126] The *New York Times* similarly designed its platform, Stela, to be meaningful to journalists and "narrow the distance between reporters and analytics data,"[127] while the team designing NPR's dashboards took a more participatory design approach, surveying competitors' systems and interviewing NPR employees before building a platform designed to speak to all aspects of the organization.[128] NPR's dashboards are not publicly available, but it has said that it will share them with the competitors they interviewed (the *New York Times*, *BuzzFeed*, the *Atlantic*, *Huffington Post*, *USA Today*, and the *Guardian*), suggesting that there are shared understandings of newsroom metrics among organizations with enough resources to develop in-house systems. Organizations without such resources still use third-party platforms like Chartbeat and Google Analytics, as well as platform-specific tools like those Facebook provides for news organizations to track content.[129] Several trade stories stress the importance of Facebook analytics.

The final question the trade press seems to be asking of analytics systems is, How should news organizations use them? Even though journalists often officially say that they pay little attention to traffic metrics, for years the trade press has been a place where journalists have acknowledged that analytics and content optimization impacts their work.[130] As Caitlin Petre (2015, n.p.) writes, "Metrics inspire a range of strong feelings in journalists, such as excitement, anxiety, self-doubt, triumph, competition, and demoralization." Sometimes the power of such systems is openly acknowledged by news organizations themselves. The *Washington Post* acknowledges that its Bandito system lets editors "enter different article versions with varying headlines, images and teaser text" and then "detects which version readers are clicking or tapping on more, and automatically serves that version more frequently on the homepage and other areas of the Post's site."[131] The *New York Times*'s Package Mapper tool took a similar approach but analyzed how audiences traversed the website and then dynamically offered personalized recommendations of paths that it thought particular users were most likely to follow.[132] These systems show how analytics are balances between personalization and site-level patterns: news organizations are trying to create close relationships with individual readers while still giving the impression that they are offering a general news experience shared by all.

The trade press openly debates how metrics should influence news work. Although some news organizations that developed in-house analytics dashboards are trying to make reporters more aware of metrics on their stories, others keep those systems from writers. At the *Verge* and MIT's *Technology Review*, only the "senior editorial leadership team"—not reporters—can see Chartbeat and Google Analytics dashboards. The *San Francisco Chronicle*'s managing editor disagreed with such an approach, saying "we pay [reporters] to sift through information and come up with logical stories and points of views," so "why can they not do that with their own data?"[133] But famed *New York Times* media critic David Carr cautioned that "just because something is popular does not make it worthy."[134]

This debate plays out in the sociotechnical details of how news organizations use metrics. The *Daily Caller* created "a hybrid pay arrangement in which staffers receive base pay plus an incentive for the performance of their work on the Internet," the details of which were not made public.[135] *Gawker* was seen as an industry leader in traffic incentives, creating a Recruits program that paid writers for each one thousand unique monthly visitors and rewarded them with longer-term contracts if they met their traffic targets.[136] Similarly, business news site *TheStreet.com* paid writers for page views ($20 for twenty thousand views in a seven-day period),[137] Advance gave bonuses to reporters who "post frequently and join comment chains,"[138] and the Apple news site 9to5Mac gave reporters a share of the Google AdSense revenue earned on their stories.[139] And in the process of trying to decide which writers it would lay off, Time Inc. ranked individual reporters from one to ten based on how "beneficial" they were to advertisers.[140] Some organizations—like Demand Media and AOL's Seed, which described themselves as quasi-news organizations while others referred to them as Web content farms—went so far as to create on-demand workforces. They would analyze search engine query patterns and, in near real time, hire people to create content relevant to those patterns. Such companies were largely disavowed in the trade press, representing an extreme, unethical end of a spectrum of metrics uses.[141]

The use of analytics and traffic incentives highlighted divergent views of press freedom. For some journalists and news organizations, autonomy means mandating that reporters have *freedom from* metrics that are assumed to be corrupting, privileging the reporter's image of the public interest. Others, though, say that such freedom harms journalism's potential to impact the world, discover audiences' interests, and generate revenue by writing popular stories. Most commentators discussed the need for proper metrics and good incentives, without articulating exactly how such balances should be struck.[142]

News organizations define their relationships to reporters, technology companies, and audiences through analytics.[143] What they choose to measure indicates what they are willing to let influence them—that is, which forces they see as relevant and willing to engage with and which they see as incompatible and needing distance from. The trade press does not have a uniform appreciation of autonomy or what it needs to be free from. It is engaged in an open debate about which analytics are anathema and which are essential to what it sees as good journalism. Some see metrics dashboards as essential to bringing reporters closer to audiences, listening to them, and enacting audiences' definition of the public interest. Others see such proximity as fundamentally problematic and emblematic of eroding press autonomy and journalists' freedom to enact their vision of the public. Larger news organizations with strong resources and reputations can make their own in-house metrics systems, selectively use third-party systems, and take time to create the ideal distances between their workforces and metrics systems. Smaller, newer entrants to online journalism must more closely align with third-party systems created by Chartbeat, Google, and Facebook.

A public right to hear comes not from journalists separating themselves from or integrating with dashboards. Such systems are actors in their own right in inseparable relationships with humans that together suggest what publics could be or might mean.

Timing

The press has always reflected and created structures of time,[144] existing at and shaping the intersection of what I elsewhere (Ananny, 2016b) call the "inside-out" time of news organizations (which initiates, schedules, and controls coverage of events beyond the newsroom) and the "outside-in" time of factors outside the newsroom (which forces journalists to reorient their rhythms and deadlines). Although the internet is often spoken as a place of "timeless time"—where an "elimination of sequencing creates undifferentiated time, which is tantamount to eternity" (Castells, 1996, p. 494)—news time has not disappeared but has become embedded in the networked press's sociotechnical structures. It continues to exist in the professional spaces and routines of traditional mainstream journalism (Carey, 1989b; Schudson, 1986), but it also is increasingly intertwined with how nonjournalists and technologies that are not overtly grounded in journalistic cultures organize journalists and audiences alike around new rhythms and deadlines.[145] The temporal patterns of the networked press—when audiences can participate, when sources are invoked, when accounts are produced, what kind of events register as news, and how often audiences encounter news—are all increasingly intertwined with a network of human and nonhuman actors. The power to speed up or slow down is not simply about journalists being free from audiences, advertisers, or technologies. As with other dimensions of networked press freedom, the networked press's time—and thus, the timeliness of the publics it can create—emerges from sociotechnical negotiations.

The trade press is filled with commentaries and thought pieces on the novelty of contemporary news time,[146] the ways online reporters balance "immediacy versus importance,"[147] the possible need to change journalistic ethics during breaking news,[148] and the ways social media saves or consumes audiences' time in ways that help or hinder journalism.[149] Beyond these general concerns, several patterns appear in the stories journalists tell themselves about networked news time—namely, how to align with or resist technology's dominant focus on real time, manage journalistic memory and make room for historical points of view when relevant data often exists outside of news organizations and technology platforms favor newness, delay and protect news as a scarce resource that journalists primarily create, work with technology infrastructures that have their own often invisible temporal priorities, synchronize with the time habits of news readers who are also technology users, and anticipate scenarios beyond what current networks show.

Real-Time First, the trade press is focused largely on creating real-time content that it thinks can compete with the real-time focus of social media. (In 2011, the Pulitzer Prize board changed a local "breaking news" category to reward "real-time" reporting.)[150] Relatively early on, *HuffPost* focused on hiring live bloggers who could practice what it saw as the lost journalistic genre of real-time reporting in ways that would attract the attention of search engines and social media platforms,[151] and the *New York Times* recently created an Express Team tasked with covering "trends and breaking news that bubble up online and might fall between the cracks of our traditional desk structure."[152] In addition to initiatives focused on journalistic labor, news organizations also invested in creating technologies for real-time publishing: *HuffPost* and *Boston.com* both created live channels designed to attract and keep viewers;[153] ITV created a "rolling news stream" that aimed to mirror the real-time content of social media channels;[154] the *Wall Street Journal* created its Markets Pulse platform to provide continuously updated financial news; and *BuzzFeed* updated how it republished wire stores, creating sharable snippets of new visual information as opposed to following the traditional practice of updating wire stories from the top and editing from the bottom.[155] *New York Magazine* even boasted in 2011 that its new policy was to publish new content every six minutes between 8:30 a.m. and 7 p.m. (Eastern time),[156] and in 2016 NPR added the phrase "live from *NPR News* in Washington" to the beginning of its newscasts "to reinforce one of terrestrial radio's greatest virtues, which is live-ness and a sense of immediacy" in an era where social media promises both.[157] And beyond journalists' own real-time initiatives, they also debate the merits of having technology companies encourage and sometimes commission news for real-time formats such as Facebook Live, Twitter's Periscope, Meerkat, and Kik.[158]

This focus on real time manifests as custom news content and also as less visible internal infrastructures that are designed to represent (such as the

New York Times's social media–driven feed Watching),[159] quote (such as the *Guardian*'s use of NPR's Quotable tool),[160] analyze (such as *Quartz*'s use of Spundge),[161] or invite users into real-time social media streams (such as the *Wikipedia*-like startup *Grasswire*).[162] The real-time speed of some domains also creates infrastructural feedback loops. For example, as high-frequency algorithms speed up stock trading, news organizations like the Associated Press (AP) (using Automated Insight's Wordsmith platform) and *Forbes* (using Narrative Science's Quill system) algorithmically write stories in near real-time to analyze the trades.[163] These algorithmically authored stories are then potential inputs to the Financial News system Thompson Reuters created to "scan and analyze stories on thousands of companies in real-time and feed the results" into traders' stock-management software.[164] The news loop is closed by a real-time algorithmic arms race: high-frequency algorithms make trades in near real-time, news algorithms write stories about those trades, and other news algorithms analyze those stories in near real time and provide analysis to high-frequency traders. *Sky News* turns its journalists into real-time infrastructure, equipping them with mobile technologies and speed training that make them "broadcast-ready" in ninety seconds.[165]

Readers often see the results of real-time infrastructures through push notifications. Such notifications are known to drive traffic to news apps[166] and are powerful because they can be updated automatically in light of new information,[167] personalized,[168] and targeted to readers in particular geographic locations.[169] But there is considerable concern that only news judgment and editorial principles trigger them,[170] not a desire to reflect social media trends or beat competitors.[171] The AP worries that the special significance of its flash alert—historically and rarely used to tell newsrooms about a "transcendent development" such as the moon landing or the Twin Towers collapse—is diluted as readers fail to distinguish important from mundane interruptions.[172]

Such worries are part of industrywide concerns over real-time news infrastructures, with many focusing on breaking news. News organizations are being told that they often spread news faster than Twitter,[173] that Twitter users follow breaking news,[174] and that readers look to mainstream news outlets[175] and elites[176] to confirm breaking news. In the face of such messaging, the trade press contains many warnings to journalists and readers alike about how to behave during breaking news: tweet "responsibly,"[177] offer live feeds without any commentaries or analysis,[178] avoid using personal accounts to prevent scooping the news organization you work for,[179] stay silent and resist any kind of online publishing,[180] or stay away from social media altogether.[181] Most broadly, these concerns motivate a small but vocal group of commentators and practitioners calling for a "slow news" movement,[182] and for greater attention to paid to the toll that 24/7 news cultures take on journalists' physical and mental health.[183]

Memory The networked press struggles both to control its present and to define its past. The trade press describes two types of sociotechnical challenges inherent in news organizations' memory work—being free from others to archive news as they wish and relying on the archives of others to ensure that they can report on the past.

Sociotechnical freedom from others takes a few different forms. The first is simply a freedom to delete news. *U.S. News & World Report* discovered how controversial this freedom was when it switched to a new content-management system and deleted much of its pre-2007 archive.[184] Commentators similarly challenged *BuzzFeed*'s freedom to reinvent itself after it removed over four thousand articles that it said "no longer met *BuzzFeed*'s updated editorial standards"[185] (that is, from before it considered itself a news site)— a move its editor in chief later said the organization "didn't fully think through."[186] In both cases, the sites learned that what they saw as internal reorganizations of their own archives triggered public concerns over whether news organizations had the right to alter their own pasts. Many in the trade press used such incidents to celebrate third-party projects—such as PastPages,[187] StoryTracker,[188] and NewsDiffs[189]—designed to archive and monitor changes in news sites.

This fight to control past news also manifests as a conversation about how to monetize news organizations' archives. Several news organizations routinely recycle news that has already proven valuable to advertisers and audiences alike—such as charging premium prices for access to past stories or packaging commercially valuable content for industry research firms[190] or republishing earlier stories under a new date stamp[191] or in a slightly different format to appear new to search engines that favor novelty.[192] And to protect the potential future value of their current work, some news organizations are trying to "future-proof"[193] their content-management systems to prevent their media from becoming inaccessible or corrupted as new technological formats are invented.[194]

Finally, news organizations' memories often are only as long as the data archives of the organizations they depend on. Journalists creating anniversary coverage of a protest where University of California at Davis police pepper-sprayed students and found themselves unable to access earlier media on the incident because the university had hired a Web reputation firm to remove online references to the protest.[195] And reporters wanting to cover when and why politicians delete tweets were hamstrung when Twitter blocked Politwoops (the Sunlight Foundation's archive of public figures' tweet streams) from accessing its data.[196] Twitter later restored Politwoops's access,[197] but the competing site PostGhost was not so lucky because Twitter issued a cease-and-desist order and the archive shut down. Such sites and incidents may seem idiosyncratic, but reliable access to Web archives is key as journalists are being told to give contemporary stories historical context (the core motivation of the news startup *Timeline*),[198] use social media to find new stories,[199] and investigate how new histories can be told as organizations like the Library of Congress make their archival formats more relevant to journalists.[200]

Delays   Sometimes news organizations' desires to postpone publishing may be at odds with the forces in the networked news environment. Several U.S. news organizations—and newslike information providers—have invoked the little-used "hot news doctrine" to argue that they should have the power to suspend temporarily other actors' right to disseminate information.

This doctrine first appeared after a U.S. Supreme Court 1918 decision (*International News Service v. Associated Press*) gave the AP a "quasi-property" right, for a limited period of time, to the news it produced. It prevented competing news organizations—but not the general public—from having access to this news as a way to protect the investments that publishers made in the people, materials, and communication networks that created the news (Epstein, 1992). The problems with this doctrine are made even more salient in networked environments: How long, exactly, should a news organization be able to delay others from republishing news it reported? How can a networked news organization separate the resources that it invests in a story from the resources of other people and organizations? For example, if some of the reporting uses a social media platform, should the delay be shorter? Should only human actors (other journalists) be delayed from publishing, or are nonhuman actors like computational code and databases also under the embargo? And what does it mean to have a *property* right—as opposed to a copyright—on a story? How is it possible to own facts that can trace their origins and confirmations to multiple sources that extend beyond a particular newsroom? For example, if a *Wikipedia* page was consulted as part of creating a breaking-news account, can its editorial team end the embargo?

Despite these questions and the distributed nature of news work, the trade press contains several instances of news organizations claiming hot news doctrine protection. In 2009, in *Associated Press v. All Headline News*, the AP claimed that All Headline News repackaged stories it found online—including AP wire stories—and sold them to "newspapers, Internet web portals, websites, and other redistributors of news content." The case was ultimately settled, but not before the U.S. District Court for the southern district of New York agreed to AP's claim of "hot news misappropriation."[201] In 2010, in *Barclays Capital v. FlyOnTheWall.com* (a financial news website), before the decision was overturned on appeal, the U.S. District Court for the southern district of New York required "*Fly* to wait until 10 a.m. EST before publishing the facts associated with analyst research released before the market opens, and to postpone publication for at least two hours for research issued after the opening bell."[202] And in 2014, Dow Jones won a $5 million judgment against the UK-based financial news site *Ransquawk* after using the hot news doctrine to claim that the site was "pirating its content by broadcasting news within seconds of publication to traders and other subscribers."[203] It had earlier claimed hot news misappropriation and won an undisclosed settlement against *Briefing.com* for the site's "systematic and often instantaneous misappropriation of Dow Jones headlines and articles."[204]

Even without bringing suit or claiming hot news misappropriation, news can be delayed when private hosts of newsworthy events meter the speed of reporters' social media usage. The University of Washington reprimanded a reporter with the *Tacoma News Tribune* for sending so many tweets during a basketball game (fifty-three) that they amounted to "live broadcasting," a violation of the school's policy on unlicensed real-time coverage.[205]

Temporal Infrastructures   Such temporal control can exist not only in the laws and policies regulating news technologies but also in the technical architectures of media infrastructures inseparable from digital news organizations.

The trade press describes several types of control through temporal infrastructure. One entails content-neutral media platforms deciding—or being forced—to use time as an organizing strategy. For example, although the articles still exist on the news organizations' own sites, the European Union's "right to be forgotten" legislation forces intermediaries like Google to remove certain content from its search index, effectively making news from sites like the *New York Times*,[206] the BBC,[207] and others invisible to many Web users.

Other time-based decisions are made by the intermediaries themselves. When Google updated its search engine in 2011 to favor content that is about "recent events, hot topics, current reviews and breaking news items,"[208] news organizations were forced to reformat stories quickly in ways that appealed to Google's new algorithm.[209] When news organizations choose to offer content through Snapchat, they know that their content will disappear from the platform "after 24 hours or much less."[210] And when news organizations started sharing video through Facebook and Twitter, they found themselves beholden to the platforms' decisions to make videos play automatically—decisions that the trade press quickly criticized as editorially unacceptable after, in 2015, social media users scrolling through Twitter and Facebook were forced to watch footage of two Virginia journalists murdered on air.[211]

In other instances, news organizations—especially those concerned with serving mobile content quickly[212]—sign on to use media platforms in exchange for access to much faster and more robust infrastructures. In the case of Facebook's Instant Articles, news content loads faster when news organizations agree to place content entirely within Facebook's architecture, share usage data, and enter into advertising agreements.[213] In the case of Google's Accelerated Mobile Pages (AMP) project (where content stays in the open Web and news organizations use an AMP version of HTML), increased mobile load times come with access to Google's advertising network and paywall system.[214] Some publishers have expressed reservations about AMP, noting that, in exchange for speed, their stories appear with a google.com URL, and it is difficult for readers to reach the publisher's own website (and advertisers).[215]

Sometimes the sociotemporal patterns of social media platforms force news organizations to reorganize their own understandings of news time. For example, journalists are told that tweets from BBC News circulate on

Twitter for the longest period of time.[216] Knowing that news spreads faster and further on social media depending on the day of the week and time of day,[217] the *Miami Herald* tries to tweet breaking news in the morning and conversational news in the afternoon.[218] In an attempt to maintain visibility to social media in time zones around the world, many publishers are told to devise hand-off procedures among their global newsrooms that ensure there are no temporal breaks in coverage.[219]

Such persistence, though, brings journalists into tense relationships with social media infrastructure. They know they are in competition with platforms like *Wikipedia*[220] and *Reddit*[221] that are developing their own in-house live and breaking news teams. They also are constantly having to rebut the timeliness of old or distant stories that, for unclear reasons, suddenly appear on social media platforms and seem new and relevant. For example, "news" of the death of Nigerian author Chinua Achebe widely circulated in March 2015, even though he died two years earlier in March 2013.[222] Journalists are told to expect such things when social media makes it look like "everything happens all the time."[223]

Reader Rhythms The sociotechnical dimensions of networked news time also lead news organizations to make guesses about how the rhythms of readers are changing in new technological contexts. Even if news organizations could create news times separate from platform infrastructures, they would reencounter them as soon as they tried to reach audiences whose paces and patterns are heavily influenced by technologies.[224]

For example, the *Times* of London and the *Sunday Times* changed when they updated their website, phone, and tablet apps after analyzing their traffic to find that four updates per day are optimal for reaching their subscribers.[225] Vox decided that 8 p.m. is the best time to update its readers, and the Toronto tabloid *Twelve Thirty Six* is entirely organized around providing news that it says is most attractive to readers at 12:36 p.m.[226]

Beyond choosing the best time to update news for readers, news organizations also make content align with how long they think readers will read, using different technologies. The *Guardian*[227] and the *New York Times*[228] invented new one-sentence story forms designed to be read at a glance on the Apple Watch.[229] The *Financial Times* created FastFT to give users "tweet-like" stories designed to keep readers on their site during breaking news events.[230] The startup *News on Demand* was founded to give readers articles that people could read in the time they said they could spare.[231] And journalists are being told that readers will consumer longer stories on mobile phones, but only for about two minutes.[232]

Other consumer-oriented innovations in news time focus on managing time for readers. The *Washington Post* updated its mobile app with a display that shows Uber riders how long is left in their trip to reduce readers' tendency to switch out of the news app.[233] The *New Yorker* is similarly concerned with readers' wandering attentions: it "tries to anticipate when a reader is about to close out of a story and pops up asking if the reader wants an emailed reminder to come back to the spot where they were left off."[234] The *Economist* refuses to link to other websites from within its stories in an effort to give its readers a "sense of completion" and calm any worries that "that they weren't being completely informed,"[235] while *Newsbound* ran a sitewide experiment to adjust how a story was segmented, finding an optimal size of information chunks that resulted in the greatest number of people finishing the story.[236] KPCC radio's website simply tells readers at the bottom of a story that it is no longer being updated and not to expect any new information,[237] while *Quartz*, *Time.com*, and the *Los Angeles Times* use an "infinite scroll" technique to show readers new stories, keeping them in suspense and giving the impression that they will miss out if they leave the site.[238]

Anticipation   Finally, some news organizations often engage in what science and technology scholar Adele Clark (2016) calls "anticipation work"— "tacking back and forth" (p. 90) between empirical information and suspicions about what the future may hold; "deleting, sorting, rearranging, [and] (re)presenting" (p. 94) information with the goal of simplifying data and environments; and hoping for futures that align with suspicions and simplifications. There is little empirical evidence yet in journalism studies of the sociotechnical anticipation work Clark describes,[239] but the trade press shows how some journalists focus on overcoming the surfeits of information they are expected to process by designing systems to predict and manage newsworthy events.

One such project is a relatively simple initiative to take information that reporters need to cover future, predictable events (event anniversaries, elections, holidays) that often exists in calendars, text files, spreadsheets, or human memory and move it to a standardized data structure that can easily be updated and used to organize reporting work.[240]

Other examples are more complex. For example, *Breaking News* created an "emerging story alerts" system that uses a mix of editorial judgment, eyewitness reports, and computational pattern matching to "notify users that a story *could* evolve into a major story."[241] The aim is to scoop competitors, set readers' expectations, and assemble an attentive audience that can be quickly informed if the event turns out to be newsworthy. Reuters has taken this notion in an even more computationally intensive direction, building its News Tracer platform to "monitor Twitter for major breaking news events" and algorithmically "assign verification scores to tweets based on 40 factors, including whether the report is from a verified account, how many people follow those who reported the news, whether the tweets contain links and images, and, in some cases, the structure of the tweets themselves." Its creator says it works best for "'witnessable events' such as bombings and natural disasters" and helps shift some of the burden of witnessing" away from humans to algorithms that can act as pattern-searching watchdogs.[242]

This somewhat lengthy discussion—of how the networked press handles real-time news, creates its memory, delays publication, intersects with platform infrastructures, understands readers' rhythms, and anticipates the future—is meant to demonstrate that a desire for autonomy always involves temporal separations and dependencies among humans and nonhumans. Journalists must fight for independence from what platforms define as the past or urgent or likely to happen, but they also must stay close enough to technological infrastructures to know how and when to assemble audiences and give historical context. As with the other dimensions of press freedom, these temporal twists and turns beg a fundamental question of the networked press: what kind of publics can and should it create with these separations and dependencies? If temporal infrastructures need to change in order to realize new types of publics, we need grounded theories of how sociotechnical infrastructures make time and why those infrastructures are most likely to give us the new publics we need.

Security

The press's ability to guarantee safe and reliable collection and publication of information appears in the trade press as two concerns—the security of journalists and sources and the security of news audiences.

Protecting Journalists and Sources Sociotechnical security for news organizations and sources manifests in several different ways. Journalists are encouraged to use a new set of technologies (such as encrypted phone and texting apps and traffic-anonymizing Tor networks that obscure packet origins and destinations) as well as new practices (such as creating strong passwords, locking devices, and directing colleagues and potential sources to similarly secure environments). The Freedom of the Press Foundation launched a campaign to fund journalistic security.[243] Researchers at Columbia and the University of Washington created a security-minded journalist toolkit (Dispatch)[244] for journalists who were being warned against using cloud-based services like Evernote, Dropbox, and Google Drive that may be mined for data or have connections to third-party data services.[245] The story of Glen Greenwald, who almost missed out on connecting with Edward Snowden because Greenwald did not use PGP encryption, is now an object lesson in professional preparedness,[246] and freelancer Quinn Norton tells in rich detail how her secure work practices helped *ProPublica* expose Russian state corruption.[247] Snowden announced that he is planning to "develop a modified version of Apple's iPhone for journalists who are concerned that they may be the target of government surveillance,"[248] and reporters vulnerable to doxing—that is, having personal information or documents (dox) publicly revealed by hackers as a means of harassing or harming—are instructed in what to do in the event of an attack.[249] Some journalists are even warned against engaging in investigative reporting practices that look like hackers' methods to avoid being labeled as such.[250] Journalists who expertly use information-security tools and habitually follow strong encryption practices may be seen by sources as more reliable reporters.[251] It is professionally beneficial for them to be close to sociotechnical security cultures, but such proximity brings personal risks. There is no one right distance that ensures both autonomy and security.

Much of the trade press discourse focuses on how to make news organizations become sociotechnically safe places for sources to approach.[252] This means hiring journalists who appreciate the value of secure tools and practices and creating initiatives that make it easy for sources to deliver sensitive information. SecureDrop—a tool originally developed by security and information advocate Aaron Swartz that lets whistleblowers leave files for news organizations anonymously using the Tor network—is now being used by the *Guardian*, the *New Yorker*, *ProPublica*, and the *Intercept*.[253] The

New York Times has a similar system called StrongBox,"[254] and *Forbes*'s is called SafeSource.[255] News organizations without such systems are seen as far less likely to receive sensitive information. Their freedom to do investigative reporting projects is intertwined with the stability and reputation of the Tor network and a host of other technologies that make it possible to mask internet addresses and protect source identities.

News organizations describe being concerned about their journalists' security skills, their sources' identities, and their own publishing systems. Google researchers warned news organizations that they are particularly vulnerable to attacks,[256] and news organizations are regularly told to upgrade their sites' security (for example, by using the HTTPS protocol)[257] and respond quickly to security vulnerabilities (such as the OpenSSL authentication bug known as Heartbleed).[258] Yet the trade press describes several incidents of news organizations being hacked. A public radio station nearly lost its entire archive of interviews, music, stories, donor information, and sales data when hackers demanded a bitcoin ransom in exchange for unlocking files it had encrypted;[259] the *New York Times* website went down twice in one month after being attacked by the Syrian Electronic Army;[260] the *Guardian* had eleven of its Twitter accounts hacked by the same group;[261] and a $136 billion U.S. stock market drop was attributed to the group after it hacked into the Associated Press's Twitter account and falsely reported that the White House had been bombed and that President Obama had been injured.[262] In the case of the Twitter hacks, news organizations' closeness to the platform—relying on its security infrastructure to archive and deliver news—meant that they shared in the platform's security vulnerabilities. After the attacks, Twitter warned news organizations that more attacks were likely to come and asked news organizations to help thwart them.[263] Securing the press's freedom to report safely and reliably became a shared concern because news organizations and social media platforms had become tightly intertwined.

Protecting Identities of Audiences The second main theme in the trade press's discussion of security focused on protecting the identities of audiences—groups that are increasingly convened through technologies with uneven records of protecting peoples' privacy. Although journalists were told that people do not mind trading personal information for free digital services,[264] they also learned that people are most comfortable talking about sensitive topics like government surveillance anywhere but on social media platforms[265]—precisely the places where news organizations are increasingly trying to meet audiences. In response to these observations, many writers suggest that perhaps news organizations should be concerned about audiences' privacy.[266] They should alert readers to the fact that comments left under news stories may be subpoenaed by law enforcement because they are not covered under shield law protections,[267] and they should create sites that limit the collection of personal information and insulate readers from systems that commodify them for advertisers.[268] Such concern is rarely translated to action, though, because the trade press usually describes news organizations that are trying to learn about and commodify audiences as much as they can[269] and are engaging in a technological arms race with ad-blocking software by devising new ways of blocking blockers.[270] Although scholars have not yet investigated the issue in detail, these trade press conversations suggest a nascent concern that the right to hear news may require privacy, protection, and disconnection that news organizations and social media platforms are only beginning to appreciate—the opportunity to encounter news and participate in news environments without being tracked and named. When should news consumption be a solitary, private experience, and when should it be a collective, visible event?

News audiences also can find themselves unwittingly becoming sources in news stories as social media platforms mediate between them and journalists. If their social media accounts have open privacy settings, then posts, comments, and connections that make sense in one context can quickly become part of news stories in ways that the trade press struggles to describe: "Is it like quoting something overheard on the street or at a public event? Or is it more like eavesdropping on a conversation at a private party?"[271] Likewise, some writers warned journalists not to treat anonymous sources on secret-sharing sites such as Whisper and Secret—which traffic in both healthy self-disclosure and unsubstantiated gossip—as they would other social media platforms that require people to register.[272] Similarly, several writers posed an ethical dilemma to the press: during protests, how should journalists cover official police statements when they know that law enforcement surveils protesters' social media posts without their knowledge or consent?[273] Reporters could simply repeat official statements without comment because they believe it is not for journalists to decide if police surveillance is lawful or ethical, or they could let audiences know that such statements emerge from warrantless surveillance. Reporters can quickly learn much more about sources than they might ever have revealed in an interview, simply because both audiences and journalists are brought together by social media platforms that collapse contexts (Marwick & boyd, 2011).

Finally, a set of emerging technologies that is becoming part of journalism and publishing is beginning to raise privacy and security questions. Many news organizations are creating virtual reality experiences that immerse audiences in custom-built, three-dimensional worlds.[274] These spaces can be powerful and evocative, but they also are highly instrumented environments that can track not just a user's presence but a host of signals that news readers have never had monitored—exactly where someone looks, what she hears, how long she speaks, what facial expressions elicited responses, which virtual objects she manipulated and for how long, and more.[275] The potential for surveillance in virtual news worlds where almost everything can be measured is unmatched. Similarly, as news organizations like *Quartz* create chat bots designed to integrate with Amazon Echo and Google Home, the voices and habits of news audiences will be recorded, modeled, and connected to third-party databases—actions that have already prompted law enforcement to try to gain access to such systems when they are thought to be relevant to investigations (Sauer, 2017).

Each new platform that news organizations design for or partner with is a potential surveillance environment. As journalists move closer to such technologies and create news experiences that are inseparable from media platforms, they bring audiences along with them. A public right to hear news in such spaces creates opportunities to listen in on audiences, often without their informed consent. If the press is to be seen as a trusted institution by sources and audiences who take risks by letting its infrastructures into their online environments and homes, it will need to show how it distances itself from surveillance architectures. This may mean that the networked press foregoes some connections, relationships, or sources of revenue, but such separations may give it greater legitimacy with publics who need the press's discretion, in turn bringing sources and audiences closer to journalists.

Audiences

News organizations have long struggled with how to see readers simultaneously as consumers whose preferences they are trying to meet, citizens whose opinions they are trying to inform, and sources with information

they need.[276] Press freedom has not been about trying to achieve independence from audiences and their demands. It has been about negotiating an
ideal distance that keeps journalists close enough to audiences to be relevant
and distant enough to maintain a distinct journalistic perspective separate
from what audiences might want. As with other dimensions of networked
press freedom, what we see in the trade press are news organizations continu-
ing to strike these balances but doing so in sociotechnical environments
with new forces of proximity.

Most fundamentally, journalists find themselves trying to distinguish
human versus computational audiences (Lokot & Diakopoulos, 2016;
Woolley & Howard, 2016). They are warned that much of the internet's traffic actually comes from automated bots. These rule-following computer programs can create expressions on social media platforms that are scheduled
or instantaneous and are often indistinguishable from humans to all but
skeptical observers aware of their ubiquity and sophistication. They generate large amounts of bogus traffic,[277] corrupt advertising markets,[278] are seen
as responsible for significant amounts of misinformation during the 2016
U.S. election,[279] and are forcing news organizations to be newly skeptical
of their site analytics[280]—but they also are presented as potential tools for
journalists and as ways to automate public-interest reporting[281] or counter
misinformation instantaneously.[282] Underlying journalists' concerns about
how close they should be to online audiences is a more fundamental question of what exactly defines a news audience in sociotechnical environments populated by humans and nonhumans.

Beyond this existential question, two patterns emerge in trade press
discourse showing how networked press freedom entails negotiating sociotechnical distances with audiences—in how news organizations interact
with audiences through commenting and engagement systems and in
how news organizations give audiences views inside newsrooms and invite
collaboration.

Commenting and Engagement Journalists are overwhelmingly focused
on how they can communicate with audiences constructively when their
systems and habits seem so ill-suited to the scale, speed, and diversity of
online communication. Audiences are communicating with journalists in
larger numbers, faster, and in more ways than ever before—and journalists
are unsure how to respond.[283]

Although news organizations say they value reader comments,[284] see commenters as potential sources,[285] and are told that people leave comments for many different reasons,[286] the vast majority of news organizations are shutting down or fundamentally rethinking their commenting systems.[287] They offer different motivations for doing so. It is too much to ask readers to comment[288] when good feedback is lost among vitriolic comments designed to cause conflict and confusion,[289] and it is too much to ask journalists to reply to comments when news organizations lack the staff to moderate comments properly[290] or the budget required to hire and manage outside moderators.[291] News organizations say that the stories with the most comments unintentionally end up being the most popular stories because the overwhelmingly negative comments draw traffic,[292] and although they are internally skeptical of the value of anonymous comments,[293] they are confusingly told that requiring real names both improves comment quality[294] or has no effect.[295]

They also find that comments can make it harder for readers to understand news stories. *Popular Science* discontinued comments on its stories because it saw hostile and ill-informed commenters spreading misinformation and unfounded doubt among its readers.[296] (It did allow bloggers hosted on its site to decide for themselves whether to enable comments.)[297] The *Los Angeles Times* similarly silenced voices when it announced that it would no longer publish letters denying that humans cause climate change.[298] Both *Popular Science* and the *Times* essentially decided that to serve the parts of their audiences they wanted to engage with and keep close, they were willing to silence and distance themselves from others they thought were not qualified to speak. Many news organizations—Reuters,[299] *Motherboard*,[300] the *Verge*,[301] *The Week*,[302] *HuffingtonPost*,[303] and NPR[304]—agreed and publicly stated that they were discontinuing comments because labor costs were high, better alternatives existed on social media sites, or as the *Chicago Sun-Times* said, it simply did not know how to "foster a productive discussion rather than an embarrassing mishmash of fringe ranting and ill-informed, shrill bomb-throwing."[305] *Reddit* founded its news spinoff, *UpVoted*, in part on the principle that comments harmed audiences.[306]

When news organizations decided to leave comments on their sites, the trade press offered advice on how to do it[307] and news organizations partnered with technology companies[308] and design communities[309] to reinvent audience engagement. And news organizations individually experimented with different approaches. *The Verge* hosted general, open forums instead of story-specific comments.[310] The *New York Times* limited the number of stories it opened for comments each day[311] and encouraged commenters to moderate themselves, creating badges and rewards systems that gave privileges to commenters with good track records.[312] Reuters restricted comments to opinion pieces,[313] the *National Journal* let only subscribers comment,[314] and *Tablet* tried to charge readers for the privilege of commenting[315] before ultimately moving its audience engagement to Facebook.[316] Several news sites also edged closer to social media: *BuzzFeed* required Facebook accounts to access its chat bots,[317] and after finding itself deleting approximately 75 percent of its site's comments,[318] the *HuffingtonPost* required commenters to log in with Facebook accounts[319] and also required that such accounts be verified by having users give Facebook their phone numbers.[320] That is, to keep commenters on its site, *HuffPo* also forces them away: by outsourcing moderation and verification, it moves readers closer to Facebook, forcing them to accept that company in exchange for proximity to *HuffPo*.

Similarly, when news organizations abandoned custom commenting systems for social media platforms, the trade press traced their different approaches. Reuters conducted scheduled, topic-specific Twitter chats in which its journalists answered readers' questions and listened to feedback. *Mic* chooses particular stories to post to its Facebook, Twitter, and Tumblr accounts, stressing that it "doesn't just leave it alone from there" but moderates conversations on its stories wherever it finds them. Deciding that it was "fine" with its "communities organizing off-site, which is what they're going to do anyway, whether we have comments or not," *USA Today*'s FTW site added WhatsApp and SMS feedback channels; it also uses tools like SimpleReach, Chartbeat, and CrowdTangle to watch how its stories are being talked about on social media, choosing to "engage in those conversations where they're happening, or not."[321] The BBC more actively tries to engage audiences by hosting conversations on new platforms as they appear, most recently using WhatsApp, WeChat, Line, and Yik Yak to interact with readers.[322] Finally, although *Popular Science* uses social media platforms to engage with audiences, it also still exchanges hand-written letters with readers and hosts events where they can gather and converse.[323]

All of these negotiations involve tensions between positive and negative freedom. News organizations' capacity to host verified commenters means that commenters must relinquish their freedom from social media platforms. News organizations' ability to enact their editorial principles means accepting social media platforms' community guidelines—tying their news judgments to the technology companies' policies, norms, and algorithms and accepting the ways that platforms foster or silence debate.[324] And getting closer to platforms' users can mean getting further away from other audiences and demographics that use social media less or in different ways.[325] Finally, meeting audiences off site does not necessarily alleviate the risks that news organizations will meet communities they were trying to avoid, as the *Wall Street Journal* learned when Anonymous held a "comment flashmob" on its Facebook page.[326]

Access and Collaboration   Although in much of the sociotechnical work of interacting with audiences, news organizations create strategic relationships to platforms that limit readers' participation, at other times news organizations are trying to create closer direct relationships with audiences as they try to produce news with them. Early examples of these coproductions involved news organizations that invited readers to submit media and then tried to figure out how to distinguish this content from professionally produced media within existing notions of journalistic quality. CNN's iReport was an early and particularly successful example,[327] but initiatives like the *Guardian*'s GuardianWatch have continued to appear.[328]

Beyond systems for accepting user-generated content, several news organizations have created views into news work and infrastructures for collaborating with audiences. One tension these projects revealed was just how much access to give to the audience. In 2011, the *Guardian* created its Open Newslist project to let audiences see story topics and assignments as they evolved and provide feedback to editors and sources to reporters using the Twitter hashtag #opennews and an on-site liveblog.[329] Although the initiative earned praise from some as an example of journalistic collaboration,[330] others questioned whether it was just a performance of coproduction because ultimate power still rested with editorial staff and the added visibility guaranteed no additional media accountability.[331] Other organizations give audiences curated views or brief glimpses into their news work. The *New York Times* Insider offers premium subscribers behind-the-scenes accounts of how journalists work,[332] and *BuzzFeed* briefly made its internal analytics dashboard open for public viewing.[333] In all cases, news organizations are not offering truly unfettered access to journalists and newsrooms but are carefully configuring systems and views of those systems in ways that give audiences limited opportunities to see and engage with news work.

Other collaborations are less performative and more complex and have journalistic outputs. For example, several news organizations offer application programming interfaces (APIs) that are essentially software toolkits to give outsiders access to some news organization data, under certain conditions, letting them create new sites and apps that repurpose journalistic work.[334] The *New York Times*, the *Guardian*, NPR, and *USA Today* all offer such APIs, sustaining a small but active community of entrepreneurs, hobbyists, students, and researchers whose projects depend on how well news organization maintain their data infrastructures, what policies they set, and whether they answer programmers' questions.[335] In exchange for providing such access and services, news organizations gain visibility, fulfill organizational missions, discover technical problems with their infrastructures, and sometimes earn small amounts of licensing revenue from premium API subscribers.

An alternative form of collaboration entails crowdsourced work that requires no programming skills or interest. An early example was the *Guardian*'s Expense Scandal project in which it asked audiences to help find patterns and anomalies in large databases of government expenses records.[336] NPR affiliate WNYC built a site for people to provide geotagged reports of cicada sightings during a once-in-seventeen-years surge in the insect's population, and the NPR apps team built a mobile phone app to crowdsource reports of children's playgrounds, trigging a series of stories about the lack of sites accessible to children with disabilities.[337]

ProPublica is a leader in this type of collaboration and has organized several similar initiatives, maintaining a Get Involved site to show readers how they can contribute to data-driven reporting.[338] To track lawmakers' positions on a gun reform bill, it asked readers to "find the contact information for their local senator's office using *ProPublica*'s extensive Senate office database, find a statement or contact the office to get a comment on the bill, and fill out a quick survey on *ProPublica*'s website."[339] To analyze a large database of records on election spending quickly and uncover any potential abuses, it "got hundreds of readers to sift through television ad spending records" and report back with patterns.[340] And it even created a "reporting recipe"[341] to help journalists at other news organizations use its free, publicly available, geotagged database of incidents in which local public schools restrained or secluded children.[342] (*ProPublica* once even asked *Reddit* users what data-driven investigative projects it should tackle next.)[343] In all cases, in exchange for creating and managing such infrastructures of collaboration, news organizations are able to do large-scale data-driven projects that they could never accomplish with existing staff. Rather than trying to keep audience members at bay, these news organizations are trying to attract readers, make them collaborators, and benefit from their free labor. They use sociotechnical systems to bring themselves closer to audiences and enable their freedom to tell particular data-intensive stories.

Finally, some news organizations are working with audiences to develop entirely new products or improve existing ones. Finnish magazine *Olivia* developed custom collaboration software to let journalists and readers co-create an issue. They worked together to find "a story topic, angle, and interviewees" and shared "experiences and expertise," and with "the crowd's input," journalists drafted stories, with audiences following along and chiming in as writing progressed.[344] *BuzzFeed* prototyped a new version of its newsletter by showing drafts to audiences, asking for feedback, and implementing suggestions,[345] and *Gawker* let readers create their own headlines and introductions for stories they shared from the site on social media.[346] In other instances, audiences helped news organizations format existing content and, in turn, attract new audiences. Viewers of PBS's *NewsHour* translated videos into non-English languages, helping the show attract new demographics,[347] and *New York Times* readers helped the paper index its archives, creating new collections of content that the paper can market and sell.[348]

Across these points of access and collaboration, we see negotiations of what Jan-Hinrik Schmidt and Wiebke Loosen (2015) might call "inclusion distance"—expectations between readers and journalists alike about why audiences participate, how their roles differ from reporters, what types of participation are more or less important, and what impact audiences can have on news work when they are included in journalists' networks. The added dimension here, though, is that many of these negotiations live among both people and nonhumans—social platforms with verification systems that require documentation, popularity algorithms whose calculations cannot distinguish well-meaning comments from uncivil trolling, analytics systems that track conversations across social media platforms, APIs that limit how often and under what conditions hobbyist programmers can query data, and large-scale databases with nonexistent or nonsensical metadata that cry out for human organization. It seems strange now to think that, to be free, news organizations need only distance from their audiences. In fact, they need to negotiate sociotechnical separations and dependencies—getting closer to or farther from humans and nonhumans—as they try to convene publics. I offer here no pronouncement of what kind of proximity these humans and nonhumans should construct but suggest that different versions of networked press freedom—and thus different types of publics—will emerge from different types of sociotechnical proximity.

Revenue

The networked press has been in a revenue crisis for years. Print circulation and its lucrative advertising revenue have been dwindling, and digital advertising fails to make up the difference; consumers accustomed to getting news for free are reluctant to pay for online journalism; and few news organizations know exactly what makes subscription plans successful (Arrese, 2015; R. Fletcher & Nielsen, 2016; Myllylahti, 2016; Pickard & Williams, 2014; Socolow, 2010). In this crisis, the press is searching for money, but it also is trying to find business models that align with its self-image as an industry that historically has carved out editorial independence and provided investors with lucrative returns (E. L. Cohen, 2002) while leveraging two main revenue sources—advertisers wanting to reach consumers and audiences willing to pay for news (J. T. Hamilton, 2006).

In the networked press, there is an additional actor beyond journalists, advertisers, and audiences—the sociotechnical systems whose configurations can commodify news and deliver revenues but sometimes at the expense of the industry's self-image as an editorially independent field beholden to neither readers nor markets. As the press becomes increasingly intertwined with commodification technologies, the definitions and achievements of editorial independence are called into question anew. The trade press is preoccupied with this question of how to earn revenue through sociotechnical systems—a preoccupation that, when examined for its separations and dependencies, reveals a networked press struggling to reconcile economic security with institutional autonomy. The trade press reveals six dimensions to the sociotechnical construction of press revenue—configuring paywalls, commodifying readers, crowdfunding, commodifying journalistic expertise, creating sponsored content, and designing partnerships.

Paywalls   The trade press describes an ongoing search for revenue,[349] primarily by figuring out how to create a virtual "barrier between an internet user and a news organization's online content" (Pickard & Williams, 2014, p. 195) that can be crossed only by paying money. The short and ongoing history of news paywalls is the story of news organizations trying to band together, distinguish themselves from others, court some audiences while shunning others, and ask hard questions about how their value should be commodified through pricing technologies that could change at any time, for unclear reasons. Early stories revolved around the novelty that online news organizations would charge readers at all.[350] Because audiences had grown accustomed to online news being free, there was a great deal of skepticism that anyone would ever pay for news.[351] Hoping for an industry-wide shift that would free them from having to negotiate their own individual strategies, news organizations wondered how many others would build paywalls,[352] how many readers paywalls would affect,[353] how much they should charge and if charges should differ across devices,[354] and whether their paper was sufficiently unique enough (that is, distant from competitors)[355] to support paid subscriptions. They were consistently told that few people would pay for online news (only 10 percent in 2014)[356] and that any increases in revenue would come with reduced traffic,[357] which worried them that paywalls would drive away readers[358] or enable journalists to connect only with affluent readers.[359]

News organizations' concerns about how close to get to readers—and which readers—has manifested in a series of paywall experiments. How many articles should be offered for free before charging? Estimates range from one to twenty per month and have changed over time.[360] Too many free articles makes readers think they never will be charged—and they are insulted when the time comes to pay—but not enough free articles makes it hard for readers to see the value of the product they eventually will be charged for.[361] Some news organizations have tried charging for access to certain content[362] (a move the *Los Angeles Times* quickly reversed after charging for its calendar of events caused a 97 percent drop in traffic),[363] for each article,[364] for access to particular journalists,[365] or for premium sites with fewer ads and better interface designs.[366] One proposal entailed letting readers themselves set the prices of articles, making the price of a story drop the more people clicked on it—essentially aligning news organizations with a logic of popularity that made some articles more likely to be purchased.[367] In all these experiments, news organizations were trying to figure out which parts of themselves to commodify for which audiences, balancing unfettered connections with readers against the promise of revenue.

Another class of experiments focused on fundamentally rethinking the paywall. Some focused on language-specific content. The Dutch news startup *Blendle* banded Dutch newspapers and magazines together into a single repository of Dutch-language news in which readers would pay only for articles they read.[368] Piano Media similarly tried to create a paywall covering all news organizations in Slovenia, but the experiment failed after the Slovenian market proved too small for a single paywall and individual news organizations left to try their own paywall configurations.[369] The paywall itself became a diagnostic of how audiences and journalist alike saw news as like or unlike that of competitors.

Some news organizations—*Slate*,[370] the *Los Angeles Times*,[371] and the *Wall Street Journal*[372]—tried to avoid the paywall stigma by calling subscriptions "memberships" that would give audiences closer, long-term relationships with news organizations. Others tried to capitalize on readers' close associations with social media platforms, offering unmetered access to stories shared via Twitter or Facebook,[373] or they leveraged readers' own relationships, trying to convert nonsubscribers by giving subscribers "gift" articles that they could share and let others read for free.[374]

Despite these different experiments, the trade press still sees paywalls as dynamic and unstable. People routinely evade them by altering URLs, deleting browser histories, refusing cookies, and sharing passwords,[375] and many news organizations have uneven policies on when to use paywalls, dropping them idiosyncratically for public emergencies, special events, and advertising partnerships.

Commodified Readers   News organizations also use their knowledge of audiences to turn readers and subscribers into revenue generators.[376] Many news organizations sell to advertisers the data they gather when people sign up for subscriptions, the traffic patterns they observe on their websites, or the right to use tracking software to surveil visitors. Even readers who do not pay are still commodified as data sources: the closer news organizations can get to paying and nonpaying readers, they more they can earn from advertisers.[377] Some news organizations also entice site visitors into answering surveys for technology companies and marketers, giving them news access in exchange for their opinions as consumers.[378] The German news site *Neue Zürcher Zeitung* tracks all of its visitors and, without their knowledge, profiles them and targets personalized marketing and free content to those it thinks are most likely to become paid subscribers. The idea of being free from all readers and their preferences in order to pursue a pure editorial vision is not part of these tracking and commodification strategies. News organizations are using analytics and marketing systems to try to get very close to readers, especially those they see as being most valuable.

Crowdfunding   Another reason to get close to readers is to make them investors in addition to subscribers. Separate from news organizations' paywalls, a flurry of crowdfunding platforms has arisen to generate funds for specific people and projects. These sites have fostered a new class of reader patrons who pledge small amounts of money to help journalists and news organizations realize projects. The closer they can get to potential donors, the greater chance they have of achieving financial freedom—although questions linger about what kind of professional autonomy emerges from such relationships.[379]

Many different people use news crowdfunding sites. Freelancers are able to raise money and reputations on such sites,[380] for-profit news organizations have used them to fund beat reporting and get access to data,[381] nonprofit news organizations have used them to hire interns,[382] and a team of professional journalists crowdfunded money to teach a course on data journalism.[383] *Spot.us* was an early example of a crowdfunding website focused on journalism, but several variants have arisen. The Dutch news site *De Correspondent* funds its own organization through crowdfunding,[384] *NewsFreed* focuses on crowdfunding investigative reporting,[385] *Emphas.is* focuses on photojournalism,[386] *Contributoria* crowdfunds news projects that are then developed in the open while visible to the funding community,[387] and *Beacon* places a fee on top of all crowdfunded stories to create a bonus pool shared among writers whose stories patrons recommend.[388] The popular general crowdfunding site Kickstarter eventually created a special section for journalism projects.[389] Across all variants, there are goals to create close relationships with particular funding communities to build with patrons a sense that projects are co-constructed and that donations are actually investments. The trade press is rife with stories about how to make journalism projects succeed on crowdfunding sites[390] and how to create new crowdfunding communities.[391]

As sociotechnical sites of networked press freedom, crowdfunding communities are one of the clearest examples of journalists using communication platforms to get close enough to people to make them patrons and audiences while trying to maintain enough distance to avoid being drawn into clientlike relationships in which journalists sacrifice their power to tell audiences things they do not want to hear. This concern appears in both the trade press and academic scholarship: some journalists see crowdfunding as a way to involve audiences and create what they see as publicly relevant news,[392] while other commentators caution that proximity to donors brings clientlike responsibility.[393] This tension is confirmed by crowdfunding scholars who find that "journalists who crowdfund strongly believe in the journalistic norm of autonomy, but at the same time feel a great deal of responsibility towards their funders" (Hunter, 2015, p. 272).

Commodified Journalistic Expertise   Because news organizations are seen as sites of traditional journalistic practice as well as places where information is created, verified, and disseminated, news organizations are beginning to capitalize on their currencies as information professionals. For example, the nonprofit news site *ProPublica* earned approximately $30,000 in revenue by selling data that its journalists gathered, vetted, and offered access to through custom-built APIs.[394] The organization's data expertise—and its brand as a trusted source of information—leads purchasers to see it less as a traditional news organization and more as a trusted knowledge broker. Other news organizations have similarly positioned parts of themselves closer to data work than to journalism, creating APIs that give premium access—and the right to create new commercial ventures—to those who pay.[395] The *Guardian* offers a "bespoke" API license to those wanting to place advertisements alongside API content, and *USA Today* similarly offers premium, paid API accounts to those building projects that require unlimited data access and permission to earn revenue.[396] These two news organizations—through their API commodifications—move themselves closer to commercial domains. In contrast, public broadcaster NPR specifies in its API terms of use that API data is only for "personal, non-commercial use."[397]

Sponsored Content   Academic research (Brandstetter & Schmalhofer, 2014; Carlson, 2015c; Wojdynski, 2016) and trade press discourse[398] agree that sponsored content—sometimes called native advertising, paid content, or promoted stories[399]—confuses most readers by making content that advertisers commission resemble news that journalists produce. Despite (or because of) this confusion and because such content can earn far more revenue than other types of advertising,[400] the trade press is filled with discussions of how to make sponsored content that both generates revenue and meets editorial standards.

Some news organizations, though, describe wanting little separation between commercial and journalistic content. *BuzzFeed* took media posted by *Reddit* users, repackaged it as sponsored content (which accounts for "nearly all the company's revenues"), and claimed that such advertisements were copyright-protected transformative uses.[401] The company's strategy is acrobatic—staying close enough to *Reddit* to mimic its users, collapsing distinctions between its commercial and journalistic content, and then arguing that its sponsored content is sufficiently distinct from *Reddit* media, making its revenue generation acceptable under copyright law's transformative-uses exemption. *HuffingtonPost*'s approach is simpler: it calls for sponsored content that "looks and feels similar to its editorial environment."[402]

Other news organizations try to strike balances when displaying sponsored content. But such balances are hard to strike when online environments vary greatly in their visual styles and interaction designs. There are no clear standards to rely on when trying to distinguish commercial and journalistic content, so each news organization invents its own method. For example, in announcing the company's new "native advertising platform," the *New York Times*'s publisher promised clear differences between commercial and journalistic work: "a distinctive color bar, the words 'Paid Post,' the relevant company logo, a different typeface and other design cues to let readers know exactly what they are looking at." (The *Times* also promised to use analytics to alert it if readers appeared to be confusing the two types of content but did not reveal how it would see such patterns of confusion.)[403] The *Washington Post* allows paid posts within its comments sections but calls them "sponsored views."[404] *Sports Illustrated* experimented with forcing readers to watch a video advertisement before reading a story, creating a perceived connection between the story and the advertiser, even when none existed or was intended.[405] *Quartz* created a new data-driven story format that uses statistics and numbers to explain issues, but it intersperses what it calls "sponsored data points" among news stories. Finally, the *MinnPost* created a "funded beats strategy" in which editorial leadership identifies newsworthy topics and issues that the board of directors then tries to match with individual funders, creating a close—but firewalled, the paper says—connection between wealthy donors interested in producing news on particular topics and journalists tasked with reporting on those beats.[406] Another strategy is to create workforce separations—to hire former journalists to create branded online content that inevitably reads like news stories but that can honestly be described as originating from the business part of an organization and not from its news part.[407]

Sometimes, trying to separate sponsored and journalistic content implicates social media platforms, relying on their designs, habits, and expectations. For example, in 2013, the Associated Press created a minor concern in the trade press[408] when it began putting out sponsored tweets under its own Twitter handle. Such tweets began with the words "SPONSORED CONTENT," but some worried that such labels made little sense outside of news site contexts, that the AP could not adequately track whether the tweets confused users, that it was hard to understand what retweets of such advertisements meant, and that such tweets seemed similar to the "promoted tweets" format that Twitter introduced in 2010[409] but that AP was not using. Although the Twitter corporation did not mind the potential confusion, Google has for several years warned publishers that it would not include in its search index pages that were solely or primarily paid links and has told news organizations that they must clearly separate sponsored content from their journalistic stories or risk having their entire sites removed from the search engine's index.

In sponsored content, we see several kinds of separations and dependencies at play. Some news organizations seem apathetic about separating commercial and journalistic content or are designing for some amount of revenue-generating confusion. Others are resigned to the fact that some readers will be confused but try to create distinctions through design techniques and labor strategies. And others seem content to let distinctions reside on social media platforms that they use to serve both commercial and journalistic work. Through this messy mix, the press must find a way to signal that its journalism is independent from sponsored content. But such signals must not be so strong that they ward off the revenue-generating clicks, tweets, and likes of confused readers or readers who see the differences but are unbothered by news organizations that intersperse commercial and journalistic content.

Partnerships   Some forms of revenue come when news organizations partner with technology companies or create partnerships through new technology infrastructures, with trade press stories focusing on how news organizations can earn revenue by staying close to and distinct from competitors and social media platforms. The Associated Press showed how news organizations can band together to fight a technology that was thought to be harming revenues. In 2012, the AP and twenty-eight other news organizations launched NewsRight, a consortium designed to charge licensing fees to aggregators that were algorithmically repackaging and selling its news content.[410] The consortium was meant to demonstrate the power that news organizations can wield when they set aside competitive rivalries in the service of industrywide action, but the initiative eventually fell apart as the technology to track aggregated content failed and individual publishers decided to pursue their own individual monetization strategies.[411] Other technology-focused partnerships among news organizations have proved more successful. After the *Washington Post* offered free digital access to its site for any subscriber to a local newspaper within the consortium it assembled,[412] both *Post* traffic and local paper subscriptions increased.[413] The strategy showed how news organizations can create complementary online access schemes by agreeing to leverage their respective differences and segment audiences and advertising markets.

In other partnerships, news organizations have leveraged the publishing channels of third-party platforms, both using and critiquing their revenue models. In 2011, the trade press tried to make sense of Apple's plan to let content providers sell subscriptions on apps that ran on Apple hardware. The company originally said that price of subscriptions sold outside the apps "can be no lower than the price offered inside the app" (effectively capping news organizations' subscription revenue) and that "customer data for in-app purchases will remain with Apple" (cutting news organizations off from a vital source of information about their audiences and a potential source of revenue).[414] After industry uproar, exceptions to these policies eventually were made for news organizations, and not long afterward, Google offered a competing platform that publishers saw as more flexible and lucrative,[415] and news publishers focused on creating mobile websites that existed outside of apps and thus beyond the reach of app store makers like Apple and Google.[416] These news app incidents revealed a situation in which news organizations were sufficiently beholden to Apple to make such exceptions necessary, Apple was eager enough to host news apps that it conceded, and Google was interested in enough in news that it offered a competing product. The definitions and viabilities of news apps emerged only when journalists forced a technology company to distinguish the news business from other types of content production and when they began exploring technologies that would let them avoid app markets altogether. The networked press's freedom to set subscription prices and reach mobile audiences required negotiations of policy and technology that both connected and distanced news organizations from platform makers.

Other news and tech partnerships are more focused on generating new content, sharing advertising revenue, and creating new audiences. Snapchat's media partnership program shares advertising revenue with news organizations,[417] and Facebook's Live program pays news organizations to create original and exclusive video experiences that are posted directly to Facebook, generating advertising income for both the platform and news organizations. For news organizations, the tradeoff with such proximity to Facebook is agreeing to work within its video format, house news content on its system, and know that only Facebook users see that news.[418] Other partnerships look more like brand relationships. The *New York Times* offered people free access to its website but only when readers accessed the sites through a Starbucks network,[419] guests staying at Trump hotels got free online access to the *New York Times* because it was "Donald Trump's favorite newspaper,"[420] the Associated Press experimented with technology that would automatically print its latest bulletins on restaurant receipts,[421] and a limited-term subscription to the *Washington Post* (owned by Amazon founder and CEO Jeff Bezos) offered a membership to Amazon's Prime program.[422] As news organizations affiliate with brands through infrastructural partnerships, they become closer to certain consumers and demographics and potentially further from an image as a general public information provider.[423]

Finally, some types of partnerships are virtually invisible to readers but still powerfully shape news revenue generation. Many news organizations use software to block ad-blocking technologies, essentially engaged in an ongoing, largely hidden technological arms race to ensure that their advertisers' messages reach readers actively trying to distance themselves from advertising.[424] And separate from news organizations and their use of paywalls, several of the companies that make paywall technologies have merged, rapidly shrinking the competitive landscape of paywall infrastructures.[425] Piano Media[426] and Press+[427] were founded to create and manage paywalls, direct news organizations on how best to configure their systems, and share research on what made paywalls successful (for example, sites with more daily stories sold more subscriptions),[428] but as they merged with each other and then paywall maker Tinypass, they created a single entity that is in a far more powerful position to dictate the features of paywall technologies and the terms of agreements with news organizations. (This power may be challenged with Google's addition of a paywall feature to its AMP publishing system.)[429]

Across these different partnerships, the networked press emerges as a distributed and somewhat unstable entity whose autonomy depends on why and how it affiliates with or breaks free from competitors, sponsors, and technology companies, each of which values news differently. Networked press freedom is not simply about being *free from* markets or commercial revenue. Indeed, it is often difficult for news organizations to trace exactly where funding originates, under what circumstances it flows, and whom it benefits. But revenue could become a diagnostic of press freedom—a way for news organizations to take stock of where their infrastructures intersect with those of revenue sources and ask what kind of publics such intersections underwrite. The key lesson here is not that news organizations are too dependent or not dependent enough on online revenue sources but that through their separations from and relationships with online funders, news organizations have an opportunity to indicate what kind of publics their funders support.

Facts

Journalists make and analyze what they see as facts. The history of press objectivity is, in part, the story of how social, technological, economic, and cultural forces shape how news is seen as separate from reporters' own interests and values and instead simply reflects truths that are assumed to exist regardless of whether reporters provide accounts of them. Although there are stable, news-relevant facts that are beyond the reach of this constructivist view of truth, scholars have largely debunked the presumption that facts are easily separated from values. Most scholars see journalistic truth as an achievement: forces align to make value-laden accounts born of particular contexts into facts that are stable and legitimate enough to circulate largely without challenge.[430] The press's autonomy requires freedom from forces that undermine its ability to make and publish what it sees as facts, as well as the capacity to connect to and work with sources that enrich and protect its definitional work. Because social facts are largely made and not found, the freedom to create truths requires both separations and dependencies.

Today, many scholars see the power to create journalistic truths as intertwined with sociotechnical systems: structured and standardized content-management systems archive events and classify information, journalists acquire and make databases in the course of investigative reporting, fact-checking software and websites constantly rank and grade the truthfulness of sources, and algorithms claim to provide neutral results but often are inseparable from systematic bias (C. W. Anderson & Kreiss, 2013; Bucher, 2017b; Dörr & Hollnbuchner, 2016; Godler & Reich, 2012; Graves, 2016; S. C. Lewis & Westlund, 2015; Parasie, 2015; M. L. Young & Hermida, 2015). The likelihood that journalists think a particular piece of evidence counts or can be trusted emerges less from traditional processes of reporting and verification and more from what is known about the source of the assertion (C. W. Anderson, 2018). In some ways, this is an old story of journalists figuring out how to trust sources, but in other ways, it is a newer phenomenon in which trust cannot emerge from the newsroom and be created by journalists but lives instead in a distributed set of human and nonhuman actors working together to make truths legitimate, stable, and portable. The networked press's autonomy lies in its freedom from some of these actors and its capacity to engage, configure, and challenge others. Three dynamics characterize much of the trade press discourse on the press's sociotechnical construction of truth—collaborative facts, architectural facts, and probable facts.

Collaborative Facts   Much of the trade press describes journalists, technologists, and technologies as co-constructing facts. Andy Carvin (then a reporter with NPR) provided a relatively early example of collaborative fact making when, from Washington, DC, he used social media to report on the 2011 Arab Spring uprisings. He openly acknowledged that he shared information that he could not verify himself and asked his network of followers to determine whether claims about people and events were true.[431] Such outreach verification also can happen less urgently. After working with experts, *New York Times* reporter C. J. Chivers could not verify the "identify an unusual cluster bomb found in Libya," so he asked for help from a blog he trusted to give accurate information and not scoop his story,[432] and several reporters use the question-and-answer platform Quora to learn about locations they cannot visit and gauge how much interest there is in a story before investing time and energy verifying information.[433] This same ethic drives the news aggregator *Storyful*, which published a list of questions it asks of social media content as it tries to determine its veracity, including "Are streetscapes similar to geo-located photos on Panoramio or Google Street View?" and "Are there any landmarks that allow us to verify the location via Google Maps or Wikimapia?"[434] *Carvin* and *Storyful* expect their audiences to be active, committed to the search for high-quality information, and skilled with the social media platforms that can provide the accuracy journalists cannot. Several dangers arise from such closeness to audiences and technologies. For example, 23 percent of U.S. adults have knowingly or unknowingly shared a false story;[435] until it made changes to its algorithm, Google regularly ranked holocaust deniers high in its search rankings;[436] and Twitter quickly spread a false report that South Carolina Governor Nikki Haley was about to be indicted,[437] a claim that could not be practically countered or corrected because it was virtually impossible to reassemble the Twitter audience that had seen and shared the lie. (The AP includes in its social media guidelines instructions on how to correct erroneous tweets.)[438] Relying on audiences and platforms to produce high-quality information and act as verification networks requires that journalists have a kind of second-order trust—a faith in people, policies, and technologies that are often invisible or unexaminable but that become journalists' collaborators.

In 2016, there were several instances of failed collaborative fact production among humans and nonhumans. After firing the team of former journalists that it had hired to curate its Trending Topics section, Facebook saw a dramatic uptick in the amount of fake news being spread through the section.[439] Facebook's failure to find a good balance between editorial and algorithmic labor meant that its site became a source of misinformation and "fake news," creating a major scandal several months later and after the U.S. presidential election as the dissemination of fake news became a major focus of the field. Journalists debated how much fake news had spread, who was responsible for its dissemination, why anyone would produce such information, what partnerships (among journalists, technology companies, audiences, educators, and government regulators) would fix the problem, and whether the problem was new and worthy of attention.[440] In the wake of the fake news scandal, a number of sociotechnical initiatives emerged, including a crowdsourced list of design ideas for journalists and technology companies alike, started by Eli Pariser, who coined the term "filter bubble";[441] a Harvard-MIT hackathon to invent new truth-making technologies;[442] an Indiana University project to visualize false news and show people how sharing spreads misinformation;[443] and HoaxBot, a Twitter account that automatically responded to people who shared fake news.[444]

Recognizing their joint responsibility—Twitter's former head of news said that "social media companies alone shouldn't have to manage fake news"[445]—news organizations and technology companies created a formal consortium to address the problem. Called FirstDraft, it aims to define fake news and work to limit its production and dissemination[446] and recently created a "trust kit" of best practices and technological tools designed to "rebuild trust with communities."

These collaborative efforts at creating facts and policing those who spread misinformation reflect a new kind of press autonomy. Journalists cannot simply distance themselves from audiences for fear of encountering falsities because those same audiences are often the ones they need to work with to verify information. Similarly, journalists cannot separate themselves from technology companies that may be more tolerant of misinformation than they are because these same companies are also news distribution channels. The public right to hear and determine the veracity of information is intertwined with a network of journalistic and technological actors with both competing and complementary truth goals.

Architectural Facts   In other moments, the construction of journalistic truth lives in technological architectures—databases and interface designs that certify and signal the veracity of data. Not only is data-driven journalism an increasingly visible and prominent part of the field—there is now an entire news awards program dedicated to data journalism[447]—but data journalism has long been offered as a reason that government databases need to be opened and cleaned and that state officials need to be able to describe the data contained therein.[448] The data that such journalism uses are often seen to possess an inherent truth separate from reporters' analyses of the data or journalistic judgments about newsworthiness of the stories that use the data. (In contrast, although the *Guardian* maintains an extensive data journalism team under the motto "Facts Are Sacred,"[449] it is self-described as an editorial staff whose work is integral, not ancillary, to story judgments.[450] And although *ProPublica* provides and sells data through its online data store, it offers rich context on how data were generated, what they may mean, and how it thinks reporters should use them.)[451] Others, though, seem to suggest separations. The *Dallas Morning News* is partnering with government officials to collect and visualize data that combines state and user-submitted reports. The project removes data generation from the newsroom, with a *Morning News* editor saying "we're the experts at communicating to the public, and they're the experts at gathering police data."[452] Similarly, Detective.io, a platform created by a "network of data journalists and developers" called *Journalism++*, "lets users input large data sets, predominantly of people or organizations, and then maps the connections between them into an easily searchable database."[453] Some writers suggest that data are facts that come first and are distinct from stories *about* data, while others caution that data and the facts they suggest must appear in social contexts[454] (people may agree on a fact's existence but disagree about its significance) and that "interpreting and presenting data requires making judgments and possibly mistakes" that journalists need to reflect on and audiences deserve to know about.[455]

Outside of news organizations, social media platforms are wrestling with the issue of whether they are or should be sources of facts versus sites of conversation. After the 2016 presidential election's uproar about fake news, one Facebook executive—after several weeks of disclaiming responsibility for the site hosting fake news and learning that even its "verified" sites spread misinformation[456]—admitted that "we resisted having standards on fake news. That was wrong."[457] The company then created an initiative to prevent fake news providers from using its advertising network, made design changes that would caution users against sharing fake news, and gave fact-checking sites access to parts of its architecture that could label misinformation—but Facebook did not define how *it* defined "fake news,"[458] nor did it provide funding to fact-checking sites it partnered with (ABC News, Snopes, PolitiFact, FactCheck.org, and AP),[459] expecting the extra work to occur without compensation.[460] It seemed to presume that an understanding of the phenomenon existed somewhere, elsewhere, and that its job was to implement that understanding. Similarly, but before the presidential election, Google added "fact-checked" tags to news articles, working with a community of news organizations to "follow the commonly accepted criteria for fact checks" and create an algorithm that "determines whether an article might contain fact checks."[461] In both cases, platforms are struggling to locate fact checking within computational infrastructure, developing with journalists automated and algorithmic processes designed to approximate their expertise.

Probable Facts   The idea of approximation—Google's fact-checking algorithm promises to determine "whether an article might contain fact checks"[462]—and related notions of probability and likelihood appear throughout trade press discussions of the sociotechnical systems that make journalistic facts. The networked press's freedom to make and publish what it considers to be "true" information is only a probable freedom—an autonomy tied to information infrastructures designed to offer likelihoods, not categorical conclusions. The chance of the press trafficking in what it would consider truthful information lives in distributed architectures that, at any given moment and for any particular distribution, only approximate facts.

For example, several news organizations have created fact-checking algorithms that aim to operate at large scale and in real time and to address as many falsities as architectures allow. In 2012, the *Washington Post* proposed the idea of a real-time fact-checking app that would dynamically "parse audio from a speech or TV ad" and "use speech-to-text technology to gather the audio and compare it against a database of statements, stats and other data that had been fact-checked." Ambitiously called Truth Teller, the project was scaled back to a simpler internal database of fact-checked statements[463] and later expanded to a real-time video analyzer that evaluated transcripts for misinformation,[464] but the vision of a real-time, real-world truth meter appears in several discussions of what journalists ideally want in order to manage the misinformation in media environments.[465] Although skepticism of automated fact-checking persists among journalists experienced with the challenges of fact-checking political statements,[466] the United Kingdom's independent fact-checking organization Full Fact published a "roadmap" of automated fact-checking technologies,[467] including the University of Texas at Arlington's ClaimBuster platform, which uses machine learning techniques to identify potentially false statements that users can manually annotate;[468] *Le Monde*'s "decoding machine," which helps readers search through politicians' previously fact-checked statements and reduce the likelihood that they will believe and share erroneous statements;[469] the news photography service Scoopshot and the *Guardian*'s GuardianWitness project, which rely partly on analyzing an image's embedded metadata and comparing it against an analysis of the image itself, with the aim being to alert readers and journalists alike to images that may have been tampered with;[470] and Reuters's News Tracer algorithm, which was designed to predict the likely emergence of breaking news on Twitter and uses a complex set of dynamic signals to evaluate a tweet's authenticity (its designer remarked, for example, that "a tweet that is entirely in capital letters is less likely to be true").[471]

No sociotechnical system claims to guarantee the truth or accuracy of any of the information it processes, but each is designed to reduce the likelihood that people share misinformation and increase the chances that machines will flag and reject falsities.

Resemblances

A somewhat small and abstract—but growing and powerful—dimension of networked press freedom centers on the sociotechnical creation of familiarity or difference—technologies and practices designed to automate news translations, simulate social environments, and collapse international distances. The *Washington Post*, for example, is experimenting with processes to translate its online stories into languages other than English so that it can create dynamic multilingual versions of content that will let users switch between languages. The main hurdle to overcome in creating more multilingual content is finding staff time for the translations and thinking through the implications of hosting multiple versions of a single story, which are bound to have different nuances in different languages.[472] The European network VoxEurop has solved this by creating a consortium of news organizations that share stories and translations, coordinating through a custom platform designed to create fast and vetted translations.[473] Some writers are concerned, though, that projects such as these—which focus on human translations by news professionals—will be rapidly eclipsed by systems that automatically translate news stories. In the summer of 2016, for example, Facebook introduced its "multilingual composer" system, which lets authors create posts that Facebook can then translate to forty-five other languages.[474] The company acknowledges the limitations of machine translation but gives authors the opportunity to edit translations and thus improve its algorithm. For news organizations, there is a tradeoff: they have an opportunity to translate content into a host of other languages automatically (and thus gain access to new audiences and advertisers), but they also risk publishing translations that contain errors and that lack the subtle nuances reporters use to create compelling narratives that people enjoy reading.

A related challenge is the opportunity to create computationally simulated news environments—augmented reality (AR) and virtual reality (VR) experiences designed to create empathy among viewers as well as contexts they could never experience without such technology.[475] The *New York Times*,[476] the *Guardian*,[477] the *Verge*,[478] *Frontline*,[479] and several other Knight Foundation projects have developed journalism AR and VR projects.[480] Some commentators claim that they foster empathy among audiences[481]— a goal in Schudson's (2008b) ideal model of the press—and that they offer a new form of storytelling that news organizations should invest in.[482] Others question whether journalism should be in the business of simulating environments that do not or could not exist without technology.[483] The crux of the issue is one of separations and dependencies: new technologies may be able to collapse the distances audiences feel from people and places, but such proximity may not be what ethical journalistic witnessing needs, and such simulations may not bear enough resemblance to offline environments to create the kind of empathy that public change demands.[484] Perhaps people should feel distance in order to realize the power they have to help sufferers, or it may be that too much closeness can create compassion fatigue that prevents long-term witnessing and sustained action (Ananny, 2015; Chouliaraki, 2006; Silverstone, 2007).

Finally, this question of "proper distance" (Silverstone, 2003) is addressed as news organizations both re-create and challenge what it means for online news to be "foreign." WNYC's *On the Media* weekly radio program asked why terrorist attacks in Paris received far more attention than those in Baga—a question it and its guest Ethan Zuckerman answered, in part, by arguing that online news bubbles leave many readers in highly localized contexts, despite the potential for news technology to help them care about other places.[485] *BuzzFeed* addressed this question by jettisoning the structure of foreign news entirely, building its coverage around what it called "themes" instead of geography.[486] And Facebook's safety notification system is a kind of foreign news agenda setter, checking in with users and issuing alerts after disasters in certain locations only—notifications that trigger news coverage.[487] Through a set of sociotechnical moves, the networked press signals which proximities are salient and powerful—which publics and issues it sees as within its purview and relevant to its autonomy.

Affect

Although the first image of the Western press is often that of a deliberative institution designed to equip rational citizens with good information (Schudson, 2003a), emotion has always played an important but usually overlooked role in journalism (Beckett & Deuze, 2016; J. M. Fishman, 2003). Journalists often create stories that are purposefully designed to move audiences and enroll them as collective witnesses, helping them feel connected to each other and able to appreciate the shared "structures of feeling" that make empathy and collective action possible (Maier, Slovic, & Mayorga, 2016; R. Williams, 1977; Zelizer, 2010). Emotional storytelling is often a way for journalists to sidestep the usual rituals of detached objectivity, revealing their own feelings and modeling for audiences how they might feel, as long as such feelings align with dominant cultural expectations of how people are supposed to feel in a particular context. Many of history's Pulitzer Prize–winning stories are not exemplars of unemotional neutrality but are accounts that adhere to rituals of objectivity while simultaneously using "subjective language" to make "emotive appeals" to readers (Wahl-Jorgensen, 2013, p. 305). Although still understudied, emotion also plays a key role in the networked press, with audience emotions (Papacharissi, 2015) and algorithmically induced feelings (Bucher, 2017a) found to be key organizing structures of online culture.

Affect is a key dimension of press autonomy: it involves the power to author a story's tone, imbue feelings with audiences, set the emotional tenor of media events, and select which audience emotions to sense and acknowledge. These dynamics are not only about journalists becoming free to pursue emotion as they see fit but also about the networked press's collective capacity to realize affect—and publics through affect.

As with the theme of resemblance, affect is a small but increasingly prevalent element of trade press discourse on the press's sociotechnical dynamics. For example, the *New York Times* highlighted its "Snow Fall" story—a "compelling destination" with a highly evocative aesthetic in which readers were immersed in a multimedia narrative—as a powerful and emotionally suggestive piece,[488] and other news organizations immediately followed suit. A *Quartz* editor remarked, "We are focused on building tools to create Snow Falls every day, and getting them as close to reporters as possible.... I'd rather have a Snow Fall builder than a Snow Fall."[489] The story stood out not just as an example of evocative storytelling but as an inspiration to develop infrastructures—tools, people, practices—that could infuse affect across the news.

The affective dimension of networked press autonomy is largely the story of having the power to control emotion through infrastructure. Shortly after Facebook expanded its Like button to include a fixed set of emotions that people can use to standardize reactions to stories (and make such emotions easier to track and commodify), technology startup Antenna attempted to replicate the model for news. Its software—which requires a Facebook account to use—lets publishers create a customized set of emotional responses that readers can then apply to headlines, story text, or associated media. It is billed as "a nearly abuse-proof way to get feedback from an audience, and in a way that reinforces the brand language." Predefined categories of emotions are seen as a way to get closer to audiences, be consistent with a brand, and build data models of readers' affective states.

Sometimes, though, infrastructures force readers to be close to or far from highly charged media. For example, Google News's editorial staff decided that it wanted to highlight upbeat stories while creating "factoids" of 2014 World Cup searches, but it directed its team of writers and data scientists to avoid stories it saw as negative (those containing words like *destroy, defeat, humiliate,* and *shame*). In choosing which search patterns to highlight as trends, it avoided language it thought was pessimistic or off-putting. As one staffer put it "a negative story ... won't necessarily get a lot of traction in social [media]."[490] Journalists citing Google's online trends as neutral statistics would leave audiences with the impression that people were far more upbeat and positive than their searches suggested.

Such close associations with technology companies can create incorrect assumptions for news audiences and also elicit unintended emotions. When "horrifying video of two journalists being shot and killed ... in Virginia during a live broadcast on WDBJ-TV"[491] was copied from news sites' online streams and shared on social media, some people became unintended audiences. At the time, Facebook and Twitter both played videos automatically, so people scrolling through their tweet streams or news feeds were immediately shown an emotionally charged scene that they may not have chosen to watch and that news organizations customarily issue warnings about before showing.[492] In the past, news organizations have mistakenly shown graphic scenes because of their desire to stay close to live events. For example, against the wishes of the anchor, Fox News mistakenly showed a suicide during live coverage of a car chase and immediately apologized for doing so.[493] The difference in this case is that the decision to broadcast or watch emotionally charged material was not a conscious one made by news organizations, social media platforms, or audiences but instead was the product of a confluence of forces. The public right to hear—or avoid—disturbing content was an infrastructural outgrowth of editorial judgment, technological design, and audience practices.

Conclusion

Networked press freedom is the story of people and machines coming together and pulling away from often invisible and unacknowledged assumptions about what kind of press publics need. Paywalls bring revenue but shut out unpaying audiences; social media platforms deliver news faster to more audiences but at the expense of privacy, fact checking, and emotional ethics; data-driven newsrooms offer real-time images of audiences and the value of journalists' labor but often uneasily integrate editorial and commercial standards; and crowdfunding sites bring new sources of revenue but can turn readers into clients and subtly suggest that journalists should work on what crowds see as popular instead of what they see as important. The separations and dependencies that structure each dimension of press autonomy beg larger questions: what exactly should the press be, and how can normative balances be struck through sociotechnical infrastructures?

I do not claim that this typology captures every dimension of the networked press from 2010 to 2016. I could have discussed different examples, and I am probably unaware of others. Additionally, the stories analyzed here do not necessarily contain the conclusions that scholars would draw about these people, technologies, organizations, or events. Researchers would likely dispute many of the accounts that journalists offer about what they do, why it matters and what role technologies play in networked journalism.

Instead, the typology is an account of the themes that dominate the stories the networked press tells itself about itself as well as an interpretation of how these themes reveal separations and dependencies among the humans and machines that, together, create the conditions under which journalists work, news is produced, audiences convene—and publics form. It is meant to be both a snapshot of a moment in time as well a framework for examining future examples and sociotechnical forces. New stories will arise, new technologies will be invented, and new claims will be made, but what I suspect will endure is a new way of thinking about press autonomy. Instead of seeing press freedom as journalists' freedom from anyone but themselves to pursue their visions of the public, it might more accurately be described as the coming together of humans and nonhumans—often unintentionally, invisibly, and with different types of power—to make publics. If you want a particular type of public, you need a certain type of free press and thus a specific set of relationships among journalism's humans and machines. Conversely, going forward, as journalists and technologists invent new types of human and machine relationships, they might do so with the knowledge that they are simultaneously creating publics. If such arrangements result in publics that are defensible—that ensure, for example, the public right to hear that individuals need to self-govern—then we might look to them as exemplars of how to create proximity among journalism's humans and machines. But if we find ourselves with unacceptable publics or too narrow a set of possible publics, then we might purposefully intervene in the networked press's separations and dependencies to create new normative visions of journalism and self-governance.

6 Conclusion

My aim has been to show a new way of thinking about press freedom—one that moves us beyond the image of heroic, individual journalists defining what they think the public is, and claiming that their unfettered right to speak sustains it. I have argued that, for the press to legitimately earn and normatively defend its freedom as an institution of democratic self-governance, it needs to show how its separations and dependencies ensure not only individual rights to speak but collective rights to hear. Especially in eras of extreme social and technological flux, press freedom can be more than a tired or anachronistic trope that rests upon the myth of journalists' separation from nonjournalists.

Instead, it can be a powerful concept to think with and ask questions: What image of the public is assumed in the press's separations and dependencies? Do these relationships give us the publics we need? Who has the power to imagine and sustain the press's relationships to states, markets, technologies, audiences, or advertisers? What other publics are possible or necessary, and what kinds of press freedom would they require? Rather than revisit the same old debates about who is a journalist or which government officials are harming the traditional press, we might see this moment of sociotechnical, economic, and normative upheavals as an opportunity to reimagine, recreate, and redefend the press. But if we are to do so, we have to know where this press is, how its autonomy emerges, and why exactly we want to defend one version of it versus another.

My contribution to these debates starts by arguing that democratic autonomy and self-governance mean more than individuals being free from unreasonable constraints. To realize ourselves more fully, we need not only the right to access information, share opinions, and choose associations.

We also need to see ourselves as publics—and question whether our publics have capacities to hear people and ideas that we would not choose to encounter.

Such publics and capacities are products of history, and depend on more than just journalistic definitions of public interest, or media technologies that engineer serendipity, calculate relevance, or manipulate attention. They require communication systems that help people discover and manage their shared social and material conditions—that show them how thriving requires more than personalized information, self-selected communities, and freedom from unwanted influences.

Because the press is a key institution of public communication, its autonomy cannot be seen simply as freedom from those who prevent it from pursuing whatever it thinks the public is. Rather, the press and its autonomy—as they always have been—are separations and dependencies that work together to help publics form. The press must not be defended blindly; it has no monopoly on defining the public interest and its autonomy should only be protected insofar as it helps to create and sustain defensible publics. A robust and self-aware press speaks the language of publics, appreciates its public-making role, and eloquently articulates why it works to create some publics over others. This kind of press is one of democracy's most powerful and essential institutions. Its freedom is worth defending.

And because today's press is inextricably embedded within sociotechnical contexts where both people and machines have power, the networked press's freedom—and therefore its power to realize networked publics—depends on how humans and nonhumans join and split through a variety of sociotechnical dynamics. The power to imagine and realize contemporary, networked press freedom is the power to create and influence these dynamics.

Accepting this argument requires seeing two kinds of freedom—individual and institutional—as relational achievements that entail balancing two other kinds of freedom—negative *freedom from* and affirmative *capacity to*. It is nonsensical to pretend that individuals can achieve autonomy without institutions (and vice versa) or that negative or positive freedom can exist without each other. Add to this framework the observation that today's institutional press is not only a social, legal, economic, or cultural achievement but also products of technological arrangements we struggle to understand and private actors who eschew public accountability, and the model of networked press freedom becomes one in which autonomy must be traced across multiple sites with varied sensitivities.

My goal has been to suggest a different way of thinking about press freedom that might speak to this historical moment and the days ahead. But beyond the argument that the sociotechnical press creates sociotechnical publics, why might this way of thinking about press freedom matter?

The press is an ideal that is made and remade in each historical moment. But this ideal needs to be interrogated and critiqued (Downey, Titley, & Toynbee, 2014), not just described, if we are to understand why we have the press we have. These interrogations and critiques require a new skill that the press and its critics are only just starting to develop—the ability to read sociotechnical relationships for their power to create the conditions under which people become publics. Research on media accountability and journalistic ethics requires seeing how normativity is inseparable from technological infrastructures. Since networked technologies are not broadcast technologies, we need a language of press freedom that speaks to today's sociotechnical landscape.

The concern is urgent. We currently are debating which parts of the press can or should be automated; whether social media is just a publishing channel or beat or an integral part of the press; why news organizations should invest in making their own technologies versus adopting those of Silicon Valley; what obligations social media platforms have to democratic processes; and what power news organizations have to resist the metrics and advertising regimes of social media platforms with narrow, opaque, and unaccountable visions of the public. The power to design the networked press is currently unevenly distributed among journalists, publishers, technology companies, and audiences. Too many decisions about how publics are made live in private organizations and proprietary technologies with thin, transactional, or nonexistent theories of autonomy and self-governance. In many ways, news organizations are still playing catch-up and still dealing with the shock of early internet incursions into what was a stable and conservative business of elite gatekeeping and mass broadcasting. Scholars and journalists alike have often seen new technologies as professional threats, distribution channels, or economic competitors, but rarely have they been seen as ubiquitous infrastructures with existential power to change the conditions under which the press imagines itself and realizes publics. As companies like Facebook and Google increasingly capture and monopolize revenue and attention, they consolidate the power to make publics within inscrutable and unaccountable sociotechnical systems, seeing public outcries as public relations problems to be ameliorated or endured. Such companies are not simply threats to the journalistic freedom, but to the very idea of autonomous, self-governing publics.

There is a flip side to the press's crisis: technology companies are generally not as adept as the news industry is at talking about publics and democracy. Technologists are often shy about using such language. They talk about communities, groups, users, sharing, content, and individual choice—but beyond platitudes about the "democratization of computation" or the "power of connection," they seem largely incapable of grappling with hard questions about self-government, democracy, and publics. As the history of press freedom has shown, journalists have a long if uneven past thinking about how their work relates to democracy. Often unconsciously, they created separations and dependencies designed to realize an image of the public. They may not have said so explicitly, or they may have fallen back on tropes of their own, but embedded in the profession of journalism and the missions of many publishers were ideas about how they thought they were helping democracies, what they defined as the public interest, how they knew they needed to act if they were to be anything other than just another business. As we saw, such commitments ebbed and flowed over time, took on varied forms, suffered from problematic relationships, and often were not as well developed as critics would have liked, but the very best and most self-reflective journalists do not shy away from seeing their work as part of democratic culture and respond maturely to critical and constructive critiques. As technology companies and social media platforms try to decide what exactly they are and who their constituents are, they often only awkwardly and shallowly invoke democracy and self-governance, preferring instead the safer terrain of users, customers, communities, personalization, and optimization.

There is an opportunity, then, for a new kind of press and a new defense of press freedom. Thoughtful journalists who understand both the history of their profession and the potential of sociotechnical systems could lead technologists to richer, more subtle, and defensibly ethical relationships with publics. Journalists, technologists, and audiences could create new sociotechnical contracts and contact languages that let them talk about what the networked press is, could be, and should be at any given moment.[1] As this book tries to do, they could look deeply and honestly at the networked press's separations and dependencies and ask if they are creating the publics people need. Instead of being enamored with every new technology Silicon Valley offers—such as augmented reality, virtual reality, drones, big data, and machine learning—or narrowly framing their work as storytelling, journalists could instead ask questions: how are these technologies actually sociotechnical relationships, what are their separations and dependencies, what kind of autonomy do they make possible, and does it help to create normatively defensible publics? This is a big ask. Although U.S. news organizations struggle for financial revenue and public trust, journalistic practitioners, scholars, and activists could band together and use their collective cultural power to resist the thin democratic thinking of Silicon Valley. The press could redefine and reassert its moral authority and demand new sociotechnical relationships for new kinds of publics. If journalists simply see their relationship to technology in terms of storytelling innovation, audience distribution, and content monetization, they cede the high ground of democratic debate to technology companies that cannot or will not prioritize publics.

As strange as it may sound, machines need to be part of this conversation. Data, algorithms, machine learning models, and artificial intelligences of all stripes need to be seen not as precursors, channels, or products of news but as powerful and often invisible agents creating the conditions under which journalists work, news emerges, audiences convene, and publics form. The networked press is made up of humans with different traditions and affiliations, but it also is populated by nonhumans with considerable and largely unaccountable power—proprietary algorithms that resist auditing, data sets with embedded and invisible biases, and surveillance and personalization technologies that watch and influence human actions. These are not just tools that the press might decide to use; they are infrastructures the press is already embedded within and often has little knowledge of or control over them. Without seeing itself as infrastructure, how will the networked press be able to see all the ways it might be being censored, all the relationships that are not being created, all the stories that are not being heard, and all the publics that are not forming?

The infrastructural view of the press and its autonomy calls for science and technology studies (STS) to be at the core of journalism scholarship that integrates democratic theory, media ethics, and sociotechnical epistemology. It does not mean applying STS to journalism as if STS were just a methodology or analytical perspective. A sociotechnical view of the press fundamentally sees journalism's people and machines as intertwined and inseparable. It calls for categories of inquiry that rise above lists of influences or isolated meetings of humans and nonhumans. Scholars of the networked press interested in creating alternative models of journalistic autonomy would do well to revisit the work of feminist writers like Wendy Brown, Judith Butler, and Sandra Harding and feminist STS scholars like Adele Clark, Donna Haraway, Susan Leigh Star, Lucy Suchman, and Judy Wajcman. Such a focus on alternative forms of power might help develop an explicitly feminist theory of networked press freedom that values listening and situated knowledge, and that challenges the dominance of voice and objectivist epistemologies. More critical, cultural, feminist scholarship is required to understand the "deep structures" (Hall, 1997) of the networked press that make some publics more possible than others.

This way of seeing press freedom is meant as a constructive challenge to rethink what the press could be, in three directions. First, designers may think about what publics could be—what kind of publics they want the press to convene—and assemble human and nonhuman actors to achieve it (Dunne & Raby, 2013). Deliberative, agonistic, enclave, decentered, affective, recursive, participatory, and counter publics all require different types of presses—and therefore different types of sociotechnical separations and dependencies. How might the twelve dimensions of networked press autonomy be combined and remixed to realize different types of publics? These dimensions are the exclusive domain of neither journalist nor technologists. They cut across questions of design, optimization, ethics, publics, and democracy. I am not saying that journalists and technologists simply need to collaborate to create new storytelling tools or turn editorial decisions into algorithms. I am arguing for an entirely new ethic of production focused on understanding, making, and defending sociotechnical publics. Editorial judgments and technology design decisions will become increasingly intertwined, and my fear is that a focus on publics will suffer irrevocably—at the hands of dominant concepts like audiences, users, customers, and communities—if networked press designers, scholars, and policymakers do not foreground and prioritize them.

Second, this way of rethinking what the press can be is not just a mode of design but a publics-driven mode for critique. If publics are failing to produce normatively acceptable outcomes—for example, if people are systematically excluded or oppressed, ideas are routinely marginalized, dissent is squashed, resources are mismanaged, or elections are stolen—then we might look at the sociotechnical conditions under which people are convened or served by the press. If the networked press is seen as a system of relationships among humans and nonhumans, with different degrees of freedom and control, then its breakdowns might be diagnosed as failures that can be ameliorated with a different set of separations or dependencies. The shortcomings of social media platforms could be seen not as failures to live up to the traditions of journalism—they do not want to be news organizations anyway—but as shortcomings in the "system of freedom of expression" (Emerson, 1970) that highlight how the power to create the conditions under which people can hear is unevenly distributed. More simply, how could Facebook be held accountable as a listening platform? How does Twitter help or harm a public right to hear? What new types of power would news organizations need with such companies if they were to use their expertise as creators of sociotechnical publics to change social media?

These questions might help journalism see itself not as a profession fighting for cultural legitimacy or economic viability but as sociotechnical makers and defenders of networked publics (Creech & Mendelson, 2015; Kunelius & Ruusunoksa, 2008). Social media companies may have greater power to create networked technologies, and regulators may have greater power to force normative change—but journalists could become the essential hybrid professionals of networked publics. They might understand not only how technologies work but also how sociotechnical systems behave as communication institutions with normative power. This shifts conversations about journalism education beyond narrow questions of whether students should be taught to code or hack or what kind of storytelling is possible with digital technologies. It pushes students to learn their professional freedom as the right and obligation to help create publics by configuring relationships among humans and nonhumans. Their autonomy could be taught as the creation and defense of the sociotechnical systems that make publics. And if someone asks "Is she a journalist?," "Is that journalism?," or "Does she need independence?," the answers might be yes to all three questions if she and her actions help to create a public right to hear.

Third, foregrounding the networked press's capacity to realize a public right to hear might help journalists and technologists look anew at questions of information overload or communication fatigue (Ananny, 2017). Instead of seeing their profession as the production of information—faster, more immersive, more shocking—journalists might see themselves as creators of listening environments. It would be a long-term project and one that would be challenging to mount in the face of the constant pressure to produce, but journalists could say that because their professional autonomy partly depends on enabling a public right to hear, they are sometimes ethically obligated *not* to add to the surfeit of online information and must instead create sociotechnical environments that help publics hear. Such courage might be supported by editors, technology companies, professional organizations, and sociotechnically literate audiences that understand the value and necessity of periodic silence.

The press's job is not to listen to us or for us but to help us hear ourselves well enough to understand how we are inextricably linked. It achieves only part of its mission—and deserves only limited autonomy—if it simply speaks to us in ways it assumes we need. If instead it is an infrastructure for both speaking and hearing—for individual and collective autonomy and for positive and negative freedom—then it is perhaps our most critically important institution and needs ongoing and robust protection.

The U.S. press currently seems to be in an "infrastructural drift" (Ciborra & Hanseth, 2001, p. 4). The current president has publicly denounced the idea of the free press, suggested the need for new libel laws, fed panic about fake news and leaks, and spread misinformation at White House press conferences while barring their broadcast. Social media bots and platforms, many of which are controlled or influenced by foreign adversaries with explicitly anti-democratic aims, swamp Western democracies with disinformation designed to sway elections and discredit results. Twitter has announced its intention to let users flag tweets as fake news, and Facebook and Google have created complex international partnerships to outsource truth judgments to proprietary, algorithmically driven infrastructures and hand-picked news and fact-checking organizations. Surveys of U.S. news audiences find that they are concerned about fake news and have little trust in traditional institutions, but they also admit to sharing stories they know to be untrue and acknowledge that they are largely held captive by unaccountable social media platforms. The press's current existential crisis is far more fundamental than concerns over declining revenues or definitions of a journalist. In the United States, at least, many are asking whether democracy can survive if we are unable to learn about, convene with, and trust each other through digital media.

There has rarely been a better and more urgent time to figure out exactly what the press is and how its freedom can and should be defended. Just as the U.S. press in colonial times was not the same as the press of the muckraking, McCarthy, and Watergate eras—press freedom meant different things then—the contemporary press faces unique challenges. I have tried to argue that in the midst of technological hype and uncertainty, today's networked press would do well to define itself as a *public* institution concerned with how *publics* are made and sustained—to ask hard questions of itself and its relationships. This demands that journalists quickly and confidently reinvent themselves as sociotechnically savvy, reflective practitioners who are concerned not only about their individual right to speak but also about a public's right to hear. This moment offers journalism an opportunity. Instead of being held captive by a mythology of autonomy that strives only for freedom from or being overtaken by thin technological rhetoric, the networked press—made of humans and nonhumans—might thoughtfully, playfully, skillfully, and powerfully reimagine itself as an institution that deftly uses separations and dependencies to make and defend entirely new publics.

Appendix: A Discussion of Method

From June 2010 through December 2016, I built a corpus of trade press stories focused on the networked press's sociotechnical dynamics. I subscribed to the newswire and digest services of the Nieman Journalism Lab, the Poynter Institute, the blog *Romenesko*, the radio program *On the Media*, the American Press Institute, the *Columbia Journalism Review*, the Pew Research Center's Journalism & Media project, *AdWeek*'s Media Bistro, and the *New York Times*'s Bits blog, Media Equation, and Media Decoder columns. These sites and services were chosen because they are often mentioned and feature prominently in the professional discourse of online journalists. They offer frequent and timely accounts of both breaking news and longer-term trends; frequently converge on similar issues, creating a well-bounded and sometimes redundant space of discourse in which themes frequently reappear; and link to stories in other media outlets, acting as observers and catalogs of media commentary beyond themselves. Throughout this time, I read each digest and selected stories that I judged to have both journalistic and technological relevance. For example, a story about a media merger or journalistic ethics that made no explicit mention of technological factors was not selected. Likewise, a story that focused exclusively on a new iPhone feature or a Twitter redesign that did not contain a clear link to a journalistic or editorial issue was not selected.

After reading each digest, I placed relevant stories into one or more of twenty-five categories that were iteratively developed over the six-year timeframe. These categories included topics like Analytics, Automation, Funding, Geolocation, and Investigative. Following an "open coding" approach (J. Corbin & Strauss, 2007; Creswell, 1998) in which new stories were compared against existing categories for both fit and novelty, the categories were developed iteratively and periodically renamed or combined to reflect both which scholarly issues were emerging (my tracking of academic discourse on the networked press) and how the trade press was changing over time. The corpus is thus historical in that it contains items spanning a six-year time period, but it was not designed to track how trade press discourse developed. This method captured 2,944 articles, which I read and coded individually. I identified, at the level of headline and lede, the article's main theme and classified it as such, but I also approached this classification process iteratively, using an axial coding technique to create new themes as I combined or renamed old themes in light of new article topics. Only categories I judged to be saturated (containing at least three different articles from three different sources over a six-month time period) were retained and considered as candidates for the typology offered below.

I want to stress two additional points. First, some technical details contained within the stories may not be correct. For example, research focused on particular algorithm, paywall, or database may show that it works differently than the story describes. I concede that not every assertion within metajournalistic discourse is technically correct but see such descriptions, claims, and assertions as part of how journalists in this historical moment discuss among themselves how they think systems work. Second, the stories do not necessarily capture what scholars would say about these systems. Deep research on any of the systems discussed here may come to different conclusions. Again, I do not defend the analyses contained within these stories; rather, they are the empirical materials I am working with in my own analysis. In chapter 5, I provide the URLs for all primary sources to distinguish between assertions made within news stories and my own analysis.

It is possible that I missed seeing themes and patterns in trade press discourse by limiting myself to these sources and selection heuristics, but my confidence in the value of these categories and the typology stems not only from this multiyear process of reading and iteratively classifying trade press discourse but also from my observations at professional and academic meetings focused on journalism and news technology. I do not describe my attendance at these gatherings as anything like the participant observation that formal ethnographies involve, but I have participated in meetings of NewsFoo, MozFest, the Online News Association, South by Southwest, and several topic-specific workshops touching on news technology themes at Columbia's Tow Center for Digital Journalism, Data & Society, Harvard's Berkman Klein Center for Internet & Society, Stanford's Center for Internet and Society, and Yale Law School's Information Society Project. These events and affiliations have helped shape my perspectives and analyses.

Notes

Chapter 1

1. For an excellent exploration of how the press's role as a guarantor of affirmative freedom has historically appeared in media reform movements, see Victor Pickard (2014a).

Chapter 2

1. This idea of unseen influences and hegemonic force has a long and complex history, a complete review of which is beyond the scope of this discussion. This idea of autonomy as a negotiation between individual agency and structures of influence and domination is more fully explored in such works as Hannah Arendt's *The Human Condition* (1958), in which she argues that an "active life" requires seeing oneself as never fully in control of one's personality because it is always subject to constructs beyond one's control (the best we can do is promise ethical behavior and forgive lapses thereof); Michel Foucault's *Discipline and Punish: The Birth of the Prison* (1979) and "Governmentality" (1991), in which he traces a series of social control techniques that reconfigure citizens' behaviors and identities in ways that best suit the aims of the state and coercive power; and Antonio Gramsci's *Prison Letters* (1988), in which he argues that an individual's freedom (particularly for workers who historically have had little access to many different forms of power) depends not only on securing economic or political capital for one's own personal use but also on critically understanding and mastering often unseen cultural influences and social systems that control the ideas that an individual might be able to imagine.

2. For an excellent intellectual history of positive and negative freedoms as communication phenomena, see Clifford G. Christians and P. Mark Fackler (2014).

3. Avital Simhony (1993) argues that autonomy is better described as struggle between internal-facing and external-facing capacities. That is, autonomy depends on abilities that reside within the single individual (things that he or she is able or not able to do at any moment) and abilities that exist within the social environment

surrounding the individual (things that collectives are able to do and things that collectives allow individuals to do, with allowances made through coercive force or cultural signaling).

4. For more on the differences between media products and other commodities, on the role played by markets in creating social order, and on the moral limits of markets, see C. Edwin Baker (2002, pp. 7–40), Ronald H. Coase (1974), Marion Fourcade (2007), Onora O'Neill (2009), Debra Satz (2010), and Kathleen M. Sullivan (1994).

5. In an important response to Post's critique of Meiklejohn, Fiss (1995) cautions against Post's uncritical embrace of civil society's ability to self-regulate speech and his general rejection of state participation in the public sphere. Agendas, Fiss argues, can come not only from town hall managers but, more insidiously, from largely unseen cultural and economic forces that can set and control topics of discussion free of any requirements to be transparent or inclusive. For example, through advertising, campaign sponsorship, or direct control of media companies, private corporations can have significant power to set public discourse agendas. Fiss instead envisions the state serving in a parliamentarian-like role that lightly administers "time, place and manner" restrictions on speech and creates a set of incentives and disincentives to encourage equitable participation by a diverse range of speakers (guarding against the "heckler's veto") (Fiss, 1995, p. 86). Fiss's position here is consistent with his earlier argument (Fiss, 1986, p. 1412) that the most powerful regulator of free speech, pragmatically, is not necessarily the courts or the state but the "forces that dominate the social structure." Indeed, Fiss points to the need to engage critically with different understandings of participation and not simply assume its inherit merit to democracy. For more complex views of civic participation in and through media systems, see W. Lance Bennett (2012), Nico Carpentier (2011), James Hay and Nick Couldry (2011), Henry Jenkins (2013), and Jenkins and Carpentier (2013).

6. On this tension between individual liberty and equality in speech environments, also see Fiss (1996).

7. See Randall P. Bezanson and William Buss (2001) for an extensive review of scenarios in which the state speaks and legal judgments thereof. They go further than Emerson's focus on constraining government speech to argue that, in democratic societies that value two-way communication between the state and the citizenry, the government has an obligation to participate in speech systems.

8. I focus here on the U.S. Constitution, its First Amendment cases, and legal philosophy emerging from U.S. perspectives.

9. For excellent overviews and contextualization of this relatively small number of cases, see Bezanson (2003a) and Lee C. Bollinger (1991).

10. An affirmative interpretation of press freedom as ensuring a public right to hear historically has not been a popular analytical framework within U.S. traditions that

equate free markets with a free press. For excellent overviews of this tradition, see Bezanson (2012), Thomas Irwin Emerson (1981), Fiss (1996), and Stein (2004, 2006).

11. See Leonard Williams Levy (1960, 2004) for controversial histories of press clause interpretation, including a claim that the framers intended only to prevent prior restraint of the press, and David A. Anderson (1983) for a good overview of historical tensions in press clause history.

12. The following chapter goes into greater detail about the various kinds of publics the press might assume to exist or create as it does its work.

13. In contrast to the originalist approach of Justice Antonin Scalia (1997) that focuses on the framers' intentions and meanings, Justice Stephen Breyer (2005) describes a "pragmatic" approach to constitutional interpretation in which he says that judges use five elements in interpreting the Constitution—statute language, jurisprudential history, legal traditions, case law precedents, constitutional purpose, and pragmatic consequences—but that, ideally, they should ground their decisions in understanding the overall *purpose* of the Constitution and interpret that purpose in contemporary terms. Scalia's originalist approach and Breyer's pragmatic view can both be considered influences on what David A. Strauss (2010) defines as the U.S.'s "living constitution"—the principles, amendments, and precedents that, taken together, create a kind of common law jurisprudence that is always changing. For an excellent critique of originalism, see Paul Brest (1980).

14. In his study of lower-court decisions focused on the meaning of the press clause in digital contexts, Jared Schroeder (2014) finds that the courts focus on examining the processes and acts of journalism rather than on creating any strict categorical definitions of *journalism* and *journalist*.

15. Such mentions of the press have not always occurred in majority rulings or controlling precedents but instead appear in the dicta of opinions—text that is not part of a ruling's core but nonetheless is evidence of judicial thinking. For more on the value of reading the full texts of court decisions and not just their holdings, see George P. Fletcher (1981), and for more on the role played by dicta in court decisions and precedents, see Frederick Schauer (1987, 1995).

16. For a thoughtful and comprehensive analysis of how this decision fits within larger, historical media reform movements that center on affirmative communication rights and a rejection of corporate libertarianism, see Victor Pickard's (2014a) excellent *America's Battle for Media Democracy*.

17. In 1976, Gallup (2016) found that 72 percent of Americans had "a great deal" or "a fair amount" of trust in the mass media. The number has never been that high since that year. In 2016, it was 32 percent. A recent Pew Research Center (2013) study found that only 28 percent of U.S. adults think journalists contribute "a lot to society's well-being."

18. Nine years before Justice Stewart's more famous speech, another justice, William J. Brennan (1965), gave somewhat similar public remarks at Brown University as part of the Alexander Meiklejohn Lecture Series. In his speech, Brennan seemed to agree with Meiklejohn's argument that the state is responsible for providing publics with the conditions that enable individual self-government. In mentioning the then recent *New York Times v. Sullivan* (1964) case, he stated that so long as a free press provides speech of "redeeming social value," it plays a valuable constitutional role in securing individual self-government.

19. In the same public remarks in which he argued for a structural understanding of the press, Justice Stewart (1975, p. 633) states that "the Free Press Clause extends protection to an institution. The publishing business is, in short, the only organized private business that is given explicit constitutional protection." In doing so, Stewart collapses two ideas—the press as an institution and the press as a publishing business. Chapter 3 addresses this question directly, but for now, it is worth noting that a business is not the same thing as an institution. A business typically focuses on the production and distribution of commodified goods and services, whereas an institution might best be thought of more broadly as a system of associations in which power, legitimacy, regulation, and norms are negotiated among a variety of actors, organizations, professions, and social contexts (DiMaggio & Powell, 1991).

20. Also see Bezanson (2003a) for an excellent overview of federal appellate and Supreme Court press cases, C. Edwin Baker (2007a) for a review of how press constitutional protections differ from those available to individuals, Richard A. Parker (2003) for a collection of insightful analyses of Supreme Court free-speech cases, and Anthony Lewis (2008) for a popular overview of First Amendment issues.

21. Similarly, in *Richmond Newspapers v. Virginia* (1980), the Court found a "right of access to criminal trials for both the press and the public ... [to help create] an informed public capable of self-government" (Dyk, 1992, p. 934). And in *Globe Newspaper Co. v. Superior Court* (1982), the Court "struck down a Massachusetts statute requiring courtrooms to be closed whenever a minor victim of a sexual crime was testifying" (Bollinger, 1991, p. 17).

22. See chapter 3 for a discussion of how the press asserts its autonomy, in part, by strategically distancing itself *from* publics.

23. See Erik Ugland (2008, 2009) for excellent historical overviews of newsgathering rights within evolving constitutional frameworks.

24. As of September 2017, thirty-seven states had either absolute or qualified protections for journalistic sources (Reporters Committee for Freedom of the Press, n.d.).

25. This is a collection of cases anchored around this decision.

26. Although some groups—scholars (Nestler, 2005), members of the press (American Society of Newspaper Editors, 2013; Newspaper Association of America, 2013),

and even the state (Favole & Kendall, 2013)—advocate for a federal shield law—a "defensive" right that Baker (1989, p. 246) likens to freedom from searches and seizures—to prevent the chilling, cooptation, or surveillance of reporting, others caution that for such a law to be useful, especially in a contemporary context of online reporting, it needs to clarify exactly who would be protected (Fargo, 2006).

27. As Bollinger (2010, pp. 27–28) notes, though, one case seems to be an exception to cases that limit the press's right to perform reporting that it deems to be of public value. In *Richmond Newspapers v. Virginia* (1980), the Court ruled that the public and the press have a right to attend criminal trials because such access may create "greater public confidence in the criminal justice system and better decisions in trials." (Bollinger, 2010, p. 28)

28. A complementary legal doctrine not explicitly focused on the press (often invoked on questions of library policies and censorship) concerns a right to receive information within a marketplace model of speech. Historically, it has been used in three scenarios: (1) "the use of the right to prevent the government from placing barriers between speakers and listeners of constitutionally protected speech; (2) the use of the right to require government intervention to compel affirmative actions by the press; and (3) the use of the right to claim access to information that is in the government's possession due to funding constraints to facilitate the free exchange of information and an informed public" (Kennedy, 2005, p. 791). For good overviews, see Jamie Kennedy (2005), William E. Lee (1987), and Susan Nevelow Mart (2003).

29. This is not to suggest that audiences are homogeneous wholes that understand speech in the same way to mean a single thing. In additional to foundational critical writing on audiences as constructions and the sociocultural processes of audience making by James S. Ettema and David Charles Whitney (1994) and Raymond Williams (1983), see Wiebke Loosen and Jan-Hinrik Schmidt (2012), Sonia Livingstone and Ranjana Das (2013), Jim Macnamara (2013), Denis McQuail (2013), and Philip M. Napoli (2011) for more contemporary critiques.

30. For an excellent critique of Facebook's argument that it is merely a technology company and not a media organization, see Napoli and Robyn Caplan (2017).

31. There is good evidence that people's information choices tend not to align with what the media would choose for them to read (Boczkowski & Mitchelstein, 2013; Boczkowski, Mitchelstein, & Walter, 2010; Boczkowski & Peer, 2011); that choice makes it possible for people to create "echo chambers" for themselves (Pariser, 2011; Sunstein, 2001, 2004); and that some people are likely to have more political knowledge than others (Prior, 2007), especially about current affairs (D. Trilling & Schoenbach, 2013). Choice-driven environments also tend to reinforce partisan political divides (Stroud, 2011) and encourage people simply to ignore information (Aalberg, Blekesaune, & Elvestad, 2013).

32. There is an emerging literature on the importance of understanding the nonuse of media technologies (S. K. Lee & Katz, 2014; Oudshoorn & Pinch, 2003; Plaut, 2015; Wyatt, 2003); the avoidance of news media (Edgerly, 2016; T. B. Ksiazek, Malthouse, & Webster, 2010; Woodstock, 2014); the ways that social media entails listening and not "lurking" (Crawford, 2009, 2011); the ways that organizations designed for listening result in a greater diversity of speakers (Macnamara, 2015); and the power of unseen technologies to surveil and model social media users, regardless of whether they contribute content (Solove, 2011; Stutzman, Grossy, & Acquisti, 2012).

33. See Jared Schudson (1978, pp. 88–120) for a discussion of the "information ideal" of citizenship and journalism's role in supporting it.

Chapter 3

1. The notion of possibility infuses much of the study of structures of social organization. Bourdieu's phrase "space of possibles" echoes Lewin's concept of "possible life spaces" and presages John F. Padgett and Walter W. Powell's (2012, p. 4) study of the new organizations emerging from a "topology of the possible." Given that, at any particular moment, field-level institutional forces make only certain concepts of free press possible, my aim is to move toward a study of press freedom in which these possibilities might be read as more or less desirable—for example, as helping or harming a public right to hear.

2. Bourdieu means *laws* not in a narrow sense of formal, state-authored regulations but as a general term describing the actions and dispositions that socially constructed norms consider to be more or less permissible. Similarly, *capital* means not only currency or commodities but also socially created resources (like reputation, class, and family lineage) that can be recognized both in formal systems (such as military ranks, university degrees, and caste systems that create clear hierarchies) and in informal, implicit ways (for example, a worker's perceived value in an interview setting may be a function not only of her employment history and letters of reference but also her dress, accent, demeanor, and the reputations of others who may have similar work histories or educational backgrounds).

3. See Pierre Marlière (2000) and Schudson (2005) for particularly pointed critiques.

4. There has been no modern historical shortage of inquiry into how the press and political systems enable each other—essentially, era-specific attempts to answer field-level questions like "Why is the press as it is?" (Hallin & Mancini, 2004, p. 2) and "What type of free press does democracy need and why does democracy need it?" (Baker, 2002, p. 125). In his critical study of the communicative forces that created and sustained nationalism and colonialism, Benedict Anderson (1983, p. 62) describes how early newspapers emerged by creating an "imagined community among a specific assemblage of fellow-readers." In the aftermath of the press's failure to challenge government accounts of World War I, Walter Lippmann (1920,

p. 11) argued that "All that the sharpest critics of democracy have alleged is true, if there is no steady supply of trustworthy and relevant news." In applying Chicago School social theories to that era's version of community journalism, Robert E. Park (1923, p. 669) claimed that the "extent to which news circulates determines the extent to which the members of a society participate in its political action." As part of his worry that profit-driven journalism would impoverish democratic societies, John Dewey (1935/2004, p. 209) worried that a "public, debauched by the ideal of getting away with whatever it can, will hardly turn away from a press that is getting away with murder." In their survey of Cold War era journalism—an implicit celebration of Western, liberal media policy (Nerone, 1995)—Fred Seaton Siebert, Theodore Peterson, and Wilbur Schramm (1963, p. 1) trace how the press "takes on the form and coloration of the social and political structures within which it operates"—structures that Victor Pickard (2014a, p. 3) shows had just been settled on after a particularly vibrant "decade of transition and reform" in U.S. media policymaking during which "national and geopolitical power relations were in flux." Even more narrowly focused sociological and ethnographic studies of the press are usually motivated by journalism's democratic essence: "I sought to study what this society tells itself about itself through the news and why" (Gans, 1979, p. xxi); local journalism's "vision of itself ... is a noble vision of tremendous democratic importance" (C. W. Anderson, 2013a, p. 3); "journalism will always express the dominant sensibilities of the public culture in which it is practiced" (Ryfe, 2012, p. 18).

5. For an argument that attempts to construct a general theory of communicative normativity using Bourdieu's notions of field, habitus, and capital, see Liane Tessa Rothenberger, Claudia Auer, and Cornelius B. Pratt (2017).

6. Cook's (1998) account is focused on what Robert M. Entman (2005) calls the "traditional journalism" of reporters who adhere to five key standards of news production—accuracy and factual claim making, the balance and separation of personal views, the allowing of news judgments to override profit considerations, a focus on checking sources of power, and the separation of news and editorial staffs. He contrasts this reporting against advocacy journalism that has a change-making agenda, tabloid journalism that is designed for profit, amusement, and policy influence, and entertainment that is targeted to meet the desires of audiences. These categories are not mutually exclusive—and are implicitly critiqued by Christians, Glasser, McQuail, Nordenstreng, and White (2009)—but they help to narrow the claims Cook makes about the press's field-level patterns.

7. Bourdieu (1996a, p. 35) called them "good guests" who "you can always invite because you know they'll be good company and won't create problems."

8. The press actually limits its authority and relevance when it tries to retain the illusion of independence—when it hews too closely to the idea that all stories have two sides, that all bureaucratically credible sources need balancing, and that journalistic interpretations unacceptably mix facts and values. For example, in their study of the

coverage of climate change debates by the U.S. "prestige press" (the *New York Times,* the *Washington Post,* the *Los Angeles Times,* and the *Wall Street Journal*), Maxwell T. Boykoff and Jules M. Boykoff (2004) observed the papers consistently juxtaposing widespread scientific consensus that global warming is caused by humans with claims by "big oil companies, conservative policy research organizations and trade associations" (p. 133) that the science was unproven: "This bias, hidden behind the veil of journalistic balance," created "both discursive and real political space for the U.S. government to shirk responsibility and delay action" (p. 134).

9. In terms of broader communication theories, the information ideal might best be thought of in terms of a transmission model in which messages are "transmitted and distributed in space for the control of distance and people" (Carey, 1989a, p. 15), where communications are successful if a receiver gets an exact copy of a sender's message (W. Weaver & Shannon, 1963), while the story ideal might be considered closer to a ritual model in which communication functions to maintain society, construct meaning, negotiate among beliefs, and discover shared consequences of communal living (Carey, 1989a, p. 18; Dewey, 1954).

10. The value of such reporting traditions, steeped in a professionalized goal of objectivity, is debatable and not universal among reporters. Daniel C. Hallin and Paolo Mancini (2004) report that an expectation of objectivity can make reporters *less* autonomous within the global profession. European journalists "would say that the Americans were 'unprofessional' because they were so constrained by the routines of balance and 'objectivity' that they didn't exercise independent judgment" (p. 226).

11. Although the Hutchins Commission is often remembered as a unique call for press accountability distinct from the forces of commercial markets, its members were by no means aligned in their understandings of freedom. Because it "agreed on publishing a report ... with a single voice," the Commission's report "often speaks in generalities that result from compromise" (Christians & Fackler, 2014, p. 339). The outgoing chair of Harvard's philosophy department, William Hocking, advocated that the press embrace "social responsibility theory" (seeing press accountability in terms of its duty to others), while Zechariah Chafee Jr. favored a "liberal emphasis on [press] rights and a suspicion of government action" that might limit their exercise in the name of collective action (p. 339). Harold Lasswell advocated that the report compromise and "endorse both negative and positive liberty" (Nerone, 1995, pp. 93–94).

12. See Miranda Joseph (2002) for an excellent discussion of the dangers of grounding images of public life too deeply within a "romance of community."

13. This is a large and nuanced body of literature, but for excellent overviews, see C. Edwin Baker (2002), Richard Butsch (2008), Christians, Glasser, McQuail Nordenstreng, and White (2009), James S. Ettema and David Charles Whitney (1994), Hallin and Mancini (2004), Sonia Livingstone (2013), and Philip M. Napoli (2011).

Chapter 4

1. For excellent discussions of these questions, see Christopher W. Anderson (2015a, 2015b, 2018), Mark Coddington (2014), and Sylvain Parasie (2015).

2. See Cristina Archetti (2013), Arnold S. de Beer (2010), Peter Berglez (2008), Peter Dahlgren (2013), Brian Ekdale (2013), Steven Livingston and Gregory Asmolov (2010), Lars Willnat, David H. Weaver, and Jihyang Choi (2013), and Ethan Zuckerman (2013).

3. See Christopher W. Anderson (2013a); Renee Barnes (2013); Joshua A. Braun and Tarleton Gillespie (2011); Alessio Corina, Annika Sehl, and Rasmus Kleis Nielsen (2016); Yacov Netzer, Keren Tenenboim-Weinblatt, and Limor Shifman (2014); Steve Paulussen, Ari Heinonen, David Domingo, and Thorsten Quandt (2007); Sue Robinson (2007); David M. Ryfe (2012); Philip Schlesinger and Gillian Doyle (2015); Jonathan Scott, David Millard, and Pauline Leonard (2015); Nikki Usher (2014); Karin Wahl-Jorgensen (2007); Patrick Weber (2013); and Andy Williams, Clarie Wardle, and Karin Wahl-Jorgensen (2010).

4. See Christopher W. Anderson (2010, 2013a), Charlie Beckett and Robin Mansell (2008), Matt Carlson (2015a), Mark Deuze (2007, 2008a), Seth C. Lewis (2012), David M. Ryfe (2012), and Nikki Usher (2014).

5. See Christopher W. Anderson (2011b, 2013b), Michael A. DeVito (2016), Nicholas Diakopoulos (2015), Konstantin Nicholas Dörr (2015), Dörr and Katharina Hollnbuchner (2016), Jan Kleinnijenhuis, Friederike Schultz, Dirk Oegema, and Wouter van Atteveldt (2013), and Arjen van Dalen (2012).

6. A recent and notable effort to focus explicitly on online journalism's normative dimensions is Chris Peters and Marcel Broersma (2017).

7. By no means do I think that learning or practicing crafts is undertheorized or simple. Scholars have traced how journalists can engage in communities of "reflective practice" (Schön, 1983) and how deeply practitioners can articulate what they define as good work (Gardner, Csikszentmihalyi, & Damon, 2002) if given the opportunity.

8. For a good short introduction to the field's history and core concepts, see Sergio Sismondo (2009).

9. See Manuel DeLanda (2006) and George E. Marcus and Erkan Saka (2006) for good reconstructions and contextualizations of Deleuze and Guattari's theory and Martin Müller (2015) for a helpful comparison of assemblage and actor-network theories.

10. This mention of difference begs the question of what constitutes a meaningful difference, hinting at a pragmatic standard that Noortje Marres (2012) develops in

her account of how Deweyan publics arise and focus on issues through a mix of social and technological conditions.

11. It is beyond the scope of this book to review the rich literature on participatory design and people's understandings of publicness, but see Carl DiSalvo (2009, 2014, 2016); DiSalvo, Marti Louw, David Holstius, Illah Nourbakhsh, and Ayça Akin (2012); Bruno Latour and Peter Weibel (2005); Christopher A. Le Dantec et al. (2010); LeDantec and Carl DiSalvo (2013); Alison Powell (2016); and Tommaso Venturini, Donato Ricci, Michele Mauri, Lucy Kimbell, and Axel Meunier (2015) for excellent recent discussions. For rich accounts of how software hackers imagine publics through their design activities and political interventions, see Gabriella Coleman (2011, 2013), Thomas James Lodato and Carol DiSalvo (2016), and Andrew R. Schrock (2016).

12. See Joshua A. Braun (2015) for a conceptually and empirically rich application of networked organizational studies and heterogeneous engineering to media distribution networks, and see Christian Katzenbach (2011) and Philip M. Napoli (2014) and for strong arguments that seeing algorithms as institutions can help scholars see how algorithms "facilitate and constrain the behaviors and cognitions of both media organizations and media users" (Napoli, 2014, p. 353).

13. For recent discussions of how the normative vision of journalism is changing see Matt Carlson (2017) and John Steel (2017). And for a good overview of the public-interest issues raised by news platforms and technology companies that refuse to see themselves as media companies, see Napoli (2015) and Napoli and Robyn Caplan (2017).

Chapter 5

1. http://niemanreports.org/articles/a-brief-guide-to-robot-reporting-tools.

2. http://www.niemanlab.org/2014/09/watching-what-happens-the-new-york -times-is-making-a-front-page-bet-on-real-time-aggregation.

3. http://www.poynter.org/2013/propublica-releases-simple-tool-for-searching -instagram/212719.

4. http://www.niemanlab.org/2015/06/how-a-group-of-researchers-tried-to-use -social-media-data-and-algorithms-to-find-breaking-news.

5. Although it did not appear in the trade press corpus, see Neil Thurman, Steve Schifferes, Richard Fletcher, Nic Newman, Stephen Hunt, and Aljosha Karim Schapals (2016) for a thoughtful scholarly account of a similar tool, SocialSensor, which was designed by European researchers to help journalists identify trending stories.

6. http://www.theatlantic.com/business/archive/2016/12/information-bubbles /509039; https://www.opensecrets.org/resources/learn/anomalies.php.

7. https://projects.propublica.org/docdollars.

8. https://www.propublica.org/getinvolved/item/reporting-recipe-investigating -restraint-and-seclusion-in-us-schools.

9. https://www.propublica.org/datastore.

10. http://www.dronejournalismlab.org/manual.

11. http://www.nytimes.com/2015/01/16/business/media/10-companies-join-effort -to-test-drones-for-newsgathering.html.

12. http://www.poynter.org/2015/what-the-faas-newly-proposed-drone-rules-mean -to-journalists/320079.

13. http://www.cjr.org/q_and_a/new_drone_rules_journalists_faq.php.

14. https://www.noflyzone.org.

15. http://www.roboticstrends.com/article/dji_blocks_drone_flights_in_washington _dc_after_white_house_crash.

16. https://www.nytimes.com/2014/11/03/us/police-targeted-media-with-no-fly -zone-over-ferguson-tapes-show.html.

17. See Matt Carlson (2016) and Andreas Graefe (2016) for recent summaries of this domain; Michael A. Beam (2014); Graefe, Mario Haim, Bastian Haarmann, and Hans-Bernd Brosius (2016) for a study of people's perception of algorithmically generated news stories; Neil Thurman et al. (2016) for an account of creating algo-rithmically produced news; and Tetyana Lokot and Nicholas Diakopoulos (2016) for a review of bot-based journalism.

18. See Christopher W. Anderson (forthcoming a) for a historical and contemporary account of structured data's influence on journalistic production.

19. http://www.niemanlab.org/2014/03/when-robots-help-human-journalists-this -post-was-created-by-an-algorithm-written-by-the-author; http://www.nytimes.com /2015/03/08/opinion/sunday/if-an-algorithm-wrote-this-how-would-you-even-know .html.

20. http://niemanreports.org/articles/automation-in-the-newsroom.

21. https://www.propublica.org/nerds/item/how-to-edit-52000-stories-at-once.

22. http://www.theatlantic.com/technology/archive/2014/03/earthquake-bot-los -angeles-times/359261; http://www.theatlantic.com/technology/archive/2014/03/how -a-california-earthquake-becomes-the-news-an-extremely-precise-timeline/284506.

23. https://insights.ap.org/industry-trends/study-news-automation-by-ap-increases -trading-in-financial-markets.

24. http://www.niemanlab.org/2016/10/the-new-york-times-is-using-a-facebook -messenger-bot-to-send-out-election-updates.

25. http://digiday.com/platforms/washington-chatbots-news.

26. http://www.niemanlab.org/2016/07/developed-with-young-readers-in-mind -cnns-new-kik-bot-gives-you-the-basics-on-big-news-stories.

27. http://variety.com/2015/digital/news/nbc-news-is-first-tv-news-service-to -connect-with-kik-mobile-chat-service-1201462575.

28. http://www.niemanlab.org/2016/02/with-an-interface-that-looks-like-a-chat -platform-quartz-wants-to-text-you-the-news-in-its-new-app.

29. http://www.niemanlab.org/2016/11/quartz-launches-its-bot-studio-with-a -quarter-million-from-knight-and-plans-for-slack-and-amazon-echo.

30. www.niemanlab.org/2016/05/the-washington-post-tests-personalized-pop-up -newsletters-to-promote-its-big-stories.

31. http://www.niemanlab.org/2016/02/how-the-washington-post-built-its-tool-to -re-engage-the-attention-of-distracted-readers-on-mobile.

32. http://www.nytimes.com/interactive/2015/12/15/upshot/the-best-places-for -better-cheaper-health-care-arent-what-experts-thought.html.

33. http://publiceditor.blogs.nytimes.com/2015/12/17/when-news-gets-too -personal.

34. http://www.niemanlab.org/2016/10/the-ap-wants-to-use-machine-learning-to -automate-turning-print-stories-into-broadcast-ones.

35. For overviews of computational and communicative issues in designing embod- ied conversational agents, see Timothy Bickmore and Justine Cassell (2005) and Cassell, Joseph Sullivan, Scott Prevost, and Elizabeth F. Churchill (2000).

36. He defines the best dialogues as civil, governed by norms and theories of public- ness, and integrated with other types of media.

37. In December 2016, Facebook CEO Mark Zuckerberg acknowledged that Facebook is not a "traditional" media company, saying "we do a lot more than just distribute news, and we're an important part of the public discourse" (Gibbs, 2016, n.p.). And in 2011, Google's Larry Page stated that "trying to improve media" was part of Google's responsibility (Myers, 2011, n.p.).

38. https://www.facebook.com/notes/facebook-media/12-best-practices-for-media -companies-using-facebook-pages/518053828230111.

39. https://support.google.com/news/publisher/answer/40787?hl=en.

40. http://www.niemanlab.org/2011/06/twitter-for-newsrooms-as-a-relationship
-building-guide.

41. http://www.wsj.com/articles/facebook-signs-deals-with-media-companies
-celebrities-for-facebook-live-1466533472.

42. http://adage.com/article/media/twitter-partners-bbc-news-embargo-8/244897.

43. http://www.niemanlab.org/2015/03/a-wave-of-distributed-content is coming
-will-publishers-sink-or-swim.

44. http://www.nytimes.com/2015/05/13/technology/facebook-media-venture-to
-include-nbc-buzzfeed-and-new-york-times.html.

45. http://www.poynter.org/2016/facebook-is-opening-up-instant-articles-to
-newsrooms-everywhere-will-a-flood-of-distributed-content-follow/397305.

46. https://media.fb.com/2015/05/12/instantarticles.

47. http://www.adweek.com/socialtimes/the-new-york-times-notes/426652.

48. http://www.niemanlab.org/2016/02/diving-all-in-or-dipping-a-toe-how
-publishers-are-approaching-googles-accelerated-mobile-pages-initiative; http://www
.niemanlab.org/2016/02/a-qa-with-googles-head-of-news-richard-gingras-on-its-vision
-for-the-accelerated-mobile-pages-project.

49. http://www.niemanlab.org/2015/10/twitter-unveils-its-own-news-digests-with
-mentions-and-some-news-orgs-can-participate.

50. http://www.niemanlab.org/2015/09/snapchat-wants-to-slip-a-little-news-into
-teens-social-smartphone-time.

51. http://www.niemanlab.org/2015/09/from-two-day-shipping-to-news-a-cheaper
-washington-post-is-now-an-amazon-prime-benefit.

52. http://www.businessinsider.com/facebook-news-feed-update-banishes-memes
-2013-12.

53. http://www.journalism.org/2015/07/14/news-habits-on-facebook-and-twitter;
http://www.poynter.org/2011/yahoo-users-searched-for-more-international-news
-than-bing-users/154690.

54. http://www.niemanlab.org/2011/09/with-its-standout-tag-google-news-is
-giving-publishers-new-incentive-to-credit-the-competition.

55. http://www.nytimes.com/2016/04/25/business/vox-media-tries-something-old
-on-something-new.html.

56. http://www.niemanlab.org/2016/08/alexa-give-me-the-news-how-outlets-are
-tailoring-their-coverage-for-amazons-new-platform.

57. http://www.niemanlab.org/2014/01/now-thats-adaptive-design-the-verge-show-different-versions-of-a-story-to-apple-google-or-microsoft-users.

58. http://www.poynter.org/2013/new-york-times-experiments-with-tweetable-highlights-in-snl-story/221911.

59. http://www.niemanlab.org/2015/10/instant-articles-get-shared-more-than-old-fashioned-links-plus-more-details-from-facebooks-news-push.

60. https://media.fb.com/2016/12/01/how-instant-articles-benefits-local-news.

61. http://www.niemanlab.org/2012/02/how-npr-drove-traffic-to-a-local-station-by-geotargeting-stories-on-facebook.

62. http://www.businessinsider.com/facebook-news-feed-update-banishes-memes-2013-12; http://www.adweek.com/news/technology/facebook-algorithm-tweaks-hurt-viral-sites-more-other-publishers-156533.

63. http://mashable.com/2014/07/13/facebook-politics-partisan-newsfeed.

64. http://www.nytimes.com/2016/06/30/technology/facebook-to-change-news-feed-to-focus-on-friends-and-family.html.

65. http://www.nytimes.com/2016/08/05/technology/facebook-moves-to-push-clickbait-lower-in-the-news-feed.html.

66. http://digiday.com/publishers/publishers-enjoy-facebook-traffic-boon; http://www.niemanlab.org/2014/08/sharing-on-facebook-surges-at-the-telegraph.

67. https://theawl.com/platform-patched-38e0a127576f#.kjzrboa4d; https://gigaom.com/2014/02/18/reality-check-no-upworthys-traffic-didnt-get-crushed-by-facebooks-algorithm-change.

68. http://www.niemanlab.org/2014/08/mastering-the-dark-arts-facebook-has-been-the-key-to-mother-jones-growing-popularity-online.

69. http://www.poynter.org/2014/mental-floss-a-big-winner-after-facebooks-mysterious-high-quality-algorithm-change/239917.

70. http://digiday.com/publishers/bleacher-report-facebook-proofing-traffic.

71. http://www.niemanlab.org/2010/01/what-qualifies-as-a-spotlight-story-on-google-news-heres-a-few-clues; http://www.niemanlab.org/2013/08/googles-new-search-feature-makes-it-easier-to-find-seminal-articles-on-big-topics.

72. http://www.niemanlab.org/2011/09/with-its-standout-tag-google-news-is-giving-publishers-new-incentive-to-credit-the-competition.

73. https://support.google.com/news/publisher/answer/93992?hl=en; https://support.google.com/news/publisher/answer/4582731.

74. http://www.poynter.org/2013/new-facebook-feature-suggests-which-content-news-orgs-should-share/226689.

75. http://www.adweek.com/socialtimes/twitter-embedding-articles/487203.

76. As Susan Leigh Star (1999, p. 382) argues, the "normally invisible quality of working infrastructure becomes visible when it breaks … [creating] the basis for a much more detailed understanding of the relational nature of infrastructure."

77. http://www.cjr.org/analysis/facebook_and_media.php; http://www.cjr.org/tow_center/facebook_zuckerberg_trump_election.php.

78. http://www.poynter.org/2013/twitter-apologizes-for-blocking-newspapers-urls/228372.

79. http://www.pottsmerc.com/article/20130810/NEWS01/130819954#full_story.

80. http://www.npr.org/sections/thetwo-way/2016/09/09/493267919/after-facebook-censors-iconic-photo-norwegian-newspaper-pushes-back.

81. http://www.nytimes.com/2016/09/10/technology/facebook-vietnam-war-photo-nudity.html.

82. Although not a news organization, the American Civil Liberties Union had its account suspended after it "posted a link on Facebook to a blog post about the debate over a statue in a public part outside of Kansas City, which depicts a nude woman taking a photo of her exposed breasts" (D. Cohen, 2013, n.p.).

83. http://mashable.com/2014/08/18/washington-post-amazon-buy-button/#yE0OgGN2asqL.

84. https://www.theguardian.com/technology/2014/aug/21/twitter-free-speech-champion-selective-censor.

85. https://www.fastcompany.com/3008881/tracking/circas-object-oriented-approach-to-building-the-news.

86. http://www.niemanlab.org/2013/06/when-editors-design-controlling-presentation-in-structured-content.

87. https://www.propublica.org/nerds/item/why-develop-in-the-newsroom; https://hackerjournalist.net/2013/07/18/why-i-work-in-a-newsroom.

88. https://source.opennews.org/en-US/articles/boyer-interview; https://www.journalism.co.uk/news/recalculating-the-newsroom-the-rise-of-the-journo-coder-/s2/a555646.

89. http://www.niemanlab.org/2013/03/jake-levine-why-learning-to-code-isnt-as-important-as-learning-to-build-something.

90. http://www.niemanlab.org/2014/01/the-new-york-times-rd-lab-is-building-a-quantified-self-semantic-analysis-tool-to-track-web-browsing.

91. http://www.niemanlab.org/encyclo/hackshackers.

92. http://www.niemanlab.org/2013/03/opennews-learning-wants-to-provide-lessons-to-developers-in-and-out-of-newsrooms.

93. http://www.niemanlab.org/2011/08/transparency-iteration-standards-knight-mozillas-learning-lab-shares-lessons-of-open-source-for-journalism.

94. http://www.niemanlab.org/2012/07/context-code-and-community-source-is-one-stop-shopping-for-newsroom-developers.

95. http://www.niemanlab.org/2013/10/qa-guardian-social-and-community-editor-joanna-geary-heads-off-to-twitter-u-k.

96. http://money.cnn.com/2015/09/29/media/liz-heron-facebook-huffington-post/index.html.

97. http://www.wsj.com/articles/the-rise-of-the-publishing-platform-specialist-1458896683.

98. https://www.theguardian.com/technology/2016/dec/12/facebook-advertises-for-head-of-news-us-election-concerns-fake-news.

99. http://www.poynter.org/2015/eric-zuckerman-named-news-partnerships-manager-at-twitter/355615.

100. http://www.poynter.org/2011/bbc-reporter-takes-her-60000-twitter-followers-to-competitor-itv/140566.

101. http://mediashift.org/2014/07/remix-put-data-journalism-into-every-entry-level-j-school-class; http://www.cjr.org/analysis/data.php; http://www.niemanlab.org/2011/01/dave-winer-how-can-universities-educate-journo-programmers.

102. http://www.niemanlab.org/2016/10/facebook-launches-online-courses-for-journalists-about-what-else-using-facebook.

103. http://www.niemanlab.org/2015/12/a-new-class-at-usc-is-teaching-students-how-to-produce-stories-specifically-for-social-media.

104. http://knightlab.northwestern.edu/2016/09/15/software-developers-interested-in-journalism-northwestern-and-the-washington-post-want-you.

105. https://journalists.org/programs/ap-google-scholarship.

106. http://www.niemanlab.org/2011/11/how-time-inc-is-preparing-for-a-future-in-digital-news-with-a-j-school-of-its-own.

107. http://www.adweek.com/fishbowlny/code-with-me-journalist-training-workshop-headed-to-portland/259146.

108. http://gizmodo.com/they-treated-us-like-garbage-former-trending-news-writ-1789248355; http://gizmodo.com/want-to-know-what-facebook-really-thinks-of-journalists-1773916117.

109. http://www.forbes.com/sites/leifwalcutt/2016/08/26/facebook-lays-off-journalists-from-trending-topics-replaces-with-algorithm/#71e0d9fa341b.

110. http://www.cjr.org/innovations/tony_haile_chartbeat.php.

111. http://www.poynter.org/2011/new-generation-of-web-analytics-applies-big-data-to-newsroom-decisions-visual-revenue-jumptime/143389.

112. http://www.nytimes.com/2010/09/06/business/media/06track.html.

113. http://www.niemanlab.org/2012/08/metrics-metrics-everywhere-how-do-we-measure-the-impact-of-journalism; http://www.greglinch.com/2012/01/quantifying-impact-a-better-metric-for-measuring-journalism.html.

114. https://www.journalism.co.uk/news/measuring-the-news-what-are-the-alternatives-to-pageviews-/s2/a556640.

115. https://source.opennews.org/en-US/articles/promotion-pageviews.

116. http://www.niemanlab.org/2013/11/the-only-metric-that-matters-total-time-reading.

117. http://www.adweek.com/fishbowlny/upworthy-ditches-pageviews-and-uniques/266828.

118. http://newsroom.fb.com/news/2015/06/news-feed-fyi-taking-into-account-time-spent-on-stories.

119. http://www.adweek.com/fishbowlny/guardian-attention-analytics/266853.

120. http://streetfightmag.com/2014/06/12/attention-and-timing-are-the-new-clicks-chartbeat-says.

121. https://gigaom.com/2014/09/29/chartbeat-gets-certified-to-measure-attention-tries-to-move-advertising-away-from-clicks-and-pageviews.

122. www.niemanlab.org/2016/08/the-daily-signal-created-a-custom-engagement-index-to-help-it-prioritize-all-its-platforms.

123. http://digiday.com/publishers/christian-science-monitor-going-maximum-engagement.

124. http://www.niemanlab.org/2015/06/tracking-impact-newslynx-goes-beyond-google-analytics-to-measure-a-storys-path-in-the-real-world.

125. http://thenextweb.com/media/2015/04/13/how-the-guardians-ophan-analytics-engine-helps-editors-make-better-decisions.

126. http://www.niemanlab.org/2016/03/the-ft-is-launching-a-new-analytics-tool -to-make-metrics-more-understandable-for-its-newsroom.

127. http://www.niemanlab.org/2016/07/the-new-york-times-is-trying-to-narrow -the-distance-between-reporters-and-analytics-data.

128. http://www.niemanlab.org/2014/04/building-an-analytics-culture-in-a -newsroom-how-npr-is-trying-to-expand-its-digital-thinking.

129. http://www.niemanlab.org/2015/09/facebook-rolls-out-new-tools-to-help -reporters-share-their-work-and-choose-who-sees-it.

130. http://www.niemanlab.org/2014/08/when-it-comes-to-chasing-clicks -journalists-say-one-thing-but-feel-pressure-to-do-another; http://www.niemanlab .org/2010/09/what-impact-is-seo-having-on-journalists-reports-from-the-field; http:// towcenter.org/research/traffic-factories.

131. http://www.wsj.com/articles/washington-posts-bandit-tool-optimizes-content -for-clicks-1454960088.

132. http://www.niemanlab.org/2014/05/watching-the-audience-move-a-new-york -times-tool-is-helping-direct-traffic-from-story-to-story.

133. http://ajr.org/2014/03/19/analytics-news-sites-grapple-can-see-data.

134. https://www.nytimes.com/2014/03/24/business/media/risks-abound-as -reporters-play-in-traffic.html.

135. https://www.washingtonpost.com/blogs/erik-wemple/wp/2014/02/26/daily -caller-implements-hybrid-salaryinternet-incentive-pay-plan.

136. http://ajr.org/2014/03/27/pay-per-visit-debate-chasing-viral-traffic-hurting -journalism.

137. http://talkingbiznews.com/1/thestreet-com-seeks-contributors.

138. http://www.poynter.org/2014/advance-defends-bonuses-for-reporters-who -post-frequently-and-join-comment-chains/244808.

139. http://www.niemanlab.org/2014/10/an-interesting-way-to-pay-reporters-give -them-the-revenue-from-their-own-google-adsense-ads.

140. http://gawker.com/time-inc-rates-writers-on-how-beneficial-they-are-to -1623253026.

141. http://pressthink.org/2010/10/the-100-percent-solution-for-innovation-in-news; http://mediashift.org/2010/07/your-guide-to-next-generation-content-farms200.

142. http://www.poynter.org/2014/as-reporters-get-measured-why-even-buzzfeed -upworthy-arent-beholden-to-numbers/244541; http://ajr.org/2014/04/15/give-jour nalists-right-metrics-pay-performance.

143. http://www.niemanlab.org/2016/02/the-next-step-moving-from-generic -analytics-to-editorial-analytics.

144. A complete review of journalism's temporalities is beyond the scope of this book, but for excellent general discussions of how journalism shapes and reflects social senses of time, see Kevin G. Barnhurst (2011); Allan Bell (1995); Dan Berkowitz (1992); Daniel Dayan and Elihu Katz (1994); Jill A. Edy (1999); Richard B. Kielbowicz (2015); Harvey Molotch and Marilyn Lester (1974), Motti Neiger, Oren Meyers, and Eyal Zandberg (2011); Neiger and Keren Tenenboim-Weinblatt (2016); Michael Schudson (1986); Tenenboim-Weinblatt (2013, 2014); and Zelizer (2014).

145. For discussions of contemporary networked news temporality, see Mike Ananny (2016b); Henrik Bødker (2017); Frode Guribye and Lars Nyre (2016); Matthew Jones, Kamal Munir, Wanda Orlikowski, and Jochen Runde (2008); Christine Larson (2015); Zvi Reich and Yigal Godler (2014); James Stanyer and Sabrina Mihelj (2016); Judy Wajcman (2014); Esther Weltevrede, Anne Helmond, and Carolin Gerlitz (2014).

146. http://www.niemanlab.org/2013/09/journalism-has-become-unstuck-in-time.

147. http://www.niemanlab.org/2014/05/immediacy-vs-importance-the-tension -underlying-how-the-nytimes-com-homepage-gets-made.

148. http://www.bbc.com/news/blogs-echochambers-27553248.

149. http://www.theatlantic.com/business/archive/2015/03/facebook-google-and -the-economics-of-time/387877.

150. http://www.poynter.org/2011/pulitzers-shift-to-all-digital-entry-format /154546.

151. http://www.niemanlab.org/2011/10/is-the-huffington-post-reinventing-the -art-of-liveblogging; http://www.niemanlab.org/2012/03/practice-pray-and-have -redundancies-on-the-imperfect-science-of-liveblogging.

152. https://www.washingtonpost.com/blogs/erik-wemple/wp/2015/10/14/what-is -the-new-york-times-doing-with-breaking-news-unit.

153. http://www.niemanlab.org/2012/08/live-broadcast-why-the-huffington-post -and-boston-com-are-getting-into-streaming-media.

154. http://www.niemanlab.org/2012/03/embracing-the-stream-itvs-new-twitter -inspired-news-site-breaks-the-days-news-into-pieces.

155. http://www.niemanlab.org/2012/07/how-buzzfeed-wants-to-reinvent-wire -stories-for-social-media; http://www.theatlantic.com/technology/archive/2013/04 /breaking-news-is-broken-could-buzzfeed-be-the-one-to-fix-it/275310.

156. http://www.niemanlab.org/2011/10/adam-moss-ny-mag-publishes-new -content-every-six-minutes.

157. http://www.npr.org/sections/ombudsman/2016/02/18/467123974/live-from-d
-c-its-the-npr-newscast.

158. https://www.poynter.org/2015/how-should-journalists-navigate-meerkat
-periscope-kik-and-what-the-heck-is-tarsii/331251; http://www.ibtimes.com/twitters
-periscope-infiltrates-tv-newsrooms-reporters-cnn-cbs-nbc-others-try-live-1866848;
http://www.recode.net/2016/4/6/11585888/facebook-paying-media-partners-like
-buzzfeed-to-livestream.

159. http://www.niemanlab.org/2014/09/watching-what-happens-the-new-york
-times-is-making-a-front-page-bet-on-real-time-aggregation; https://www.journalism
.co.uk/news/why-the-new-york-times-has-launched-new-homepage-stream
-watching-/s2/a562568.

160. http://sarahmarshall.io/post/107708899448/using-the-quotable-tool-for-real
-time-social.

161. http://www.niemanlab.org/2012/09/first-look-spundge-is-software-to-help
-journalists-to-manage-real-time-data-streams.

162. https://gigaom.com/2014/05/16/grasswire-founder-austen-allred-is-trying-to
-build-a-wikipedia-style-platform-for-real-time-news.

163. http://www.nytimes.com/2015/03/08/opinion/sunday/if-an-algorithm-wrote
-this-how-would-you-even-know.html.

164. http://thomsonreuters.com/content/dam/openweb/documents/pdf/tr-com
-financial/news-analytics-product-brochure--oct-2010.pdf.

165. https://www.journalism.co.uk/news/mobile-journalism-sky-news-reporters
-broadcast-ready-in-90-seconds-/s2/a555282.

166. http://www.niemanlab.org/2016/06/the-guardian-is-experimenting-with
-interactive-auto-updating-push-alerts-to-cover-big-stories.

167. http://www.niemanlab.org/2016/06/the-guardian-is-experimenting-with
-interactive-auto-updating-push-alerts-to-cover-big-stories.

168. http://www.niemanlab.org/2016/04/you-can-now-get-personalized-breaking
-news-alerts-on-slack.

169. http://www.niemanlab.org/2014/06/the-notification-knows-where-you-are
-breaking-news-debuts-news-alerts-tied-to-your-location.

170. http://www.cjr.org/tow_center/mobile_notifications_changing_new_york
_times.php; http://www.nytimes.com/times-insider/2015/04/01/this-just-in-behind
-the-news-alert.

171. https://www.washingtonpost.com/pr/wp/2016/03/23/how-the-washington
-post-improved-the-speed-of-breaking-news-email-alerts/?utm_term=.710e92e75e1f;

http://bleacherreport.com/articles/1124741-inside-media-on-breaking-news
-sourcing-credit-scoops-in-sports.

172. http://www.poynter.org/2013/ap-sends-rare-flash-for-mandelas-death/232611.

173. http://www.adweek.com/socialtimes/study-twitter-rarely-beats-news-outlets-to
-breaking-news/132842.

174. http://www.journalism.org/2015/07/14/the-evolving-role-of-news-on-twitter
-and-facebook.

175. http://www.poynter.org/2012/when-news-breaks-most-americans-seek-a
-second-trusted-source-for-more-info/190640.

176. http://www.niemanlab.org/2014/05/how-is-twitter-different-during-a-big
-news-event-personal-chatter-goes-down-attention-shifts-to-elites.

177. http://www.theatlantic.com/technology/archive/2012/11/how-to-tweet
-responsibly-during-a-breaking-news-event/264386; http://www.adweek.com/fish
bowlny/5-things-tweeting-a-tragedy/257761; https://www.washingtonpost.com
/lifestyle/style/news-outlets-often-stumble-in-quest-for-speed-and-accuracy/2013
/09/16/e5444820-1f19-11e3-8459-657e0c72fec8_story.html.

178. http://www.adweek.com/lostremote/ap-offering-slow-tv-for-breaking-news
/50267.

179. http://www.poynter.org/2012/bbc-news-when-to-break-news-on-twitter
/162588.

180. http://www.niemanlab.org/2013/04/breaking-news-pragmatically-some
-reflections-on-silence-and-timing-in-networked-journalism.

181. https://gigaom.com/2013/07/08/if-you-dont-like-the-chaos-of-breaking-news
-you-should-probably-stay-off-twitter.

182. http://www.niemanlab.org/2012/12/from-real-time-to-slow-social; http://www
.cjr.org/the_kicker/what_we_need_is_a_slow_news_mo.php; https://www.theguard
ian.com/commentisfree/2013/apr/23/ap-twitter-hack-hoax-digital-media.

183. http://www.nytimes.com/2012/05/13/magazine/joe-weisenthal-vs-the-24
-hour-news-cycle.html; http://www.poynter.org/2012/kim-bui-growing-demands-on
-reporters-time-is-worrisome/161267.

184. http://jimromenesko.com/2014/02/18/u-s-news-deletes-content-published
-before-2007.

185. http://gawker.com/over-4-000-buzzfeed-posts-have-completely-disappeared
-1619473070.

186. http://www.poynter.org/2014/buzzfeeds-ben-smith-we-didnt-fully-think
-through-the-removal-of-old-posts/264007.

187. http://www.niemanlab.org/2012/06/great-idea-pastpages-offers-automated-citations-for-researchers.

188. http://www.niemanlab.org/2014/11/storytracker-is-a-new-tool-to-track-how-news-homepages-change.

189. http://www.cjr.org/watchdog/newsdiffs_new_york_times.php.

190. http://www.niemanlab.org/2013/04/the-newsonomics-of-recycling-journalism.

191. http://digiday.com/publishers/publishers-evergreen-content-strategy-make-the-old-new-again.

192. http://open.blogs.nytimes.com/2016/07/26/the-future-of-the-past-modernizing-the-new-york-times-archive.

193. http://mediashift.org/2014/04/future-proofing-news-apps.

194. http://www.cjr.org/behind_the_news/minus_proper_archives_many_new.php.

195. http://www.sacbee.com/news/local/education/article71659992.html.

196. http://www.huffingtonpost.com/2015/06/04/twitter-revokes-politwoops_n_7512892.html.

197. http://mobile.nytimes.com/2016/01/01/technology/twitter-politwoops.html.

198. https://www.fastcompany.com/3040983/meet-timeline-a-mobile-news-app-with-a-long-long-memory.

199. http://www.poynter.org/2013/5-ways-journalists-can-use-social-media-to-resurface-old-content/197991.

200. https://medium.com/@adriennelaf/what-will-yesterdays-news-look-like-tomorrow-7f82290ab8d0#.t58uvn3ig.

201. http://www.niemanlab.org/2010/09/whats-the-law-around-aggregating-news-online-a-harvard-law-report-on-the-risks-and-the-best-practices.

202. http://www.niemanlab.org/2010/03/the-barclays-case-will-hot-news-limit-the-right-to-aggregate-news.

203. http://www.niemanlab.org/2014/10/the-hot-news-doctrine-lives-and-earns-dow-jones-a-5-million-ruling.

204. http://globenewswire.com/news-release/2010/11/15/434451/207063/en/Dow-Jones-Successfully-Resolves-Lawsuit-Aimed-at-Protecting-Its-Content.html.

205. http://www.poynter.org/2012/university-of-washington-limits-reporters-live-tweets-during-games/195653.

206. https://www.nytimes.com/2014/10/04/business/media/times-articles-removed
-from-google-results-in-europe.html.

207. https://www.americanpressinstitute.org/need-to-know/offshore/bbc-listing-its
-pages-removed-from-google-as-part-of-europes-right-to-be-forgotten-law.

208. https://techcrunch.com/2011/11/03/googles-new-algorithm-update-impacts
-35-of-searches.

209. http://mobile.nytimes.com/blogs/bits/2011/11/03/google-changes-search
-algorithm-trying-to-make-results-more-timely.

210. http://www.nytimes.com/2016/04/25/business/media/snapchat-election
-campaign-news.html.

211. http://digiday.com/platforms/news-crew-shooting-shows-perils-auto-play
-videos-twitter-facebook.

212. http://www.niemanlab.org/2014/09/how-nytimes-com-cut-load-times-and-got
-faster-for-users.

213. http://www.poynter.org/2016/facebook-is-opening-up-instant-articles-to
-newsrooms-everywhere-will-a-flood-of-distributed-content-follow/397305.

214. http://www.niemanlab.org/2016/02/a-qa-with-googles-head-of-news-richard
-gingras-on-its-vision-for-the-accelerated-mobile-pages-project; http://www.niemanlab
.org/2016/02/diving-all-in-or-dipping-a-toe-how-publishers-are-approaching
-googles-accelerated-mobile-pages-initiative; http://www.nytco.com/the-new-york
-times-participates-in-google-amp-project.

215. http://www.nytimes.com/2017/01/01/technology/google-amp-mobile
-publishing.html.

216. http://www.poynter.org/2012/study-bbc-articles-live-longest-on-twitter
/191793.

217. http://www.adweek.com/socialtimes/best-time-to-post-social-media/504222;
https://www.americanpressinstitute.org/publications/reports/survey-research/how
-americans-get-news/, https://blog.bufferapp.com/best-time-to-tweet-research.

218. http://www.niemanlab.org/2013/05/at-the-miami-herald-tweetings-about
-breaking-news-in-the-a-m-and-conversation-in-the-p-m.

219. http://www.niemanlab.org/2014/07/report-around-the-clock-how-some-news
-orgs-use-time-zones-to-their-advantage-to-operate-247.

220. http://www.niemanlab.org/2014/02/who-edits-breaking-news-articles-on
-wikipedia.

221. https://gigaom.com/2014/02/25/reddit-embraces-its-role-as-a-journalistic
-entity-with-new-live-reporting-feature.

222. http://www.niemanlab.org/2015/03/r-i-p-chinua-achebe-again-the-unstuck-in -time-life-of-social-media.

223. http://www.theatlantic.com/technology/archive/2015/03/on-social-media -everything-happens-all-the-time/388469.

224. See Wajcman (2014) for an excellent survey of the technological dimensions of contemporary time cultures.

225. http://www.niemanlab.org/2016/03/the-uks-times-and-sunday-times-are -structuring-their-new-apps-and-website-around-peak-traffic-times.

226. http://www.niemanlab.org/2015/10/is-there-an-ideal-time-of-day-to-read -news-a-site-called-twelve-thirty-six-has-one-idea-youll-never-guess.

227. https://www.theguardian.com/help/insideguardian/2015/mar/09/introducing -moments-from-the-guardian-app-built-for-apple-watch.

228. http://www.nytco.com/the-times-rolls-out-one-sentence-stories-on-apple-watch.

229. http://www.niemanlab.org/2015/03/the-next-stage-in-the-battle-for-our -attention-our-wrists.

230. https://gigaom.com/2013/05/29/ft-launches-breaking-news-tool-when-140 -characters-doesnt-cut-it.

231. https://www.journalism.co.uk/news/news-on-demand-to-offer-articles-based -on-readers-attention/s2/a556587.

232. http://www.niemanlab.org/2016/05/good-news-publishers-people-will-read -your-long-stories-on-their-phones-for-two-minutes-anyway.

233. http://www.niemanlab.org/2016/11/you-can-now-connect-your-washington -post-app-to-uber-for-more-efficient-in-car-reading.

234. http://www.niemanlab.org/2015/10/cant-finish-a-new-yorker-story-online-the -magazine-will-now-send-you-an-email-reminder-to-come-back.

235. http://www.mathewingram.com/work/2015/04/01/the-economist-wants-to -give-you-a-sense-of-completeness-even-if-thats-an-illusion.

236. https://medium.com/@jkalven/watch-out-a-cliff-d2312cbb1fc4#.xy3dejhe8.

237. For example, http://www.scpr.org/news/2016/08/30/64142/fast-moving-river side-county-fire-burns-120-acres.

238. http://digiday.com/publishers/four-tactics-publishers-use-get-readers-stick -around; http://digiday.com/brands/definitive-digiday-guide-whats-whats-2017

239. For more on anticipation as sociotechnical work, see Steven J. Jackson (2016); Jackson, David Ribes, Ayse Buyuktur, and Geoffrey C. Bowker (2011); and Stephanie B. Steinhardt and Jackson (2014, 2015).

240. http://www.niemanlab.org/2014/06/can-you-turn-future-news-events-into
-structured-data; https://wicknews.wordpress.com/2014/06/12/is-future-news-the
-news-of-the-future.

241. http://www.niemanlab.org/2015/08/push-it-how-breaking-news-notifies
-users-of-news-stories-before-they-become-big; http://blog.breakingnews.com/post
/124267649514/know-faster-with-emerging-story-alerts.

242. http://www.niemanlab.org/2016/11/reuters-built-its-own-algorithmic
-prediction-tool-to-help-it-spot-and-verify-breaking-news-on-twitter.

243. http://mediashift.org/2013/12/freedom-of-the-press-foundation-steps-up
-encryption-efforts-for-journalists; http://www.niemanlab.org/2013/12/91274.

244. http://www.cjr.org/analysis/security_tools.php.

245. http://www.niemanlab.org/2014/12/algorithm-fatigue-what-evernotes-news
-recommending-product-can-tell-us-about-privacy; http://www.newsweek.com/wary
-privacy-issues-ditch-dropbox-and-avoid-google-says-edward-snowden-276956.

246. http://www.huffingtonpost.com/2013/06/10/edward-snowden-glenn
-greenwald_n_3416978.html.

247. http://www.cjr.org/feature/the_back_door.php.

248. http://www.nytimes.com/2016/07/22/technology/edward-snowden-to-help
-develop-a-safer-phone-for-journalists.html.

249. http://niemanreports.org/articles/how-to-deter-doxxing.

250. http://www.niemanlab.org/2014/03/hacking-in-the-newsroom-what
-journalists-should-know-about-the-computer-fraud-and-abuse-act.

251. In the opening of his book *No Place to Hide*, Glenn Greenwald (2014) describes
how Edward Snowden refused to communicate with him until Greenwald had created an encryption key and demonstrated his proficiency with secure communication techniques.

252. http://niemanreports.org/articles/how-to-keep-sources-secure-from-surveillance;
http://towcenter.org/digital-security-and-source-protection-for-journalists-research
-by-susan-mcgregor.

253. http://www.niemanlab.org/2014/06/the-guardian-introduces-securedrop-for
-document-leaks.

254. http://www.niemanlab.org/2013/05/the-new-yorker-launches-strongbox-what
-are-the-experts-saying.

255. http://www.cjr.org/behind_the_news/securedrop_etc.php.

256. http://www.reuters.com/article/us-media-cybercrime-idUSBREA2R0EU
20140328.

257. http://www.cjr.org/first_person/_by_joel_simon_the.php; http://www.nieman
lab.org/2016/04/wireds-making-the-long-and-slow-switch-to-https-and-it-wants-to
-help-other-news-sites-do-the-same; http://www.niemanlab.org/2015/07/s-is-for
-secure-why-news-organizations-are-ditching-or-should-ditch-http-for-https.

258. http://www.niemanlab.org/2014/04/what-does-heartbleed-mean-for
-journalists.

259. http://www.niemanlab.org/2014/11/how-a-virus-demanding-a-bitcoin-ransom
-almost-destroyed-a-public-radio-stations-archives.

260. http://www.theatlantic.com/national/archive/2013/08/new-york-times
-website-crashes-again/311706.

261. http://www.theverge.com/2013/4/29/4282202/the-guardian-falls-victim
-syrian-electronic-army-11-twitter-accounts-hacked.

262. https://www.washingtonpost.com/news/worldviews/wp/2013/04/23/syrian
-hackers-claim-ap-hack-that-tipped-stock-market-by-136-billion-is-it-terrorism
/?utm_term=.950ff350da43.

263. https://www.buzzfeed.com/jwherrman/twitter-warns-journalists-we-believe
-that-these-attacks-will?utm_term=.lxV29535G#.if4GYkBk0; http://www.marketing
pilgrim.com/2013/04/twitter-doesnt-exactly-instill-confidence-in-memo-to-jour
nalists.html.

264. http://www.poynter.org/2014/new-pew-study-finds-most-people-ok-trading
-privacy-for-valued-digital-services/309055.

265. http://www.pewinternet.org/2014/08/26/social-media-and-the-spiral-of-silence.

266. http://www.niemanlab.org/2013/05/should-media-companies-be-doing-more
-to-protect-their-readers-and-commenters-right-to-privacy.

267. http://www.niemanlab.org/2013/05/should-media-companies-be-doing-more
-to-protect-their-readers-and-commenters-right-to-privacy; http://www.poynter.org
/2012/judge-orders-spokesman-review-to-id-anonymous-commenter/183698; http://
www.poynter.org/2014/judge-oks-subpoena-for-nola-com-commenters-identities
/236722.

268. http://www.niemanlab.org/2015/12/love-thy-reader-securely.

269. https://theconversation.com/think-youre-reading-the-news-for-free-new
-research-shows-youre-likely-paying-with-your-privacy-49694.

270. https://www.buzzfeed.com/matthewzeitlin/the-washington-post-begins
-blocking-ad-blockers?utm_term=.woRVeX0Xr#.fcJp3odo4.

271. http://www.cjr.org/realtalk/facebook_as_a_reporting_tool.php.

272. http://www.niemanlab.org/2014/04/how-some-journalists-are-using -anonymous-secret-sharing-apps.

273. http://www.reuters.com/article/facebook-privacy-warrants-idUSL1N101 16220150721?irpc=932; https://www.engadget.com/2016/10/11/aclu-police-use-twitter -facebook-data-to-track-protesters; http://m.computerworld.com/article/2494830/data -privacy/twitter-gives-up-user-data-to-feds-69--of-the-time.html.

274. http://www.cjr.org/the_feature/virtual_reality_facebook_second_life.php; http: //www.niemanlab.org/2015/11/the-new-york-times-hopes-its-first-virtual-reality -film-the-displaced-kicks-off-mass-adoption-of-vr; http://www.niemanlab.org/2015 /10/what-was-it-like-watching-a-vr-stream-of-last-nights-democratic-debate-hot-and -heavy; https://medium.com/viewing-the-future-virtual-reality-in-journalism.

275. https://theintercept.com/2016/12/23/virtual-reality-allows-the-most-detailed -intimate-digital-surveillance-yet.

276. For an excellent review of the gap between what journalists and audiences see as valuable news in online environments, see Pablo J. Boczkowski and Eugenia Mitchelstein (2013).

277. http://www.niemanlab.org/2013/10/when-readers-are-robots-tracking-bogus -botnet-traffic.

278. https://www.bloomberg.com/features/2015-click-fraud.

279. http://www.nytimes.com/2016/11/18/technology/automated-pro-trump-bots -overwhelmed-pro-clinton-messages-researchers-say.html.

280. http://www.niemanlab.org/2015/09/beware-the-bots-some-best-practices-to -combat-the-fraudulent-traffic-industry.

281. http://www.niemanlab.org/reading/can-news-bots-do-public-interest -journalism.

282. https://medium.com/thoughts-on-journalism/we-built-a-twitter-bot-that -replies-to-people-who-share-fake-news-d23127c1ed15#.aw8h9uiww.

283. The academic scholarship on comments is large and tends to focus on what kind of commenting features news sites offer, what motivates readers to comment, what the quality of comments is, whether anonymity helps or hurts comments, how journalists perceive such comments, and whether they influence news production. For good recent studies, see Annika Bergström and Ingela Wadbring (2015); Kevin Coe, Kate Kenski, and Stephen A. Rains (2014); Stephanie Craft, Tim P. Vos, and J. David Wolfgang (2016); Sanne Hille and Piet Bakker (2014); Laura Hlavach and William H. Freivogel (2011); Thomas B. Ksiazek, Peer, and Lessard (2015); Thomas B. Ksiazek, Limor Peer, and Kevin Zivic (2016); Fabian Prochazka, Patrick Weber, and Wolfgang Schweiger (2016); Bill Reader (2012); Zvi Reich (2011); Nina

Springer, Ines Engelmann, and Christian Pfaffinger (2015); Patrick Weber (2014); Rodrigo Zamith and Seth C. Lewis (2014); and Marc Ziegele, Timo Breiner, and Oliver Quiring (2014).

284. http://www.niemanlab.org/2014/07/newspaper-editors-strongly-support -online-comments-about-their-daily-content.

285. http://publiceditor.blogs.nytimes.com/2014/03/17/for-some-reader -contributions-become-a-new-reporting-tool.

286. http://www.niemanlab.org/2016/03/who-is-posting-comments-on-news -stories-and-why-do-they-do-it.

287. https://www.wired.com/2015/10/brief-history-of-the-demise-of-the-comments -timeline; http://www.cjr.org/behind_the_news/demise_of_comment_sections_or .php; http://www.nytimes.com/2013/09/22/magazine/no-comments.html; https:// www.washingtonpost.com/lifestyle/style/some-news-sites-cracking-down-on-over -the-top-comments/2014/05/07/4bc90958-d619-11e3-95d3-3bcd77cd4e11_story .html?utm_term=.de633af18333; http://www.poynter.org/2012/why-well-never-stop -struggling-over-comment-sections/167214.

288. http://www.niemanlab.org/2014/04/some-news-orgs-are-killing-comments -but-not-just-because-their-commenters-are-terrible-at-being-humans.

289. http://www.poynter.org/2013/nyt-community-manager-good-comments -shouldnt-sit-among-those-designed-to-cause-conflict/224101.

290. http://www.niemanlab.org/2015/09/what-happened-after-7-news-sites-got-rid -of-reader-comments; http://www.popsci.com/science/article/2013-09/why-were -shutting-our-comments.

291. http://www.niemanlab.org/2011/04/the-writing-on-the-wall-why-news -organizations-are-turning-to-outside-moderators-for-help-with-comments.

292. http://www.niemanlab.org/2015/09/what-happened-after-7-news-sites-got-rid -of-reader-comments.

293. http://www.nytimes.com/2010/04/12/technology/12comments.html.

294. http://www.poynter.org/2012/new-study-real-names-improve-quality-of -website-comments/183275.

295. https://techcrunch.com/2012/07/29/surprisingly-good-evidence-that-real -name-policies-fail-to-improve-comments. For a thoughtful recent review of lit- erature on requiring real names in online environments, see J. Nathan Matias (2017).

296. http://www.popsci.com/science/article/2013-09/why-were-shutting-our -comments.

297. http://www.adweek.com/fishbowlny/popular-science-blog-network-comments -jacob-ward/98632.

298. https://www.americanpressinstitute.org/need-to-know/up-for-debate/la-times -wont-print-letters-denying-humans-cause-global-warming.

299. http://blogs.reuters.com/great-debate/2014/11/07/editors-note-reader -comments-in-the-age-of-social-media.

300. http://motherboard.vice.com/read/im-on-twitter-too.

301. http://www.theverge.com/2015/7/6/8901753/so-comments-have-been-turned -off.

302. http://theweek.com/articles/441774/theweekcom-closing-comments-section.

303. http://www.niemanlab.org/2013/08/the-huffington-post-is-killing-anonymous -comments.

304. http://www.npr.org/sections/ombudsman/2016/08/17/489516952/npr -website-to-get-rid-of-comments.

305. http://www.poynter.org/2014/sun-times-kills-comments-until-it-can-fix -morass-of-negativity-racism-and-hate-speech/247525.

306. https://www.wired.com/2015/10/no-comments-allowed-reddits-new-news-site -upvoted.

307. https://www.americanpressinstitute.org/publications/reports/strategy-studies /choose-commenting-platform/single-page.

308. http://www.niemanlab.org/2014/06/why-the-new-york-times-and-the -washington-post-and-mozilla-are-building-an-audience-engagement-platform -together; http://www.niemanlab.org/2015/10/the-coral-project-is-building-its-first -product-a-listening-tool.

309. http://www.niemanlab.org/2016/06/here-are-some-of-the-best-and-most -interesting-ideas-from-the-guardians-comments-focused-hack-day.

310. http://www.niemanlab.org/2015/09/what-happened-after-7-news-sites-got-rid -of-reader-comments.

311. http://publiceditor.blogs.nytimes.com/2012/10/15/questions-and-answers-on -how-the-times-handles-online-comments-from-readers.

312. http://publiceditor.blogs.nytimes.com/2015/11/20/change-needed-for -commenting-that-favors-the-verified; http://www.nytimes.com/interactive/2015/11 /23/nytnow/23commenters.html.

313. http://www.niemanlab.org/2015/09/what-happened-after-7-news-sites-got-rid -of-reader-comments.

314. http://www.poynter.org/2014/national-journal-eliminates-comments-from
-non-members/252404.

315. http://www.niemanlab.org/2015/02/troll-toll-tablet-is-now-charging-its
-readers-for-the-right-to-comment.

316. http://www.niemanlab.org/2015/06/after-deciding-to-charge-for-comments
-tablets-conversation-moves-to-facebook.

317. https://www.buzzfeed.com/amandahickman/in-cleveland-meet-buzzbot.

318. http://www.poynter.org/2013/huffington-post-deletes-75-percent-of-incoming
-comments/222059.

319. http://www.niemanlab.org/2014/06/want-to-comment-on-a-huffington-post
-article-youll-need-to-use-facebook-now.

320. http://www.poynter.org/2013/want-to-comment-on-huffpost-just-give
-facebook-your-phone-number-first/233193.

321. http://www.niemanlab.org/2015/09/what-happened-after-7-news-sites-got-rid
-of-reader-comments.

322. http://digiday.com/publishers/how-bbc-is-using-yik-yak-to-talk-to-millennials
-and-get-them-to-talk-back.

323. http://www.niemanlab.org/2015/09/what-happened-after-7-news-sites-got-rid
-of-reader-comments.

324. https://www.nytimes.com/2014/08/27/upshot/how-social-media-silences
-debate.html.

325. https://www.americanpressinstitute.org/publications/reports/survey-research
/millennials-news; http://www.journalism.org/2016/05/26/news-use-across-social
-media-platforms-2016.

326. http://www.poynter.org/2012/wsj-facebook-pages-hit-by-comment-flashmob
/163822.

327. http://www.niemanlab.org/2011/08/ireport-at-5-nearly-900000-contributors
-worldwide.

328. http://www.adweek.com/fishbowlny/guardian-launches-user-generated
-content-platform-guardianwatch/259500?red=kw.

329. https://www.theguardian.com/news/series/open-newslist; https://www.theguard
ian.com/help/insideguardian/2011/oct/17/guardian-newslist; https://www.journalism
.co.uk/news/open-journalism-guardian-newslist/s2/a549794.

330. https://gigaom.com/2011/10/10/memo-to-newspapers-let-your-readers-inside
-the-wall.

331. http://www.adweek.com/fishbowlny/new-experiment-lets-readers-influence -editorial-decision-making-process-at-the-guardian/248469?red=kw.

332. http://www.nytimes.com/subscriptions/switch/lp8964W.html.

333. https://gigaom.com/2010/09/02/buzzfeed-opens-up-access-to-its-viral -dashboard; https://storify.com/patrickruffini/what-buzzfeed-s-analytics-dashboard -tells-us-about.

334. For a scholarly discussion focused on how news organizations use APIs to nego- tiate distances with audiences, see Mike Ananny (2013). For other studies of journal- istic uses of APIs, see Tanja Aitamurto and Seth C. Lewis (2011, 2012), Michael Lahey (2016), and Yuanbo Qiu (2016).

335. http://www.niemanlab.org/2012/05/the-guardian-creates-an-api-for-n0tice-its -open-news-platform; http://www.poynter.org/2011/beginners-guide-for-journalists -who-want-to-understand-api-documentation/138211; https://www.poynter.org/2012 /8-apis-your-news-organization-should-start-using-today/165347.

336. http://www.niemanlab.org/2009/06/four-crowdsourcing-lessons-from-the -guardians-spectacular-expenses-scandal-experiment.

337. http://towcenter.org/npr-news-app-team-experiments-with-making-data -driven-public-media-with-the-public.

338. https://www.journalism.co.uk/news/propublica-puts-spotlight-on -collaborative-opportunities-for-readers/s2/a552286.

339. http://www.adweek.com/fishbowlny/propublica-crowdsources-gun-control -bill-with-trackthevote/259280?red=kw.

340. http://www.niemanlab.org/2012/12/crowdsourcing-campaign-spending-what -propublica-learned-from-free-the-files.

341. http://www.niemanlab.org/2014/08/how-propublica-uses-a-reporting-recipe -to-cook-up-collaboration.

342. https://www.propublica.org/getinvolved/item/reporting-recipe-investigating -restraint-and-seclusion-in-us-schools.

343. http://www.adweek.com/fishbowlny/propublica-asks-reddit-what-should-we -cover/258733?red=kw.

344. http://mediashift.org/2013/06/challenges-cocreating-magazine-journalism -reader-input.

345. https://www.buzzfeed.com/millietran/what-we-learned-from-a-week-of -prototyping-a-newsletter-in-p?utm_term=.tfwZKWYWv#.hlZx8kRk3.

346. http://www.niemanlab.org/2013/07/gawker-is-letting-readers-rewrite-head lines-and-reframe-articles.

347. http://www.niemanlab.org/2012/08/pbs-newshours-viewers-are-translating-its -videos-into-52-languages-and-counting.

348. http://www.niemanlab.org/2014/10/why-the-new-york-times-built-a-tool-for -crowdsourced-time-travel.

349. https://theconversation.com/newspapers-ongoing-search-for-subscription -revenue-from-paywalls-to-micropayments-40726.

350. http://www.wsj.com/articles/SB10001424052748704213404576100033883758 352.

351. http://www.poynter.org/2011/why-would-anyone-pay-to-read-the-new-york -times-online/142936; http://www.cjr.org/the_audit/shirky_and_paywalls.php; http:// www.npr.org/2012/01/30/146093302/how-online-paywalls-are-changing-journalism.

352. http://www.niemanlab.org/2012/04/wait-so-how-many-newspapers-have -paywalls.

353. http://www.poynter.org/2012/paywalls-now-affect-one-third-of-daily -newspaper-readers/180323.

354. http://www.niemanlab.org/2012/04/the-newsonomics-of-99-cent-media.

355. http://www.adweek.com/fishbowlny/usa-today-publisher-paper-not-unique -enough-for-paywall/257265?red=kw.

356. http://www.poynter.org/2014/only-about-10-percent-of-online-readers-pay-for -news/255507.

357. https://www.minnpost.com/david-brauer-blog/2011/12/strib-metered-pay -wall-web-traffic-down-10-15-percent-revenue#.Tt5Um96dWws.twitter.

358. http://www.poynter.org/2012/new-york-times-traffic-flat-since-paywall /160780.

359. http://www.niemanlab.org/2011/03/the-price-you-pay-for-asking-people-to -pay-the-price-gerry-marzorati-on-class-and-the-nyt-paywall.

360. http://www.niemanlab.org/2012/04/the-newsonomics-of-99-cent-media; http: //www.poynter.org/2012/naa-list-shows-newspaper-paywalls-typically-allow-11 -free-articles/183295; http://www.poynter.org/2012/raju-narisetti-says-free-samples -can-lead-to-paid-subscribers/180709; http://www.niemanlab.org/2013/02/the-boston -globe-tightens-up-as-executives-seek-the-optimal-balance-between-free-and-paid.

361. http://www.poynter.org/2012/changes-to-new-york-times-paywall/167147.

362. https://www.cnet.com/news/sf-chronicle-erects-paywall-for-premium-content; http://www.medialifemagazine.com/slate-tries-new-sort-paywall.

363. http://www.niemanlab.org/2009/02/will-paid-content-work-two-cautionary
-tales-from-2004.

364. http://www.niemanlab.org/2015/04/the-winnipeg-free-press-is-launching-a
-paywall-that-lets-readers-pay-by-the-article; https://medium.com/on-blendle/blendle-a
-radical-experiment-with-micropayments-in-journalism-365-days-later-f3b799022edc#
.ufmqg34fw.

365. https://gigaom.com/2013/02/08/five-ways-media-companies-can-build
-paywalls-around-people-instead-of-content; http://www.niemanlab.org/2013/04/get
ting-personal-a-dutch-online-news-platform-wants-you-to-subscribe-to-individual
-journalists.

366. http://ajr.org/2013/12/16/beyond-paywalls-new-ways-charge-news.

367. https://gigaom.com/2013/07/11/what-if-the-price-you-had-to-pay-to-read-a
-story-dropped-as-more-people-clicked-on-it.

368. https://medium.com/on-blendle/the-dutch-revolution-in-journalism-all
-newspapers-behind-one-paydike-a2031594e430#.an6omo2xz.

369. http://digiday.com/publishers/countrywide-paywall-faltered.

370. https://gigaom.com/2014/04/21/slate-tries-to-buck-the-paywall-trend-by
-focusing-on-membership.

371. http://www.niemanlab.org/2012/03/what-kind-of-challenges-does-the-l-a
-times-face-in-creating-a-membership-program.

372. http://www.niemanlab.org/2014/09/wall-street-journal-turns-subscribers-into
-members-with-wsj.

373. http://www.recode.net/2016/3/28/11587326/the-new-york-times-may-make-it
-harder-to-use-facebook-and-twitter-to.

374. http://www.niemanlab.org/2013/11/minnpost-funds-reporting-through-new
-donor-backed-beats.

375. http://nymag.com/daily/intelligencer/2013/02/new-york-times-closes-url
-paywall-loophole.html; http://publiceditor.blogs.nytimes.com/2013/04/10/times
-writer-tangles-with-the-ethics-of-password-sharing.

376. For excellent general discussions of how readers, users, and their attention
streams are commodified for advertisers (even when they are consuming seemingly
free content) and how hard it is for people to extract themselves from such commodified surveillance, see Mark Andrejevic (2003), Julia Angwin (2014), Joseph Turow
(2011), and Tim Wu (2016).

377. https://theconversation.com/think-youre-reading-the-news-for-free-new
-research-shows-youre-likely-paying-with-your-privacy-49694.

378. http://www.poynter.org/2012/google-customer-survey-questions-are-an-offbeat
-alternative-to-a-paywall/168333; http://www.niemanlab.org/2011/10/how-google
-is-quietly-experimenting-in-new-ways-for-readers-to-access-publishers-content; http://
www.columbiamissourian.com/opinion/local_columnists/dear-reader-missourian
-site-is-ending-its-time-paywall-and/article_38bb43f7-3e37-5a14-8132-2ce04a95d9e3
.html.

379. For theorizations and case studies of crowdfunding public-facing industries
like journalism and the arts, see Tanja Aitamurto (2011); Daren C. Brabham (2017);
Miguel Carvajal, José A. Garcia-Aviles, and José L. Gonzalez (2012); Roei Davidson
and Nathaniel Poor (2015); Rodrigo Davies (2014); Andrea Hunter (2015); and Lian
Jian and Jieun Shin (2015).

380. http://mediashift.org/2013/05/crowdfunding-journalism-a-new-financing
-model-for-freelancers.

381. http://www.adweek.com/fishbowlny/kickstarter-campaign-the-magazine
/265648?red=kw; http://www.niemanlab.org/2014/08/the-huffington-post-wants-you
-to-help-pay-for-its-future-coverage-in-ferguson; http://www.niemanlab.org/2011/10
/bringing-a-crowd-to-a-records-fight-the-columbia-missourian-uses-spot-us-to-raise
-money-for-data-request.

382. http://www.adweek.com/fishbowlny/how-propublica-used-kickstarter-to-fund
-a-reporting-internship/261742?red=kw.

383. http://www.adweek.com/fishbowlny/for-journalism-news-developers-launch
-kickstarter-to-raise-money-to-teach-data-journalism-for-all/257959?red=kw.

384. http://www.niemanlab.org/2013/04/a-dutch-crowdfunded-news-site-has
-raised-1-3-million-and-hopes-for-a-digital-native-journalism.

385. http://techcitynews.com/2013/05/29/newsfreed-crowdfunding-investigative
-journalism.

386. http://thenextweb.com/media/2012/02/26/like-a-kickstarter-for-photojournal
ism-emphas-is-helps-finance-visual-storytelling.

387. https://gigaom.com/2014/01/08/contributorias-founders-talk-about-why-they
-are-building-an-open-community-for-crowdfunding-journalism.

388. https://techcrunch.com/2014/02/12/beacon-y-combinator-launch.

389. http://www.poynter.org/2014/kickstarter-adds-official-category-for-journalism
/255526.

390. http://www.niemanlab.org/2012/10/how-to-make-your-journalism-project
-succeed-on-kickstarter; http://www.adweek.com/fishbowlny/how-to-crowdfund-your
-journalism-project/257893?red=kw.

391. http://mashable.com/2013/06/26/kickstarter-propublica-journalism/#G0EQ
.ysTXPq8; http://www.niemanlab.org/2015/02/heres-a-recipe-for-successfully-crowd
funding-journalism-in-2015.

392. http://www.journalism.org/2016/01/20/crowdfunded-journalism.

393. https://www.journalism.co.uk/news/-value-for-money-how-crowdfunding
-journalism-affects-reader-relationships/s2/a562942.

394. http://www.niemanlab.org/2014/07/propublica-sees-30000-in-new-revenue
-from-data-store.

395. For a more complete discussion of APIs as infrastructures of networked press
autonomy, see Ananny (2013).

396. http://www.niemanlab.org/2011/10/usa-today-toys-with-a-side-business-selling
-commercial-access-to-its-data.

397. http://www.niemanlab.org/2011/04/new-name-new-mission-npr-digital
-services-expands-hoping-to-help-streamline-local-journalism; http://www.npr.org
/about-npr/179876898/terms-of-use.

398. http://www.niemanlab.org/2016/12/native-ads-are-still-very-confusing-to
-many-readers-a-new-survey-suggests; https://www.theguardian.com/commentis
free/2014/feb/25/yahoo-opens-gemini-native-advertising.

399. http://www.niemanlab.org/2016/09/recommended-content-widgets-still-have
-major-disclosure-and-clickbait-problems-says-a-new-report.

400. http://www.politico.com/media/story/2013/12/sulzbergers-native-advertising
-manifesto-001772.

401. http://www.poynter.org/2013/the-problem-with-buzzfeeds-sponsored-posts
/200214.

402. https://www.journalism.co.uk/news/native-advertising-how-news-sites
-separate-church-and-state/s2/a554648.

403. http://www.politico.com/media/story/2013/12/sulzbergers-native-advertising
-manifesto-001772.

404. http://www.adweek.com/fishbowlny/post-announces-sponsored-views
/261134?red=kw.

405. http://www.adweek.com/news/press/sports-illustrated-testing-new-type
-paywall-152935.

406. http://www.niemanlab.org/2013/11/minnpost-funds-reporting-through-new
-donor-backed-beats.

407. https://www.journalism.co.uk/news/native-advertising-how-news-sites
-separate-church-and-state/s2/a554648.

408. http://www.niemanlab.org/2013/01/the-ap-is-selling-ads-in-its-tweets-but
-twitter-doesnt-mind; http://www.adweek.com/socialtimes/ap-sharing-sponsored
-tweets-and-panicking-reporters/475311.

409. https://blog.twitter.com/2010/promoted-tweets-testing-in-the-timeline.

410. http://www.poynter.org/2012/ap-28-news-orgs-launch-newsright-to-collect
-licensing-fees-from-aggregators/157817.

411. http://www.niemanlab.org/2013/05/the-newsonomics-of-where-newsright
-went-wrong.

412. http://www.niemanlab.org/2014/03/the-washington-post-goes-national-by
-offering-free-digital-access-to-readers-of-local-newspapers.

413. http://www.niemanlab.org/2014/06/that-washington-post-deal-with-local
-newspapers-is-generating-decent-numbers.

414. http://www.niemanlab.org/2011/02/what-apples-new-subscription-policy
-means-for-news-new-rules-new-incentives-new-complaints.

415. http://www.niemanlab.org/2011/02/take-that-cupertino-google-undercuts
-apples-subscription-plan-with-a-cheaper-one-of-its-own.

416. http://www.poynter.org/2012/with-new-tablet-web-app-new-york-times-may
-avoid-apples-fees/190297.

417. http://www.recode.net/2016/10/18/13326196/snapchat-discover-ad-sales
-plan-change.

418. http://www.poynter.org/2016/heres-why-facebook-is-paying-news
-organizations-millions-of-dollars/418132; http://www.wsj.com/articles/facebook
-signs-deals-with-media-companies-celebrities-for-facebook-live-1466533472.

419. https://gigaom.com/2013/02/27/new-york-times-gives-starbucks-visitors-15
-free-stories-a-day.

420. See http://www.poynter.org/2014/trump-hotel-guests-get-free-online-access-to
-the-new-york-times-the-donalds-favorite-paper/255532.TheNewYorkTimesmaynolon
gerbeDonaldTrump'sfavoritenewspaper.

421. http://www.poynter.org/2013/sponsored-treats-ap-prints-news-on-restaurant
-receipts/200081.

422. http://www.niemanlab.org/2015/09/from-two-day-shipping-to-news-a
-cheaper-washington-post-is-now-an-amazon-prime-benefit.

423. News organizations and commercial brands have a long history of intermin-
gling. In the early days of radio and television news, entire bulletins and programs

were visibly sponsored by advertisers like Goodyear, Glo-Coat, and Camel cigarettes, with on-air personalities reading endorsements (Ponce de Leon, 2015).

424. http://www.niemanlab.org/2016/07/the-financial-times-is-testing-blocking -the-adblockers-by-blocking-actual-words-from-its-stories; http://fortune.com/2016 /06/08/the-new-york-times-is-preparing-to-step-up-its-war-on-ad-blockers.

425. http://www.niemanlab.org/2014/09/the-newsonomics-of-the-pianopress -merger-creating-the-worlds-largest-paywall-tech-company; http://www.niemanlab .org/2015/08/tinypass-and-piano-media-merge-and-embrace-paywall-as-a-fluid -concept.

426. http://www.niemanlab.org/2012/02/piano-media-bumps-up-slovak-paywall -price-25-percent.

427. http://www.poynter.org/2012/press-passes-300-clients-now-using-metered -model-to-charge-for-online-news/168712.

428. http://www.poynter.org/2012/more-stories-result-in-more-subscription -revenue-press-says/180554.

429. https://www.bloomberg.com/news/articles/2016-02-24/google-gives-publish ers-what-facebook-apple-haven-t-a-paywall.

430. For excellent discussions of epistemological tensions underlying journalistic professionalism, see Mark W. Brewin (2013), Theodore L. Glasser and James S. Ettema (1993), Raymond W. K. Lau (2012), Dan Schiller (1979), Michael Schudson (1978), Schudson and Christopher W. Anderson (2008), Steven C. Ward (1996), Stephen J. A. Ward (2005), and Kate Wright (2011).

431. http://www.poynter.org/2012/andy-carvin-explains-how-twitter-is-his-open -source-newsroom/157874.

432. http://www.poynter.org/2012/stumped-new-york-times-reporter-crowdsources -id-of-a-rare-bomb/161533.

433. http://www.poynter.org/2011/6-ways-journalists-can-use-quora-as-a-tool-for -reporting-sharing-ideas/114314.

434. http://niemanreports.org/articles/finding-the-wisdom-in-the-crowd; http:// niemanreports.org/articles/the-process-of-verification.

435. http://www.journalism.org/2016/12/15/many-americans-believe-fake-news-is -sowing-confusion.

436. https://gizmodo.com/google-changes-algorithm-to-remove-holocaust-denying -re-1790500861.

437. http://www.nytimes.com/2012/04/10/us/politics/false-nikki-haley-twitter -report-spreads-fast.html.

438. http://www.poynter.org/2012/ap-tells-staff-how-to-correct-erroneous-tweets
-in-new-social-media-guidelines/159622.

439. https://www.washingtonpost.com/news/the-intersect/wp/2016/08/29
/a-fake-headline-about-megyn-kelly-was-trending-on-facebook/?utm_term=
.f78bd9b2b01e.

440. https://www.buzzfeed.com/craigsilverman/partisan-fb-pages-analysis?utm_
term=.sfpL5R6Rm#.unABJjbjv; https://medium.com/@BiellaColeman/on-truth-and
-lies-in-a-pragmatic-performative-sense-with-my-respects-to-nietzsche-or-why-reality
-5c8400bd9ac2#.z0fi6lac4; https://firstdraftnews.com/almost-half-of-americans-beli
eve-government-responsible-for-tackling-fake-news; http://www.npr.org/sections
/ed/2016/12/22/505432340/the-classroom-where-fake-news-fails; http://www.politico
.com/magazine/story/2016/12/fake-news-history-long-violent-214535; https://medium
.com/thoughts-on-journalism/we-built-a-twitter-bot-that-replies-to-people-who-share
-fake-news-d23127c1ed15#.fwrcykuev.

441. https://www.theguardian.com/technology/2016/nov/29/facebook-fake-news
-problem-experts-pitch-ideas-algorithms.

442. http://www.niemanlab.org/2012/03/hacking-for-truth-whatever-that-is-ideas
-to-fight-misinformation.

443. http://hoaxy.iuni.iu.edu.

444. https://medium.com/thoughts-on-journalism/we-built-a-twitter-bot-that
-replies-to-people-who-share-fake-news-d23127c1ed15#.fwrcykuev.

445. http://www.npr.org/2016/11/20/502770866/ex-head-of-twitter-news-social
-media-companies-alone-shouldn-t-regulate-fake-new.

446. http://www.niemanlab.org/2016/09/facebook-twitter-and-30-other-orgs-join
-first-drafts-partner-network-to-help-stop-the-spread-of-fake-news.

447. https://www.theguardian.com/technology/blog/2013/jul/01/data-journalism
-awards-improving.

448. http://radar.oreilly.com/2010/12/data-journalism.html.

449. https://www.theguardian.com/news/series/facts-are-sacred.

450. https://www.theguardian.com/news/datablog/2013/apr/04/data-journalism
-guardian-rusbridger.

451. https://www.propublica.org/datastore/about.

452. http://www.niemanlab.org/2013/03/dallas-morning-news-partners-with-local
-government-group-to-gather-clean-universal-crime-data.

453. https://www.journalism.co.uk/news/detective-io-launches-to-search
-connections-in-datasets/s2/a555266.

454. http://towcenter.org/what-the-tesla-affair-tells-us-about-data-journalism.

455. https://qz.com/189703/the-problem-with-data-journalism.

456. http://www.huffingtonpost.co.uk/entry/facebook-fake-news_uk_582c20b7e4b
08b8e51a43bc2.

457. http://www.vox.com/policy-and-politics/2016/12/2/13812818/facebook-fake
-news-think-before-you-share.

458. http://newsroom.fb.com/news/2016/12/news-feed-fyi-addressing-hoaxes-and
-fake-news.

459. https://www.ap.org/ap-in-the-news/2016/facebook-finally-gets-serious-about
-fighting-fake-news.

460. https://www.technologyreview.com/s/603188/the-limits-of-fact-checking
-facebook.

461. http://www.pri.org/stories/2016-10-14/fact-check-tags-added-google-news.
https://blog.google/topics/journalism-news/labeling-fact-check-articles-google
-news.

462. http://www.pri.org/stories/2016-10-14/fact-check-tags-added-google-news.

463. http://www.poynter.org/2012/washington-posts-truthteller-project-hopes-to
-birth-real-time-fact-checking/183774.

464. https://www.washingtonpost.com/news/ask-the-post/wp/2013/09/25
/announcing-truth-teller-beta-a-better-way-to-watch-political-speech/?utm_term=
.62d0bbe2c7c5; http://www.knightfoundation.org/articles/debuting-truth-teller
-washington-post-real-time-lie-detection-service-your-service-not-quite-yet.

465. http://thefjp.org/2013/03/can-robots-tell-the-truth.

466. http://www.poynter.org/2016/who-decides-whats-true-in-politics-a-history-of
-the-rise-of-political-fact-checking/429326.

467. https://fullfact.org/blog/2016/aug/automated-factchecking.

468. http://www.poynter.org/2016/report-automated-fact-checking-is-coming-and
-soon/426370.

469. http://www.poynter.org/2016/le-monde-wants-to-build-a-b-s-detector-2
/440078.

470. http://www.poynter.org/2013/new-guardian-scoopshot-efforts-bring-elements
-of-automation-to-photo-verification/212585; http://mashable.com/2013/04/16/the
-guardianwitness/#Z75KU_idQPqQ.

471. http://www.niemanlab.org/2016/11/reuters-built-its-own-algorithmic
-prediction-tool-to-help-it-spot-and-verify-breaking-news-on-twitter.

472. http://www.niemanlab.org/2016/06/the-washington-post-is-dabbling-in -translations-to-reach-a-growing-non-english-speaking-audience.

473. http://www.niemanlab.org/2016/08/european-publishers-are-teaming -together-to-translate-the-news-to-reach-broader-audiences.

474. https://www.wired.com/2016/07/fb-2.

475. https://www.gitbook.com/book/towcenter/virtual-reality-journalism/details; http://www.theverge.com/a/virtual-reality.

476. www.poynter.org/2016/how-the-new-york-times-used-its-archives-to-make -the-past-a-virtual-reality; http://www.niemanlab.org/2016/05/the-new-york-times -is-trying-to-make-vr-films-that-arent-one-offs-and-that-keep-readers-coming-back.

477. http://www.theguardian.com/world/ng-interactive/2016/apr/27/6x9-a-virtual -experience-of-solitary-confinement.

478. http://www.theverge.com/a/virtual-reality.

479. http://www.niemanlab.org/2015/11/what-frontlines-team-learned-producing -its-new-vr-documentary.

480. http://www.knightfoundation.org/media/uploads/publication_pdfs/VR _report_web.pdf.

481. http://www.niemanlab.org/2016/08/designing-news-products-with-empathy -how-to-plan-for-individual-users-needs-and-stresses.

482. http://www.cjr.org/innovations/virtual_reality_journalism.php.

483. http://www.cjr.org/the_feature/virtual_reality_facebook_second_life.php; http:// www.wired.com/2016/02/vr-moral-imperative-or-opiate-of-masses.

484. For a more in-depth discussion of how sociotechnical separations and depen- dencies influence journalistic ethics of witnessing, see Mike Ananny (2015).

485. http://www.wnyc.org/story/why-paris-not-baga.

486. http://www.niemanlab.org/2013/12/where-in-the-world-is-buzzfeed-building -foreign-news-around-themes-rather-than-geography.

487. http://www.cjr.org/analysis/facebook_as_state.php.

488. http://publiceditor.blogs.nytimes.com/2012/12/27/snow-fall-tells-a-story -about-an-avalanche-and-a-newspapers-reinvention.

489. http://www.niemanlab.org/2014/05/the-leaked-new-york-times-innovation -report-is-one-of-the-key-documents-of-this-media-age.

490. http://www.npr.org/sections/alltechconsidered/2014/07/09/330003058/in -google-newsroom-brazil-defeat-is-not-a-headline.

491. https://digiday.com/media/news-crew-shooting-shows-perils-auto-play-videos -twitter-facebook.

492. http://digiday.com/platforms/news-crew-shooting-shows-perils-auto-play -videos-twitter-facebook.

493. http://mediadecoder.blogs.nytimes.com/2012/09/28/as-it-followed-a-car-chase -fox-news-showed-a-man-kill-himself.

Chapter 6

1. For a discussion of how a new type of public editor might speak this language, see Mike Ananny (2016a).

References

Aalberg, T., Blekesaune, A., & Elvestad, E. (2013). Media choice and informed democracy: Toward increasing news consumption gaps in Europe? *International Journal of Press/Politics, 18*(3), 281–303.

Abbott, A. (1988). *The system of professions: An essay on the division of expert labor.* Chicago, IL: Chicago University Press.

Ahmad, A. N. (2010). Is Twitter a useful tool for journalists? *Journal of Media Practice, 11*(2), 145–155. doi:10.1386/jmpr.11.2.145_1

Ahva, L., & Heikkila, H. (2016). Mass, audience, and the public. In T. Witschge, C. W. Anderson, D. Domingo, & A. Hermida (Eds.), *Handbook of digital journalism* (pp. 315–325). New York, NY: Sage.

Aitamurto, T. (2011). The impact of crowdfunding on journalism: Case study of Spot.Us, a platform for community-funded reporting. *Journalism Practice, 5*(4), 429–445.

Aitamurto, T. (2016). Crowdsourcing as a knowledge-search method in digital journalism. *Digital Journalism, 4*(2), 280–297. doi:10.1080/21670811.2015.1034807

Aitamurto, T., & Lewis, S. C. (2011, April 1). Open APIs and news organizations: A study of open innovation in online journalism. Paper presented at the International Symposium on Online Journalism, Austin, TX. Retrieved from http://online .journalism.utexas.edu/2011/papers/AitamuroLewis2011.pdf

Aitamurto, T., & Lewis, S. C. (2012). Open innovation in digital journalism: Examining the impact of open APIs at four news organizations. *New Media & Society, 15*(2), 314–331.

Althaus, S. L. (2003). When news norms collide, follow the lead: New evidence for press independence. *Political Communication, 20*(4), 381–414.

American Society of Newspaper Editors. (2013, May 21). Encourage your congressperson to support Free Flow of Information Act [Blog]. Retrieved from http://asne .org/blog_home.asp?Display=1601

Ananny, M. (2013). Press-public collaboration as infrastructure: Tracing news organizations and programming publics in application programming interfaces. *American Behavioral Scientist, 57*(5), 623–642.

Ananny, M. (2014). Networked press freedom and social media: Tracing historical and contemporary forces in press-public relations. *Journal of Computer-Mediated Communication, 19*(4), 938–956. doi:10.1111/jcc4.12076

Ananny, M. (2015). Creating proper distance through networked infrastructure: Examining Google Glass for evidence of moral, journalistic witnessing. In M. Carlson & S. C. Lewis (Eds.), *Boundaries of journalism: Professionalism, practices, and participation* (pp. 83–99). New York, NY: Routledge.

Ananny, M. (2016a, March 17). It's time to reimagine the role of a public editor, starting at *The New York Times*. Nieman Lab. Retrieved from http://www.niemanlab.org/2016/03/mike-ananny-its-time-to-reimagine-the-role-of-a-public-editor-starting-at-the-new-york-times

Ananny, M. (2016b, February 6). Networked news time: How slow—or fast—do publics need news to be? *Digital Journalism, 4*(4), 414–431. doi:10.1080/21670811.2015.1124728

Ananny, M. (2017). The whitespace press: Designing meaningful absences into networked news. In P. J. Boczkowski & C. W. Anderson (Eds.), *Remaking the news* (pp. 129–146). Cambridge, MA: MIT Press.

Ananny, M., & Bighash, L. (2016). Why drop a paywall? Mapping industry accounts of online news decommodification. *International Journal of Communication, 10*, 3359–3380.

Ananny, M., & Crawford, K. (2015). A liminal press: Situating news app designers within a field of networked news production. *Digital Journalism, 3*(2), 192–208. doi:10.1080/21670811.2014.922322

Anderson, B. (1983). *Imagined communities* (Rev. ed.). London, UK: Verso.

Anderson, C. W. (2010). Journalistic networks and the diffusion of local news: The brief, happy news life of the "Francisville Four." *Political Communication, 27*(3), 289–309.

Anderson, C. W. (2011a). Between creative and quantified audiences: Web metrics and changing patterns of newswork in local U.S. newsrooms. *Journalism: Theory, Practice, Criticism, 12*(5), 550–566.

Anderson, C. W. (2011b). Deliberative, agonistic, and algorithmic audiences: Journalism's vision of its public in an age of audience transparency. *International Journal of Communication, 5*, 529–547.

Anderson, C. W. (2011c, April 1). What aggregators do: Rhetoric, practice, and cultures of digital and analog evidence in Web-era journalism. Paper presented at the

International Symposium on Online Journalism, Austin, TX. Retrieved from http://online.journalism.utexas.edu/2011/papers/Anderson2011.pdf

Anderson, C. W. (2013a). *Rebuilding the news: Metropolitan journalism in the digital age.* Philadelphia, PA: Temple University Press.

Anderson, C. W. (2013b). Towards a sociology of computational and algorithmic journalism. *New Media & Society, 15*(7), 1005–1021. doi:10.1177/1461444812465137

Anderson, C. W. (2015a). Between the unique and the pattern: Historical tensions in our understanding of quantitative journalism. *Digital Journalism, 3*(3), 349–363. doi:10.1080/21670811.2014.976407

Anderson, C. W. (2015b). Drawing boundary lines between journalism and sociology, 1895–2000. In M. Carlson & S. C. Lewis (Eds.), *Boundaries of journalism: Professionalism, practices, and participation* (pp. 201–217). New York, NY: Routledge.

Anderson, C. W. (2018). *Apostles of certainty: Data journalism and the politics of doubt.* Oxford, UK: Oxford University Press.

Anderson, C. W., & Kreiss, D. (2013). Black boxes as capacities for and constraints on action: Electoral politics, journalism, and devices of representation. *Qualitative Sociology, 36*, 365–382.

Anderson, C. W., & Maeyer, J. D. (2015). Objects of journalism and the news. *Journalism, 16*(1), 3–9.

Anderson, D. A. (1983). The origins of the press clause. *UCLA Law Review, 30*, 455–541.

Anderson, D. A. (2002). Freedom of the press. *Texas Law Review, 80*(3), 429–530.

Anderson, R. E. (1973). *Branzburg v. Hayes:* A need for statutory protection of new sources. *Kentucky Law Journal, 61*, 551–559.

Anderson, S. P., & Gabszewicz, J. J. (2006). The media and advertising: A tale of two-sided markets. In V. A. Ginsburgh & D. Throsby (Eds.), *Handbook of the economics of art and culture* (Vol. *25*, pp. 567–614). Amsterdam: Elsevier.

Andrejevic, M. (2003). *Reality TV: The work of being watched.* New York, NY: Rowman & Littlefield.

Angwin, J. (2014). *Dragnet nation.* New York, NY: Times Books.

Archetti, C. (2013). Journalism in the age of global media: The evolving practices of foreign correspondents in London. *Journalism, 14*(3), 419–436.

Arendt, H. (1958). *The human condition.* Chicago, IL: University of Chicago Press.

Armstrong, C. L., & Gao, F. (2010). Now tweet this: How news organizations use Twitter. *Electronic News, 4*(4), 218–235.

Arneson, R. (1985). Freedom and desire. *Canadian Journal of Philosophy, 15*, 425–448.

Arrese, Á. (2015). From gratis to paywalls: A brief history of a retro-innovation in the press's business. *Journalism Studies, 17*(8), 1051–1067. doi:10.1080/14616 70X.2015.1027788

Atton, C., & Hamilton, J. F. (2008). *Alternative journalism.* New York, NY: Sage.

Baker, C. E. (1989). *Human liberty and freedom of speech.* Oxford, UK: Oxford University Press.

Baker, C. E. (1998). The media that citizens need. *University of Pennsylvania Law Review, 147*(2), 317–408.

Baker, C. E. (2002). *Media, markets, and democracy.* Cambridge, UK: Cambridge University Press.

Baker, C. E. (2007a). The independent significance of the press clause under existing law. *Hofstra Law Review, 35*, 955–1026.

Baker, C. E. (2007b). *Media concentration and democracy: Why ownership matters.* Cambridge, UK: Cambridge University Press.

Balkin, J. M. (2008). The future of free expression in a digital age. *Pepperdine Law Review, 36*, 101–118.

Ball-Rokeach, S. J. (1985). The origins of individual media-system dependency: A sociological framework. *Communication Research, 12*(4), 485–510. doi:10.1177/0093 65085012004003

Bandura, A. (1986). *Social foundations of thought and action: A social cognitive theory.* Englewood Cliffs, NJ: Prentice-Hall.

Barnes, R. (2013). The "ecology of participation": A study of audience engagement on alternative journalism websites. *Digital Journalism, 2*(4), 542–557. 10.1080 /21670811.2013.859863

Barnhurst, K. G. (2010a). The form of reports on U.S. newspaper Internet sites, an update. *Journalism Studies, 11*(4), 555–566.

Barnhurst, K. G. (2010b). Technology and the changing idea of news: 2001 U.S. newspaper content at the maturity of internet 1.0. *International Journal of Communication, 4*, 1082–1099.

Barnhurst, K. G. (2011). The problem of modern time in American journalism. *KronoScope, 11*(1–2), 98–123. doi:10.1163/156852411X595297

Barnhust, K. G., & Mutz, D. (1997). American journalism and the decline in event-centered reporting. *Journal of Communication, 47*(4), 27–53.

Barnhurst, K. G., & Nerone, J. (2001). *The form of news: A history*. New York, NY: Guilford Press.

Barry, A. (2013). *Material politics: Disputes along the pipeline*. New York, NY: Wiley-Blackwell.

Baughman, J. L. (2006). *The republic of mass culture: Journalism, filmmaking, and broadcasting in America since 1941* (3rd ed.). Baltimore, MD: Johns Hopkins University Press.

Baym, N. (2015). *Personal connections in the digital age*. New York, NY: Polity Press.

Beam, M. A. (2014). Automating the news: How personalized news recommender system design choices impact news reception. *Communication Research, 41*(8), 1019–1041. doi:10.1177/0093650213497979

Beck, U. (2002). *Individualization: Institutionalized individualism and its social and political consequences*. London, UK: Sage.

Beckett, C., & Deuze, M. (2016). On the role of emotion in the future of journalism. *Social Media + Society, 2*(3). doi:10.1177/2056305116662395

Beckett, C., & Mansell, R. (2008). Crossing boundaries: New media and networked journalism. *Communication, Culture & Critique, 1*, 92–104.

Beer, D., & Burrows, R. (2010). The sociological imagination as popular culture. In J. Burnett, S. Jeffers, & G. Thomas (Eds.), *New social connections: Sociology's subjects and objects* (pp. 233–252). Basingstoke, UK: Palgrave.

Bell, A. (1995). News time. *Time & Society, 4*(3), 305–328.

Belman, L. S. (1977). John Dewey's concept of communication. *Journal of Communication, 27*(1), 29–37.

Benkler, Y. (2006). *The wealth of networks: How social production transforms markets and freedom*. New Haven, CT: Yale University Press.

Benkler, Y. (2011). A free irresponsible press: Wikileaks and the battle over the soul of the networked fourth estate. *Harvard Civil Rights–Civil Liberties Law Review, 46*, 311–397.

Benn, S. I. (1988). *A theory of freedom*. Cambridge, UK: Cambridge University Press.

Bennett, W. L. (1990). Toward a theory of press-state relations. *Journal of Communication, 40*(2), 103–125.

Bennett, W. L. (1996). An introduction to journalistic norms and representations of politics. *Political Communication, 20*, 381–414.

Bennett, W. L. (2007). *News: The politics of illusion*. New York, NY: Pearson Longman.

Bennett, W. L. (2012). The personalization of politics: Political identity, social media, and changing patterns of participation. *Annals of the American Academy of Political and Social Science, 644*, 20–39. doi:10.1177/0002716212451428

Bennett, W. L., Lawrence, R. G., & Livingston, S. (2006). None dare call it torture: Indexing and the limits of press independence in the Abu Ghraib scandal. *Journal of Communication, 56*, 467–485.

Bennett, W. L., Lawrence, R. G., & Livingston, S. (2007). *When the press fails: Political power and the news media from Iraq to Katrina*. Chicago, IL: University of Chicago Press.

Benson, R. (1999). Field theory in comparative context: A new paradigm for media studies. *Theory and Society, 28*, 463–498.

Benson, R. (2004). Bringing the sociology of media back in. *Political Communication, 21*(3), 275–292.

Benson, R. (2005). American journalism and the politics of diversity. *Media Culture & Society, 27*(1), 5–20.

Benson, R. (2006). News media as a "journalistic field": What Bourdieu adds to new institutionalism, and vice versa. *Political Communication, 23*(2), 187–202.

Benson, R. (2009). Shaping the public sphere: Habermas and beyond. *American Sociologist, 40*, 175–197.

Benson, R., & Neveu, E. (2005a). Introduction: Field theory as a work in progress. In R. Benson & E. Neveu (Eds.), *Bourdieu and the journalistic field* (pp. 1–25). Cambridge, UK: Polity Press.

Benson, R., & Neveu, E. (Eds.). (2005b). *Bourdieu and the journalistic field*. Cambridge, UK: Polity Press.

Berger, P., & Luckman, T. (1967). *The social construction of reality*. New York, NY: Anchor Books.

Berglez, P. (2008). What is global journalism? *Journalism Studies, 9*(6), 845–858.

Bergström, A., & Wadbring, I. (2015). Beneficial yet crappy: Journalists and audiences on obstacles and opportunities in reader comments. *European Journal of Communication, 30*(2), 137–151. doi:10.1177/0267323114559378

Berkowitz, D. (1992). Non-routine news and newswork: Exploring a what-a-story. *Journal of Communication, 42*(1), 82–94.

Berlin, I. (1969). *Four essays on liberty*. Oxford, UK: Oxford University Press.

Bernstein, B. (1962). Social class, linguistic codes and grammatical elements. *Language and Speech, 5*(4), 221–240.

Bezanson, R. P. (1999). The developing law of editorial judgment. *Nebraska Law Review, 78*(4), 754–857.

Bezanson, R. P. (2003a). *How free can the press be?* Urbana, IL: University of Illinois Press.

Bezanson, R. P. (2003b). The structural attributes of press freedom: Private ownership, public orientation, and editorial independence. In C. LaMay (Ed.), *Journalism and the debate over privacy* (pp. 17–60). London, UK: Routledge.

Bezanson, R. P. (2012). Whither freedom of the press? *Iowa Law Review, 97,* 1259–1274.

Bezanson, R. P., & Buss, W. G. (2001). The many faces of government speech. *Iowa Law Review, 86,* 1377–1511.

Bezanson, R. P., Cranberg, G., & Soloski, J. (1987). *Libel law and the press: Myth and reality.* New York, NY: Free Press.

Bickford, S. (1996). *The dissonance of democracy: Listening, conflict, and citizenship.* Ithaca, NY: Cornell University Press.

Bickmore, T., & Cassell, J. (2005). Social dialogue with embodied conversational agents. In J. C. J. van Kuppevelt, L. Dybkjær, & N. O. Bernsen (Eds.), *Advances in natural multimodal dialogue systems* (pp. 23–54). Dordrecht, the Netherlands: Springer Netherlands.

Blasi, V. (1977). The checking value in first amendment theory. *American Bar Foundation Research Journal, 2*(3), 521–649.

Blumer, H. (1939). The field of collective behavior. In R. E. Park (Ed.), *An outline of the principles of sociology* (pp. 245–247). New York, NY: Barnes & Noble.

Blumer, H. (1969). *Symbolic interactionism: Perspective and method.* Berkeley, CA: University of California Press.

Blumler, J. G., & Cushion, S. (2014). Normative perspectives on journalism studies: Stocktaking and future directions. *Journalism, 15*(3), 259–272. doi:10.1177/146488 4913498689

Boczkowski, P. J. (2004a). *Digitizing the news: Innovation in online newspapers.* Cambridge, MA: MIT Press.

Boczkowski, P. J. (2004b). The mutual shaping of technology and society in videotex newspapers: Beyond the diffusion and social shaping perspectives. *Information Society, 20*(4), 255–267.

Boczkowski, P. J. (2004c). The process of adopting multimedia and interactivity in three online newsrooms. *Journal of Communication, 54* (2), 197–213.

Boczkowski, P. J. (2010). *News at work: Imitation in an age of information abundance.* Chicago, IL: University of Chicago Press.

Boczkowski, P. J. (2015). The material turn in the study of journalism: Some hopeful and cautionary remarks from an early explorer. *Journalism, 16*(1), 65–68. doi:10.1177/1464884914545734

Boczkowski, P. J., & Mitchelstein, E. (2012). How users take advantage of different forms of interactivity on online news sites: Clicking, e-mailing, and commenting. *Human Communication Research, 38,* 1–22.

Boczkowski, P. J., & Mitchelstein, E. (2013). *The news gap: When the information preferences of the media and the public diverge.* Cambridge, MA: MIT Press.

Boczkowski, P. J., Mitchelstein, E., & Walter, M. (2010). Convergence across divergence: Understanding the gap in the online news choices of journalists and consumers in Western Europe and Latin America. *Communication Research, 38*(3), 376–396.

Boczkowski, P. J., & Peer, L. (2011). The choice gap: The divergent online news preferences of journalists and consumers. *Journal of Communication, 61,* 857–876.

Bødker, H. (2017). The time(s) of news websites. In B. Franklin & S. Eldridge II (Eds.), *The Routledge companion to digital journalism studies* (pp. 55–63). London, UK: Routledge.

Boeyink, D. E. (1990). Anonymous sources in news stories: Justifying exceptions and limiting abuses. *Journal of Mass Media Ethics, 5*(4), 233–246.

Bollinger, L. C. (1991). *Images of a free press.* Chicago, IL: University of Chicago Press.

Bollinger, L. C. (2010). *Uninhibited, robust and wide-open: A free press for a new century.* Oxford, UK: Oxford University Press.

Bouk, D. (2015). *How our days became numbered: Risk and the rise of the statistical individual.* Chicago, IL: University of Chicago Press.

Bourdieu, P. (1990). *The logic of practice* (R. Nice, Trans.). Stanford, CA: Stanford University Press.

Bourdieu, P. (1993). *The field of cultural production.* New York, NY: Columbia University Press.

Bourdieu, P. (1996a). *On television.* New York, NY: New Press.

Bourdieu, P. (1996b). *The rules of art: Genesis and structure of the literary field.* Stanford, CA: Stanford University Press.

Bourdieu, P. (2005). The political field, the social science field, and the journalistic field. In R. Benson & E. Neveu (Eds.), *Bourdieu and the journalistic field* (pp. 29–48). Cambridge, UK: Polity Press.

Bowker, G. C., & Star, S. L. (1999). *Sorting things out: Classification and its consequences.* Cambridge, MA: MIT Press.

Boykoff, M. T., & Boykoff, J. M. (2004). Balance as bias: Global warming and the U.S. prestige press. *Global Environmental Change, 14*, 125–136.

Boyte, H. C. (1995). Public opinion as public judgment. In C. T. S. Theodore L. Glasser (Ed.), *Public opinion and the communication of consent* (pp. 417–436). New York, NY: Guilford Press.

Brabham, D. C. (2017). How crowdfunding discourse threatens public arts. *New Media & Society, 19*(7), 983–999. doi:10.1177/1461444815625946

Brandstetter, B., & Schmalhofer, J. (2014). Paid content: A successful revenue model for publishing houses in Germany? *Journalism Practice, 8*(5), 499–507. doi:10.1080/1 7512786.2014.895519

Brandtzaeg, P. B., Lüders, M., Spangenberg, J., Rath-Wiggins, L., & Følstad, A. (2016). Emerging journalistic verification practices concerning social media. *Journalism Practice, 10*(3), 323–342. doi:10.1080/17512786.2015.1020331

Braun, J. A. (2014). Transparent intermediaries: Building the infrastructures of connected viewing. In J. Holt & K. Sanson (Eds.), *Connected viewing: Selling, streaming and sharing media in the digital era* (pp. 124–143). New York, NY: Routledge.

Braun, J. A. (2015). *This program is brought to you by … : Distributing television news online*. New Haven, CT: Yale University Press.

Braun, J. A., & Gillespie, T. (2011). Hosting the public discourse, hosting the public: When online news and social media converge. *Journalism Practice, 5*(4), 383–398.

Breed, W. (1955). Social control in the newsroom: A functional analysis. *Social Forces, 33*, 326–355.

Brennan, W. J. (1965). The Supreme Court and the Meiklejohn interpretation of the First Amendment. *Harvard Law Review, 79*(1), 1–20.

Brest, P. (1980). The misconceived quest for the original understanding. *Boston University Law Review, 60*, 204–238.

Brewin, M. W. (2013). A short history of the history of objectivity. *Communication Review, 16*(4), 211–229.

Breyer, S. (2005). *Active liberty: Interpreting our democratic constitution*. New York, NY: Knopf.

Bright, J. (2016). The social news gap: How news reading and news sharing diverge. *Journal of Communication, 66*(3), 343–365. doi:10.1111/jcom.12232

Brown, J. A. (1998). Media literacy perspectives. *Journal of Communication, 48*(1), 44–57.

Brown, W. (1998). Freedom's silences. In R. C. Post (Ed.), *Censorship and silencing: Practices of cultural regulation* (pp. 313–327). Los Angeles, CA: Getty Research Institute.

Bryant, J., & Miron, D. (2002). Entertainment as media effect. In J. Bryant & D. Zill-mann (Eds.), *Media effects: Advances in theory and research* (2nd ed., pp. 549–582). Mahwah, NJ: Lawrence Erlbaum.

Bucher, T. (2017a). The algorithmic imaginary: Exploring the ordinary affects of Facebook algorithms. *Information Communication and Society, 20*(1), 30–44. doi:10.10 80/1369118X.2016.1154086

Bucher, T. (2017b). "Machines don't have instincts": Articulating the computational in journalism. *New Media & Society, 19*(6), 807–825. doi:10.1177/1461444815624182

Butsch, R. (2008). *The citizen audience: Crowds, publics, and individuals.* New York, NY: Routledge.

Calame, B. (2006, January 1). Behind the eavesdropping story, a loud silence. *New York Times.* Retrieved from http://www.nytimes.com/2006/01/01/opinion/behind -the-eavesdropping-story-a-loud-silence.html

Caldwell, J. T. (2008). *Production culture: Industrial reflexivity and critical practice in film and television.* Durham, NC: Duke University Press.

Calhoun, C. (1992). Introduction: Habermas and the public sphere. In C. Calhoun (Ed.), *Habermas and the public sphere* (pp. 1–48). Cambridge, MA: MIT Press.

Calhoun, C. (1998). The public good as a social and cultural project. In W. Powell & E. Clemens (Eds.), *Private action and the public good* (pp. 20–35). New Haven, CT: Yale University Press.

Callison, C. (2014). *How climate change comes to matter: The communal life of facts.* Durham, NC: Duke University Press.

Canter, L. (2015). Personalised tweeting: The emerging practices of journalists on Twitter. *Digital Journalism, 3*(6), 888–907. 10.1080/21670811.2014.973148

Carey, J. W. (1987). The press and the public discourse. *Center Magazine, 20,* 4–15.

Carey, J. W. (1989a). A cultural approach to communication. In *Communication as culture: Essays on media and society* (pp. 13–36). New York, NY: Routledge.

Carey, J. W. (1989b). Technology and ideology: The case of the telegraph. In *Communication as culture: Essays on media and society* (pp. 201–230). New York, NY: Routledge.

Carey, J. W. (1995). The press, public opinion, and public discourse. In T. L. Glasser & C. T. Salmon (Eds.), *Public opinion and the communication of consent* (pp. 373–402). New York, NY: Guilford Press.

Carey, J. W. (1997). The communications revolution and the professional communica-tor. In E. S. Munson & C. A. Warren (Eds.), *James Carey: A critical reader* (pp. 128–144). Minneapolis, MN: University of Minnesota Press.

Carey, J. W. (2000). Some personal notes on U.S. journalism education. *Journalism*, *1*(1), 12–23.

Carlson, M. (2009). Dueling, dancing, or dominating? Journalists and their sources. *Sociology Compass*, *3*(4), 526–542. doi:10.1111/j.1751-9020.2009.00219.x

Carlson, M. (2011). *On the condition of anonymity: Unnamed sources and the battle for journalism*. Chicago, IL: University of Illinois Press.

Carlson, M. (2015a). The many boundaries of journalism. In M. Carlson & S. C. Lewis (Eds.), *Boundaries of journalism: Professionalism, practices and participation* (pp. 1–18). New York, NY: Routledge.

Carlson, M. (2015b). Metajournalistic discourse and the meanings of journalism: Definitional control, boundary work, and legitimation. *Communication Theory*, *26*(4), 349–368. doi:10.1111/comt.12088

Carlson, M. (2015c). When news sites go native: Redefining the advertising–editorial divide in response to native advertising. *Journalism*, *16*(7), 849–865. doi:10.1177/1464884914545441

Carlson, M. (2016). Automated journalism: A posthuman future for digital news? In B. Franklin & S. Eldridge (Eds.), *The Routledge companion to digital journalism studies* (pp. 226–234). London, UK: Routledge.

Carlson, M. (2017). Establishing the boundaries of journalism's public mandate. In C. Peters & M. Broersma (Eds.), *Rethinking journalism again: Societal role and public relevance in a digital age* (pp. 49–63). London, UK: Routledge.

Carpentier, N. (2011). Contextualising author-audience convergences: "New" technologies' claims to increased participation, novelty and uniqueness. *Cultural Studies*, *25*(4–5), 517–533.

Carvajal, M., Garcia-Aviles, J. A., & Gonzalez, J. L. (2012). Crowdfunding and non-profit media: The emergence of new models for public interest journalism. *Journalism Practice*, *6*(5–6), 638–647. doi:10.1080/17512786.2012.667267

Cassell, J., Sullivan, J., Prevost, S., & Churchill, E. F. (Eds.). (2000). *Embodied conversational agents*. Cambridge, MA: MIT Press.

Cassirer, E. (1946). *Language and myth* (S. K. Langer, Trans.). New York, NY: Harper & Brothers.

Cassirer, E. (1953). *Substance and function, and Einstein's theory of relativity*. New York, NY: Dover. (Original work published 1923)

Cassirer, E. (1960). *The logic of the humanities* (C. S. Howe, Trans.). New Haven, CT: Yale University Press. (Original work published 1942)

Castells, M. (1996). *The rise of the network society*. London, UK: Blackwell.

Catledge, T. (1971). *My life and the Times*. New York, NY: Harper & Row.

Chadwick, A. (2013). *The hybrid media system: Politics and power*. Oxford, UK: Oxford University Press.

Chen, A. (2014, October 23). The laborers who keep dick pics and beheadings out of your Facebook feed. *Wired*. Retrieved from http://www.wired.com/2014/10/content -moderation

Chomsky, D. (1999). The mechanisms of management control at the New York Times. *Media, Culture & Society, 21*(5), 579–599.

Chomsky, D. (2006). "An interested reader": Measuring ownership control at the New York Times. *Critical Studies in Mass Communication, 23*(1), 1–18.

Chouliaraki, L. (2006). *The spectatorship of suffering*. London, UK: Sage.

Christians, C. G., & Fackler, P. M. (2014). The genesis of social responsibility theory: William Ernest Hocking and positive freedom. In R. S. Fortner & P. M. Fackler (Eds.), *The handbook of media and mass communication* (pp. 333–356). New York, NY: John Wiley.

Christians, C. G., Glasser, T. L., McQuail, D., Nordenstreng, K., & White, R. A. (2009). *Normative theories of the media*. Urbana, IL: University of Illinois Press.

Christman, J. (1988). Constructing the inner citadel: Recent work on the concept of autonomy. *Ethics, 99*(1), 109–124.

Christman, J. (1991). Liberalism and individual positive freedom. *Ethics, 101*(2), 343–359.

Chung, D. S. (2008). Interactive features of online newspapers: Identifying patterns and predicting use of engaged readers. *Journal of Computer-Mediated Communication, 13*(3), 658–679.

Chung, D. S., & Yoo, C. Y. (2008). Audience motivations for using interactive features: Distinguishing use of different types of interactivity on an online newspaper. *Mass Communication and Society, 11*(4), 375–397.

Ciborra, C. U., & Hanseth, O. (2001). *From control to drift: The dynamics of corporate information infrastructures*. Oxford, UK: Oxford University Press.

Clark, A. E. (2016). Anticipation work: Abduction, simplification, hope. In G. C. Bowker, S. Timmermans, A. E. Clarke, & E. Balka (Eds.), *Boundary objects and beyond: Working with Leigh Star* (pp. 85–120). Cambridge, MA: MIT Press.

Cline, A. R. (2008). Ethics and ethos: Writing an effective newspaper ombudsman position. *Journal of Mass Media Ethics, 23*(2), 79–89.

Coase, R. H. (1974). The market for goods and the market for ideas. *American Economic Review, 64*(2), 384–391.

Coddington, M. (2012). Defending a paradigm by patrolling a boundary: Two global newspapers' approach to WikiLeaks. *Journalism & Mass Communication Quarterly*, *89*(3), 377–396.

Coddington, M. (2014). Clarifying journalism's quantitative turn. *Digital Journalism*, *3*(3), 331–348. doi:10.1080/21670811.2014.976400

Coe, K., Kenski, K., & Rains, S. A. (2014). Online and uncivil? Patterns and determinants of incivility in newspaper website comments. *Journal of Communication, 64*(4), 658–679. doi:10.1111/jcom.12104

Cohen, D. (2013, September 26). ACLU Facebook post deleted (then restored), group temporarily blocked from posting. *Social Times*. Retrieved from http://www.adweek.com/socialtimes/aclu-censorship/428713

Cohen, E. L. (2002). Online journalism as market-driven journalism. *Journal of Broadcasting & Electronic Media, 46*(4), 532–548.

Cohen, J. (1997). Procedure and substance in deliberative democracy. In J. Bohman & W. Rehg (Eds.), *Deliberative democracy: Essays on reason and politics* (pp. 407–437). Cambridge, MA: MIT Press.

Coleman, G. (2011). Hacker politics and publics. *Public Culture, 23*(3), 511–516.

Coleman, G. (2013). *Coding freedom: The ethics and aesthetics of hacking*. Princeton, NJ: Princeton University Press.

Coleman, G. (2014). *Hacker, hoaxer, whistleblower, spy: The many faces of Anonymous*. New York, NY: Verso.

Collins, R. (1992). The romanticism of agency/structure versus the analysis of micro/macro. *Current Sociology, 40*(1), 77–97.

Cook, T. E. (1998). *Governing with the news*. Chicago, IL: University of Chicago Press.

Cook, T. E. (2000). The future of institutional media. In W. L. Bennett & R. M. Entman (Eds.), *Mediated politics: Communication in the future of democracy* (pp. 182–200). Cambridge, UK: Cambridge University Press.

Cook, T. E. (2006). The news media as a political institution: Looking backward and looking forward. *Political Communication, 23*, 159–171.

Corbin, C. M. (2009). The First Amendment right against compelled listening. *Boston University Law Review, 89*, 939–1016.

Corbin, J., & Strauss, A. (2007). *Basics of qualitative research: Techniques and procedures for developing grounded theory* (3rd ed.). New York, NY: Sage.

Corina, A., Sehl, A., & Nielsen, R. K. (2016). *Private sector media and digital news*. Reuters Institute for the Study of Journalism, Oxford University. Retrieved from http://reutersinstitute.politics.ox.ac.uk/sites/default/files/Cornia%20-%20Private %20Sector%20Media%20and%20Digital%20News%20FINAL.pdf

Couldry, N. (2009). Rethinking the politics of voice. *Continuum, 23*(4), 579–582.

Couldry, N., & Jenkins, H. (2014). Participations: Dialogues on the participatory promise of contemporary culture and politics. *International Journal of Communication, 8.*

Craft, S., Vos, T. P., & Wolfgang, J. D. (2016). Reader comments as press criticism: Implications for the journalistic field. *Journalism, 17*(6), 677–693. doi:10.1177/1464884 915579332

Crawford, K. (2009). Following you: Disciplines of listening in social media. *Continuum, 23*(4), 525–535.

Crawford, K. (2011). Listening, not lurking: The neglected form of participation. In H. Greif, L. Hjorth, A. Lasén, & C. Lobet-Maris (Eds.), *Cultures of participation: Media practices, politics and literacy* (pp. 63–74). Berlin, Germany: Peter Lang.

Creech, B., & Mendelson, A. L. (2015). Imagining the journalist of the future: Technological visions of journalism education and newswork. *Communication Review, 18*(2), 142–165. doi:10.1080/10714421.2015.1031998

Creswell, J. W. (1998). *Qualitative inquiry and research design: Choosing among five traditions.* Thousand Oaks, CA: Sage.

Dahl, R. A. (1989). *Democracy and its critics.* New Haven, CT: Yale University Press.

Dahlgren, P. (1992). Introduction. In P. Dahlgren & C. Sparks (Eds.), *Journalism and popular culture* (pp. 1–23). New York, NY: Sage.

Dahlgren, P. (2013). Online journalism and civic cosmopolitanism: Professional vs. participatory ideals. *Journalism Studies, 14*(2), 156–171.

Darnton, R. (1975). Writing news and telling stories. *Daedalus, 104*(2), 175–194.

Davidson, R., & Poor, N. (2015). The barriers facing artists' use of crowdfunding platforms: Personality, emotional labor, and going to the well one too many times. *New Media & Society, 17*(2), 289–307. doi:10.1177/1461444814558916

Davies, R. (2014). Three provocations for civic crowdfunding. *Information Communication and Society, 18*(3), 342–355.

Dayan, D., & Katz, E. (1994). *Media events: The live broadcasting of history.* Cambridge, MA: Harvard University Press.

de Beauvoir, S. (1948). *The ethics of ambiguity.* New York, NY: Citadel Press.

de Beer, A. S. (2010). News from and in the "dark continent": Afro-pessimism, news flows, global journalism and media regimes. *Journalism Studies, 11*(4), 596–609.

DeLanda, M. (2006). *A new philosophy of society: Assemblage theory and social complexity*. New York, NY: Bloomsbury Academic.

Deleuze, G., & Guttari, F. (1987). *A thousand plateaus: Capitalism and schizophrenia*. Minneapolis, MN: University of Minnesota Press.

Deuze, M. (2004). What is multimedia journalism? *Journalism Studies, 5*(2), 139–152.

Deuze, M. (2005). What is journalism? Professional identity and ideology of journalists reconsidered. *Journalism, 6*(4), 442–464.

Deuze, M. (2007). *Media work*. Cambridge, UK: Polity Press.

Deuze, M. (2008a). The changing context of news work: Liquid journalism and monitorial citizenship. *International Journal of Communication, 2*, 848–865.

Deuze, M. (2008b). The professional identity of journalists in the context of convergence culture. *Observatorio (OBS*), 2*(4), 103–117.

Deuze, M. (2010). Journalism and convergence culture. In S. Allan (Ed.), *The Routledge companion to news and journalism* (pp. 267–276). New York, NY: Routledge.

Deuze, M., & Marjoribanks, T. (2009). Newswork. *Journalism, 10*(5), 555–561.

DeVito, M. A. (2016). From editors to algorithms: A values-based approach to understanding story selection in the Facebook newsfeed. *Digital Journalism, 5*(6), 753–773. doi:10.1080/21670811.2016.1178592

Dewey, J. (1954). *The public and its problems*. New York, NY: Swallow Press.

Dewey, J. (1963). *Reconstruction in philosophy*. Boston, MA: Beacon Press.

Dewey, J. (1997). *Experience and education*. New York, NY: Free Press.

Dewey, J. (2004). Our un-free press. In R. W. McChesney & B. Scott (Eds.), *Our unfree press: One hundred years of radical media criticism* (pp. 207–210). New York, NY: New Press. (Original work published 1935)

Dewey, J. (2008). Practical democracy: Review of Walter Lippmann's "Phantom Public." In J. A. Boydston (Ed.), *John Dewey: The later works, 1925–1953, Vol. 2, 1925–1927: Essays, reviews, miscellany, and The public and its problems* (pp. 213–225). Carbondale, IL: Southern Illinois University Press.

Diakopoulos, N. (2015). Algorithmic accountability: Journalistic investigation of computational power structures. *Digital Journalism, 3*(3), 398–415. doi:10.1080/21670811.2014.976411

Digital Media Law Project. (2009a, September 13). *Enterline v. The Pocono Record*. Retrieved from http://www.dmlp.org/threats/enterline-v-pocono-record

Digital Media Law Project. (2009b, October 17). Illinois v. The Alton Telegraph. Retrieved from http://www.dmlp.org/threats/illinois-v-alton-telegraph

Digital Media Law Project. (2013, May 24). State shield laws. Berkman Center for Internet & Society. Retrieved from http://www.dmlp.org/state-shield-laws

DiMaggio, P. J. (1991). Constructing an organizational field as a professional project: U.S. art museums, 1920–1940. In P. J. DiMaggio & W. Powell (Eds.), *The new institutionalism in organizational analysis* (pp. 267–292). Chicago, IL: University of Chicago Press.

DiMaggio, P. J., & Powell, W. W. (1991). Introduction. In W. W. Powell & P. J. DiMaggio (Eds.), *The new institutionalism in organizational analysis* (pp. 1–38). Chicago, IL: University of Chicago Press.

DiSalvo, C. (2009). Design and the construction of publics. *Design Issues, 25*(1), 48–63.

DiSalvo, C. (2014). Critical making as materializing the politics of design. *Information Society, 30*(2), 96–105. doi:10.1080/01972243.2014.875770

DiSalvo, C. (2016). Design and prefigurative politics. *Journal of Design Strategies, 8*(1), 29–35.

DiSalvo, C., Louw, M., Holstius, D., Nourbakhsh, I., & Akin, A. (2012). Toward a public rhetoric through participatory design: Critical engagements and creative expression in the neighborhood networks project. *Design Issues, 28*(3), 48–61.

Dobson, A. (2014). *Listening for democracy: Recognition, representation, reconciliation.* Oxford, UK: Oxford University Press.

Domingo, D. (2015). Research that empowers responsibility: Reconciling human agency with materiality. *Journalism, 16*(1), 69–73. doi:10.1177/1464884914545738

Dörr, K. N. (2015). Mapping the field of algorithmic journalism. *Digital Journalism, 4*(6), 700–722. doi:10.1080/21670811.2015.1096748

Dörr, K. N., & Hollnbuchner, K. (2016). Ethical challenges of algorithmic journalism. *Digital Journalism, 5*(4), 404–419. doi:10.1080/21670811.2016.1167612

Douglas, S. J. (1989). *Inventing American broadcasting, 1899–1922.* Baltimore, MD: Johns Hopkins University Press.

Douglas, S. J. (2004). *Listening in: Radio and the American imagination.* Minneapolis, MN: University of Minnesota Press.

Downey, J., Titley, G., & Toynbee, J. (2014). Ideology critique: The challenge for media studies. *Media Culture & Society, 36*(6), 878–887, doi:10.1177/0163443714536113

Downs, A. (1957). *An economic theory of democracy.* New York, NY: Harper & Row.

Dreher, T. (2009). Listening across difference: Media and multiculturalism beyond the politics of voice. *Continuum, 23*(4), 445–458.

Dunne, A., & Raby, F. (2013). *Speculative everything: Design, fiction, and social dreaming.* Cambridge, MA: MIT Press.

Dworkin, G. (1981). The concept of autonomy. In R. Haller (Ed.), *Science and ethics* (pp. 203–213). Amsterdam, The Netherlands: Rodopi.

Dworkin, G. (1988). *The theory and practice of autonomy.* Cambridge, UK: Cambridge University Press.

Dyk, T. B. (1992). Newsgathering, press access, and the first amendment. *Stanford Law Review, 44*(5), 927–960.

Edgerly, S. (2016, December 19). Seeking out and avoiding the news media: Young adults' proposed strategies for obtaining current events information. *Mass Communication and Society, 20*(3), 358–377. doi:10.1080/15205436.2016.1262424

Edy, J. A. (1999). Journalistic uses of collective memory. *Journal of Communication, 49*(2), 71–85.

Ehrlich, M. C. (1996). Using "ritual" to study journalism. *Journal of Communication Inquiry, 20*(2), 3–17.

Ekdale, B. (2013). "I wish they knew that we are doing this for them": Participation and resistance in African community journalism. *Journalism Practice, 8*(2), 181–196. doi:10.1080/17512786.2013.859833

Ellison, N. B., & boyd, d. (2013). Sociality through social network sites. In W. H. Dutton (Ed.), *The Oxford handbook of Internet studies* (pp. 151–172). Oxford: Oxford University Press.

Emerson, T. I. (1970). *The system of freedom of expression.* New York, NY: Random House.

Emerson, T. I. (1981). The affirmative side of the first amendment. *Georgia Law Review, 15,* 795–849.

Emery, E. (1950). *History of the American Newspaper Publishers Association.* Minneapolis, MN: University of Minnesota Press.

Emery, E., & McKerns, J. P. (1987). AEJMC: Seventy-five years in the making. *Journalism Monographs, 104,* 1–91.

Entman, R. M. (2005). The nature and sources of news. In G. Overholser & K. H. Jamieson (Eds.), *The press* (pp. 48–65). Oxford, UK: Oxford University Press.

Epstein, R. A. (1992). *International News Service v. Associated Press*: Custom and law as sources of property rights in news. *Virginia Law Review, 78*(1), 85–128.

Ettema, J. S., & Glasser, T. L. (1987a). On the epistemology of investigative journalism. In M. Gurevitch & M. R. Levy (Eds.), *Mass communication review yearbook 6* (pp. 338–361). Newbury Park, CA: Sage.

Ettema, J. S., & Glasser, T. L. (1987b). Public accountability or public relations? Newspaper ombudsmen define their role. *Journalism Quarterly, 64*(1), 3–12.

Ettema, J. S., & Glasser, T. L. (1998). *Custodians of conscience*. New York, NY: Columbia University Press.

Ettema, J. S., & Whitney, D. C. (Eds.). (1994). *Audiencemaking: How the media create the audience*. London, UK: Sage.

Evans, K. G. (2001). Dewey and the dialogical process: Speaking, listening and today's media. *International Journal of Public Administration, 24*(7–8), 771–798.

Fallon, R. H. (1994). Two senses of autonomy. *Stanford Law Review, 46*(4), 875–905.

Fargo, A. L. (2006). Analyzing federal shield law proposals: What Congress can learn from the states. *Communication Law and Policy, 11*(1), 35–82.

Favole, J. A., & Kendall, B. (2013, May 15). President pushes for shielding journalists. *Wall Street Journal*. Retrieved from http://online.wsj.com/article/SB10001424127887 3240826045784852408638385124.html

Feenberg, A. (1999). *Questioning technology*. New York, NY: Routledge.

Fishkin, J. S. (2009). *When the people speak: Deliberative democracy and public consultation*. New York, NY: Oxford University Press.

Fishman, J. M. (2003). News norms and emotions: Pictures of pain and metaphors of distress. In L. Gross, J. S. Katz, & J. Ruby (Eds.), *Image ethics in the digital age* (pp. 53–70). Minneapolis, MN: University of Minnesota Press.

Fishman, M. (1980). *Manufacturing the news*. Austin, TX: University of Texas Press.

Fiske, J. (2002). *Television culture*. London, UK: Routledge.

Fiss, O. (1986). Free speech and social structure. *Iowa Law Review, 71*, 1405–1425.

Fiss, O. (1995). The right kind of neutrality. In D. S. Allen & R. Jensen (Eds.), *Freeing the first amendment: Critical perspectives on freedom of expression* (pp. 79–92). New York, NY: New York University Press.

Fiss, O. (1996). *The irony of free speech*. Cambridge, MA: Harvard University Press.

Flanagan, M., Howe, D., & Nissenbaum, H. (2008). Embodying values in technology: Theory and practice. In J. van den Hoven & J. Weckert (Eds.), *Information technology and moral philosophy* (pp. 322–353). Cambridge, UK: Cambridge University Press.

Fletcher, G. P. (1981). Two modes of legal thought. *Yale Law Journal, 90*(5), 970–1003.

Fletcher, R., & Nielsen, R. K. (2016, October 28). Paying for online news. *Digital Journalism*, 1–19. doi:10.1080/21670811.2016.1246373

Fligstein, N., & McAdam, D. (2012). *A theory of fields*. Oxford, UK: Oxford University Press.

Folkerts, J. (2014). History of journalism education. *Journalism & Communication Monographs, 6*(4), 227–299. doi:10.1177/1522637914541379

Foucault, M. (1979). *Discipline and punish: The birth of the prison*. New York, NY: Random House.

Foucault, M. (1991). Governmentality. In G. Burchell, C. Gordon, & P. Miller (Eds.), *The Foucault effect: Studies in governmentality with two lectures by and an interview with Michel Foucault* (pp. 87–104). Chicago, IL: University of Chicago Press.

Fourcade, M. (2007). Theories of markets and theories of society. *American Behavioral Scientist, 50*(8), 1015–1034.

Fowler, M. S., & Brenner, D. L. (1982). A marketplace approach to broadcast regulation. *Texas Law Review, 60*, 207–258.

Fraser, N. (1990). Rethinking the public sphere: A contribution to the critique of actually existing democracy. *Social Text, 25/26*, 56–80.

Friedman, B., Kahn, P. H., & Borning, A. (2006). Value sensitive design and information systems. In P. Zhang & D. Galletta (Eds.), *Human-computer interaction in management information systems: Foundations* (pp. 348–372). London, UK: M. E. Sharpe.

Friedman, B., & Nissenbaum, H. (1996). Bias in computer systems. *ACM Transactions on Information Systems, 14*(3), 330–347.

Fung, A. (2003). Associations and democracy: Between theories, hopes, and realities. *Annual Review of Sociology, 29*, 515–539.

Gallup. (2016, September 14). Americans' trust in mass media sinks to new low. Gallup Politics. Retrieved from http://www.gallup.com/poll/195542/americans-trust-mass-media-sinks-new-low.aspx

Gallup, G. (1939). *Public opinion in a democracy: Stafford Little lectures*. Princeton, NJ: Princeton University Press.

Gamson, W. (1992). *Talking politics*. Cambridge, UK: Cambridge University Press.

Gans, H. (1979). *Deciding what's news*. New York, NY: Vintage.

Garden, C. (2014). Meta rights. *Fordham Law Review, 83*(2), 855–906.

Gardner, H., Csikszentmihalyi, M., & Damon, W. (2002). *Good work: When excellence and ethics meet* (pp. 179–206). New York, NY: Basic Books.

Garry, P. M. (1994). *Scrambling for protection: The new media and the first amendment*. Pittsburgh, PA: University of Pittsburgh Press.

Gentzkow, M., & Shapiro, J. M. (2008). Competition and truth in the market for news. *Journal of Economic Perspectives, 22*(2), 133–154.

Gerbner, G., & Gross, L. (1976). Living with television: The violence profile. *Journal of Communication, 26*(2), 172–194.

Gerbner, G., Gross, L., & Morgan, M., Signorielli, N., & Shanahan, J. (2002). Growing up with television: Cultivation processes. In J. Bryant & D. Zillmann (Eds.), *Media effects: Advances in theory and research.* Mahwah, NJ: Lawrence Erlbaum.

Gerlitz, C., & Helmond, A. (2013). The like economy: Social buttons and the data-intensive Web. *New Media & Society, 15*(8), 1348–1365. doi:10.1177/1461444812472322

Gibbs, S. (2016, December 22). Mark Zuckerberg appears to finally admit Facebook is a media company. *The Guardian.* Retrieved from https://www.theguardian.com /technology/2016/dec/22/mark-zuckerberg-appears-to-finally-admit-facebook-is-a -media-company

Giddens, A. (1984). *The constitution of society: Outline of the theory of structuration.* London, UK: Polity Press.

Gieryn, T. F. (1983). Boundary-work and the demarcation of science from non-science: Strains and interests in professional ideologies of scientists. *American Sociological Review, 48*(6), 781–795.

Gillespie, T. (2017). Governance of and by platforms. In J. Burgess, A. Marwick, & T. Poell (Eds.), *Sage handbook of social media* (pp. 254–278). London, UK: Sage.

Gillmor, D. (2004). *We the media: Grassroots journalism by the people, for the people.* Sebastopol, CA: O'Reilly Media.

Gitlin, T. (1980). *The whole world is watching: Mass media in the making and unmaking of the new left.* Berkeley, CA: University of California Press.

GLAAD. (2014, August). GLAAD media reference guide. Retrieved from http://www .glaad.org/sites/default/files/GLAAD%20MRG_9th.pdf

Glasser, T. L. (2000). The politics of public journalism. *Journalism Studies, 1*(4), 683–686.

Glasser, T. L., Awad, I., & Kim, J. W. (2009). The claims of multiculturalism and journalism's promise of diversity. *Journal of Communication, 59*(1), 57–78.

Glasser, T. L., & Ettema, J. S. (1993). When the facts don't speak for themselves: A study of the use of irony in daily journalism. *Critical Studies in Mass Communication, 10*(4), 322–338.

Glasser, T. L., & Gunther, M. (2005). The legacy of autonomy in American journalism. In G. Overholser & K. H. Jamieson (Eds.), *The press* (pp. 384–399). Oxford, UK: Oxford University Press.

Glasser, T. L., & Lee, F. L. F. (2002). Repositioning the newsroom: The American experience with public journalism. In R. Kuhn & E. Neveu (Eds.), *Political journalism: New challenges, new practices* (pp. 203–224). London, UK: Routledge.

Godler, Y., & Reich, Z. (2012). How journalists think about facts: Theorizing the social conditions behind epistemological beliefs. *Journalism Studies, 14*(1), 94–112.

Goffman, E. (1959). *The presentation of self in everyday life.* London, UK: Penguin.

Goldhaber, M. H. (1997). The attention economy and the Net. *First Monday, 2*(4).

Gotfried, J., & Shearer, E. (2016, May 26). News use across social media platforms. Pew Research Center. Retrieved from http://www.journalism.org/2016/05/26/news -use-across-social-media-platforms-2016

Graefe, A. (2016, January). Guide to automated journalism. Columbia Tow Center for Digital Journalism. Retrieved from http://towcenter.org/research/guide-to -automated-journalism

Graefe, A., Haim, M., Haarmann, B., & Brosius, H.-B. (2016). Readers' perception of computer-generated news: Credibility, expertise, and readability. *Journalism,* 1–16. doi:10.1177/1464884916641269

Gramsci, A. (1988). *Prison letters.* London, UK: Pluto Press.

Graves, L. (2016). *Deciding what's true: The rise of political fact-checking in American journalism.* New York, NY: Columbia University Press.

Greenwald, G. (2014). *No place to hide.* New York, NY: Metropolitan Books.

Guest, J. A., & Stanzler, A. L. (1969). The constitutional argument for newsmen concealing their sources. *Northwestern University Law Review, 64*(1), 18–61.

Guribye, F., & Nyre, L. (2016, December 5). The changing ecology of tools for live news reporting. *Journalism Practice.* doi:10.1080/17512786.2016.1259011

Gutman, A., & Thompson, D. (2004). *Why deliberative democracy?* New Haven, CT: Princeton University Press.

Gutmann, A. (1987). *Democratic education.* Princeton, NJ: Princeton University Press.

Haas, T. (2004). The public sphere as a sphere of publics: Rethinking Habermas's theory of the public sphere. *Journal of Communication, 54*(1), 178–184.

Haas, T. (2005). From "public journalism" to the "public's journalism"? Rhetoric and reality in the discourse on weblogs. *Journalism Studies, 6*(3), 387–396.

Habermas, J. (1989). *The structural transformation of the public sphere.* Cambridge, MA: MIT Press.

Haiman, F. S. (1981). *Speech and law in a free society.* Chicago, IL: University of Chicago Press.

Hall, S. (Ed.). (1997). *Representation: Cultural representations and signifying practices.* London, UK: Sage.

Hallin, D. C. (1985). The American news media: A critical theory perspective. In J. Forester (Ed.), *Critical theory and public life* (pp. 121–146). Cambridge, MA: MIT Press.

Hallin, D. C. (1986). *The uncensored war: The media and Vietnam.* New York, NY: Oxford University Press.

Hallin, D. C. (2000). Commercialism and professionalism in the American news media. In J. Curran & M. Gurevitch (Eds.), *Mass media and society* (pp. 218–237). London, UK: Arnold.

Hallin, D. C., & Mancini, P. (2004). *Comparing media systems.* New York, NY: Cambridge University Press.

Hamilton, J. M. (2009). *Journalism's roving eye: A history of American foreign reporting.* Baton Rouge, LA: Louisiana State University Press.

Hamilton, J. T. (2006). *All the news that's fit to sell.* Princeton, NJ: Princeton University Press.

Hansen, E. (2013). Aporias of digital journalism. *Journalism, 14*(5), 678–694.

Hansen, E. (2014). The positive freedom of the public sphere: The need for courageous truth-tellers. *Journalism Studies, 16*(6), 767–781. doi:10.1080/1461670X.2014.943937

Hansmann, H. (1980). The role of nonprofit enterprise. *Yale Law Journal, 89*(5), 835–901.

Hanusch, F. (2016). Web analytics and the functional differentiation of journalism cultures: Individual, organizational and platform-specific influences on newswork. *Information Communication and Society, 20*(10), 1571–1586. doi:10.1080/1369118X.2016.1241294

Hare, K. (2014, January 22). Court OKs subpoena for Nola.com commenters' identities. *Poynter.* Retrieved from http://www.poynter.org/news/mediawire/236722/judge-oks-subpoena-for-nola-com-commenters-identities

Harris, R. J., & Scott, C. L. (2002). Effects of sex in the media. In J. Bryant & D. Zillmann (Eds.), *Media effects: Advances in theory and research* (2nd ed., pp. 307–332). Mahwah, NJ: Lawrence Erlbaum.

Hatch, N. O. (1988). Introduction: The professions in a democratic culture. In N. O. Hatch (Ed.), *The professions in American history* (pp. 1–13). Notre Dame, IN: University of Notre Dame Press.

Hay, J., & Couldry, N. (2011). Rethinking convergence/culture. *Cultural Studies*, *25*(4–5), 473–486.

Hayles, N. K., & Crofts Wiley, S. B. (2012). Media, materiality, and the human. In J. Packer & S. B. Crofts Wiley (Eds.), *Communication matters: Materialist approaches to media, mobility, and networks* (pp. 17–34). London, UK: Routledge.

Held, D. (2006). *Models of democracy* (3rd ed.). Stanford, CA: Stanford University Press.

Herbst, S. (1993). The meaning of public opinion: Citizens' constructions of political reality. *Media Culture & Society*, *15*, 437–454.

Herbst, S. (1995). *Numbered voices: How opinion polling has shaped American politics.* Chicago, IL: University of Chicago Press.

Hermes, J. (2013, May 7). When comments turn ugly: Newspaper websites and anonymous speech. Citizen Media Law Project. Retrieved from http://www.dmlp .org/blog/2013/when-comments-turn-ugly-newspaper-websites-and-anonymous -speech

Hermida, A. (2009). The blogging BBC: Journalism blogs at "the world's most trusted news organisation." *Journalism Practice*, *3*(3), 1–17.

Hermida, A. (2012). Tweets and truth: Journalism as a discipline of collaborative verification. *Journalism Practice*, *6*(5–6), 659–668.

Hermida, A. (2013). #Journalism. *Digital Journalism*, *1*(3), 295–313. doi:10.1080/2167 0811.2013.808456

Hermida, A. (2015). Nothing but the truth: Redrafting the journalistic boundary of verification. In M. Carlson & S. C. Lewis (Eds.), *Boundaries of journalism: Professionalism, practices, and participation* (pp. 37–50). New York, NY: Routledge.

Hille, S., & Bakker, P. (2014). Engaging the social news user: Comments on news sites and Facebook. *Journalism Practice*, *8*(5), 563–572. doi:10.1080/17512786.2014. 899758

Hindman, M. (2008). *The myth of digital democracy.* Princeton, NJ: Princeton University Press.

Hlavach, L., & Freivogel, W. H. (2011). Ethical implications of anonymous comments posted to online news stories. *Journal of Mass Media Ethics*, *26*(1), 21–37.

Horwitz, R. B. (2006). Or of the blog. *Nexus*, *11*, 45–68.

Houston, B. (2015, November 12). Fifty years of journalism and data: A brief history. Global Investigative Journalism Network. Retrieved from http://gijn.org/2015/11/12 /fifty-years-of-journalism-and-data-a-brief-history

Hughes, T. P. (2004). *Human-built world: How to think about technology and culture.* Chicago, IL: Chicago University Press.

Hunter, A. (2015). Crowdfunding independent and freelance journalism: Negotiating journalistic norms of autonomy and objectivity. *New Media & Society, 17*(2), 272–288. doi:10.1177/1461444814558915

Husband, C. (2009). Between listening and understanding. *Continuum, 23*(4), 441–443.

Hutchins Commission on Freedom of the Press. (1947). *A free and responsible press.* Chicago, IL: University of Chicago Press.

Igo, S. (2007). *The averaged American: Surveys, citizens, and the making of a mass public.* Cambridge, MA: Harvard University Press.

Jackson, S. J. (2013). Rethinking repair. In T. Gillespie, P. J. Boczkowski, & K. A. Foot (Eds.), *Media technologies: Essays on communication, materiality, and society* (pp. 221–239). Cambridge, MA: MIT Press.

Jackson, S. J. (2016). Speed, time, infrastructure: Temporalities of breakdown, maintenance, and repair. In J. Wajcman & N. Dodd (Eds.), *The sociology of speed: Digital, organizational, and social temporalities* (pp. 169–186). Oxford, UK: Oxford University Press.

Jackson, S. J., Ribes, D., Buyuktur, A., & Bowker, G. C. (2011). Collaborative rhythm: Temporal dissonance and alignment in collaborative scientific work. Paper presented at CSCW 2001, the Proceedings of the ACM Conference on Computer-Supported Cooperative Work, Hangzhou, China.

James, W. (1914). *Habit.* New York, NY: Henry Holt.

James, W. (1981). *Pragmatism.* Indianapolis, IN: Hackett. (Original work published 1907)

Jenkins, H. (1992). *Textual poachers: Television fans and participatory culture.* Oxford, UK: Routledge Press.

Jenkins, H. (2013). Rethinking "rethinking convergence culture." *Cultural Studies, 28*(2), 267–297. doi:10.1080/09502386.2013.801579

Jenkins, H., & Carpentier, N. (2013). Theorizing participatory intensities: A conversation about participation and politics. *Convergence.* doi:10.1177/1354856513482090

Jian, L., & Shin, J. (2015). Motivations behind donors' contributions to crowdfunded journalism. *Mass Communication & Society, 18*(2), 165–185. doi:10.1080/15205436.2014.911328

John, N. A. (2012). Sharing and Web 2.0: The emergence of a keyword. *New Media & Society, 15*(2), 167–182. doi:10.1177/1461444812450684

Johnson, S. (1998). Public journalism and newsroom structure: The Columbia, S.C., model. In E. B. Lambeth, P. E. Meyer, & E. Thorson (Eds.), *Assessing public journalism* (pp. 123–142). Columbia, MO: University of Missouri Press.

Johnston, J., & Wallace, A. (2016). Who is a journalist? *Digital Journalism, 5*(7), 850–867. doi:10.1080/21670811.2016.1196592

Jones, M., Munir, K., Orlikowski, W., & Runde, J. (2008). About time too: Online news and changing temporal structures in the newspaper industry. Paper presented at the Twenty-ninth International Conference on Information Systems, Paris, France.

Joseph, M. (2002). *Against the romance of community*. Minneapolis, MN: University of Minnesota Press.

Josephi, B. (2009). Journalism education. In K. Wahl-Jorgensen & T. Hanitzsch (Eds.), *The handbook of journalism studies* (pp. 42–58). New York, NY: Routledge.

Kahneman, D. (2003). Maps of bounded rationality: Psychology for behavioral economics. *American Economic Review, 93*(5), 1449–1475.

Kant, I. (2002). *Groundwork for the metaphysics of morals* (A. W. Wood, Trans.). Binghamton, NY: Vail-Ballou Press. (Original work published 1785)

Kaplan, R. L. (2002). *Politics and the American press: The rise of objectivity, 1865–1920*. Cambridge, UK: Cambridge University Press.

Kaplan, R. L. (2006). The news about new institutionalism: Journalism's ethic of objectivity and its political origins. *Political Communication, 23*(2), 173–185.

Karppinen, K., & Moe, H. (2016). What we talk about when we talk about "media independence." *Javnost—The Public, 23*(2), 105–119. doi:10.1080/13183222.2016.1162986

Katz, E. (1957). The two-step flow of communication: An up-to-date report on an hypothesis. *Public Opinion Quarterly, 21*(1), 61–78. doi:10.1086/266687

Katzenbach, C. (2011). Technologies as institutions: Rethinking the role of technology in media governance constellations. In M. Puppis & N. Just (Eds.), *Trends in communication policy research* (pp. 117–138). London, UK: Intellect.

Keith, S. (2015). Horseshoes, stylebooks, wheels, poles, and dummies: Objects of editing power in twentieth-century newsrooms. *Journalism, 16*(1), 44–60. doi:10.1177/1464884914545732

Kelty, C. M. (2005). Geeks, social imaginaries, and recursive publics. *Cultural Anthropology, 20*(2), 185–214.

Kelty, C. M. (2014). The fog of freedom. In T. Gillespie, P. J. Boczkowski, & K. A. Foot (Eds.), *Media technologies: Essays on communication, materiality, and society* (pp. 195–220). Cambridge, MA: MIT Press.

Kelty, C. M., Panofsky, A., Currie, M., Crooks, R., Erickson, S., Garcia, P., et al. (2015). Seven dimensions of contemporary participation disentangled. *Journal of the Association for Information Science and Technology, 66*(3), 474–488.

Kennedy, J. (2005). Right to receive information: The current state of the doctrine and the best application for the future. *Seton Hall Law Review, 35*(2), 789–821.

Kerslake, E., & Kinnell, M. (1998). Public libraries, public interest and the information society: Theoretical issues in the social impact of public libraries. *Journal of Librarianship and Information Science, 30*(3), 159–167.

Kielbowicz, R. B. (2015). Regulating timeliness: Technologies, laws, and the news, 1840–1970. *Journalism & Communication Monographs, 17*(1), 5–83. doi:10.1177/1077699 014566380

Kleinnijenhuis, J., Schultz, F., Oegema, D., & van Atteveldt, W. (2013). Financial news and market panics in the age of high-frequency sentiment trading algorithms. *Journalism, 14*(2), 271–291. doi:10.1177/1464884912468375

Kovach, B., & Rosenstiel, T. (2014). *The elements of journalism* (3rd ed.). New York, NY: Three Rivers Press.

Kreiss, D., & Brennen, J. S. (2016). Normative models of digital journalism. In T. Witschge, C. W. Anderson, D. Domingo, & A. Hermida (Eds.), *Handbook of digital journalism* (pp. 299–314). New York, NY: Sage.

Ksiazek, T. B., Malthouse, E. C., & Webster, J. G. (2010). News-seekers and avoiders: Exploring patterns of total news consumption across media and the relationship to civic participation. *Journal of Broadcasting & Electronic Media, 54*(4), 551–568.

Ksiazek, T. B., Peer, L., & Lessard, K. (2015). User engagement with online news: Conceptualizing interactivity and exploring the relationship between online news videos and user comments. *New Media & Society.* doi:10.1177/1461444814545073

Ksiazek, T. B., Peer, L., & Zivic, A. (2016). Discussing the news: Civility and hostility in user comments. *Digital Journalism, 3*(6), 850–870. doi:10.1080/21670811.2014.97 2079

Kunelius, R., & Ruusunoksa, L. (2008). Mapping professional imagination: On the potential of professional culture in the newspapers of the future. *Journalism Studies, 9*(5), 662–678.

Lacey, K. (2006). The invention of a listening public: Radio and its audiences. In C. Ross & K. C. Fuehrer (Eds.), *Mass media, culture and society in twentieth-century Germany* (pp. 61–79). Basingstoke, UK: Palgrave.

Lacey, K. (2013). *Listening publics: The politics and experience of listening in the media age.* Cambridge, UK: Polity.

Lahey, M. (2016). Invisible actors: Web application programming interfaces, television, and social media. *Convergence, 22*(4), 426–439. doi:10.1177/1354856516641915

Larson, C. (2015). Live publishing: The onstage redeployment of journalistic authority. *Media Culture & Society, 37*(3), 440–459. doi:10.1177/0163443714567016

Larson, M. L. (1977). *The rise of professionalism: A sociological analysis.* Berkeley, CA: University of California Press.

Latour, B. (1992). Where are the missing masses? The sociology of a few mundane artifacts. In W. E. Bijker & J. Law (Eds.), *Shaping technology / building society: Studies in sociotechnical change* (pp. 225–258). Cambridge, MA: MIT Press.

Latour, B. (1993). *We have never been modern* (C. Porter, Trans.). Cambridge, MA: Harvard University Press.

Latour, B. (2004). Why has critique run out of steam? From matters of fact to matters of concern. *Critical Inquiry, 30*(2), 225–248.

Latour, B. (2005). *Reassembling the social: An introduction to actor-network-theory.* Oxford, UK: Oxford University Press.

Latour, B., & Weibel, P. (Eds.). (2005). *Making things public: Atmospheres of democracy.* Cambridge, MA: MIT Press.

Lau, R. W. K. (2012). Re-theorizing news' construction of reality: A realistic-discourse-theoretic approach. *Journalism, 13*(7), 886–902. doi:10.1177/1464884911432660

Law, J. (1987). Technology and heterogeneous engineering: The case of Portugese expansion. In W. E. Bijker, T. P. Hughes, & T. Pinch (Eds.), *The social construction of technological systems* (pp. 111–134). Cambridge, MA: MIT Press.

Law, J. (1992). Notes on the theory of the actor-network: Ordering, strategy, and heterogeneity. *Systemic Practice and Action Research, 5*(4), 379–393.

Law, J., & Callon, M. (1992). The life and death of an aircraft: A network analysis of technical change. In W. E. Bijker & J. Law (Eds.), *Shaping technology/building society: Studies in sociotechnical change* (pp. 21–52). Cambridge, MA: MIT Press.

Law, J., & Mol, A. (1995). Notes on materiality and sociality. *Sociological Review, 43*(2), 274–294.

LeCam, F. (2015). Photographs of newsrooms: From the printing house to open space offices. Analyzing the transformation of workspaces and information production. *Journalism, 16*(1), 134–152. doi:10.1177/1464884914558347

Lecheler, S., & Kruikemeier, S. (2016). Re-evaluating journalistic routines in a digital age: A review of research on the use of online sources. *New Media & Society, 18*(1), 156–171. doi:10.1177/1461444815600412

LeDantec, C. A., Christensen, J. E., Bailey, M., Farrell, R. G., Ellis, J. B., & Danis, C. M., … Edwards, W. K. (2010). A tale of two publics: Democratizing design at the margins. In *DIS '10: Proceedings of the Conference on Designing Interactive Systems* (pp. 11–20). New York, NY: ACM.

LeDantec, C. A., & DiSalvo, C. (2013). Infrastructuring and the formation of publics in participatory design. *Social Studies of Science, 43*(2), 241–264. doi:10.1177 /0306312712471581

Lee, S. K., & Katz, J. E. (2014). Disconnect: A case study of short-term voluntary mobile phone non-use. *First Monday, 19*(12). doi:10.5210/fm.v19i12.4935

Lee, W. E. (1987). The Supreme Court and the right to receive expression. *Supreme Court Review*, 303–344.

Leonardi, P. M. (2012). Materiality, sociomateriality, and socio-technical systems: What do these terms mean? How are they related? Do we need them? In P. M. Leonardi, B. A. Nardi, & J. Kallinikos (Eds.), *Materiality and organizing: Social interaction in a technological world* (pp. 25–48). Oxford, UK: Oxford University Press.

Leonardi, P. M. (2013). Theoretical foundations for the study of sociomateriality. *Information and Organization, 23*(2), 59–76. doi:10.1016/j.infoandorg.2013.02.002

Levin, S., Wong, J. C., & Harding, L. (2016, September 9). Facebook backs down from "napalm girl" censorship and reinstates photo. *The Guardian*. Retrieved from https://www.theguardian.com/technology/2016/sep/09/facebook-reinstates-napalm -girl-photo

Levy, L. W. (1960). *Legacy of suppression: Freedom of speech and press in early American history* (2nd ed.). Cambridge, MA: Belknap Press of Harvard University Press.

Levy, L. W. (2004). *Emergence of a free press*. Chicago, IL: Ivan R. Dee.

Lewin, K. (1951). *Field theory in social science: Selected theoretical papers*. D. Cartwright (Ed.). Westport, CT: Greenwood.

Lewis, A. (2008). *Freedom for the thought we hate*. New York, NY: Basic Books.

Lewis, S. C. (2012). The tension between professional control and open participation: Journalism and its boundaries. *Information Communication and Society, 15*(6), 836–866.

Lewis, S. C., & Usher, N. (2016). Trading zones, boundary objects, and the pursuit of news innovation: A case study of journalists and programmers. *Convergence, 22*(5), 543–560. doi:10.1177/1354856515623865

Lewis, S. C., & Westlund, O. (2015). Big data and journalism: Epistemology, expertise, economics, and ethics. *Digital Journalism, 3*(3), 447–466. 10.1080/21670811. 2014.976418

Liao, T. (2014). Augmented or admented reality? The influence of marketing on augmented reality technologies. *Information Communication and Society, 18*(3), 310–326. doi:10.1080/1369118X.2014.989252

Lichtenberg, J. (1987). Foundations and limits of freedom of the press. *Philosophy & Public Affairs, 16*(4), 329–355.

Lichtenberg, J. (2000). In defence of objectivity revisited. In J. Curran & M. Gurevitch (Eds.), *Mass media and society* (pp. 225–242). London, UK: Arnold.

Lipari, L. (1996). Journalistic authority: Textual strategies of legitimation. *Journalism & Mass Communication Quarterly, 73*(4), 821–834.

Lipari, L. (2010). Listening, thinking, being. *Communication Theory, 20,* 348–362.

Lippmann, W. (1920). *Liberty and the news.* New York, NY: Harcourt, Brace and Howe.

Lippmann, W. (1922). *Public opinion.* New York, NY: Free Press.

Lippmann, W. (1925). *The phantom public.* Edison, NJ: Transaction.

Livingston, S., & Asmolov, G. (2010). Networks and the future of foreign affairs reporting. *Journalism Studies, 11*(5), 745–760.

Livingston, S., & Bennett, W. L. (2003). Gatekeeping, indexing, and live-event news: Is technology altering the construction of news? *Political Communication, 20*(4), 363–380.

Livingstone, S. (2013). The participation paradigm in audience research. *Communication Review, 16*(1–2), 21–30.

Livingstone, S., & Das, R. (2013). The end of audiences? Theoretical echoes of reception amidst the uncertainties of use. In J. Hartley, J. Burgess, & A. Bruns (Eds.), *A companion to new media dynamics* (pp. 104–121). New York, NY: Wiley-Blackwell.

Lodato, T. J., & DiSalvo, C. (2016). Issue-oriented hackathons as material participation. *New Media & Society, 18*(4), 539–557. doi:10.1177/1461444816629467

Lokot, T., & Diakopoulos, N. (2016). News bots: Automating news and information dissemination on Twitter. *Digital Journalism, 4*(6), 682–699. doi:10.1080/21670811.2015.1081822

Loosen, W., & Schmidt, J.-H. (2012). (Re-)discovering the audience. *Information Communication and Society, 15*(6), 867–887.

Lynch, L. (2010). "We're going to crack the world open": Wikileaks and the future of investigative reporting. *Journalism Practice, 4*(3), 309–318.

MacCallum, G. C. J., Jr. (1967). Negative and positive freedom. *Philosophical Review, 76*(3), 312–334.

MacGregor, P. (2007). Tracking the online audience: Metric data start a subtle revolution. *Journalism Studies, 8*(2), 280–298.

Machill, M., & Beiler, M. (2009). The importance of the Internet for journalistic research. *Journalism Studies, 10*(2), 178–203. doi:10.1080/14616700802337768

MacKinnon, R. (2012). *Consent of the networked: The worldwide struggle for Internet freedom.* New York, NY: Basic Books.

Macnamara, J. (2013). Beyond voice: Audience-making and the work and architecture of listening as new media literacies. *Continuum, 27*(1), 160–175.

Macnamara, J. (2015). *Organizational listening: The missing essential in public communication.* London, UK: Peter Lang.

Maier, S. R., Slovic, P., & Mayorga, M. (2016). Reader reaction to news of mass suffering: Assessing the influence of story form and emotional response. *Journalism.* doi:10.1177/1464884916663597

Mansbridge, J. (1999). On the idea that participation makes better citizens. In S. L. Elkin & K. E. Soltan (Eds.), *Citizen competence and democratic institutions* (pp. 291–325). University Park, PA: Pennsylvania State University Press.

Marcus, G. E., & Saka, E. (2006). Assemblage. *Theory, Culture & Society, 23*(2–3), 101–106. doi:10.1177/0263276406062573

Marlière, P. (2000). The impact of market journalism: Pierre Bourdieu on the media. In B. Fowler (Ed.), *Reading Bourdieu on society and culture* (pp. 199–211). London, UK: Blackwell.

Marres, N. (2012). *Material participation: Technology, the environment and everyday publics.* London, UK: Palgrave Macmillan.

Mart, S. N. (2003). The right to receive information. *Law Library Journal, 95,* 175–190.

Marvin, C. (1990). *When old technologies were new: Thinking about electric communication in the late nineteenth century* (Reprint ed.). New York, NY: Oxford University Press.

Marwick, A., & boyd, d. (2011). I tweet honestly, I tweet passionately: Twitter users, context collapse, and the imagined audience. *New Media & Society, 13*(1), 114–133.

Matias, J. N. (2017, January 3). The real name fallacy. Coral Project. Retrieved from https://blog.coralproject.net/the-real-name-fallacy

McCombs, M. E., & Reynolds, A. (2002). News influence on our pictures of the world. In J. Bryant & D. Zillmann (Eds.), *Media effects: Advances in theory and research* (2nd ed., pp. 1–18). Mahwah, NJ: Lawrence Erlbaum.

McCombs, M. E., & Shaw, D. L. (1972). The agenda-setting function of mass media. *Public Opinion Quarterly, 36*(2), 176–187.

McKenna, K. (1993). The loneliest job in the newsroom. *American Journalism Review, 15*(2), 40–44.

McManus, J. (1994). *Market-driven journalism.* Newbury Park, CA: Sage.

McMillian, J. (2011). *Smoking typewriters: The sixties underground press and the rise of alternative media in America.* Oxford, UK: Oxford University Press.

McQuail, D. (2013). The media audience: A brief biography—stages of growth or paradigm change? *Communication Review, 16*(1–2), 9–20.

Mead, G. H. (1967). *Mind, self, and society.* Chicago, IL: University of Chicago Press. (Original work published 1934)

Meiklejohn, A. (1948). *Free speech and its relation to self-government.* New York, NY: Harper.

Meyer, M. J. (1987). Stoics, rights, and autonomy. *American Philosophical Quarterly, 24,* 267–271.

Meyer, P. (1973). *Precision journalism.* Bloomington, IN: Indiana University Press.

Meyers, C. (2000). Creating an effective newspaper ombudsman position. *Journal of Mass Media Ethics, 15*(4), 248–256.

Mill, J. S. (1974). *On liberty.* London, UK: Penguin Books. (Original work published 1859)

Mills, C. W. (2000). *The sociological imagination.* Oxford, UK: Oxford University Press. (Original work published 1959)

Mindich, D. (1998). *Just the facts: How "objectivity" came to define American journalism.* New York, NY: New York University Press.

Mitchelstein, E., & Boczkowski, P. (2009). Between tradition and change: A review of recent research on online news production. *Journalism, 10*(5), 562–586.

Mitchelstein, E., & Boczkowski, P. J. (2013). Tradition and transformation in online news production and consumption. In W. H. Dutton (Ed.), *The Oxford handbook of Internet studies* (pp. 378–400). Oxford, UK: Oxford University Press.

Mol, A. (1999). Ontological politics: A word and some questions. *Sociological Review, 47*(S1), 74–89. doi:10.1111/j.1467-954X.1999.tb03483.x

Molotch, H., & Lester, M. (1974). News as purposive behavior: On the strategic use of routine events, accidents, and scandals. *American Sociological Review, 39*(1), 101–112.

Mouffe, C. (2005). *On the political.* London, UK: Routledge.

Müller, M. (2015). Assemblages and actor-networks: Rethinking socio-material power, politics, and space. *Geography Compass, 9*(1), 27–41. doi:10.1111/gec3.12192

Murasky, D. M. (1974). The journalist's privilege: *Branzburg* and its aftermath. *Texas Law Review, 52*(5), 829–917.

Murdock, G. (1977). *Patterns of ownership: Questions of control.* Milton Keynes, UK: Open University Press.

Myers, S. (2011, September 29). Larry Page: "Trying to improve media" is part of Google's responsibility. *Poynter.* Retrieved from http://www.poynter.org/2011/larry-page-trying-to-improve-media-is-part-of-googles-responsibility/147711

Myllylahti, M. (2016). Newspaper paywalls and corporate revenues: A comparative study. In B. Franklin & S. Eldridge (Eds.), *The Routledge companion to digital journalism studies* (pp. 166–175). London, UK: Routledge.

Nagel, T. (1998). Concealment and exposure. *Philosophy & Public Affairs, 27*(1), 3–30.

Napoli, P. M. (1997). The media trade press as technology forecaster: A case study of the VCR's impact on broadcasting. *Journalism & Mass Communication Quarterly, 74*(2), 417–430.

Napoli, P. M. (2011). *Audience evolution: New technologies and the transformation of media audiences.* New York, NY: Columbia University Press.

Napoli, P. M. (2014). Automated media: An institutional theory perspective on algorithmic media production and consumption. *Communication Theory, 24*(3), 340–360. doi:10.1111/comt.12039

Napoli, P. M. (2015). Social media and the public interest: Governance of news platforms in the realm of individual and algorithmic gatekeepers. *Telecommunications Policy, 39*(9), 751–760. doi:10.1016/j.telpol.2014.12.003

Napoli, P. M., & Caplan, R. (2017). Why media companies insist they're not media companies, why they're wrong, and why it matters. *First Monday, 22*(5).

Neely, W. (1974). Freedom and desire. *Philosophical Review, 83*, 32–54.

Neff, G. (2015). Learning from documents: Applying new theories of materiality to journalism. *Journalism, 16*(1), 74–78. doi:10.1177/1464884914549294

Neiger, M., Meyers, O., & Zandberg, E. (2011). On media memory: Editors' introduction. In M. Neiger, O. Meyers, & E. Zandberg (Eds.), *On media memory: Collective memory in a new media age* (pp. 1–26). London, UK: Palgrave-Macmillan.

Neiger, M., & Tenenboim-Weinblatt, K. (2016). Understanding journalism through a nuanced deconstruction of temporal layers in news narratives. *Journal of Communication, 66*(1), 139–160. doi:10.1111/jcom.12202

Nemeth, N. (2003). *Newspaper ombudsmen in North America: Assessing an experiment in social responsibility.* Westport, CT: Praeger.

Nerone, J. (2013). The historical roots of the normative model of journalism. *Journalism, 14*(4), 446–458. doi:10.1177/1464884912464177

Nerone, J. (2015). *The media and public life: A history.* London, UK: Polity.

Nerone, J. (Ed.). (1995). *Last rights: Revisiting Four Theories of the Press.* Chicago, IL: University of Illinois Press.

Nestler, J. S. (2005). The underprivileged profession: The case for Supreme Court recognition of the journalist's privilege. *University of Pennsylvania Law Review, 154*(1), 201–256.

Netzer, Y., Tenenboim-Weinblatt, K., & Shifman, L. (2014). The construction of participation in news websites: A five-dimensional model. *Journalism Studies, 15*(5), 619–631. doi:10.1080/1461670X.2014.895527

Neveu, E. (2007). Pierre Bourdieu. *Journalism Studies, 8*(2), 335–347.

Newspaper Association of America. (2013, May 15). Newspaper Association of America welcomes reintroduction of Free Flow of Information Act. NAA. Retrieved from http://www.naa.org/en/News-and-Media/Press-Center/Archives/2013/NAA-Welcomes-Reintroduction-of-Free-Flow-of-Information-Act.aspx

Nissenbaum, H. (2001, March). How computer systems embody values. *IEEE Computer*, 118–120.

O'Donnell, P. (2009). Journalism, change and listening practices. *Continuum, 23*(4), 503–517.

O'Neill, O. (2009). Ethics for communication? *European Journal of Philosophy, 17*(2), 167–180.

Oliver, M. B. (2002). Individual differences in media effects. In J. Bryant & D. Zillmann (Eds.), *Media effects: Advances in theory and research* (2nd ed., pp. 507–524). Mahwah, NJ: Lawrence Erlbaum.

Opgenhaffen, M., & Scheerlinck, H. (2014). Social media guidelines for journalists: An investigation into the sense and nonsense among Flemish journalists. *Journalism Practice, 8*(6), 726–741. doi:10.1080/17512786.2013.869421

Ophir, E., Nass, C., & Wagner, A. D. (2009). Cognitive control in media multitaskers. *Proceedings of the National Academy of Sciences of the United States of America, 106*(37), 15583–15587.

Orlikowski, W. (2008). Sociomateriality: Challenging the separation of technology, work and organization. *Academy of Management Annals, 2*(1), 433–474.

Orlikowski, W. (2010). The sociomateriality of organisational life: Considering technology in management research. *Cambridge Journal of Economics, 34*(1), 125–141.

Oudshoorn, N., & Pinch, T. (2003). How users and non-users matter. In N. Oudshoorn & T. Pinch (Eds.), *How users matter: The co-construction of users and technology* (pp. 1–25). Cambridge, MA: MIT Press.

Padgett, J. F., & Powell, W. W. (2012). *The emergence of organizations and markets.* Princeton, NJ: Princeton University Press.

Page, B. I., & Shapiro, R. Y. (1992). *The rational public.* Chicago, IL: University of Chicago Press.

Pantti, M., & Sirén, S. (2015). The fragility of photo-truth. *Digital Journalism, 3*(4), 495–512. doi:10.1080/21670811.2015.1034518

Papacharissi, Z. (2015). Toward new journalism(s): Affective news, hybridity, and liminal spaces. *Journalism Studies, 16*(1), 27–40. doi:10.1080/1461670X.2014.890328

Papacharissi, Z., & Easton, E. (2013). In the habitus of the new: Structure, agency and the social media habitus. In J. Hartley, J. Burgess, & A. Bruns (Eds.), *A companion to new media dynamics* (pp. 171–184). New York, NY: Wiley-Blackwell.

Parasie, S. (2015). Data-driven revelation? Epistemological tensions in investigative journalism in the age of "big data." *Digital Journalism, 3*(3), 364–380. doi:10.1080/2 1670811.2014.976408

Pariser, E. (2011). *The filter bubble.* New York, NY: Penguin Press.

Park, R. E. (1923). The natural history of the newspaper. *American Journal of Sociology, 29*(3), 273–289.

Park, R. E. (1940). News as a form of knowledge: A chapter in the sociology of knowledge. *American Journal of Sociology, 45*(5), 669–686.

Parker, R. A. (Ed.). (2003). *Free speech on trial: Communication perspectives on landmark Supreme Court decisions.* Tuscaloosa, AL: University of Alabama Press.

Parks, L. (2012). Technostruggles and the satellite dish: A populist approach to infrastructure. In G. Bolin (Ed.), *Cultural technologies: The shaping of culture in media and society* (pp. 64–86). London, UK: Routledge.

Parks, L., & Starosielski, N. (Eds.). (2015). *Signal traffic: Critical studies of media infrastructure.* Chicago, IL: University of Illinois Press.

Pateman, C. (1970). *Participation and democratic theory.* Cambridge, UK: Cambridge University Press.

Paulussen, S., Heinonen, A., Domingo, D., & Quandt, T. (2007). Doing it together: Citizen participation in the professional news making process. Observatorio (OBS*). *Journal, 3*, 131–154.

Perlmutter, D. D., & Schoen, M. (2007). "If I break a rule, what do I do, fire myself?" Ethics codes of independent blogs. *Journal of Mass Media Ethics, 22*(1), 37–48.

Perloff, R. M. (2002). The third-person effect. In J. Bryant & D. Zillmann (Eds.), *Media effects: Advances in theory and research* (2nd ed., pp. 489–506). Mahwah, NJ: Lawrence Erlbaum.

Peters, C., & Broersma, M. (Eds.). (2017) *Rethinking journalism again: Societal role and public relevance in a digital age.* London, UK: Routledge.

Peters, J. D. (1995). Historical tensions in the concept of public opinion. In C. T. S. Theodore L. Glasser (Ed.), *Public opinion and the communication of consent* (pp. 3–32). New York, NY: Guilford Press.

Peters, J. D. (2006). Media as conversation, conversation as media. In J. Curran & D. Morley (Eds.), *Media and cultural theory* (pp. 115–126). London, UK: Routledge.

Petre, C. (2015, May 7). The traffic factories: Metrics at Chartbeat, Gawker Media, and *The New York Times*. Tow Center for Digital Journalism. Retrieved from http://towcenter.org/research/traffic-factories

Pew Research Center. (2013, July 11). Public esteem for military still high. Pew Research Center, Religion & Public Life. Retrieved from http://www.pewforum.org/Other-Demographics/Public-Esteem-for-Military-Still-High.aspx#journalists

Pickard, V. (2014a). *America's battle for media democracy: The triumph of corporate libertarianism and the future of media reform.* Cambridge, UK: Cambridge University Press.

Pickard, V. (2014b). The great evasion: Confronting market failure in American media policy. *Critical Studies in Media Communication, 31*(2), 153–159. doi:10.1080/15295036.2014.919404

Pickard, V. (2015, December 11). The U.S. stands as a cautionary tale for what happens when a media system is dominated by market values. Democratic Audit UK. Retrieved from http://www.democraticaudit.com/2015/11/25/the-us-stands-as-a-cautionary-tale-for-what-happens-when-a-media-system-is-dominated-by-market-values

Pickard, V., & Williams, A. T. (2014). Salvation or folly? The promises and perils of digital paywalls. *Digital Journalism, 2*(2), 195–213. doi:10.1080/21670811.2013.865967

Pinch, T. J., & Bijker, W. E. (1984). The social construction of facts and artefacts: Or how the sociology of science and the sociology of technology might benefit each other. *Social Studies of Science, 14*(3), 399–441.

Pinchevski, A. (2001). Freedom from speech (or the silent demand). *Diacritics, 31*(2), 71–84.

Plantin, J.-C., Lagoze, C., Edwards, P. N., & Sandvig, C. (2016, August 4). Infrastructure studies meet platform studies in the age of Google and Facebook. *New Media & Society*. doi:10.1177/1461444816661553

Plaut, E. R. (2015). Technologies of avoidance: The swear jar and the cell phone. *First Monday*, *20*(11). doi:10.5210/fm.v20i11.6295

Plesner, U. (2009). An actor-network perspective on changing work practices: Communication technologies as actants in newswork. *Journalism*, *10*(5), 604–626.

Ponce de Leon, C. L. (2015). *That's the way it is: A history of television news in America.* Chicago, IL: University of Chicago Press.

Popkin, S. L. (1994). *The reasoning voter.* Chicago, IL: University of Chicago Press.

Post, R. C. (1993). Meiklejohn's mistake: Individual autonomy and the reform of public discourse. *University of Colorado Law Review*, *64*, 1109–1137.

Potter, W. J. (2014). A critical analysis of cultivation theory. *Journal of Communication*, *64*(6), 1015–1036. doi:10.1111/jcom.12128

Powell, A. (2016). Hacking in the public interest: Authority, legitimacy, means, and ends. *New Media & Society*, *18*(4), 535–538. doi:10.1177/1461444816629470

Powell, W. W., & DiMaggio, P. J. (Eds.). (1991). *The new institutionalism in organizational analysis.* Chicago, IL: University of Chicago Press.

Powers, M. (2012). "In forms that are familiar and yet-to-be invented": American journalism and the discourse of technologically specific work. *Journal of Communication Inquiry*, *36*(1), 24–43.

Prior, M. (2007). *Post-broadcast democracy: How media choice increases inequality in political involvement and polarizes elections.* Cambridge, UK: Cambridge University Press.

Pritchard, D. (1993). The impact of newspaper ombudsmen on journalists' attitudes. *Journalism Quarterly*, *70*(1), 77–86.

Prochazka, F., Weber, P., & Schweiger, W. (2016, March 22). Effects of civility and reasoning in user comments on perceived journalistic quality. *Journalism Studies*, 1–17. doi:10.1080/1461670X.2016.1161497

Qiu, Y. (2016). The openness of open application programming interfaces. *Information Communication and Society*, *20*(11), 1720–1736. doi:10.1080/1369118X.2016.1254268

Reader, B. (2012). Free press vs. free speech? The rhetoric of "civility" in regard to anonymous online comments. *Journalism & Mass Communication Quarterly*, *89*(3), 495–513.

Reich, Z. (2011). User comments: The transformation of participatory space. In J. B. Singer, A. Hermida, D. Domingo, A. Heinonen, S. Paulussen, T. Quandt, et al.

(Eds.), *Participatory journalism: Guarding open gates at online newspapers* (pp. 96–117). Malden, MA: Wiley-Blackwell.

Reich, Z. (2012). Journalism as bipolar interactional expertise. *Communication Theory, 22*(4), 339–358. doi:10.1111/j.1468-2885.2012.01411.x

Reich, Z., & Godler, Y. (2014). A time of uncertainty: The effects of reporters' time schedule on their work. *Journalism Studies, 15*(5), 607–618. doi:10.1080/1461670X.2014.882484

Reporters Committee for Freedom of the Press. (n.d.). Shield laws and protection of sources by state. Retrieved from http://www.rcfp.org/browse-media-law-resources/guides/reporters-privilege/shield-laws

Robinson, S. (2007). "Someone's gotta be in control here": The institutionalization of online news and the creation of a shared journalistic authority. *Journalism Practice, 1*(3), 305–321.

Rogoff, B., Paradise, R., Arauz, R. M., Correa-Chavez, M., & Angelillo, C. (2003). Firsthand learning through intent participation. *Annual Review of Psychology, 54*(1), 175–203.

Rorty, R. (1989). *Contingency, irony, and solidarity.* Cambridge, UK: Cambridge University Press.

Rose, N. (1999). *Powers of freedom: Reframing political thought.* Cambridge, UK: Cambridge University Press.

Rosen, J. (1999). *What are journalists for?* New Haven, CT: Yale University Press.

Rosen, J. (2006, June 27). The people formerly known as the audience. *Press Think.* Retrieved from http://journalism.nyu.edu/pubzone/weblogs/pressthink/2006/06/27/ppl_frmr_p.html

Rosen, J. (2008, April 22). The uncharted: From "off the bus" to "meet the press." *Huffington Post.* Retrieved from http://www.huffingtonpost.com/jay-rosen/the-uncharted-from-off-th_b_96575.html

Rothenberger, L. T., Auer, C., & Pratt, C. B. (2017). Theoretical approaches to normativity in communication research. *Communication Theory, 27*(2), 176–201. doi:10.1111/comt.12103

Rubin, A. M. (2002). The uses-and-gratifications perspective of media effects. In J. Bryant & D. Zillmann (Eds.), *Media effects: Advances in theory and research* (2nd ed., pp. 525–548). Mahwah, NJ: Lawrence Erlbaum.

Ruiz, C., Domingo, D., Micó, J. L., Díaz-Noci, J., Masip, P., & Meso, K. (2011). Public sphere 2.0? The democratic qualities of citizen debates in online newspapers. *International Journal of Press/Politics, 16*(4), 463–487.

Russell, A. (2001). Chiapas and the new news: Internet and newspaper coverage of a broken cease-fire. *Journalism, 2*(2), 197–220.

Russell, A. (2007). Digital communication networks and the journalistic field: The 2005 French riots. *Critical Studies in Media Communication, 24*(4), 285–302.

Russell, A. (2011). *Networked: A contemporary history of news in transition.* London, UK: Polity.

Ryfe, D. M. (2006). The nature of news rules. *Political Communication, 23,* 203–214.

Ryfe, D. M. (2009). Structure, agency, and change in an American newsroom. *Journalism, 10*(5), 665–683.

Ryfe, D. M. (2012). *Can journalism survive? An inside look at American newsrooms.* London, UK: Polity.

Salmon, C. T., & Glasser, T. L. (1995). The politics of polling and the limits of consent. In T. L. Glasser & C. T. Salmon (Eds.), *Public opinion and the communication of consent* (pp. 437–458). New York, NY: Guilford Press.

Sandvig, C. (2015). The Internet as the anti-television: Distribution infrastructure as culture and power. In L. Parks & N. Starosielski (Eds.), *Signal traffic: Critical studies of media infrastructures* (pp. 225–245). Champaign, IL: University of Illinois Press.

Satz, D. (2010). *Why some things should not be for sale: The moral limits of markets.* Oxford, UK: Oxford University Press.

Sauer, G. (2017, February 28). A murder case tests Alexa's devotion to your privacy. *Wired.* Retrieved from https://www.wired.com/2017/02/murder-case-tests-alexas -devotion-privacy

Scalia, A. (1997). *A matter of interpretation: Federal courts and the law.* Princeton, NJ: Princeton University Press.

Scanlon, T. (1972). A theory of freedom of expression. *Philosophy & Public Affairs, 1*(2), 204–226.

Schauer, F. (1982). *Free speech: A philosophical inquiry.* New York, NY: Cambridge University Press.

Schauer, F. (1987). Precedent. *Stanford Law Review, 39,* 571–605.

Schauer, F. (1995). Giving reasons. *Stanford Law Review, 47*(4), 633–659.

Schauer, F. (1998). Principles, institutions and the first amendment. *Harvard Law Review, 112,* 84–121.

Schauer, F. (2005). Towards an institutional first amendment. *Minnesota Law Review, 89,* 1256–1279.

Schifferes, S., Newman, N., Thurman, N., Corney, D., Goker, A. S., & Martin, C. (2014). Identifying and verifying news through social media: Developing a user-centred tool for professional journalists. *Digital Journalism, 2*(3), 406–418. 10.1080/21670811.2014.892747

Schiller, D. (1979). An historical approach to objectivity and professionalism in American news reporting. *Journal of Communication, 29*(4), 46–57.

Schlesinger, P., & Doyle, G. (2015). From organizational crisis to multi-platform salvation? Creative destruction and the recomposition of news media. *Journalism, 16*(3), 305–323. doi:10.1177/1464884914530223

Schmidt, J.-H., & Loosen, W. (2015). Both sides of the story: Assessing audience participation in journalism through the concept of inclusion distance. *Digital Journalism, 3*(2), 259–278. doi:10.1080/21670811.2014.930243

Schön, D. (1983). *The reflective practitioner: How professionals think in action.* New York, NY: Basic Books.

Schrock, A. R. (2016). Civic hacking as data activism and advocacy: A history from publicity to open government data. *New Media & Society, 18*(4), 581–599. doi:10.1177/1461444816629469.

Schroeder, J. (2014). Focusing on how rather than on whom: Constructing a process-based framework for interpreting the press clause in the network-society era. *Communication Law and Policy, 19*(4), 509–562. doi:10.1080/10811680.2014.955775

Schudson, M. (1978). *Discovering the news: A social history of American newspapers.* New York, NY: Basic Books.

Schudson, M. (1986). Deadlines, datelines, and history. In R. K. Manoff & M. Schudson (Eds.), *Reading the news* (pp. 79–108). New York, NY: Pantheon Books.

Schudson, M. (1988). The profession of journalism in the United States. In N. O. Hatch (Ed.), *The professions in American history* (pp. 145–161). Notre Dame, IN: University of Notre Dame.

Schudson, M. (1997). Why conversation is not the soul of democracy. *Critical Studies in Mass Communication, 14,* 297–309.

Schudson, M. (1998). *The good citizen: A history of American public life.* New York, NY: Free Press.

Schudson, M. (2001). The objectivity norm in American journalism. *Journalism, 2*(2), 149–170.

Schudson, M. (2003a). Click here for democracy: A history and critique of an information-based model of citizenship. In H. Jenkins & D. Thorburn (Eds.), *Democracy and new media* (pp. 49–60). Cambridge, MA: MIT Press.

Schudson, M. (2003b). *The sociology of news*. New York, NY: Norton.

Schudson, M. (2005). Autonomy from what? In R. Benson & E. Neveu (Eds.), *Bourdieu and the journalistic field* (pp. 214–223). Cambridge, UK: Polity Press.

Schudson, M. (2008a). The "Lippmann-Dewey debate" and the invention of Walter Lippmann as an anti-democrat 1986–1996. *International Journal of Communication, 2*, 1031–1042.

Schudson, M. (2008b). Six or seven things news can do for democracy. In *Why democracies need an unlovable press* (pp. 11–26). Cambridge, UK: Polity Press.

Schudson, M. (2008c). *Why democracies need an unlovable press*. New York, NY: Polity.

Schudson, M. (2010). Political observatories, databases and news in the emerging ecology of public information. *Daedalus, 139*(2), 100–109.

Schudson, M. (2015). What sorts of things are thingy? And what sorts of thinginess are there? Notes on stuff and social construction. *Journalism, 16*(1), 61–64. doi:10.1177/1464884914545733

Schudson, M., & Anderson, C. W. (2008). Objectivity, professionalism, and truth seeking in journalism. In K. Wahl-Jorgensen & T. Hanitzsch (Eds.), *The handbook of journalism studies* (pp. 88–101). Mahwah, NJ: Lawrence Erlbaum.

Scott, J., Millard, D., & Leonard, P. (2015). Citizen participation in news. *Digital Journalism, 3*(5), 737–758. doi:10.1080/21670811.2014.952983

Scott, W. R. (2013). *Institutions and organizations: Ideas, interests, and identities* (4th ed.). London, UK: Sage.

Seelye, K. Q. (2008, April 14). Blogger is surprised by uproar over Obama story, but not bitter. *New York Times*. Retrieved from http://www.nytimes.com/2008/04/14/us /politics/14web-seelye.html

Sewell, W. (1992). A theory of structure: Duality, agency and transformation. *American Journal of Sociology, 98*, 1–29.

Shilton, K. (2012). Value levers: Building ethics into design. *Science, Technology & Human Values, 38*(3), 374–397.

Shilton, K., Koepfler, J. A., & Fleischmann, K. R. (2013). Charting sociotechnical dimensions of values for design research. *Information Society, 29*(5), 259–271. doi:10. 1080/01972243.2013.825357

Shilton, K., Koepfler, J. A., & Fleischmann, K. R. (2014). How to see values in social computing: Methods for studying values dimensions. In *CSCW '14: Proceedings of the Seventeenth ACM Conference on Computer Supported-Cooperative Work and Social Computing* (pp. 426–435). New York, NY: ACM.

Shirky, C. (2008). *Here comes everybody: The power of organizing without organizations.* New York, NY: Penguin.

Shoemaker, P. J., Vos, T. P., & Reese, S. D. (2009). Journalists as gatekeepers. In K. Wahl-Jorgensen & T. Hanitzsch (Eds.), *The handbook of journalism studies* (pp. 73–87). New York, NY: Rutledge.

Siebert, F. S., Peterson, T., & Schramm, W. (1963). *Four theories of the press: The authoritarian, libertarian, social responsibility, and Soviet communist concepts of what the press should be and do.* Champaign, IL: University of Illinois Press.

Sigal, L. V. (1973). *Reporters and officials: The organization and politics of newsmaking.* Lexington, MA: D. C. Heath.

Sigal, L. V. (1986). Sources make the news. In R. K. Manoff & M. Schudson (Eds.), *Reading the news* (pp. 9–37). New York, NY: Pantheon Books.

Siles, I., & Boczkowski, P. J. (2012). Making sense of the newspaper crisis: A critical assessment of existing research and an agenda for future work. *New Media & Society, 14*(8), 1375–1394.

Silverstone, R. (2003). Proper distance: Towards an ethics for cyberspace. In G. Liestol, A. Morrison, & T. Rasmussen (Eds.), *Digital media revisited: Theoretical and conceptual innovations in digital domains* (pp. 469–490). Cambridge, MA: MIT Press.

Silverstone, R. (2007). *Media and morality: On the rise of the mediapolis.* Cambridge, UK: Polity Press.

Simhony, A. (1993). Beyond negative and positive freedom: T. H. Green's view of freedom. *Political Theory, 21*(1), 28–54.

Simon, H. (1978). Rationality as a process and product of thought. *American Economic Review, 68*, 1–16.

Simon, H. (1983). *Reason in human affairs.* Stanford, CA: Stanford University Press.

Sismondo, S. (2009). *An introduction to science and technology studies* (2nd ed.). London, UK: Wiley-Blackwell.

Socolow, M. J. (2010). "We should make money on our news": The problem of profitability in network broadcast journalism history. *Journalism, 11*(6), 675–691.

Solove, D. (2011). *Nothing to hide: The false tradeoff between privacy and security.* New Haven, CT: Yale University Press.

Sparrow, B. H. (1999). *Uncertain guardians: The news media as a political institution.* Baltimore, MD: Johns Hopkins University Press.

Sparrow, B. H. (2006). A research agenda for an institutional media. *Political Communication, 23*, 145–157.

Springer, N., Engelmann, I., & Pfaffinger, C. (2015). User comments: Motives and inhibitors to write and read. *Information Communication and Society*, *18*(7), 798–815. doi:10.1080/1369118X.2014.997268

Squires, C. R. (2002). Rethinking the black public sphere: An alternative vocabulary for multiple public spheres. *Communication Theory*, *12*(4), 446–468. doi:10.1111/j.1468-2885.2002.tb00278.x

Stanyer, J., & Mihelj, S. (2016). Taking time seriously? Theorizing and researching change in communication and media studies. *Journal of Communication*, *66*(2), 266–279. doi:10.1111/jcom.12218

Star, S. L. (1999). Ethnography of infrastructure. *American Behavioral Scientist*, *43*(3), 377–391.

Star, S. L., & Griesemer, J. R. (1989). Institutional ecology, "translations" and boundary objects: Amateurs and professionals in Berkeley's Museum of Vertebrate Zoology, 1907–39. *Social Studies of Science*, *19*(3), 387–420.

Star, S. L., & Ruhleder, K. (1996). Steps toward an ecology of infrastructure: Design and access for large information spaces. *Information Systems Research*, *7*(1), 111–134.

Star, S. L., & Strauss, A. (1999). Layers of silence, arenas of voice: The ecology of visible and invisible work. *Computer Supported Cooperative Work*, *8*, 9–30.

Steel, J. (2017). Reappraising journalism's normative foundations. In C. Peters & M. Broersma (Eds.), *Rethinking journalism again: Societal role and public relevance in a digital age* (pp. 35–48). London, UK: Routledge.

Steensen, S., & Ahva, L. (2014). Theories of journalism in a digital age. *Journalism Practice*, *9*(1), 1–18. doi:10.1080/17512786.2014.928454

Stein, L. (2004). Understanding speech rights: Defensive and empowering approaches to the first amendment. *Media Culture & Society*, *26*(1), 103–120.

Stein, L. (2006). *Speech rights in America: The first amendment, democracy, and the media*. Champaign, IL: University of Illinois Press.

Steinhardt, S. B., & Jackson, S. J. (2014). Reconciling rhythms: Plans and temporal alignment in collaborative scientific work. In *CSCW '14: Proceedings of the seventeenth ACM Conference on Computer-Supported Cooperative Work and Social Computing* (pp. 134–145). New York, NY: ACM.

Steinhardt, S. B., & Jackson, S. J. (2015). Anticipation work: Cultivating vision in collective practice. In *CSCW '15: Proceedings of the eighteenth ACM Conference on Computer-Supported Cooperative Work* (pp. 443–453). New York, NY: ACM.

Stephens, M. (1988). *A history of news: From the drum to the satellite*. New York, NY: Viking.

Stewart, D. R. (2013). Social media policies for journalists. In D. R. Stewart (Ed.), *Social media and the law: A guidebook for communication students and professionals* (pp. 196–211). New York, NY: Routledge.

Stewart, P. (1975). Or of the press. *Hastings Law Journal, 26,* 631–638.

Strauss, A. L., Fagerhaugh, S., Suczek, B., & Wiener, C. (1985). *Social organization of medical work.* Chicago, IL: University of Chicago Press

Strauss, D. A. (1991). Persuasion, autonomy, and freedom of expression. *Columbia Law Review, 91*(2), 334–371.

Strauss, D. A. (2010). *The living constitution.* New York, NY: Oxford University Press.

Streeter, T. (1996). *Selling the air.* Chicago, IL: University of Chicago Press.

Stroud, N. J. (2011). *Niche news: The politics of news choice.* Oxford, UK: Oxford University Press.

Stutzman, F., Grossy, R., & Acquisti, A. (2012). Silent listeners: The evolution of privacy and disclosure on Facebook. *Journal of Privacy and Confidentiality, 4*(2), 7–41.

Suchman, L. (1994). Working relations of technology production and use. *Computer-Supported Cooperative Work, 2,* 21–39.

Suchman, L. (1996). Supporting articulation work. In R. Kling (Ed.), *Computerization and controversy: Values conflicts and social choices* (pp. 407–423). San Diego, CA: Academic Press.

Suchman, L., Blomberg, J., Orr, J. E., & Trigg, R. (1999). Reconstructing technologies as social practice. *American Behavioral Scientist, 43*(3), 392–408.

Sullivan, K. M. (1994). Free speech and unfree markets. *UCLA Law Review, 42,* 949–965.

Sunstein, C. (1994). *Democracy and the problem of free speech.* New York, NY: Free Press.

Sunstein, C. (2001). *Republic.com.* Princeton, NJ: Princeton University Press.

Sunstein, C. (2004). Democracy and filtering. *Communications of the ACM, 47*(12), 57–59.

Sunstein, C. (2009). *Republic.com 2.0.* Princeton, NJ: Princeton University Press.

Swidler, A. (1986). Culture in action: Symbols and strategies. *American Sociological Review, 51*(2), 273–286.

Tandoc, E. C. (2014). Journalism is twerking? How Web analytics is changing the process of gatekeeping. *New Media & Society, 16*(4), 559–575.

Tandoc, E. C. (2015). Why Web analytics click: Factors affecting the ways journalists use audience metrics. *Journalism Studies, 16*(6), 782–799. doi:10.1080/1461670X.2014.946309

Tandoc, E. C., & Jenkins, J. (2017). The Buzzfeedication of journalism? How traditional news organizations are talking about a new entrant to the journalistic field will surprise you! *Journalism, 18*(4), 482–500. doi:10.1177/1464884915620269

Tandoc, E. C., & Thomas, R. J. (2014). The ethics of Web analytics: Implications of using audience metrics in news construction. *Digital Journalism, 3*(2), 243–258. 10.1080/21670811.2014.909122

Tenenboim-Weinblatt, K. (2014). Counting time: Journalism and the temporal resource. In B. Zelizer & K. Tenenboim-Weinblatt (Eds.), *Journalism and memory* (pp. 97–112). London, UK: Palgrave MacMillan.

Terranova, T. (2012). Attention, economy and the brain. *Culture Machine, 13*.

Tenenboim-Weinblatt, K. (2013). Bridging collective memories and public agendas: Toward a theory of mediated prospective memory. *Communication Theory, 23*(2), 91–111.

Thorson, K., & Wells, C. (2016). Curated flows: A framework for mapping media exposure in the digital age. *Communication Theory, 26*(3), 309–328. doi:10.1111/comt.12087

Thurman, N., Schifferes, S., Fletcher, R., Newman, N., Hunt, S., & Schapals, A. K. (2016). Giving computers a nose for news. *Digital Journalism, 4*(7), 838–848. doi:10.1080/21670811.2016.1149436

Trilling, D., & Schoenbach, K. (2013). Skipping current affairs: The non-users of online and offline news. *European Journal of Communication, 28*(1), 35–51. doi:10.1177/0267323112453671

Trilling, D., Tolochko, P., & Burscher, B. (2017). From newsworthiness to shareworthiness: How to predict news sharing based on article characteristics. *Journalism & Mass Communication Quarterly, 94*(1), 38–60. doi:10.1177/1077699016654682

Tuchman, G. (1972). Objectivity as strategic ritual: An examination of newsmen's notions of objectivity. *American Journal of Sociology, 77*(4), 660–679.

Tuchman, G. (1973). Making news by doing work: Routinizing the unexpected. *American Journal of Sociology, 79*(1), 110–131.

Tuchman, G. (1978). *Making news: A study in the social construction of reality.* New York, NY: Free Press.

Turner, F. (2005). Actor-networking the news. *Social Epistemology, 19*(4), 321–324.

Turow, J. (1994). Hidden conflicts and journalistic norms: The case of self-coverage. *Journal of Communication, 44*(2), 29–46.

Turow, J. (2011). *The daily you: How the new advertising industry is defining your identity and your worth.* New Haven, CT: Yale University Press.

Tylor, J. (2014). An examination of how student journalists seek information and evaluate online sources during the newsgathering process. *New Media & Society, 17*(8), 1277–1298. doi:10.1177/1461444814523079

Ugland, E. (2008). Demarcating the right to gather news: A sequential interpretation of the first amendment. *Duke Journal of Constitutional Law & Public Policy, 3,* 113–189.

Ugland, E. (2009). Newsgathering, autonomy, and the special-rights apocrypha: Supreme Court and media litigant conceptions of press freedom. *Journal of Constitutional Law, 11*(2), 375–422.

Usher, N. (2013). Al Jazeera English online: Understanding Web metrics and news production when a quantified audience is not a commodified audience. *Digital Journalism, 1*(3), 335–351. 10.1080/21670811.2013.801690

Usher, N. (2014). *Making news at The New York Times.* Ann Arbor, MI: University of Michigan Press.

Usher, N. (2015). The late great *International Herald Tribune* and *The New York Times*: Global media, space, time, print, and online coordination in a 24/7 networked world. *Journalism, 16*(1), 119–133. doi:10.1177/1464884914545743

van Dalen, A. (2012). The algorithms behind the headlines: How machine-written news redefines the core skills of human journalist. *Journalism Practice, 6*(5–6), 648–658.

van Dijck, J. (2013). *The culture of connectivity: A critical history of social media.* Oxford, UK: Oxford University Press.

Venturini, T., Ricci, D., Mauri, M., Kimbell, L., & Meunier, A. (2015). Designing controversies and their publics. *Design Issues, 31*(3), 74–87. doi:10.1162/DESI_a_00340

Verbeek, P.-P. (2006). Materializing morality: Design ethics and technological mediation. *Science, Technology & Human Values, 31*(3), 361–380. doi:10.1177/0162243905285847

Vu, H. T. (2014). The online audience as gatekeeper: The influence of reader metrics on news editorial selection. *Journalism, 15*(8), 1094–1110. doi:10.1177/1464884913504259

Wahl-Jorgensen, K. (2002). The construction of the public in letters to the editor: Deliberative democracy and the idiom of insanity. *Journalism, 3*(2), 183–204.

Wahl-Jorgensen, K. (2007). *Journalists and the public: Newsroom culture, letters to the editor, and democracy.* Cresskill, NJ: Hampton Press.

Wahl-Jorgensen, K. (2013). The strategic ritual of emotionality: A case study of Pulitzer Prize–winning articles. *Journalism, 14*(1), 129–145.

Wajcman, J. (2007). From women and technology to gendered technoscience. *Information Communication and Society, 10*(3), 287–298. doi:10.1080/13691180701409770

Wajcman, J. (2014). *Pressed for time: The acceleration of life in digital capitalism.* Chicago, IL: University of Chicago Press.

Ward, S. C. (1996). *Reconfiguring truth.* New York, NY: Rowman & Littlefield.

Ward, S. J. A. (2005). *Invention of journalism ethics: The path to objectivity and beyond.* Montreal, QC: McGill-Queen's Press.

Ward, S. J. A., & Wasserman, H. (2015). Open ethics: Towards a global media ethics of listening. *Journalism Studies, 16*(6), 834–849. doi:10.1080/1461670X.2014.950882

Warner, M. (2005). *Publics and counterpublics.* New York, NY: Zone Books.

Warren, M. E. (2000). *Democracy and association.* Princeton, NJ: Princeton University Press.

Weaver, D. H., & Willnat, L. (2016). Changes in U.S. journalism. *Journalism Practice, 10*(7), 844–855. doi:10.1080/17512786.2016.1171162

Weaver, W., & Shannon, C. E. (1963). *The mathematical theory of computation.* Chicago, IL: University of Illinois Press.

Weber, M. (2007). "Objectivity" in social science. In C. Calhoun, J. Gerteis, J. Moody, S. Pfaff, & I. Virk (Eds.), *Classical sociological theory* (2nd ed., pp. 211–217). Malden, MA: Blackwell.

Weber, P. (2014). Discussions in the comments section: Factors influencing participation and interactivity in online newspapers' reader comments. *New Media & Society, 16*(6), 941–957. doi:10.1177/1461444813495165

Webster, J. G., & Ksiaze, T. B. (2012). The dynamics of audience fragmentation: Public attention in an age of digital media. *Journal of Communication, 62*, 39–56.

Weiss, A. S., & Domingo, D. (2010). Innovation processes in online newsrooms as actor-networks and communities of practice. *New Media & Society, 12*(7), 1156–1171.

Welbers, K., van Atteveldt, W., Kleinnijenhuis, J., Ruigrok, N., & Schaper, J. (2016). News selection criteria in the digital age: Professional norms versus online audience metrics. *Journalism, 17*(8), 1037–1053. doi:10.1177/1464884915595474

Weltevrede, E., Helmond, A., & Gerlitz, C. (2014). The politics of real-time: A device perspective on social media platforms and search engines. *Theory, Culture & Society, 31*(6), 125–150. doi:10.1177/0263276414537318

Wilkinson, K. T., & Merle, P. F. (2013). The merits and challenges of using business press and trade journal reports in academic research on media industries. *Communication, Culture & Critique, 6*(3), 415–431. doi:10.1111/cccr.12019

Willey, S. (1998). Civic journalism in practice: Case studies in the art of listening. *Newspaper Research Journal, 19*(1), 16–29.

Williams, A., Wardle, C., & Wahl-Jorgensen, K. (2010). The limits of audience participation: UGC @ the BBC. In B. Franklin & M. Carlson (Eds.), *Journalists, sources, and credibility: New perspectives* (pp. 152–166). London, UK: Routledge.

Williams, R. (1977). *Structures of feeling Marxism and literature.* Oxford, UK: Oxford University Press.

Williams, R. (1983). *Culture and society: 1780–1950.* New York, NY: Columbia University Press.

Willnat, L., Weaver, D. H., & Choi, J. (2013). The global journalist in the twenty-first century: A cross-national study of journalistic competencies. *Journalism Practice, 7*(2), 163–183. doi:10.1080/17512786.2012.753210

Winner, L. (1986). *The whale and the reactor.* Chicago, IL: Chicago University Press.

Wojdynski, B. W. (2016). The deceptiveness of sponsored news articles: How readers recognize and perceive native advertising. *American Behavioral Scientist, 60*(12), 1475–1491. doi:10.1177/0002764216660140

Woodstock, L. (2014). The news-democracy narrative and the unexpected benefits of limited news consumption: The case of news resisters. *Journalism, 15*(7), 834–849. doi:10.1177/1464884913504260

Woolley, S. C., & Howard, P. N. (2016). Political communication, computational propaganda, and autonomous agents. *International Journal of Communication, 10*(9), 4882–4890.

Wright, K. (2011). Reality without scare quotes. *Journalism Studies, 12*(2), 156–171. doi:10.1080/1461670X.2010.509569

Wu, T. (2016). *The attention merchants: The epic scramble to get inside our heads.* New York, NY: Knopf.

Wyatt, S. (2003). Non-users also matter: The construction of users and non-users of the Internet. In N. Oudshoorn & T. Pinch (Eds.), *How users matter: The co-construction of users and technology* (pp. 67–79). Cambridge, MA: MIT Press.

Young, D. R. (2015). Contract failure theory. In J. S. Ott & L. A. Dicke (Eds.), *The nature of the nonprofit sector* (3rd ed., pp. 121–125). Boulder, CO: Westview Press.

Young, I. M. (1997). Difference as a resource for democratic communication. In J. Bohman & W. Rehg (Eds.), *Deliberative democracy: Essays on reason and politics* (pp. 383–406). Cambridge, MA: MIT Press.

Young, I. M. (2000). *Inclusion and democracy.* New York, NY: Oxford University Press.

Young, M. L., & Hermida, A. (2015). From Mr. and Mrs. Outlier to central tendencies: Computational journalism and crime reporting at the *Los Angeles Times. Digital Journalism, 3*(3), 381–397. doi:10.1080/21670811.2014.976409

Zaller, J., & Chiu, D. (1996). Government's little helper: U.S. press coverage of foreign policy crises, 1945–1991. *Political Communication, 13*(4), 385–405. doi:10.1080/10584609.1996.9963127

Zamith, R. (2016, December 13). On metrics-driven homepages. *Journalism Studies,* 1–22. doi:10.1080/1461670X.2016.1262215

Zamith, R., & Lewis, S. C. (2014, February 19). From public spaces to public sphere: Rethinking systems for reader comments on online news sites. *Digital Journalism,* doi:10.1080/21670811.2014.882066

Zelizer, B. (1997). Journalists as interpretive communities. In D. A. Berkowitz (Ed.), *Social meanings of news* (pp. 401–419). New York, NY: Sage.

Zelizer, B. (2004). *Taking journalism seriously: News and the academy.* London, UK: Sage.

Zelizer, B. (2010). *About to die: How news images move the public.* Oxford, UK: Oxford University Press.

Zelizer, B. (2014). Memory as foreground, journalism as background. In B. Zelizer & K. Tenenboim-Weinblatt (Eds.), *Journalism and memory* (pp. 32–49). London, UK: Palgrave MacMillan.

Zetter, K. (2008, September 8). Six-year-old news story causes United Airlines stock to plummet—UPDATE Google placed wrong date on story. *Wired.* Retrieved from http://www.wired.com/2008/09/six-year-old-st

Ziegele, M., Breiner, T., & Quiring, O. (2014). What creates interactivity in online news discussions? An exploratory analysis of discussion factors in user comments on news items. *Journal of Communication, 64*(6), 1111–1138. doi:10.1111/jcom.12123

Zucker, L. G. (1977). The role of institutionalization in cultural persistence. *American Sociological Review, 42*(5), 726–743.

Zuckerman, E. (2013). *Rewire: Digital cosmopolitans in the age of connection.* New York, NY: Norton.

Index

Giddens, Anthony, 13
Gitlin, Todd, 80–81
Gizmodo, 136
Glasser, Theodore L., 56–57, 82, 86
Goffman, Erving, 13
Google, 4, 137, 141, 148, 153, 168–170,
  173, 175–176, 185, 190, 206n37
  Accelerated Mobile Pages (AMP), 130,
  148, 171
Google Analytics, 139, 140
Google Drive, 152
Google Glass, 121
Google Home, 128, 130, 155
Google News, 132, 180
Gothamist, 125
Government
  factuality of information provided by,
  68–69
  framing of news by, 64, 79–80
  funding provided by, 38, 64
  journalists' critique of, 79–80
  press activities implicitly involving,
  59, 63–64, 200n4
Gramsci, Antonio, 195n1
Grasswire, 144
Greenwald, Glen, 152
Guardian, 131, 135, 138, 139, 144, 149,
  152, 153, 159, 160, 166, 174–175,
  177, 178
Guattari, Félix, 112

Habermas, Jürgen, 110
Habitus, 50–52
Hacks/Hackers, 135
Haiman, Franklyn S., 20
Haley, Nikki, 173
Hallin, Daniel C., 68, 80
Haraway, Donna, 188
Harding, Sandra, 188
Harvard University, 174
Heartbleed, 153
Held, David, 14–15
Heron, Liz, 135

HoaxBot, 174
Hocking, William, 202n11
Holmes, Oliver Wendell, Jr., 20
Hot news doctrine, 146–147
Huffington Post, 62, 135, 139, 143, 157,
  158, 167
Hughes, Charles Evans, 31
Hutchins Commission on Freedom of
  the Press, 73, 90, 202n11

Indiana University, 174
Information ideal, 81, 202n9
Information model of citizenship, 8
Infrastructural inversion, 111
Infrastructure, 111
Institutions, businesses compared to,
  198n19. *See also* Press, as institution
Intercept, 152
International News Service, 146
Interpretive flexibility, 111
Inverted pyramid, 79
Investigative reporting, 153
Irony, 82–83
ITV, 143

Johnson, Lyndon B., 84
Journalism, 114
Journalism++, 175
Journalism schools, 71–72, 73, 136, 189
Journalistic balance, 201n8
Journalists. *See also* Metajournalistic
  discourse; Press
  audiences as conceived/imagined by,
  85–94
  defining, 62
  dependence of, on nonjournalists, 8
  diversity of, 84
  independence of, 77
  as individual interpreters, 81–82
  myth of lone/individual/heroic, 1–2,
  8, 43, 63
  as professional communicators, 81–82
  public opinion of, 197n17